From Salisbury to Major

From Salisbury to Major

Continuity and change in Conservative politics

Brendan Evans
and
Andrew Taylor

Manchester University Press

Manchester and New York

distributed exclusively in the USA and Canada by St Martin's Press

Published by Manchester University Press
Oxford Road, Manchester M13 9NR, UK
and Room 400, 175 Fifth Avenue, New York, NY 10010, USA

Distributed exclusively in the USA and Canada
by St Martin's Press, Inc., 175 Fifth Avenue, New York, NY 10010, USA

British Library Cataloguing-in-Publication Data
A catalogue record for this book is available from the British Library

Library of Congress Cataloging-in-Publication Data
Evans, Brendan, 1944–
    From Salisbury to Major : continuity and change in conservative
politics / Brendan Evans and Andrew Taylor.
        p.   cm.
    ISBN 0–7190–4290–9 (hardback : alk. paper). — ISBN 0–7190–4291–7
(pbk. : alk. paper)
        1. Great Britain—Politics and government—20th century.
    2. Conservatism—Great Britain—History—20th century.
    3. Conservative Party (Great Britain—History.   4. Salisbury, Robert
Cecil. marquess of, 1830–1903.   5. Major, John Roy, 1943–
    I. Taylor, Andrew, 1954– .   II. Title.
    DA566.7.E93   1996
    324.24104′09′04—dc20   95–30846

ISBN 0 7190 4290 9 *hardback*
     0 7190 4291 7 *paperback*

First published 1996

99 98 97 96 95   10 9 8 7 6 5 4 3 2 1

Typeset in Great Britain
by Northern Phototypesetting Co. Ltd, Bolton
Printed in Great Britain
by Redwood Books, Trowbridge

Contents

Acknowledgements		page vi
Series editors' preface		vii
Introduction		1
1	The lineages of modern Conservatism	4
2	Conservatism in crisis, 1914–1931	26
3	Conservatism challenged, 1931–1945	50
4	Conservatism remade, 1945–1953	76
5	Prosperity and political exhaustion, 1955–1964	101
6	Heath and the Heathmen, 1965–1970	141
7	Managing party tensions, 1970–1979	183
8	The debate about Thatcherism	219
9	Conservatism and the 1990s	247
	Conclusion	277
	Index	282

Acknowledgements

The authors would like to thank the following for granting access to material consulted in the writing of this book: first the Conservative Party. The Conservative Party archivist, Dr Martin Maw (and his predecessor Dr Sarah Street), were invariably helpful in finding material in the Party archives at the Bodleian Library, Oxford. The authors would also like to acknowledge the permission of Alistair Cooke of the Conservative Research Department for permission to use the Party archives. The Public Record Office, Kew, granted access to government records and permission to quote from official documents. Thanks are also due to the House of Lords Record Office which granted permission to consult the Bonar Law, Hannon, and Davidson papers. The Woolton and Monckton papers were consulted at the Bodleian Library, and the Headlam papers at the Durham Record Office. The Manchester University Library, British Library and the Cambridge University Library were also helpful in providing access to material, and the authors would particularly like to thank the library staff at the University of Huddersfield for their help and assistance. The following individuals gave formal interviews and the authors would like to express their thanks for their insights into Conservative politics: the late Lord Thorneycroft, Lord Fraser of Kilmorack, Lord Carr of Hadley, Sir Edward Heath, Lord Lawson of Blaby, Lord Howe of Aberavon, and David Howell MP. Andrew Taylor would like to thank Robert Godber who first aroused his interest in the Conservative Party. Finally, thanks are due to our families who encouraged us in our work on the Conservative Party.

Series editors' preface

This is a new series prompted by the relative dearth of research-dedicated political science series currently available, as well as the fecund source of publication ideas provided by current political developments, both at home and abroad.

Political Analyses will focus on the wealth of new developments and events in British politics, including: the growth of sleaze and decline of public confidence in politics and politicians; the erosion of democracy through the advance of the Quango state; the evergrowing power of the media in political processes; the constant growth of the underclass and related social problems; the gradual failure of the welfare state to cope with converging demands as the end of the millennium approaches; the desperation of the Conservative leadership and the apparent renaissance of Labour; the attempts of Major to construct a viable post-Thatcher conservatism; the carefully calculated efforts of Labour to confect a programme which pleases most and offends few; and the increasing divisiveness of Europe as an issue throughout British politics.

It will also draw upon international topics, where events have been similarly exciting, if not revolutionary: the ending of the Reagan–Thatcher axis towards the end of the eighties; the parallel collapse of communism worldwide and the ongoing struggle for human rights in countries like Burma and China; the ending of the Cold War and the opening up of communist countries to western influences; the economic emergence of Pacific and Far Eastern countries; the outbreak of civil war in many parts of the world from Somalia to Yugoslavia; the emergence of international organisations to fulfil roles like peacekeeping (UN) and policing (NATO); the awareness of environmental threats worldwide and the enhanced roles of concerned pressure groups; and the globalisation of communications, via print, television and the Internet.

The series aims to explore in depth new ideas beyond the scope of the Politics Today series, and is aimed at a higher level audience including academics and the well informed reader, as well as undergraduates.

Introduction

Conservatism is a protean ideology. Throughout British political history Conservatism has been supplemented by the Conservative Party frequently taking its opponent's ideas, adapting them, and making them its own. This adaptability is Conservatism's response to its political dilemma: how could a popular element be introduced into politics in order to legitimise social, economic, and political inequality without admitting the people directly to the governing process and challenging the status quo?

The book examines the Conservative Party's ability to dominate British politics. It does so, however, by arguing that this dominance has been the result of the intermeshing of a complex internal political process whose purpose is adaptation to an often rapidly changing political environment. The conventional view is that the Conservative Party had achieved this dominance relatively easily and without substantial ideological baggage. This book challenges this view on two grounds: first, the Conservative Party has adapted but it has done so often as a result of considerable internal conflict; and second, that in this process of adaptation ideology has been of great importance. Conservatism can be defined as what the Conservative Party does as all parties must respond to events and changes in the political economy which are outside its control, but no party does so in a pragmatic, a-political way: parties are composed of individuals with ideas of what their party stands for, and they will fight for these ideas.

The structure of the book needs some explanation. Whilst it presents a comprehensive picture of the Conservative Party we have chosen to highlight those elements which shed most light on the Party's evolution as the dominant governing party. In particular, the book is concerned with the Conservative Party's changing relationship with mass democracy, hence the emphasis given to ideology and its transmission to a mass electorate. The second point which requires explanation is our choice of 1965 as the watershed of our analysis. 1965 sees a confluence of factors which had not been present in the Party before: first, an elected leader drawn from a non-aristocratic background, reflecting the social change within both the party grassroots and parliamentary elite, and, to some extent, the wider society. Second, despite (or because of) thirteen years of Conservative rule, Socialism, far from being killed by affluence, was finding a new lease of life with Harold Wilson's credo of scientific modernisation. The Conservative Party was ideologically and politically unhappy with statist modernisation, but growing numbers of Conservatives were willing to consider non-statist methods of modernisation which fitted in with the resurgence of neo-Liberalism, culminating in Thatcherism.

The first part of the book explores Conservative politics from the mid-nineteenth century to the mid-1960s. Chapter 1 considers briefly the core elements of the modern Conservative Party. It considers the growth of reformism under the slow emergence of mass democracy and the development under Salisbury and Bonar Law of anti-Socialism as a populist electoral appeal. Chapter 2 examines the extended crisis of Conservatism between 1914 and 1931 and the Party's attempts to find a response to the rise of organised labour, parliamentary Socialism, and the growth of the state. Central to this response was Baldwin's conscious development of a non-partisan, cross-class appeal. Chapter 3 explores the contrast between the different political traditions represented by Baldwin and Chamberlain (the latter being more popular with the party) and the political turbulence caused by the outbreak of war. The Second World War's impact on the Conservative Party was, first, to widen the political space available to One Nation Conservatives and limit that open to the neo-Liberals; and second, it produced a significant shift to the left which led to the Party's most devastating defeat. Chapter 4 looks at the remaking of Conservatism after 1945 and argues that the changes of 1945–9 were less important than the context in which the Conservatives were returned to government in 1951. Neo-Liberal ideas remained strong in the party but were limited in their effect by the government's determination to retain office. Chapter 5 explores the Conservative response to the post-war consensus and Macmillan's 'you've never had it so good' era. It concludes by arguing that by 1961 the conception of Conservatism which had dominated politics since the 1930s was politically exhausted, which led to the search for a new Conservative response.

The second part examines the Conservative Party from 1965 to the 1990s. Chapter 6 examines the development of the search for this new Conservatism which proved to be a turbulent period for the party. This was because of the partially concealed conflict of Heath's policies (a complex and contradictory mixture of technocratic reformism and One Nation Conservatism) with the resurgent neo-Liberal, free-market wing of the Conservative Party. Neo-Liberalism had been dormant for much of the 1950s. It re-emerged with the palpable failure of Macmillan's governments leading to electoral defeat, and a consequential intellectual counter-revolution, including the explosion of Powellism at both a populist and intellectual level in the party. This is the pivotal period in recent Conservative history, hence the emphasis placed on such a short span of time. Chapter 7 shows how Heath was compelled by this neo-liberal resurgence to adopt anti-statist policies which conflicted with both his political instincts and the then orthodox interpretation of effective governance. Paradoxically, the Party accepted Heath's 'U-turn', rounding on him only as a result of electoral defeat in 1974 but even this was qualified as in the 1975 leadership election the grassroots remained loyal to him. The emergence of Mrs Thatcher as party leader is therefore only partly an ideological phenomenon as she benefited from the party's proclivity for rejecting leaders who lose elections. The chapter concludes with a detailed analysis of internal party politics and the relationship with the mass electorate during the 1970s. Chapter 8 adopts a radically different approach to analysing the Thatcher era. In place of a chronology of her governments it analyses the nature of Thatcherism in the light of the vast academic literature spawned by these years. Far from seeing Thatcherism as a new growth it argues that it represents another, albeit more aggressive, attempt by Conservatives to respond to statism and the power of organised labour. Chapter 9 examines how a weak and intellectually confused leader sought to manage a party enthused by Thatcherism in which the traditional loyalty to the leader had been eroded. This erosion reflects growing doubts about the ability of the Major government to deliver economic and political success despite the victory of 1992.

Whilst historical parallels are never exact and usually dangerous, it may be that Major's government and the Conservative Party are in a similar condition of ideological exhaustion to the Macmillan government between 1961 and 1963. If this is so, then electoral defeat in 1996 or 1997 will be followed by a further round of bitter internal feuding over the true meaning of Conservatism. On the other hand, affluence and continuing anxiety about the Labour Party might lead to a further stage in the creation of a democratic one-party Conservative state.

1

The lineages of modern Conservatism

Modern Conservatism begins with the Whig politician Edmund Burke, and modern politics with the French Revolution against which Burke vented so much spleen.[1] Before 1789 politics was confined to a narrow aristocratic elite concerned with the distribution of the spoils generated by the existing socio-economic order. The populace had a walk-on role in an occasional riot or when their betters appealed to them as part of an intra-elite conflict. The French Revolution transformed the political role of 'the people' and entrenched the view that any political system which did not satisfy popular aspirations should be done away with, as should those who had benefited most from these arrangements. The French Revolution emphasised the redistribution of wealth and property as an essential precondition of, and support for, the redistribution of political power and thereby established the basis for Socialism. The Revolution's emphasis on reason and natural rights represented a profound challenge to Conservatism's emphasis on tradition and the imperfectibility of human kind. Finally, the French Revolution conjured up the spectre of the all-powerful state acting as the servant of the General Will, justifying any action no matter how terrible by the will of the majority as determined by the state. Confronted by such overwhelming power, the individual had the choice of submission or destruction.[2]

These political developments were accompanied in Britain by industrialisation which threatened to dissolve the bonds of civil society, making disharmony normal and creating new social forces (the industrialist and the working class) whose mutual strife threatened stability. Revolution and industrialisation shattered the eighteenth-century constitution generating a new yardstick to judge political institutions (utilitarianism), and elevated 'the people' to the centre of politics. The characteristic demand of the 'new' politics was for 'the people' to be admitted directly to government via the franchise. For this point Conservative politics was forced to confront directly the problem posed by demands for mass political participation and the related phenomena of the growth of the state.

Peel, Disraeli, and the emergence of Conservatism

The shift from a stable-agricultural to a dynamic-industrial society dominated by rapacious capitalists and desperate industrial workpeople, it was feared, would destroy the traditional bases of Conservative politics and thinking.[3] Industrialisation focused Conservative thinking on one question: how could the social order be maintained? From the 1820s, when Sir Robert Peel began to outline a moderate reformist strategy, the use of state power to maintain social and political stability has been at the core of Conservative politics.[4] By the end of the 1840s Conservatism seemed in full retreat before advancing Liberalism. Despite its restricted nature the Reform Act (1832) signalled the end of the rural-aristocratic dominance of the political system, and Disraeli's destruction of Peel's government over protection and the repeal of the Corn Laws (1846) split the party forcing Conservatism into the political wilderness until 1874. Even though Chartism was defeated in 1848 class politics were feared to be characteristic of politics in industrial society. Yet, Conservatives adapted and the origins of adaptation lie in the period when Conservatism's prospects seemed blackest.

Tory resistance to the 1832 Reform Act was rewarded with a crushing electoral rebuff: only 185 MPs out of 658 in the reformed House of Commons, but all was not lost as reform left the House of Lords and local government unaffected. The Act increased the electorate by 300,000 (80%) but it still numbered only 650,000 out of a population of 16 million. So about 4% of the population had the vote, the average constituency electorate was 948, and the franchise qualifications were extremely complex. Reform also had little perceptible effect on the composition of the political elite: the Parliaments of the 1840s were sociologically similar to those of the 1820s. Nevertheless, politicians recognised a fundamental shift had taken place.

Conservatives had three choices in the 1930s.[5] First, they could become an aristocratic-rural party of resistance, if not reaction. This was attractive to large numbers of natural Tories but the electoral base for resistance to change was too small to form a government. This strategy was not politically viable. Second, some Tories looked to a paternalist alliance of aristocrats and factory workers against the industrial middle class. Between 1830 and 1845 there seemed to be solid ideological and political grounds for such an alliance. The Factory Acts, the agitation against the new Poor Law, revulsion against the distress caused by urbanisation and the factory system, and the stirrings of the working class seemed to offer fertile ground for social Toryism. This strategy had two flaws, however. First, it challenged directly the dominant ideology of free-market capitalism, and it required a working-class electorate which no political group (with the exception of the Chartists) thought attractive. The third option was the moderate reformism associated with Canning and Peel coupled with an appeal to all in society who feared disorder. The combination of reform and strong government was to become a key important element in the Conservative Party's success.

Sir Robert Peel articulated this in his *Address to the Electors of the Borough of Tamworth* (1834) – the Tamworth Manifesto.[6] Should Tories who opposed the Reform Act, Peel asked, now withdraw from politics? The Tories should not, Peel argued, because, first, they had an obligation to carry on the King's government; and second, withdrawal would imbalance the constitution by restricting government to one section of political opinion. Peel made 'a frank and explicit declaration of principle': the Tories, he claimed, had never 'been disposed to acquiesce in acknowledged evils, either from the mere superstitious reverence for ancient usages or from the dread of labour or responsibility in the application of a remedy'. The Reform Act marked a new era and the Tories accepted it as a settlement of a debate which had threatened serious political unrest. They would not repeal or amend the Act. On reform in general, however, Peel emphatically rejected living in 'a perpetual vortex of agitation' in which politicians promised 'instant redress of anything which anybody may call abuse'. However, 'if the spirit of the Reform Bill implies merely a careful review of institutions, civil and ecclesiastical, undertaken in friendly temper, combining, with the firm maintenance of established rights, the correction of proven abuses and the redress of real grievances, in that case I can, for myself and for my colleagues, undertake to act in such a spirit and with such intentions'.

The Tamworth Manifesto is usually portrayed as Peel directing the Tories away from the path of resistance and the satisfactions of principled (if powerless) opposition towards reformism, an act which proved vital for Conservatism's adaptability and success. However, Peel remained wedded to an aristocratic political order widened to embrace the industrial wealth of the middle class, not democracy. His politics were strongly utilitarian and this made him careless of the sentiments and emotions of his less cerebral colleagues. When convinced of the rightness of a position Peel pursued his conviction irrespective of the party cost; this eroded his support and when the crisis came in 1846 his party split. Peel and his Cabinet colleagues departed and after Peel's death in 1851 the Peelites merged with the Liberal Party. Peelism with Peel was too disruptive and created a recurring problem in Conservative politics. What, many Tories now asked, distinguished them from Whigs and Liberals? What had become of principle in politics? If Tories were now reformers surely the electorate would prefer to vote for those whose reformism was based on principle not opportunism?

The Corn Law crisis and split revolved around one of the perennial questions of Conservative politics: is the preservation of the status quo best served by resisting change or by accommodating it? In 1846 the lack of cohesion in the party system allowed the controversy to split the Tory Party. This acted as a salutary warning to subsequent Conservative leaders, but after the Peelites' departure the Conservative Party emerged from the unlikely alliance of bucolic squires and foppish Young England led by Benjamin Disraeli. Disraeli is credited with the organisational and doctrinal reform which, when combined, provided the Conservative Party with a powerful lure for the affections of mass democracy: One Nation Conservatism.[7] Disraeli's early politics (notably his part in the destruction of Peel) and political writings (notably *Vindication of the English Constitution* of 1835) were reactionary. Disraeli's novels *Coningsby* (1844), *Sybil* (1845), and *Tancred* (1847) lamented the passing of the aristocratic political order and expressed the romantic medievalism of Young England but they identified the 'two nations' (*Sybil*) and argued that the Conservative task was to unite them (*Coningsby*). Even the anachronistic *Vindication* expresses two key Disraelian ideas: reverence for the monarchy and that radical parties were anti-nation.[8] The lesson of 1846 and the wilderness years was that Conservatism could not conserve if it remained confined to the narrow political base left after the split. If office was the purpose of politics Conservatives could not afford the luxury of unsullied principles and had to woo the electorate. This was recognised by Disraeli. Conservatives were seen as irresponsible and dominated by the agricultural interest, and the only way an image of incompetence in government can be dispelled is by governing. This explains why the minority Disraeli–Derby government grasped the nettle of parliamentary reform in 1867: to show Conservatives could govern effectively and that they were not the 'stupid party'.

There was considerable pressure in the country for reform counterbalanced by a deep Conservative dislike of reform which threatened a further split. Derby and Disraeli calculated that a Conservative Reform Act might capture the political initiative and by redistributing seats limit the damage caused by expanding the electorate. The Liberals, themselves divided over the extent of reform, would be discomfited by this theft of their clothes. The Conservative leadership, along with most of the political class, agreed reform would exclude the lowest elements of the urban working class, so the 1867 Act was the least radical reform which a minority Conservative government (facing considerable internal disquiet) could pass. Despite losing the 1868 election the damage inflicted was less than many Conservatives feared. After 1867 winning the support of the urban working class became critical for Conservatism's survival and success. For a party seeking a response mass-politics logic suggested making a positive appeal to the working class.[9] Between 1874 and 1878 Disraeli's government passed a wide range of social legislation: was this a new Conservatism responding to an emerging democracy? The 1870s saw Conservatism accommodate itself to the new politics but thereafter it presented itself as the party of stability and safety. The Conservative Party disliked the growth of mass politics but feared returning to the political wilderness and this gave Disraeli room for manoeuvre. The reforms 'were in no sense the product of a pre-meditated Conservative policy. They did not stem from a coherent programme aimed at winning the support of the classes whose interests they most directly touched ... They were not the planned accompaniment of the extension of the franchise'.[10]

In 1868 the Conservatives did not appeal explicitly to the working-class electorate, although the National Union tried to convince the new electorate of Conservatism's sympathy for the working class. Electioneering in the industrial boroughs did bring Conservatives (literally) face-to-face with the new working-class electorate which proved not to be composed of rabid Jacobins. This was the background to Disraeli's 1872 speeches at the Manchester Free Trade Hall (April) and Crystal Palace (July) when he declared 'another great object of the Tory party, and one not inferior to the maintenance of the Empire, or the upholding of our institutions, is the elevation of the condition of the people'.

> It must be obvious to all who consider the condition of the multitude with a desire to improve and elevate it, that no important step can be gained unless you effect some reduction of their hours of labour and humanise their toil ... the working classes of this country ... are in possession of personal privilege ... they have obtained ... a great extension of political rights ... is it at all wonderful that they should wish to elevate and improve their condition, and is it unreasonable that they should ask the Legislature to assist them ... as far as it is consistent with the general welfare of the realm? Why, the people of England would be ... idiots ... if, with their experience and acuteness, they should not long have seen that the time had arrived when social, and not political improvement is the object which they ought to pursue.

The Crystal Palace speech was significant because it accepted the inevitability of state regulation of private economic interests. Disraeli accepted it was natural and inevitable that the working class would use the vote to advance their own interests. Disraeli was, however, convinced that the working class could be trusted to better their position *within* the status quo, not destroy it.

Conservatives saw their task being to settle the country after a decade of agitation. To promote a political and social consensus the Conservatives were willing to remedy legitimate grievances and thereby broaden the basis of popular support for, and legitimacy of, the political system (and the Conservative Party). The One Nation approach associated with Disraeli emerged at a unique time in the party's history when it was entering a transitional period. Aristocratic influence was declining but still dominant, the influence of the major employer interests and the urban middle class was increasing but was still subordinate, this created a political equilibrium within Conservatism which allowed Disraeli's ideas to take shape. The reforms of the 1870s were a-typical as the social composition of the party changed and its hostility to democracy increased. Under Disraeli the party broadened its electoral base and the Burkean/Peelite tradition justified moderate reform. This enabled Conservatism to change whilst remaining within the political status quo and, relying on the tendency of the Liberal Party to split between radical and non-radical elements, encourage a drift of support away from Liberalism to Conservatism. The Conservative Party had more to gain in the long run by waiting for events to split the Liberals rather than from competing on social reform. By 1880 social reform was not a Conservative priority but the party could not abandon the working class, so by combining Monarchy and Imperialism Disraeli forged a popular appeal to hinder the development of an independent working-class political consciousness.[11]

By combining the three principles articulated in 1872 – 'to maintain the institutions of the country ... to uphold the Empire of England ... [and] the elevation of the condition of the people' – Disraeli provided the Conservative Party with a response to mass democracy. This One Nation Conservatism was set out in his Crystal Palace speech:

> the tone and tendency of Liberalism cannot be concealed. It is to attack the institutions of the country under the name of Reform (Cheers) and to make war on the manners and customs of the people of this country under the pretext of Progress (Cheers) ... Gentlemen, the Tory party, unless it is a national party, is nothing (Cheers). It is not a confederacy of nobles, it is not a democratic multitude; it is a party formed from all the numerous classes of the realm – classes alike and equal before the law, but whose different conditions and different aims give vigour and variety to our national life.

Substitute Socialism for Liberalism and the elasticity of Conservative politics is apparent. However, any programmatic appeal to the working class would run foul of the urban middle class, but to defend the interests of the propertied the Conservative Party had to engage with democracy. This pushed Conservative politics towards cross-class solidarity to inhibit the development of class consciousness.

Lord Salisbury's melancholia

In his youth Salisbury (then Viscount Cranbourne) railed against democracy, resigning from Disraeli's government over the 1867 Act.[12] As leader of the Conservative Party from 1881 to 1902 and Prime Minister for much of this time he was the first Conservative leader and premier to have to manage an emerging democracy and proved to be an accomplished player of the democratic game. 'The greatest danger of democracy', Salisbury believed, 'is, that it places supreme power in the hands of those who may be misled by hunger into acts of folly or wrong'. Democracy would transform government into the plaything of party rather than the expression of the national interest, whilst giving the vote to the working class would culminate in an orgy of property confiscation.[13] Politics was about property and the fundamental conflict was between those who had and those who lacked property.[14] Salisbury identified taxation as 'the cardinal question of our day', as in a democracy it was in the interests of the masses and those they elected to believe that 'Every deficiency can be filled up, every difficulty made straight, by a single application to the one fathomless resource' (the pockets of the propertied) though this would produce a flight of capital and economic collapse.[15]

In democracy the political elites' role of leading and guiding the masses was disrupted by demagogic party leaders striving to win votes.[16] For Salisbury the supreme political virtues were security of property, social stability, and order secured by a hierarchy with the landed aristocracy at the apex. Though profoundly pessimistic about the future, Salisbury recognised the futility of standing in the path of history. His role, as he conceived it, was to slow the inevitable drift to democracy and Socialism, a task which needed a cohesive elite conscious of their interests and determined to defend them. Political behaviour grew from self-interest. 'What grounds have we', Salisbury pondered,

> for the fond belief that if we trust the English working class with so perilous a gift [the vote], they will be proof against a temptation to which every other class that has been exposed to it has succumbed? ... When men are living on from fifteen to twenty shillings a week, money or money's worth stir in the depths of the human soul with a force which 'loyalty to institutions' or attachments of any kind cannot hope in the long run to rival.[17]

The rule of the propertied was justified pragmatically: their superior economic and political performance reflected their qualities and justified their dominance. Salisbury's analysis of the political economy of democracy has a modern ring. Democracy 'means Government by men of less independence and lower culture: it means laws which will fetter capital to favour labour, and will trammel the freedom of the owners of property to make it cheaper and more accessible to those who have it not: it means taxes levied and spent by the men that contribute to them least'.[18]

Democracy would eventually produce an independent working-class political consciousness: the working class might be ignorant but it was not stupid. Once workers had the vote they would sell it to the highest bidder and, Salisbury feared, there would be no shortage of politicians (and not just radicals) who would make these bids.[19] Conceding the vote to the working class was a revolutionary step because Salisbury, as an elitist, never regarded classes as sociological abstractions. Classes were political collectivities acting to secure their own interests and the vote translated sociological characteristics and economic interests into political power. Those who cried 'trust the people' were, Salisbury believed, deluding themselves;

workers were a class and would behave as such. In that they were no different to the aristocracy.

Salisbury's conception of the Conservative Party's political role was discussed in his ominously titled article, *Disintegration*. Disintegration was fuelled by the growing estrangement of the classes, party interest, and democratic political leadership (demagogic and redistributionist). The propertied had to resist, so democratic politics was 'civil war with the gloves on'. The problem was electoral ignorance and the growth of party: 'During the long intervals which elapse between the periods when they do give their minds to politics and pronounce an intelligent decision, they pay no attention at all. Their voice is mimicked by someone else, who speaks in their name, and affects their authority'.[20] Party was the basis of government, whose policy was formed by the competition for votes. This competition produced political instability and capriciousness. Democratic governments were shortsighted and reactive, making concessions to well-organised minorities who were, by their nature, insatiable. Traditional elites, in their anxiety to preserve the status quo undermined it and themselves by playing the electoral game.

American political institutions were designed to control democratic passions via checks and balances. This could not, however, be replicated in Britain.[21] Salisbury wanted the Conservative Party to be the equivalent of the American checks and balances, delaying democracy and blunting its worst effects. Conservatism's *raison d'être* was resisting the 'rising storm of Democratic spoilation' but this required more than a Conservative government. Salisbury saw the need for a party to defend the rights of property holders (great or small) and which could rely on 'a certain amount of Conservative opinion, and the party will have the benefit of whatever reaction [democracy] may produce'.[22] So:

> The object of our party is not, and ought not to be, simply to keep things as they are. In the first place, the enterprise is impossible, there is much in our present mode of thought and action which it is highly undesirable to conserve. What we require is the administration of public affairs, whether in the executive or the legislative department, in that spirit of the old constitution which held the nation together as a whole, and levelled its united force at objects of national import, instead of splitting it into a bundle of unfriendly and distrusted fragments.[23]

Salisbury, therefore, was building on the foundations laid by Peel and Disraeli.

The Liberal victory in 1880 was thought to represent the political future more than the Conservative victory of 1874.[24] Yet the Conservatives dominated politics between 1886 and 1902. In 1868 the Conservatives were the country party; by 1885 half the Conservative parliamentary strength came from urban constituencies and this was after the 1884 Reform Act increased the size of the working-class electorate. Salisbury accepted the inevitability of further reform but insisted it be accompanied by a redistribution of seats to prevent the swamping of the Conservative rural base and the burgeoning Conservative suburbs by the boroughs. Redistribution would create a *cordon sanitaire* of Conservative suburban and rural constituencies around the boroughs and deny power to the working class.[25] For Salisbury it was axiomatic that the Conservative Party was a natural minority (he calculated the ratio was 5 Conservative to 6 Liberal MPs), so securing representation for minorities by drawing constituency boundaries to give expression to the locally dominant interest would allow urban (or 'villa') Conservatism to emerge.[26] The basis for the growth of urban Conservatism was not due to mass Liberal conversions (though conversions there were) but the political restructuring prompted by redistribution and single-member constituencies. This ensured urban Conservatives who 'had formerly been swamped in huge constituencies ... were now high and dry on islands of their own'.[27]

The trigger for Conservative dominance after 1886 was Gladstone's conversion to Irish Home Rule and the consequent split amongst the already weakened Liberals. Though the Conservatives won the 1886 election, Liberal strength remained formidable. Conservative dominance was essentially negative and derived from Liberal failure to mobilise their maximum support, as Liberals abstained rather than vote Conservative. After 1885 there was a long-run tendency for *turnout* to increase marginally but with some dramatic variations. Turnout only returned to the 80%+ level in 1906, the year of the Liberal landslide. The period of Conservative hegemony (1886–1902) had an average turnout of 76.3%, so low turnouts tended to benefit the Conservatives. Second, the Conservative *share of the total vote* remained fairly stable, but on the three occasions (1886, 1895, and 1900) when the Conservative share of the total vote reached 50% the election was characterised by Liberal disarray. The Conservative share of the total electorate was stable in the long run despite short-term fluctuations. In the 1886, 1895, and 1900 elections the total vote the Conservative share of the *electorate* was below 30%. This suggests core Conservative support was about 25% to 30% of the electorate: support beyond this was determined by the behaviour of Liberal voters. The Conservatives won in 1895 and 1900 with a smaller share of the electorate than in 1886 and their best share of the electorate was in January 1910. The Conservative share of the electorate followed turnout and as their share of the total vote remained more or less stable Liberal abstentions crucially influenced election results. Home Rule, Liberal disunity, and the lack of a clear policy (but one sufficiently radical to worry many Liberals) contributed to a negative restructuring produced by the refusal of Liberals to vote.[28]

An important element in the Conservative dominance was constituency organisation. Originally Salisbury distrusted 'wirepullers' but the defeat of 1880 convinced him of the importance of political organisation. By the end of the 1880s R. W. E. Middleton, the Conservative principal agent, had 'stimulated and supervised the development of partisan electoral organisation to a pitch of refinement unmatched before and perhaps since'.[29] It is significant that as this machine lost its vitality after Middleton's retirement in 1903 the Conservatives suffered a catastrophic defeat.

In 1900 the Conservatives won one of their greatest election victories; in 1906 they suffered their greatest electoral defeat. Salisbury's retirement in May 1902 was followed by a series of disastrous by-election results which accurately foretell defeat in 1906.[30] Defeat cannot be blamed on either tariff reform or depression. Chamberlain's campaign was launched on 15 May 1903 after the by-elections revealed the anti-Conservative trend. Tariff reform was to split the Conservative Party and damaged it in 1906 but its immediate effect was to revive Conservative fortunes. Similarly, these electoral problems appeared before the end of the Boer War boom and Conservative fortunes revived as the economy slid into recession, worsening when recovery began. Balfour's 1902 Education Act provoked one of the bitterest controversies in modern British political history, comparable to the furore caused by the Poll Tax. Though a thoroughly needed reform of the educational system, by providing support for Anglican schools through local government rates, the Act aroused the final fury of the Nonconformist conscience, energising anti-Conservative sentiment and reviving flagging Liberal morale and organisation. A minor duty on imported corn in 1902, imposed to help pay for the Boer War, mobilised free-trade opinion. The duty was seen as a first step to protection, a perception made more credible when Chamberlain launched his tariff reform crusade. The duties were portrayed as a 'stomach tax' on working-class food, which benefited the Liberals. The end of the war in 1902 shifted attention to Conservative mismanagement of both the war and the peace. Milner's sanctioning of indentured Chinese labour in South African mines was exploited by the Liberals and aroused working-class opinion against the Conservatives. Conservative policy therefore both mobilised Liberal opinion and antagonised large numbers of working-class voters.

In 1906 the Conservatives were reduced from 402 MPs when Salisbury retired, to 157 (a 10.6% swing) producing a Liberal government with a majority of 130 over all other parties, a government, moreover, with an extensive (and expensive) programme of social reform which seemed almost Socialist in inspiration. Did 1906 represent the fulfilment of Salisbury's 1883 prediction of disintegration? How did the Conservative Party propose to respond?

The Conservative response to democracy

The catastrophe of 1906 implied an equally dramatic Conservative riposte and three such responses were current in the party: Tory democracy, tariff reform, and National Toryism. All failed because they conflicted with the realities of power in the Conservative Party.

Though derived from Disraeli, Tory democracy is usually identified with Lord Randolph Churchill, although he was by no means clear what it meant. Churchill's advocacy emerged from the defeat of 1880, the death of Disraeli in 1881, and his contempt for the leadership of Sir Stafford Northcote. Without a positive appeal Conservative 'successes will be fewer and separated from each other by intervals of growing length'; the Conservative Party should 'bring to perfection those schemes of imperial rule, of social reform which Lord Beaconsfield had only time to dream of, to hint at, and to sketch'. Within Disraeli's 1871 dictum *sanitas sanitatum, omnia sanitas* 'a careful mind will discover a scheme of social progress and reform, of dimensions so large and wide-spreading that many volumes would not suffice to explain its details ... in it is embraced, a social revolution'.[31]

Salisbury believed Tory democracy would achieve the opposite of what was intended as it would split the Conservative Party and remove from politics the only reliable defence against radicalism. 'The Tory Party', he wrote in a letter to Churchill,

> is composed of varying elements ... the 'classes and dependents of classes' are the strongest ingredients in our composition, but we have so to conduct legislation that we shall give some satisfaction to both the classes and the masses. This is especially difficult with the classes – all legislation is rather unwelcome to them, as tending to disturb a state of things with which they are rather satisfied. It is evident, therefore, that we must work at less speed and at a lower temperature than our opponents. Our bills must be tentative and cautious, not sweeping and dramatic.[32]

Churchill's disdain for 'villadom' and middle-class urban Conservatism was not shared by Salisbury who recognised that this was the Conservative hard-core. The Conservative Party could, and did, survive and prosper without Randolph Churchill or Tory democracy and its importance declined with Churchill's retirement from politics, but the problem of Conservatism's relationship with the working class remained.[33]

What was required was a means of integrating the working class into Conservatism without affecting policy or the distribution of power in the party. The instrument was the Primrose League founded in 1883 in honour of Disraeli who had died in 1881.[34] Despite its medieval-chivalric language and rituals the Primrose League responded to mass democracy by appealing to prejudices which transcended class divisions. Its community organisation translated Conservative principles into the everyday life of the population and by bringing duchesses and scullery maids into personal (albeit sporadic) contact at League social functions it sought to demonstrate the artificiality of class antagonism. The League successfully appealed to the 'respectable' working class who in earlier decades had been attracted by Liberal nonconformity and who might now be attracted to Socialism.

For Salisbury the League's value lay in its ability to delay the rise of class politics and it helped the Conservative Party reconcile itself to democracy and develop techniques of mass political management. In 1910 the League had an official enrolment of 2 million which, even allowing for the gap between membership and enrolment, makes it a very substantial political organisation. Nonetheless, the Primrose League failed. It could not stem the wider processes of social and political change in late-Victorian and Edwardian Britain. The League's promotion of controlled working-class participation via social deference could not become a political appeal robust enough to prevent the rise of class politics.

Chamberlain believed that tariff reform (protecting domestic industry from foreign competition and giving privileged access to Imperial goods) would reduce unemployment, increase wages and promote national unity by protecting property by remedying mass discontents. Furthermore, tariff reform would solve Conservatism's ambivalence towards social reform and mobilise the masses without stirring up working-class consciousness. It enabled Chamberlain to appeal to both traditional Conservative anti-*laisser-faire* and Tory democracy as a specifically Conservative response to democratic politics. This resulting political force would cross class boundaries and restrict the space available for an independent working-class consciousness and thereby promote national unity by combining employer and employee against their common enemy: foreign competition. Tariff reform would therefore marginalise class politics.[35]

Chamberlain was widely distrusted in the Conservative Party. He had split the Liberals in 1886 and now threatened to do the same for the Conservatives; the free trade/protection conflict had, remember, shattered Peel's party. Tariff reform social politics meant Conservatives competing with the Liberal and Labour parties, and the financing of social reform had taxation implications, but duties on imported foodstuffs and goods were unpopular with the working-class electorate. Conservative free traders were therefore amongst the most conservative in the party. They were deeply hostile to all forms of collectivism and state intervention, seeing Chamberlain as part of a wider collectivist drift in British politics. Tariff reformers welcomed much of the Liberal social legislation as British 'Bismarkianism' and saw protection as an effective response to growing international competition with the British Empire. Whilst many Conservatives welcomed the bolstering of Imperial power they were determined to resist collectivism even if this limited the party's attractiveness to the working class. The internal tensions generated by tariff reform were too powerful for Balfour's attempts to maintain unity and he was forced to resign in 1911.

National Toryism was not just an aristocratic reaction to modernity and democracy, but the most extreme manifestation of a wider Conservative discontent about the nation's future. They were neither organized nor unified, even on their central concerns (military preparedness, Ireland, defence of the Anglican church), nor did they vote in a unified way.[36] Fear of Socialism, democracy, and threats to the Empire (from Imperial Germany and Irish nationalism) coalesced into fears of a 'General Crisis'. This required the radical solution of 'National Toryism' which was lying dormant 'in the minds and hearts of millions of our fellow countrymen'. Its absence was the result of the ruling class abnegating their duty of providing leadership, and democracy's corruption of politics.[37] Conservative leaders in the Commons were part of a wider betrayal, produced by their infection with the bacillus of democracy. Conservative leaders were Conservative in name only and winning elections was pointless unless the party stuck to its principles. The National Tories' concern for national efficiency made them impatient at the enervating reverence accorded tradition in Conservative politics. They sought 'a doctrine, a faith, philosophy, an ideal, a frame of mind, a creed, a clarified statement of principles, a definite conception of the meaning of patriotism'.[38] They sought, in other words, an ideology. A reactionary or negative policy could not prosper in democracy, but even though Conservative governments had passed useful social legislation this 'has not created any solid attachment among the working classes'. It was the creation of these 'solid attachments' which lay at the heart of National Tory politics.[39]

Integration was to be achieved 'not so much by passing laws as by reconstructing thought ... saving the nation by leading a confused and discordant public mind back to first principles'. These principles were Disraeli's but applied with greater rigour via a positive programme. Social reform was integral to National Toryism: 'The Tories were the only Party who took any notice of the working classes before they had the vote ... we have only to return to first principles ... Toryism is not obsolete. It is only dormant'. National Toryism would weld traditional values (law, order, liberty, and religion) with a programme giving 'each individual elements that will afford him an opportunity of at least living a free and decorous existence, and the opportunity to raise himself or herself to the highest point of moral and material efficiency'. This required a contract with the working class: 'every one who is ready to work bravely and honestly shall have a living wage and a healthy home and the enjoyment of the elementary rights of citizenship'. National unity would be elevated above sectional and class interests.[40] Without such a programme the Conservative Party would conspire in its own destruction. Democracy was only the first stage of Socialism: the Conservative task was to avert this by creating an ordered national community. The masses were guaranteed a minimum level of health, education, and subsistence in return for accepting their subordination within a web of mutual obligations directed at the service of the Empire.

Despite their obvious differences these three responses had a common major weakness: they were essentially collectivist and statist in inspiration. They all envisioned a much greater level of state control over private interests and as such, were bound to be disliked by Conservatives, despite their common desire to boost national unity and Imperial power which, of course, was attractive to Conservatives. The scale of the 1906 defeat convinced many Conservatives a sea-change had occurred in British politics. The growth of trade unions and industrial unrest, the formation of the Labour Party, and the growth of state intervention all pointed to the rise of Socialism. Arthur Balfour, the party leader, wrote to Edward VII's private secretary that the election was much more 'than the swing of the pendulum'. He feared: 'We are face to face (no doubt in a milder form) with the Socialist difficulties which loom so large on the Continent. Unless I am greatly mistaken, the Election of 1906 inaugurates a new era'.[41] Many Conservatives believed that if the party was 'ever to regain its former position ... it must reconstitute itself more in harmony with the twentieth century requirements of a thoroughly up-to-date Democracy'. The electorate was 'no longer dependent on what it [was] told by the publican over a mug of beer' so Conservatives must 'seek to re-unite the party on a strong policy of social reform'.[42] If radical solutions were out of the question, what about moderate reformism?

Historians have assumed the Conservative Party under Balfour and Bonar Law had no interest in social reform and that this was a major error.[43] In fact the party developed a distinctive policy which influenced the 1914 *Campaign Guide* prepared for the forthcoming general election. The Unionist Social Reform Committee (USRC), an unofficial policy study group founded in 1911, was convinced after the failure of tariff reform that the party needed a positive appeal to the working class. The USRC looked to Disraeli and Tory democracy but was also influenced by Fabianism and a belief in the efficacy of state intervention. Despite the moderation this inheritance did not endear the USRC to the party.[44] In responding to the 1909 'People's Budget', welfare reforms, the House of Lords, and most obviously, over Home Rule and Ulster, the Conservatives appeared to become increasingly reactionary. Instead of trying to formulate a positive alternative, Conservatives flirted with extra-constitutional politics, and Balfour remained unresponsive to pleas for a positive policy which, it has been argued, led the party, by default, to *laisser-faire* and obstructionism. The strain of maintaining unity proved too great and Balfour resigned the leadership in 1911 and was replaced by Andrew Bonar Law who was even less responsive. One historian concludes that 'Adaptation ... was imperative ... the Unionist party needed to cultivate a positive and popular appeal based on a forward policy'.[45] But is this so? Did adaptation require a 'forward' social policy?

Andrew Bonar Law is crucial to the development of the modern Conservative Party. He was a dour Scots-Canadian whose oratorical style was compared to the hammering of rivets and had made his fortune in the Glasgow iron trade. In Conservative terms Law was an outsider. He has been justly described as 'the unknown Prime Minister' and was said to care about only two political issues (tariff reform and Ulster) but his importance goes far beyond this. Law had been elected unopposed as leader when Walter Long and Austen Chamberlain withdrew in the interests of party unity. Law's adoption of, and keen pursuit of, Balfour's strategy of resistance was not the result of inexperience, miscalculation, opportunism, or irresponsibility but was a sophisticated strategy intended to win the next election.[46] The difference was style: 'This melancholy teetotal widower ... *met the needs of a demoralised party* better than Balfour. It was a matter of style not policy – bluntness, vigour and invective, instead of dialectic, urbanity and subtlety'.[47]

Law's politics were based on the conviction that 'for the Conservatives social reform was not on the whole a profitable line to pursue. If the country wanted more and better social reform it would not vote Conservative'.[48] This commended itself to the party but what about the electorate? Although a tariff reformer Law recognised it had not only failed to win over the working class but had cost votes. Constituency surveys found that constitutional issues which were of fundamental importance to Conservatives had no attraction for the electorate except where anti-Catholic/anti-Irish sentiment was strong. However, these surveys also found considerable disquiet amongst Liberals over political and industrial unrest and the Asquith government's social reforms.[49] A positive appeal to working-class voters would therefore antagonise existing and potential supporters without producing any significant gains. Moreover, political developments during and after 1910 pointed to a Conservative revival, not decline. First, Conservative losses of 1906 were recouped in the 1910 elections and it was increasingly clear that the Labour and Liberal alliance was by no means solid and Labour's by-election failures pointed to a failure to achieve electoral take-off. Furthermore, the Conservative Party was gaining support in municipal politics. Secondly, the fading of industrial unrest with the failure of the London Dock Strike (1912) eased the pressure from the party on Law to 'do something'. Finally, it should be remembered that Law had secured the leadership as the unity candidate and he would do nothing to antagonise his party, hence his staunch defence of core Conservative issues.

The Conservative Party had recovered from the disaster of 1906 without a positive appeal and events confirmed Law's judgement that the party had little to gain from social reform. Research on the development of class politics in early twentieth-century British politics confirms the rationality of Law's decision not to appeal to democracy. Religious factors, not class, remained the dominant influence on electoral behaviour; only after 1918 did class gain the ascendancy. This 'sustains the traditional view of a dramatic alteration of cleavage bases between 1910 and 1918, a movement of the vote from a confessional to a class alignment'.[50] The implications of this for Conservative political strategy are obvious: the First World War was critical for the emergence of class politics. Class politics could well have emerged anyway but the war ensured that they developed far faster than if the war had not taken place. As politicians could not foresee the war they could not take remedial action to prevent the emergence of class politics and, anyway, there was little evidence that class was becoming the determinant of mass electoral behaviour. If class politics were weak and the class party (Labour) was not breaking through there was no reason for the Conservative Party to appeal to the working class as a class.

The restrictions of the pre-1918 franchise neutralised a considerable amount of non-Conservative electoral support. Conservatives were alarmed by Pease's 1912 franchise bill which would have created an electorate of 9.5 million based on virtually universal male suffrage subject to minimal residence qualifications. The bill passed its second reading undamaged but Law successfully protested that the government's inclusion of women's franchise clauses at the Committee stage rendered the bill wholly different to that approved by the House. The Speaker agreed and declared the bill invalid.[51] With Pease's bill disposed of and the restricted franchise preserved, there was again no reason for Law to alter his strategy.

Law's conviction that current politics were not hostile to Conservatism also influenced the overhaul of the party organisation conducted by Arthur Steel-Maitland (Law's Party Chairman). It had two purposes. First, it reoriented the party as the focal point for anti-progressivism in British politics; and second, it recreated the Middleton Machine to bolster the party's position within the political status quo. Party managers now recognised that short-term campaigning would not win a secure Conservative vote, this required long-term propaganda: 'the socialists do not push matters just before an election, they keep digging at the people all the year round'. The traditional functions of party organisation were augmented with an emphasis on political education, propaganda and intelligence gathering which was new to British politics.[52]

The potential of anti-Socialism as an electoral strategy can be seen in Conservative successes in local government. Municipal Socialism posed a more immediate threat to Conservatives than parliamentary Socialism in national politics. London municipal politics provide a clear example. The London Municipal Society (LMS) took control of the London County Council (LCC) in 1907 via an aggressive anti-progressive propaganda campaign attacking high rates, financial mismanagement, and municipal Socialism. The LMS was also able to exploit changes in the electorate (notably the rise of the suburban black-coated worker) and shifting patterns of party allegiance. At a time when the loyalty of the London working class to Liberalism was weakening, national and local electoral patterns were converging. So, 'whenever Conservatives could be persuaded to turn out and vote for the LMS candidates at the LCC elections, they would provide a natural majority for Municipal Reform'.[53] The Conservative local government effort inside and outside London was based on anti-Socialism and an enormous effort was made to place this message before the electorate. By 1914 there was evidence that 'opposition to all forms of municipal "extravagance", began to earn electoral dividends' and there was no reason why this strategy should not work in national politics.[54]

If reform offered no gains, resistance was equally problematic. The 1914 *Campaign Guide* contains a substantial Conservative social reform package and while the USRC's recommendations were not accepted, the influence of Conservative social reformers was largely hidden.[55] The Conservative Party was involved in subsidising anti-Socialist organisations in areas of industrial militancy, but for electoral reasons it did so covertly.[56] Law's uncompromising stand on Ulster has obscured the caution with which he approached industrial unrest. The aggressive espousal of the Ulster Unionist cause kept the grassroots contented so increasing the leadership's room for manoeuvre during the massive labour unrest of 1911–14. Law's object was to keep the Conservative Party out of industrial politics, letting the government suffer the opprobrium for the disruption and shoulder the responsibility for finding a solution.[57] Many Conservatives pressed Law to take a 'robust' stance on industrial unrest and mobilise opinion in support for harsh measures against strikers. Whilst expressing his personal sympathy for such a response Law concluded that 'an attempt to make party capital out of this disaster [the 1912 miners' strike] would do us harm not good'.[58] For the Conservative Party to embrace anti-trade unionism would be very dangerous as it might be interpreted as the party being anti-*working class* which was not the same as being *anti-Socialist*. Short of a major confrontation with the unions, requiring the massive use of state power to coerce the unions the *ad hoc* policy of the government was acceptable to the Conservative leadership.[59]

Law's leadership began with the Conservative Party's fortunes at a low ebb; three years later Conservatives were riding high with good reason to believe they would win the next general election. Thus, 'The wider party was mobilized and enthused; organization was tighter than ever before; Press support was more solid; financial backing both widespread and generous; the electoral machine finely tuned, and a membership no longer hesitant but inspired'.[60] Law's aggressive 'reactionary' politics united the party and was therefore a rational strategy; social reformism would promote party disunity. Law, however, could certainly not afford to offend large swathes of voters by blanket opposition to working-class or trade-union interests. This complex problem could be resolved by anti-Socialism, a viable electoral strategy within the status quo.

What conclusions can we draw from this brief survey of Conservative politics in the nineteenth century? First, and most important, the Conservative Party has never been a reactionary party. Whiggism, utilitarianism, and pragmatism were blended by Peel and subsequently by Disraeli into an acceptance that ignoring abuses risked discontent becoming something far more dangerous. Whilst not known for their reforming instincts, Salisbury and Law acknowledged the Conservative Party could, and should, undertake moderate reforms. Second, reformism depended on the preservation of social order, and vice versa. Peel, Disraeli, Salisbury, and Law were united by their fear of a breakdown in social order, but order and discipline were to be maintained, however, not just by coercion but by judicious and timely concession. 'Kicks and carrots' seems to sum up the Conservative approach to preserving social and political stability.

The purpose of reformism and the maintenance of order was the defence of property rights, the basis of freedom. This did not apply solely to 'big' (landed or industrial) property. One of Peel's most significant contributions to Conservative success was a recognition that those with only a small amount of property had as much (perhaps more) to fear from any threat to property as any landed aristocrat or industrialist. The Conservative role as the defender of the property rights of all classes was endorsed by Disraeli, Salisbury, and Law. Herein lie the origins of 'the property-owning democracy' of the 1950s as well as the popular capitalism of the 1980s. Furthermore, from the sanctity of property emerges the Conservative Party's conviction that it, and it alone, is the bulwark against Socialism.

Taken together these three aspects of Conservatism form the party's response to democracy. Nevertheless, the Conservative Party remained distrustful of democracy and during the century refined techniques for managing democracy. The creation of the National Union and Conservative Central Office and auxiliaries such as the Primrose League are the most obvious examples of these techniques. Historically the Conservative Party has not only been the best organised British party but also the most innovatory in adopting new propaganda and other methods so as to manage and manipulate public opinion. The importance of organisation was recognised by Disraeli, under whom the National Union and Central Office were established, by Salisbury who benefited from the Middleton Machine, and Law who presided over Steel-Maitland's regeneration of the party machine. The purpose of this organisation was the fragmentation of class consciousness. It is not too great an exaggeration to claim that the pre-eminent objective of Conservative domestic politics was to prevent, or at least stunt, the growth of an independent working-class consciousness.

These developments also created problems. The most serious, and most difficult to resolve, was reconciling party unity with electoral success. All party leaders strove to balance the party's dislike of change with the need to be electable. Reconciling party management and electoral competition was facilitated by the concentration of authority in the party leader and the party's tendency to defer to its leaders. This enabled the Conservatives to survive three major challenges: the challenge of reform after 1834, the challenge of democracy after 1867, and the challenge of Socialism from 1900. By 1914 the Conservative Party had an effective response to politics as then structured but whether or not this would have delivered victory in 1915 is, of course, unknowable but the outbreak of war clearly posed a threat to the status quo. A large-scale European war would drastically alter political life, and the longer the war lasted the greater would be its political impact.

Notes

1 R. Eccleshall, *English Conservatism since the Restoration. An Introduction and Anthology* (London: Unwin Hyman, 1990) provides a useful survey, and R. Blake, *The Conservative Party from Peel to Thatcher* (London: Fontana, 1985), pp. 1–9, considers the confused and confusing origins of the Conservative Party. B. Coleman, *Conservatism and the Conservative Party in Nineteenth Century Britain* (London: Edward Arnold, 1989) is a first-class survey of the period to the 1890s.

2 B. W. Hill (ed.), *Edmund Burke. On Government, Politics and Society* (London: Fontana, 1975), and F. O'Gorman, *Edmund Burke. His Political Philosophy* (London: Unwin Books, 1973) survey Burke's politics.

3 On the politics of this period see J. A. Phillips, *Electoral Behaviour in Unreformed England* (Princeton: Princeton University Press, 1982), and N. Gash, *Reaction and Reconstruction in English Politics 1832–52* (Oxford: Oxford University Press, 1965).

4 N. K. O'Sullivan, *Conservatism* (New York: St Martin's Press, 1976), pp. 82–92, and Eccleshall, *English Conservatism*, pp. 83–92.

5 M. Bentley, *Politics without Democracy, 1815–1914* (London: Fontana, 1984), pp. 86–95,and Blake, *The Conservative Party*, pp. 19–28.

6 For Peel see R. Steward, *The Politics of Protection* (Cambridge: Cambridge University Press, 1971), and R. Stewart, *The Foundation of the Conservative Party* (London: Longmans, 1978). More manageable is I. Newbold, 'Sir Robert Peel and the English Conservative Party, 1832–1841', *English Historical Review*, 98 (1983), pp. 529–57.

7 See R. Blake, *Disraeli* (London: Eyre & Spottiswoode, 1966), E. J. Feutchwanger, *Disraeli, Democracy and the Conservative Party* (Oxford: Oxford University Press, 1968), and J. Vincent, *Disraeli* (Oxford: Oxford University Press, 1992).

8 P. W. Buck (ed.), *How Conservatives Think* (Harmondsworth: Penguin, 1975),

pp. 68–70.

9 P. Smith, *Disraelian Conservatism and Social Reform* (London: Routledge & Kegan Paul, 1967), p. 45. See also R. Shannon, *The Age of Disraeli, 1868–1881: The Rise of Tory Democracy* (London: Longman, 1992).

10 Smith, *Disraelian Conservatism*, pp. 58 and 86.

11 P. Joyce, *Work, Society and Politics. The Culture of the Factory in Later Victorian Britain* (London: Methuen, 1980), pp. 292–303.

12 Salisbury's politics are explored in M. Pinto-Duschinsky (ed.), *The Political Thought of Lord Salisbury* (London: Constable, 1968), P. Smith (ed.), *Lord Salisbury on Politics* (Cambridge: Cambridge University Press, 1971), and Lord Blake and H. Cecil (eds.), *Salisbury, The Man and His Politics* (London: Macmillan, 1987). The best short examination of Salisbury is 'The Authentic Voice of Conservatism' in P. F. Clarke, *A Question of Leadership. From Gladstone to Thatcher* (Harmondsworth: Penguin, 1992), pp. 43–59.

13 'The Reform Bill', *Quarterly Review*, 238 (April 1866), p. 541, and 'The Budget and the Reform Bill', *Quarterly Review*, 214 (April 1860), pp. 523–4.

14 F. M. L. Thompson, 'Private Property and Public Policy', in Blake & Cecil (eds.), *Salisbury*, pp. 252–89. Significantly, one of Salisbury's few domestic reforms was to improve working-class housing.

15 'The Budget and the Reform Bill', pp. 536 and 541.

16 'The Factory Movement', *The Saturday Review*, 20 March 1858, pp. 298–9.

17 'The Reform Bill', p. 549.

18 'The Reform Bill', p. 553.

19 'The Budget and the Reform Bill', p. 523, and 'Mr Roebuck at Salisbury', *The Saturday Review*, 25 January 1862.

20 'Disintegration', *Quarterly Review* (1883), p. 567.

21 'Disintegration', pp. 568–70.

22 'The Reform Bill', p. 557.

23 'Disintegration', p. 56.

24 A. B. Cooke and J. Vincent (eds.), *The Governing Passion. Cabinet Government and Party Politics in Britain, 1885–1886* (Brighton: Harvester Press, 1975), p. 3.

25 'The Reform Bill', pp. 532–40 for Salisbury's analysis.

26 P. Marsh, *The Discipline of Popular Government, Lord Salisbury's Domestic Statecraft 1886–1902* (Brighton: Harvester Press, 1975), pp. 35–47.

27 J. Cornford, 'The Transformation of Conservatism in the Late 19th Century', *Victorian Studies*, 7 (September 1963), p. 58, and N. Blewett, *The Peers, the Parties, and the People. The General Elections of 1910* (London: Macmillan, 1972), p. 15.

28 Blewett, *The Peers, the Parties, and the People*, p. 23.

29 Marsh, *The Discipline of Popular Government*, pp. 184–9.

30 A. K. Russell, *Liberal Landslide. The General Election of 1906* (Newton Abbott: David & Charles, 1973), p. 154, and Blewett, *The Peers, the Parties, and the People*, p. 27.

31 R. S. Churchill, 'Elijah's Mantle', *Fortnightly Review*, 1 May 1883, pp. 613–21.

32 Quoted in Coleman, *Conservatism*, p. 177.

33 Marsh, *The Discipline of Popular Government*, pp. 47–59, and Blake, *The Conservative Party*, pp. 157–9.

34 M. Pugh, *The Tories and the People, 1880–1935* (Oxford: Basil Blackwell, 1985), p. 139.

35 This account is based on A. Sykes, *Tariff Reform in British Politics* (Oxford: Clarendon Press, 1979).

36 G. D. Phillips, *The Diehards. Aristocratic Society and Politics in Edwardian England* (Harvard: Harvard University Press, 1979), pp. 114 and 129ff.

37 Lord Willoughby de Broke, 'The Tory Tradition', *National Review*, 58 (1911), p. 208 for the National Tory definition of crisis, and also Phillips, *The Diehards*, p. 148, 'National Toryism', *National Review*, 59 (1912), p. 412, and 'The Tory Tradition', pp. 206–7.

38 'National Toryism', pp. 416–17, and 'The Tory Tradition', p. 208.

39 'The Tory Tradition', pp. 201–6, and 'National Toryism', p. 418.

40 'National Toryism', p. 418, 'The Tory Tradition', p. 211, and 'National Toryism', pp. 420–2.

41 Quoted in E. J. Halevy, *The Rule of Democracy 1905–1914* (London, Benn 1962), p. 92 and F. J. C. Hearnshaw, *Conservatism in England* (London: Macmillan, 1933), p. 245.

42 D. A. Cosby, 'The Conservative Disaster, and What It Signifies', *The Westminster Review*, 16(3) (March 1906), p. 237.

43 For example, M. Pugh, *The Making of Modern British Politics* (London, 1982), pp. 106–7, and A. Sykes, *Tariff Reform in British Politics, 1906–1913* (Oxford: Clarendon Press, 1979), chapter 9.

44 J. Ridley, 'The Unionist Social Reform Committee, 1911–1914: Wets Before the Deluge', *The Historical Journal*, 30(2) (1987), pp. 408–9.

45 D. S. Dutton, 'The Unionist Party and Social Policy, 1906–1914', *The Historical Journal*, 24(4) (1981), pp. 875–7.

46 J. Smith, 'Bluff, Bluster and Brinkmanship: Andrew Bonar Law and the Third Home Rule Bill', *The Historical Journal* 36(1) (1993), pp. 161–78.

47 Blake, *The Conservative Party*, p. 194. Our emphasis.

48 R. Blake, *The Unknown Prime Minister* (London: Cassell 1955), p. 140.

49 *Bonar Law Papers 26/1/76*, Walter Long to Law, November, February, and March 1911–12, Constituency Survey. Hereafter *BL*.

50 K. D. Wald, *Crosses on the Ballot. Patterns of British Voter Alignment since 1885* (Princeton: Princeton University Press, 1983), p. 214.

51 M. Pugh, *Electoral Reform in Peace and War* (London: Routledge & Kegan Paul, 1978), pp. 36–43.

52 *BL 24/5/159*, A Stringer to Law, 27 December 1911, and J. Ramsden, *The Conservative Party in the Age of Balfour and Baldwin* (London: Longman, 1978), chapters 4 and 5 for details.

53 K. Young, *Local Politics and the Rise of Party* (Leicester: Leicester University Press, 1975), pp. 96–7.

54 Young, *Local Politics and the Rise of Party*, pp. 104–12.

55 Ridley, 'The Unionist Social Reform Committee', p. 411.

56 J. Barnes and D. Nicholson, *The Leo Amery Diaries, Volume 1: 1896–1929* (London: Hutchinson, 1980), 17 February and 1 August 1912, and *BL 3/3/12*, Sir George Younger to Law, 9 October 1913.

57 *BL 33/4/34*, Law to Lord Salisbury, 3 May 1912.

58 *BL 33/4/27*, Law to Sir Hugh Graham, 29 March 1912.
59 K. Middlemas, *Politics in Industrial Society* (London: Deutsch, 1979), p. 58, and K. D. Brown, 'The Anti-Socialist Union, 1908–1949', in K. D. Brown (ed.), *Essays in Anti-Labour History* (London: Macmillan 1975), pp. 234–61.
60 Smith, 'Bluff, Bluster and Brinkmanship', p. 178.

2

Conservatism in crisis, 1914–1931

The 1914–18 war aroused Conservative fears about the growth of the state, democracy, and Socialism and fuelled the Conservative search for a modification of Law's pre-1914 strategy. The Conservative destruction of the Coalition in 1922 led the party to evolve a political style which sought to constitutionalise democracy. The success of Baldwin's 'non-partisan' politics of national integration was not pre-ordained and was not fully accepted by the party. Despite these problems Baldwin's politics of integration secured its apotheosis in the 1931 political crisis.

Conservatism and the First World War

Conservatives recognised that the longer the war lasted the greater would be its effect on politics. Production demands could only be satisfied by a mass mobilisation which brought labour (industrial and political) into politics, and this 'led the state to become increasingly involved in the direction, control and disciplining of the labour force'.[1] The Conservatives were now confronting mass democracy and the growth of the state, both of which it had long regarded as inherently Socialist. The party tried three responses: coalition, the encouragement of patriotic labour, and a Conservative union movement. All failed.

When the war did not end by Christmas the governing elites proceeded to readjust their relationship. Until May 1915 the Liberals remained in government with the Conservatives playing the increasingly frustrating role of patriotic opposition. On 6 August the National Union Executive accepted they and the Liberal Party end the publication of party propaganda and the making of partisan speeches, and on 28 August a formal electoral truce was concluded.[2] By the spring of 1915 Conservative acquiescence was wearing thin, and the emergence of the Unionist Business Committee reflected growing backbench unhappiness with the government and Law's acquiescence culminating in a rebellion over Lloyd George's plan to regulate the drink trade.[3] In May 1915 the government was restructured into a formal Coalition in which the Liberals kept the key offices of state and Law received the Colonial Office but the backbench made it clear Asquith's government was living on borrowed time.[4]

Up to December 1916 these manoeuvrings largely concerned those politicians deeply involved in high politics but the demands of the war effort were progressively closing the gap between 'high' and 'low' politics. From the attempts to resolve unrest and secure the co-operation of the unions Lloyd George emerged as the most dynamic minister.[5] The strains of war production lay at the heart of the political crisis of December 1916. Dissatisfaction over Asquith's prosecution of the war and Law's difficulties with the Unionists led him, Carson, and Lloyd George to advocate a three-member War Committee with Asquith as Premier. When Asquith rejected this the dissidents led by the Conservatives lined up behind Lloyd George: 'All he had to do was to hold a pistol at Asquith's head whenever he chose because he was the strongest man'.[6] Asquith fell.

The Second Coalition brought the Conservatives back into government where they were to remain in government (but for two brief intervals) until July 1945. The Conservatives were ambivalent towards Lloyd George but they were back in government under a Prime Minister whose commitment to winning the war could not be doubted. Furthermore, Lloyd George seemingly enjoyed a special rapport with labour. He was, however, a dangerously mercurial innovator whose pragmatic wartime expedients, many Conservatives feared, would have devastating consequences for post-war politics. For the time being Lloyd George was an indispensable asset for the Conservatives and while the war lasted the Coalition was impregnable. Lloyd George had no party until May 1918 when he created a Coalition Liberal organisation which, along with his reputation, he used to achieve a favourable allocation of seats in the electoral agreement of July 1918. Growing labour unrest in 1917 led many Conservatives to doubt that Lloyd George could handle the unions and working class, and by the Armistice there was a deep Conservative distrust of Lloyd George but, one Conservative noted, *'Unity seems to me so essential if the orderly elements are to prevail against the forces of disorder'.*[7]

Popular support for the war seemingly offered an opportunity for marginalising working-class political consciousness and isolating Socialism. Prominent in the emergence of patriotic labour was Lord Milner, who had been frustrated by the party's negativity before 1914 and its refusal to appeal to the working class. The war, it was argued, had created a group of patriotic Socialists and union leaders with whom Conservatives could co-operate, and the patriotic labour movement was both a valuable auxiliary and offered a means of dividing the Labour Party. Patriotic labour emerged in 1916 as the British Workers' League (BWL, later the National Democratic

Labour Party, NDLP) which initially was critical of all parties but was attracted to the Conservatives because of their common rejection of class politics. L. S. Amery actively promoted the BWL, arguing that 'the conflict of the future was between those who had the national and patriotic and those who had the international point of view, and that [he] was prepared to endorse and back any programme that was patriotic, even if I disagreed with its details, *providing it secured the adhesion of the working classes to the national and Imperial idea'*.[8] The difficulty was that the BWL's programme advocated massive state intervention which the Conservative Party defined as Socialism.[9]

By the end of 1916 negotiations were under way on a programme to harmonise relations between capital and labour and translate this into post-war politics. Patriotic labour agreed the Conservative Party 'should not simply adopt and patronise the BWL ... but should come out with a programme of its own not incompatible with the other'.[10] Discussions began in April 1917 on an electoral agreement covering thirty constituencies but difficulties developed in coming to an electoral accord. The BWL's importance increased with the Russian Revolution and the domestic industrial unrest of 1917 and throughout 1917 Steel-Maitland and the BWL negotiated a common programme. The Conservative Party was careful, however, to give these talks no official status.[11]

By late 1917/early 1918 it was increasingly difficult to reconcile Conservatism and patriotic labour on a positive programme. The constituencies would not accept BWL candidates unless they had been endorsed by the party leadership but endorsement would make the BWL appear a Conservative Party creature.[12] The BWL might, it was recognised, cost the party working-class support and disrupt relations with the unions whose co-operation was essential. Nonetheless, in November 1917 Bonar Law advocated the Conservative Party ally with patriotic labour.[13] By 1918 the NDLP seemed impressive but it failed to secure legitimacy with the working class, and despite having eighteen MPs in 1918 the party was wiped out in the 1922 general election. Patriotic labour was a creation of the war; once the war ended so did its rationale.

The patriotic upsurge of the war years and the leftwards drift of labour politics prompted the question of what, if any, direct link the Conservative Party ought to have with the working class. Traditionally, the Conservative Party feared the consequences of a party within a party. Class linkages violated both the One Nation self-image and threatened to limit the leadership's room for manoeuvre. The Unionist Labour Movement and the Labour Sub-Committee of the National Union were founded in 1919 on the initiative of Lancashire Conservative trade unionists.[14] Their purpose was to organise against Socialism and syndicalism in support of King, Constitution and Empire and to help secure the election of Conservative trade unionists to union office and public bodies up to and including the House of Commons.[15] The aim was not 'to fight trade unions (or) trade unionists, but ... that small and determined body which dominated the present Labour Party ... the men who would shake hands with Bolshevists and would upset the whole fabric upon which the Constitution of the country had been built'. In industry it sought 'a readjustment of the ideas between employers and the employed, whereby they might have industrial peace and goodwill amongst men'.[16] The belief was that Conservative trade unionists and voters could challenge the Labour Party–union connection if organised and mobilised but organisationally and politically the Unionist Labour Movement was a failure.[17].

The 1914–18 war 'knocked away the foundations of some cherished Conservative principles, hastened the advent of some articles of Conservative faith and raised a host of new problems that were to challenge interwar conservatism'.[18] The Conservative commitment to Ulster and free trade were undermined by the war, and most accepted that the war would lead to a further, and very major, extension of the franchise to virtually all men and some women. There remained considerable disquiet at the consequences of a large-scale intrusion of the working class into politics but the central problem of wartime politics which was not resolved was the Conservative attitude to the state. Conservatives accepted that the war could not be prosecuted without a high level of state intervention but how much of this *ad hoc* intervention should remain in peace? The instinctive Conservative reaction was to return to 'normalcy'.

The Conservative Party and the new politics

The 1918 Coalition manifesto declared, 'The principal concern of every Government is and must be the condition of the great mass of the people who live by manual toil'. The realities of power within the party and Coalition dictated that its policy would become dominated by fiscal orthodoxy and the maintenance of business condence. Could working-class opinion be reconciled with this governing mentality?

Central to the government's post-war policy was labour's marginalisation. By early 1918 ministers intended to marginalise the unions which involved drawing a distinction between 'political' and 'industrial' activity and using the resources of the state to crush the former and encourage the latter.[19] The Labour Party's marginality was demonstrated by the removal of Henderson from the War Cabinet in 1917 and Labour was swamped by the Coalition in the 1918 election. Lloyd George and Conservative politicians had a vested interest in portraying the Labour Party as extremists and allies of the Bolsheviks. The Conservatives warned that voting Labour would lead to 'A Republic in this Country, Civil War and Revolution, Lenin, Trotsky and Up with Bolshevism and Communism' and 'The "Labour" Party stands for Waste, Bankruptcy, Ruin for All. For Bolshevism! For Unemployment! For Revolution!'[20] In private the Coalition was less worried but believed it necessary to establish a connection in the electorate's mind between the Labour Party and extremism. This was used to great effect with the Zinoviev Letter (1924) and less publicly in running intelligence operations against Labour such as securing the co-operation of the Labour Party's printers so that the Conservative Party had first sight of policy and other documents.[21] To avoid losing electoral support the Labour Party would have to strive to prove its democratic credentials and drawing the Labour Party into constitutional politics would transform it into a mechanism for controlling militancy.

Conservative dominance in the Coalition and its determination to preserve business confidence ensured that the extension of political rights in 1918 was not accompanied by any significant extension of social rights. The war increased business's fear of state intervention and growing trade union power and strengthened business links with the Conservative Party.[22] This worried some Conservatives. Baldwin expressed caution about the 'hard faced men who looked as if they had done well out of the war' and Bridgeman regretted the 'strange absence of any sporting desire amongst manufacturers to take some risks with the large profits ... piled up in the War, partly of course due to labour unrest, but I fear partly due to the love of large profits'.[23] Law warned businessmen that there was 'in the House of Commons ... an element such as we have never seen before because there are enough to create a serious opposition, to that extent, our whole industrial system is challenged'.[24] The dominance of business was symbolised by the appointment of the Geddes Committee (August 1921) on public expenditure which 'was guaranteed to recommend the rich man's response, not so much to the slump as to any situation which enabled the wealthy to assert successfully their class interest – low taxation through savage cuts in state expenditure, expenditure on social programme for the less privileged'.[25]

The Coalition's original justification and attraction for the Conservatives was that it promised to marginalise Socialism. Events, such as increasing unemployment, eased one set of pressures on government but might transfer the crisis to the electoral and political system. Politicians feared unemployment would be reflected in increased electoral support for the Labour Party. Between 14 December 1918 (the general election) and 19 October 1922 (the Carlton Club meeting) there were twenty-eight by-elections. Of these the Coalition lost twenty and won three (a net loss of seventeen), and of these the Labour Party won fourteen which indicated the Coalition's inability to block Labour's advance. A closer examination of the Coalition's losses reveals a more complex picture. The Coalition Unionists lost five seats to the Liberals, four to Labour, and two to Independents; the Coalition Liberals lost seven seats to Labour, one each to an Independent and a

Conservative. From the Conservative point of view, then, it was the loss of Coalition Liberal and Unionist seats to Labour which was so serious as it pointed to a polarisation of politics. It was this which undermined support for the Coalition among the Conservatives.

Unrest amongst the Conservative junior ministers was reflected in the party in the country. From January 1922 Sir George Younger (the Party Chairman) and Sir Malcolm Fraser (Principal Agent) warned Austen Chamberlain (Law's successor as Party Leader) that an early election fought on Coalition lines would cost the Conservatives 100 seats and split the party. Chamberlain and leading Unionist ministers (except Stanley Baldwin) endorsed Lloyd George's thesis 'that in order to defeat Labour it is necessary to have a Coalition'. Senior Conservative ministers failed to appreciate the strength of feeling in the party, or that they could browbeat any opposition into submission. Law, out of politics because of ill-health but whose attitude to the continuation or otherwise of the Coalition would be crucial, was 'very pessimistic ... convinced that nothing would avert a break up and fear[ed] a long exclusion from office, something like the fate of the Party after the break between Peel and Disraeli'. If Chamberlain resigned over the Coalition's continuation Law was willing to become party leader.[26]

The meeting at the Carlton Club decided against Coalition and removed Lloyd George from office. The resignation of Chamberlain and his supporters removed, albeit temporarily, the leading ranks of Conservatives from politics and made Law party leader and Prime Minister. Although the seriousness of Law's illness was not then apparent it was suspected that he would not be Prime Minister for long and that the succession would be between Lord Curzon (who apart from his noble status had a number of personality traits which made him unsuitable for political leadership in a democracy) and the hitherto obscure Baldwin whose new eminence was due to the senior ministers' resignations. The Coalition's collapse 'was not the result of a Carlton Club plot, but came up from below with great force from the constituencies'.[27] The formation of the 1922 Committee confirmed the increasingly important element of the backbench in Conservative politics.[28] Party organisation in the country was now far more influential because of the extension of the franchise in 1918. The 'peasants' revolt' of 1922 meant that henceforth party management skills would, more than ever, be an essential attribute of a Conservative leader.

Between 1918 and 1922 Conservatives contemplated various schemes to limit the impact of the new electorate, such as proportional representation or reform of the House of Lords. By 1922 the Conservative Party had abandoned any attempt to erect structural or institutional obstacles to mass democracy.[29] This meant it had to rely on the obstacles provided by existing political arrangements. Conservative strategy was based on two elements: that mass democracy was a *fait accompli* and that the Conservative

Party had to educate the mass electorate into an appreciation of the legitimate (i.e. limited) role of government. This relied on the distortions generated by the electoral system and establishing a two-party system in which the only alternative to voting Conservative was voting Labour. The institutions of parliamentary democracy became an effective barrier to mass democracy. In the inter-war period the Conservatives won a majority of the votes cast only in 1931 and 1935 and never a majority of the electorate, but they won a majority of seats in the House of Commons in 1922, 1924, 1931 and 1935. The Conservatives were able to dominate British politics and government with an average of 45% of the votes cast and 33% of the electorate thanks to the operation of the first-past-the-post electoral system. Furthermore, it took far fewer votes to elect a Conservative MP than a Labour or Liberal.[30]

Once Labour achieved major party status in 1918 the question was which of the two other parties would become its main rival. Liberal/Conservative co-operation in 1918 and 1931 fatally undermined Liberal support as it encouraged those who wished to oppose the government to vote Labour and encouraged pro-government Liberals to vote Conservative. The Liberals became caught in a two-party squeeze which led to a decline in the number of Liberal candidacies, itself an indicator of waning organisational vitality and financial viability.[31] The last substantial Liberal challenge for government came in 1929 so the destination of the votes released by Liberal decline is a major factor in modern British politics. Evidence gathered in the early 1960s concludes that whilst 'the Labour Party succeeded to the Liberals' place as the Conservatives' main opponent in the British party system, only a minority of historical Liberal support went to Labour'.[32] The flow of the Liberal vote to the Labour and Conservative parties is a function of the emergence of class politics with Liberal voters identifying Labour's rise as responsible for Liberal decline and Socialism as antithetical to core Liberal ideas. Particularly important was the Conservative appeal to the children of working-class liberals which broadened Conservative working-class support.[33]

Under democracy Conservatives feared the House of Commons would become dominated by the party caucus faithfully reflecting the desires of an electorate manipulated by demagogues. What actually happened was that both the House of Commons and party organisation became dominated by the party leadership. The fall of the Coalition, the fragmentation of the opposition, and the electoral system ensured the Conservatives could rule on a minority of the popular vote. What mattered was preserving the unity of the party in the country and the House of Commons. This was made possible by developments produced by the emergence of mass politics in the late nineteenth century. The first of these developments was the emergence of mass parties whose essential purpose was to secure the election of MPs. This required the alignment of political parties with popular sentiment so that these parties (and their allies in the media) could influence opinion. MPs were elected on a party label and were identified with and committed to a party whose political success and grassroots organisation ensured their election. The concomitant was disciplined parties in the House of Commons under the control of the party whips and party leaders. This placed the sovereignty of Parliament and its legislative power at the disposal of the group of party leaders who controlled a disciplined majority in the House of Commons. This isolated government from direct pressures under all but the most extreme circumstances. The relative autonomy of government was further enhanced by the reorganisation and centralisation of government via the Cabinet Secretariat and the central role of the Treasury within government, and the beneficiary of this process was the Prime Minister who became the focal point of both the party and the governmental system.

Law's philosophy of government and political practice was set out in his 1922 election address:

> The crying need of the nation at this moment – and which in my judgement far exceeds any other – is that we should have tranquillity and stability both at home and abroad so that free scope should be given to the initiative and enterprise of our citizens, for it is in that way far more than by action of the Government that we can hope to recover from the economic and social results of the war.[34]

Law's main domestic policy concerns were the revival of trade and the reduction of unemployment. Government would take emergency measures but these, Law conceded, were palliatives as trade would only improve and unemployment fall following public spending and tax cuts to transfer resources to the private sector and bolster business confidence. Law acknowledged that there were many (albeit unspecified) legislative measures he would like to recommend to the electorate but confessed he could not do so because of the overriding priority of returning to 'normalcy'. The role of government was strictly limited. To a delegation of miners seeking government intervention to improve living standards Law lamented: 'What can the Government do? It is easy to say [it] is the business of Government to put it right. How can they put it right?' His industrial policy was simple, he told the TUC: 'we are doing all we can to restore sound finance'. To the TUC's suggestion that unemployment might lead to unrest Law warned that the government would not yield to unconstitutional pressure.[35]

The expansion of the electorate transformed electoral politics and party politicians had to respond to the new environment. Party managers were acutely conscious of the potential difficulties now facing the Conservatives in their relationship with the electorate. J. C. C. Davidson, for example, believed that 'Before the war it was possible with a limited and highly expert electorate to put forward Party programmes of a restricted and well defined character, but nowadays I am quite sure that while not departing from the principles of our Party we must endeavour to gain the confidence not of our own supporters but of the mugwump vote'.[36] Impressionistic confirmation of this can be seen in the changing nature of party manifestoes which up to 1918 were slim documents, couched in vague terms. The 1918 manifesto is a long document dealing in specifics, those of 1922 and 1923 see a reversion to the limited pre-1918 model, but that of 1924 is a long document making specific appeals to many groups, a trend continued by the 1929 manifesto. After making due allowance for the unique character of each election the increasing length and detailed content of Conservative manifestoes points to a change in the nature of politics, so Law's struggle for limited government was, in a sense, a doomed rear-guard action. So, 'Between 1920 and 1924 the Conservative Party made three long-term decisions. The first was to remove Lloyd George from office. The second was to take up the role of "defender of the social order". The third was to make Labour the chief party of opposition. These decisions were attempts to contain the upheaval caused by the Labour Party's arrival as a major force and to gain whatever advantage could be gained from it'.[37] Law laid the foundations of this but it was Stanley Baldwin who implemented the strategy of class integration.

Baldwin and the politics of non-partisan Conservatism

Baldwin entered Parliament in 1908 aged 41 from the family iron and steel company. He made little political impact but cultivated a reputation as a moderate, thoughtful, and reliable MP with expertise on industrial matters (he served on the USRC). Baldwin became leader of the Conservative Party by accident. In 1916 he became Law's parliamentary Private Secretary, then Financial Secretary of the Treasury, and in 1921 President of the Board of Trade. Baldwin was party leader from 1922 to 1937, Prime Minister three times (1923, 1924–9, 1935–7), and was the key figure in the National Government. To form a government the Conservative Party had to prevent a Liberal revival which would split the anti-Socialist vote and it did so by projecting itself as the party of 'common sense' for which all voters concerned with the nation's true interests could vote. The failure of the last Liberal challenge in 1929 and the obliteration of the Labour government in 1931 greatly simplified the politics enabling Baldwin to create the institutional expression of his politics: the National Government. Baldwin's appeal to a wide spectrum of support was, however, based on an unrepresentative and partisan political structure, the Conservative Party.

There was nothing inevitable about the dominance of Baldwinite Conservatism in the inter-war period. He owed his eminence to his role at the

Carlton Club meeting where he delivered a devastating attack on Lloyd George and the Coalition when every other minister spoke in favour of continued participation. Without the subsequent break-up of the Coalition and the resignations of the senior Conservative ministers Baldwin would not have become Law's Chancellor of the Exchequer and number two, and without Law's resignation due to throat cancer Baldwin would not have become party leader in 1923 and therefore Prime Minister. As a member of the Lords, Curzon was deemed unsuitable to be Prime Minister, this left only Baldwin. Furthermore, Baldwin had a number of serious scrapes with the Party over his decision to call an unnecessary election in 1923 on protection which the Conservatives lost and led to the first Labour government (over his handling of the miners in 1925, the loss of the 1929 general election, his lack of inspiration as leader of the opposition, and his India policy after 1931) events which, although he survived, demonstrate a less than enthusiastic endorsement of his leadership. That he survived is testimony to both his political skills and the fact that he offered an effective response to the most pressing problem facing the Conservatives: the rise of Labour.

The maintenance of business confidence and the centrality of business interests to Conservative politics provided a counterweight to Baldwin's One Nation politics. The Conservative focus on anti-Socialism naturally drew the party and business closer together after 1918.[38] In 1929 the party raised £125,000 from the City 'for the simple reason that they are thoroughly frightened at the prospect of a socialist Government'. This money was raised at a series of lunches where Baldwin made 'inimitable little speeches so free from Party bias that the dangers seemed all the greater as no allowance had to be made for partisanship'. Baldwin was, of course, speaking to his own kind:

> it is essentially a businessman's appeal to businessmen to help the only political party which possesses the one national organisation which is capable of fighting Socialism of which there is increasing terror amongst financiers and industrialists of the country as it becomes nearer to the realm of practical politics.[39]

In the 1930s 181 of 415 government MPs (44%) were company directors. Government MPs held 775 directorships of which the largest category was in the financial sector where 86 MPs held 109 directorships. Family business connections were equally strong: 29% of the fathers of Conservative MPs were occupied in industry, banking, and commerce.[40] The prominence of business and financial interests led one senior Conservative to lament its effect on policy. Urging the government to pass a Factory Bill and do more to safeguard manufacturing industry Bridgeman doubted 'the wisdom of paying off so much National Debt at this time – we seem to consider the Bankers only and not the industrialists'.[41] These business links represented a major limiting factor on the content of Baldwinite Conservatism's cross-class politics.

Baldwin was convinced that there was an anti-Socialist majority in the electorate but that this was not inevitably a Conservative majority. The destruction of the Coalition and the 1923 and 1924 general elections restricted the attractiveness of Conservative–Liberal coalition (as opposed to co-operation) and the Labour government (1924) made aggressive anti-Socialism a questionable electoral strategy. Baldwin's difficulty was reconciling what he interpreted as the wider needs of the political system (Labour's political integration) and the Conservative Party (electoral success on the basis of centre opinion) with the fears and prejudices of the party grassroots over the rise of Labour and Socialism. Baldwin was accused of committing two major errors when he became leader. The first was to throw away Bonar Law's 1922 majority in the 1923 election called when Baldwin became convinced that unemployment could only be resolved by protection. This united the anti-Conservative majority in defence of free trade. The second flowed from this: the first Labour government. Baldwin thought it right that the electorate should be asked to pronounce on a fundamental shift in economic policy and the result meant that Labour should be given an opportunity to form a government. In retrospect, his decision to put Labour in government was a master-stroke. Labour took office under carefully controlled conditions, the Conservative–Liberal majority could prevent any Labour adventurism which was, in any case, unlikely given Ramsay Macdonald's constitutionalism. Baldwin spent the time in opposition cultivating his natural supporters on the Conservative and Labour backbenches, leaving others to harass the government. The Labour government's failure was pre-ordained and its fall led to a general election and one of the Conservative Party's greatest electoral victories, with a majority of over 200. The Conservatives benefited from the *Daily Mail*'s 'Red Scare' stunt: the Zinoviev Letter which purported to reveal a Communist conspiracy to subvert the armed forces, but the Conservative share of the vote was such that the Zinoviev Letter did not materially affect the election's outcome. The Liberal unity of 1923 was not repeated and they were reduced to 40 MPs. Labour gained 1 million votes but lost MPs. The 1924 election provided the foundation for Baldwin's political objectives but these were not necessarily those of the Conservative Party.[42]

Baldwin's Conservatism used a unique idiom and was expressly designed for a mass democracy, drawing on the mythical certainties of England's past, employing a rural idiom designed to appeal to an uncertain urban-industrial society. The war and its lost generation, Baldwin believed, had placed a heavy responsibility on those who had been too old to fight, to reunite society. This was to be done not by 'super-men' such as Lloyd George or Mussolini but by 'the innate common-sense, integrity, courage and faith of the common men and women'.[43]

The rural imagery employed contrasted the alienation and dehumanisation of industrial life with the ordered interdependence of rural life. This was located in Disraelian One Nation Toryism, reinforced by Baldwin's business career which brought him into contact with ordinary people, convincing him of their honesty and integrity which provided the rationale for his politics: 'There is only one thing which I feel is worth giving one's whole strength to, and that is the binding together of all classes of our people in an effort to make life in this country better in every sense of the word. That is the main end and object of my life in politics'.[44] Baldwin's conception of politics as being to promote the national good gave his Toryism a non-partisan appeal. In November 1923, for example, he declared 'when one is giving one's life in service for the people of this country one is not working for any kind of abstraction or any large party of voters, but for the human men and women who are carrying on the daily toil of the world'.[45] Conservatives, Baldwin argued, 'want to help better the conditions for our own people. We want to see the people raised, not into a society of State ownership, but into a society in which, increasingly, the individual may become an owner'.[46]

Baldwin's most powerful articulation of the English rural ideal is his speech, 'On England and the West':

> To me, England is the country, and the country is England ... the tinkle of the hammer on the anvil in the country smithy, the corncrake on a dewy morning, the sound of the scythe against the whetstone, and the sight of a plough team coming over the brow of a hill, the sight that has been seen in England since England was a land, and may be seen in England long after the Empire has perished and every works in England has ceased to function, for centuries the one eternal sight of England ... These things strike down into the very depths of our nature, and touch chords that go back to the beginning of time and the human race, but they are chords that with every year of our life sound a deeper note in our innermost being.[47]

This inheritance, Baldwin argued, was common to all and transcended class, providing a sure basis for social integration.

Baldwin returned frequently to society's need to transcend class divisions. This was eloquently expressed in his March 1925 speech on the Macquisten Bill which proposed to restore contracting-in to the trade unions' political funds. Baldwin opposed the bill and called on his party to vote against it in the interests of class harmony. To support his argument Baldwin conjured up an elegiac picture of the lost harmony of his family firm:

> It was a place where I knew, and had known from childhood, every man on the ground; a place where I was able to talk with the men not only about the troubles in the works, but troubles at home and their wives. It was a place

where strikes and lock-outs were unknown. It was a place where the fathers and grandfathers of the men working there had worked, and where their sons went automatically into the business. It was also a place where nobody ever 'got the sack', and where we had a natural sympathy for those who were less concerned with efficiency than in this generation, and where large numbers of old gentlemen used to spend their days sitting on the handles of wheelbarrows, smoking their pipes.[48]

Baldwin recognised this could not be recreated but it represented an aspiration to be striven for in contemporary democratic politics.

Baldwin feared democracy's darker side.[49] Democracy had to be led and democratic leaders had to risk short-term unpopularity and take decisions which would prove correct in the long run. After the 1924 victory he told an audience of party workers and MPs that 'it is your duty, your primary duty, to educate that great democracy'. The Conservative Party, Baldwin continued, stood 'for the union of those two nations of which Disraeli spoke two generations ago; union among our own people to make one nation of our own people at home, which if secured, nothing else matters in the world'.[50]

This was complicated by the General Strike (May 1926) and Baldwin was acutely conscious of this. The General Strike represented a powerful challenge to Baldwinism and forced him to defend his approach to democracy. In his view the General Strike was not an industrial dispute but an attempt to coerce the community and its democratically elected government. For this reason it had to be defeated. Baldwin raised no objection to moderate trade unionism which, he believed, was a force for peace and stability in industry but the political use of industrial power was illegitimate. Once the strike was over, Baldwin argued, it was time for the nation to reintegrate: there should be no recriminations or revenge and the solidarity and common sense displayed by the strikers should now be used for the common good.[51]

It was vital for the Conservative Party's future that the unions were convinced that their interests could be expressed *within* the political nation. This was easily achieved because the Trades Union Congress (TUC) and the Labour Party were united in their distaste for syndicalist politics. More importantly the Conservative Party had to be made to accept that their understandable desire to punish the unions would be counterproductive. By not wreaking a terrible revenge the unions would have no reason not to accept the status quo, which, experience showed, was more likely to meet Conservative requirements than any other democratic alternative. It is for this reason that the Conservatives propounded the thesis that the General Strike proved the vitality and soundness of existing political arrangements.

The General Strike posed a major problem for Baldwinite Conservatism. Hitherto Conservative leaders had been concerned with the effect of mass democracy on Conservative interests, regarding the party as one of the main obstacles to the worst excesses of mass democracy. One of the legacies of the General Strike was to bring home forcefully to the leadership the fact that the Conservative Party was itself a creation of mass democratic politics whose members demanded government policy reflect their preferences. Understandably there was considerable demand for drastic action to be taken against the unions which compelled Baldwin to agree to legislation, but he accompanied his acceptance with a stout defence of legitimate trade unionism and Disraelian One Nation Conservatism.[52] The Trades Union and Trades Disputes Act (1927) was the minimum legislative retribution that the party would accept and the maximum Baldwin would agree to; whilst it undoubtedly annoyed the unions and the Labour Party it satisfied the party's desire for revenge and the trade union question largely disappeared from the party's agenda until 1931.

Analysis of the party's response to the General Strike has tended to focus on the 1927 Act and has ignored one of the most notable attempts at myth-making in British political history. Baldwin's intention was that the General Strike should mark a new base-line for the political system's development: the final constitutionalisation of mass democracy. For this to be achieved the General Strike had to become part of the mainstream British political tradition of Whig-like progression to political maturity. The appropriation of the General Strike by the dominant political tradition was vital as so powerful a symbol of class conflict could not be permitted to become the exclusive property of the dissenting tradition in British politics. Appropriation was also essential to prove to the Conservative Party that mass democracy did not pose a threat. Thus, 'At times one became rather sad because it was difficult to make some people understand that the Communist who fired a revolver or threw a bomb from within the ranks of the strikers against the Police or for pure mischief would have ended his days most painfully at the hands of the strikers long before he could have been rescued by the Police'. After the strike's end the emphasis shifted to stressing the loyalty and soundness of the strikers: 'if you could have moved about amongst the people it would have been borne in upon you that the heart of the people is absolutely sound and that the vast majority of the strikers themselves are not only good citizens but very patriotic'.[53] The General Strike was therefore proof of the political maturity of the people.

In this way the General Strike became part of the justification of British liberal democracy, proving the validity and vitality of established political institutions. Baldwin's oft-professed dream of industrial peace was not, and could not be, realised after 1926 because it was inconceivable that a Conservative Cabinet would coerce industrialists. Ministers were frustrated by the coal owners who had secured significant concessions from the Cabinet on the understanding that this was part of a 'gentleman's agreement' to reach a compromise settlement in the coal industry. However, 'They were obviously determined to break up the [Miners'] Federation. I asked them what harm it could do them if all the district agreements when concluded had to be ratified by the Federation, and [Mining] Association, nationally ... E. [van] Williams said "but what good?" I said "Peace" (for five years) but that did not appeal to him'.[54] This frustration did not, however, lead ministers to impose a solution on the coal owners.

When Baldwin left for Aix-les-Bains in the summer Churchill was left in charge of the negotiations. Churchill was anxious to secure a long-term settlement and several ministers feared this would lead him to committing the government to confrontation with the employers so provoking a crisis within the party. The coal owners knew the strength of their position and that the government would not coerce them.[55] The fate of Austen Chamberlain in 1922 meant that Baldwin was very conscious of what could happen to a leader who lost the party's confidence. When the temporary subsidy was granted to the coal industry in July 1925 Baldwin was warned by the Chief Whip that backbench support could only be guaranteed if there was no further subsidy to this or any other industry.[56] Baldwin's position was bolstered by natural sentiments of loyalty and the absence of any clear alternative leader, but he took very great care to meet the worries of his supporters who would not have accepted coercion of the coal owners. The limits on Baldwin and the government's willingness to coerce business in the interests of cross-class politics were therefore clear.

Conservative politics, National Government

Defeat in 1929 provoked a crisis over Baldwin's leadership and politics which he narrowly survived. If he had been removed subsequent Conservative politics would have been very different. By the end of 1928 the Cabinet appeared lacklustre and lacking a strategic vision, and Baldwin must bear some of the blame for this. The government's major reforms (Churchill's derating proposals and Chamberlain's activity at the Ministry of Health) would not take effect before the election, nor did Baldwin attempt to reinvigorate his government by a major reshuffle. This prompted Davidson, Baldwin's Party Chairman, to urge that 'a forward leap is necessary in order to give our Members and candidates something to talk about in addition to the record of the Government and the fallacies in the Socialist and Liberal programmes'.[57]

The 1924 Labour government's collapse and the defeat of the General Strike confirmed the Conservatives as the party of stability, and in preparing for the election the Liberals, not Labour, were identified as the Conservatives' main problem, for if the Liberals fielded 400–500 candidates they might split the anti-Socialist vote.[58] Davidson feared the defeat of the

General Strike would cost working-class votes but the party could not dis-
avow its actions for 'unless we adopt a vigorous policy, and act up to the
expectations of our own supporters ... we shall discourage our own people'.
This was difficult to reconcile with Baldwin's centrist rhetoric and his belief
that it was the Conservative Party's duty to lessen class antagonism, and
Baldwin was advised to concentrate on retaining and expanding the Conservative working-class electorate. Bridgeman urged Worthington-Evans,
who chaired the committee responsible for formulating the party's manifesto, to include a Factories Bill and increased safeguarding of key industries
to reduce unemployment and criticised the influence of the City over party
policy.[59] The Conservative political dilemma was expressed by Bridgeman
who advised Baldwin 'not to attempt to outbid L[loyd] G[eorge] or the
Socialists in a vote-catching programme' but he conceded the Conservatives
needed a positive appeal, as well as relying on the government's record.[60]
Baldwin's election slogan, 'Safety First', made sense in a context where the
Conservative strategy was to preserve the anti-Socialist vote. Baldwin made
this clear in private: 'If only industry as a whole realised the full dangers
which are bound to ensue were nationalisation to come into the field of
practical politics I believe there would not be much difficulty in raising the
necessary funds to defeat it. The evil effect on credit and the flight of capital would have disastrous effects just at a time when the country is beginning to emerge from the serious depression through which ... it has been
passing'.[61]

After 1929 the Conservatives remained the largest single party and the
electoral system contained the Liberal challenge but at the cost of a Labour
government. 'The election', Bridgeman wrote, 'was lost, not I think from
any wave of resentment against the Government and certainly not against
Baldwin, nor on any one particular piece of policy or legislation', but was
due to 'the love of change common to all democracies or the swing of the
pendulum'. Conservative policy was poorly projected compared to Lloyd
George's *We Can Conquer Unemployment* and Labour's appeal. This and
Lloyd George's 'insistence on fighting every seat gave Socialism a victory
which they could not have won, if arrangements had been made to avoid
three-cornered fights where it was sure to lose the seat to a Socialist'. Social
reform was not only costly but brought little electoral benefit: '*Reduction of
taxation would have done more good*'.[62]

The Liberal failure confirmed the Conservatives' identification of Labour
and Socialism as the fundamental political threat and Labour's improvement on its 1924 performance indicated its electoral support was on an
upward curve, and many Conservatives feared Lloyd George's lack of
principle would lead him to support Labour to wheedle his way back into
government. Macdonald's suspicion of Lloyd George and the Liberals was
not thought strong enough to prevent him from clinging on to office by

co-operating with Lloyd George. As Conservatives expected to be out of office for some time 'We must start getting our policy ready because the electorate do require some time to be educated'.[63] The internal party crisis focused on the style of Baldwin's leadership and the nature of his Conservatism. As in 1924 he was criticised for being too accommodating to Labour, but after 1929 Baldwinism shifted further to the left to correct the influence of the right who were disproportionately strong in safe southern constituencies. Baldwin was anxious to win back northern urban seats which were essential if the Conservative Party was to be convincingly presented as truly national and for winning a majority. He could not afford to adopt the more partisan line favoured by southern Conservatives. Two-fifths of Labour seats were won on a minority vote in three-cornered contests and aggressive partisan Conservatism might not draw off crucial Liberal support in key northern urban seats.[64]

The Labour government survived with Liberal support, which increased Conservative frustration and the party turned inwards. This implosion was fuelled by a recognition that the outcome of the leadership struggle would determine the policies and tone of the next Conservative government. The most serious threat to Baldwin came from two press lords, Beaverbrook (*Daily Express*) and Rothermere (*Daily Mail*). Beaverbrook's Empire Free Trade campaign launched in July 1929 was a wholly unrealistic attempt to create an Imperial customs union dominated by Britain but it enjoyed considerable support in the party. Beaverbrook ran Empire Free Trade candidates against official Conservatives while Rothermere, who had long been unhappy with Baldwinite Conservatism, wished to influence Baldwin's choice of colleagues by threatening to withhold from him his newspaper's support. This led Baldwin to compare press lords to harlots in his speech at Caxton Hall in June 1930, but Baldwin was compelled to sacrifice Davidson as Party Chairman replacing him with Neville Chamberlain. Nonetheless, Baldwin survived. Baldwin confronted his opponents at the meeting of Conservative MPs, peers, and candidates where he issued an open challenge to the party to 'back him or sack him'. They chose the former. By March 1931 a compromise had been reached with Beaverbrook based on a mutual desire not to divide the forces of Conservatism, and the press barons were, of course, an important element in the Conservative coalition.[65]

A second threat emerged over the government of India. Baldwin agreed with the Viceroy (Lord Irwin) that India's future was as a Dominion. This was also government policy. This consensus was challenged by Churchill who saw Dominion status for India as the end of Empire.[66] Churchill's die-hard stance on India attracted considerable support and became symbolic of wider discontents with centrist Conservatism in the party. Baldwin's speech in the Commons ('the speech of his life') on India on 12 March 'confirmed him in the Leadership, but the Party is honeycombed with faction and disloyalty and how long he can hold his position no one can tell'.[67] Churchill's crusade never coalesced with that of the Empire Free Traders (Churchill was a convinced free trader) and Churchill resigned from the Shadow Cabinet in early 1931 over India and began his long march through the political wilderness.

The crisis of 1931 is the pivotal event of inter-war politics and was of major significance to the development of modern British politics.[68] Its impact lies in its suddenness. Few Conservatives expected the Labour government to collapse and certainly not in the way that it did, nor did they expect to enter a coalition. Many hoped to use opposition to rethink Conservatism. Electorally Baldwin could feel confident about the future as by late 1930 the average swing against the government was 9% and even greater swings were registered in early 1931; more importantly these results saw the Liberal vote slip significantly.[69] In the aftermath of defeat in 1929 Bridgeman had outlined two conditions for a Conservative victory: Baldwin should retain the leadership and Liberal votes should defect back to the Conservatives. By early 1931 both conditions were being realised.[70]

A major Conservative rethink was prevented by the internal battles of 1929–31. Baldwin's survival prevented the adoption of any alternative to his Conservatism and secured his authority, and the sudden onset of the August crisis further entrenched Baldwin's position. The Conservative Party, therefore, had little to gain electorally from coalition. The Conservatives believed the solution to the economic crisis was cuts in government spending and taxation but Baldwin's original intention was to remain uninvolved in Labour's crisis. As the crisis deepened the Conservatives shifted their ground to pressurising the government to take the necessary public spending decisions or be removed from office by the House of Commons. This, however, would place some responsibility for these decisions on the Conservatives with obvious possible adverse electoral consequences: with this prospect in mind a national government became increasingly attractive. When the Labour Cabinet split over the economies recommended by the May Committee the crisis deepened as without these economies there would be no foreign loan. Pressure for a national government came from King George V who on 23 August asked Baldwin whether he was willing to serve under the Labour Prime Minister, Ramsay Macdonald. Baldwin could hardly refuse but consoled himself with the thought that this was hardly likely to happen and that the most likely outcome was that the Labour government would fall and he would be asked to form a government. After meeting Baldwin the King flattered and browbeat Macdonald into not resigning but becoming the leader of a coalition. Once Baldwin had agreed to serve all the Conservatives options, other than the national government, were closed down and the National Government was formed on the basis of Conservative acquiescence.[71]

Many Conservatives saw the National Government as a temporary expedient to force through public spending cuts and defend the Gold Standard, and once the economy stabilised the parties would then fight an election which Labour would lose. Events dictated otherwise. Despite increased taxation and cuts in public spending put through by Philip Snowden, the ex-Labour now National Chancellor, the economic spiral continued, accelerating when the Atlantic Fleet at Invergordon mutinied (15 September) over pay cuts. This crisis of confidence forced the pound off the Gold Standard (20 September). Baldwin, the Lord President and the real power in the government, saw this as an opportunity to fight an election on tariff reform and protection. The Conservative Party in Parliament and the country was strongly in favour of an immediate election using a National appeal to smash Labour. This was reinforced by pressure from the City who pressed for speedy action and supported the ideas of a National Government. The Governor of the Bank of England told Baldwin 'that the Election ought to be today, if not today, then tomorrow. The foreigner regards this as a makeshift government with no strong majority' whereas a strong majority would restore confidence.[72] Baldwin had little option other than to defer, especially when the King's influence was thrown into the balance. Macdonald's disquiet over the idea of a National election counted for little especially when the King assured him of his indispensability, and that it was his duty to front the National electoral appeal so his resignation would not be accepted. On 5 October the Cabinet agreed to go to the country as a National Government, albeit with three manifestoes.

The Conservatives stressed the idea of 'equality of sacrifice' to counter a Labour 'squeeze the rich' platform. Public spending cuts (especially in unemployment pay) would be accompanied by tax increases (albeit minimal) and it was essential to have Labour and Liberal participation so as to spread any unpopularity as widely as possible. So, for many Conservatives the National Government represented a potential counter-revolution: the means whereby the growth of the state might be halted and Socialism banished to the margins of the political system. As he watched the massive Conservative gains piling up on election night Tom Jones felt 'glad the National Cause has won. I voted Conservative for the first time in my life ... "Labour" had to be thrashed, but it cannot be destroyed'.[73]

In fact, Labour was very nearly destroyed. The Conservatives and their allies returned 471 MPs, Labour 52, and Labour's leadership was decimated: only one Cabinet minister and two junior ministers survived. As the Liberals were prisoners of the Conservatives politics had now simplified into Socialism versus anti-Socialism. Nonetheless, Labour's popular vote was higher than in 1929, holding up well in predominantly working-class areas and areas of high unemployment. For a politician of Baldwin's stamp and for a 'National' government this was worrying as it indicated the growing strength of class in British politics, and its eventual reinforcement when the pendulum swung against the National Government. Paradoxically, the scale of the National victory in 1931 made it more difficult to carry out the counter-revolution envisaged by the bulk of Conservatives, and by default the Conservative Party found itself further enmeshed in Baldwin's non-political Conservatism. To what extent, however, was the Conservative Party wedded to Baldwinism?

Notes

1 K Burgess, *The Challenge of Labour. Shaping British Society 1850–1930* (London: Croom Helm, 1980), p. 155.

2 *National Union Executive Committee*, 6 August 1914.

3 J. Stubbs, 'The Impact of the Great War on the Conservative Party' in G. Peele and C. Cook (eds.), *The Politics of Reappraisal, 1918–1939* (London: Macmillan, 1975), pp. 23–6 and P. Williamson (ed.), *The Modernisation of Conservative Politics. The Diaries and Letters of William Bridgeman, 1904–1935* (London: The Historian's Press, 1988), entry 29 November 1914. Hereafter, *Bridgeman Diaries*.

4 *Bridgeman Diaries*, entry for May 1915.

5 C. J. Wrigley, *David Lloyd George and the British Labour Movement* (Brighton: Harvester Press, 1976), pp. 91–109.

6 *Bridgeman Diaries*, entry for Autumn 1916.

7 *Bridgeman Diaries*, Bridgeman to C. Bridgeman, 24 November 1918. Our emphasis.

8 J. Barnes and David Nicholson (eds.), *Leo Amery Diaries, Volume 1: 1896–1929* (London: Hutchinson, 1980), 8 November 1917. Our emphasis. Hereafter, *Leo Amery Diaries*.

9 R. Douglas, 'The National Democratic Labour Party and the British Workers' League', *Historical Journal*, 15(3) (1972), pp. 533–52, and J. Stubbs, 'Lord Milner and Patriotic Labour', *English Historical Review*, 87 (October 1972), pp. 717–54.

10 *Leo Amery Diaries*, 8 November 1917.

11 Stubbs, 'Lord Milner and Patriotic Labour', pp. 741–2.

12 *NUA 2/1/35*, Special Conference on the Representation of the People Bill, 30 November 1917, p. 8.

13 *The Times*, 2 November 1917.

14 *AREA 3/13/1*, Lancashire Trade Union Sub-Committee, 12 February 1918, and *Central Council Meeting*, 20 May 1919.

15 NUA Pam 1982 (1920/42), *The Why and Wherefore of the Unionist Labour Committee, or, The Labour Wing of the Unionist Party*.

16 NUA Pam 1976 (March 1920), *The Labour Committee National Unionist Conference at Southport*, pp. 5 and 8.

17 *NUA 6/1/1–3*, Report of the Principal Agent, July 1924.

18 Stubbs, 'The Impact of the Great War on the Conservative Party', p. 11.

19 K. Middlemas, *Politics in Industrial Society* (London: Deutsch, 1979), pp. 129–33. For the state's role in industrial unrest see K. Jeffery and P. Hennessy, *States of Emergency, British Governments and Strikebreaking since 1919* (London: Routledge & Kegan Paul, 1983), R. Geary, *Policing Industrial Disputes 1893 to 1985* (London: Methuen, 1985), and S. Peak, *Troops in Strikes. Military Intervention in Industrial Disputes* (London: The Cobden Trust, 1984). C. J. Wrigley, *Lloyd George and the Challenge of Labour. The Post-war Coalition, 1918–1922*, (Brighton: Harvester, 1990), examines the Coalition's relations with Labour.

20 NUA Pam 1951 (1920/1), *What the 'Labour' Party Wants*, and NUA Pam 1948 (1920/7), *What the 'Labour' Party Has Done*.

21 R. Rhodes James (ed.), *Memoirs of a Conservative. J. C. C. Davidson's Memoirs and Papers, 1910–1937* (London: Weidenfeld and Nicolson, 1969), p. 272. Davidson also employed Sir Joseph Ball (who resigned from MI5 to work for Davidson but who retained his links with the intelligence community returning to MI5 in the late 1930s) to run the Conservative Party's moles in Labour's headquarters.

22 J. Turner, 'The Politics of "Organised Business" in the First World War', in J. Turner (ed.), *Businessmen and Politics* (London: Heinemann, 1984), pp. 33–49 and J. Turner, 'The British Commonwealth Union and the General Election of 1918', *English Historical Review*, 93 (1978), pp. 528–59.

23 *Bridgeman Diaries*, entry for 30 March 1919.

24 *BL 116/3/1*, Notes on a Deputation from the Railway Companies, 28 November 1922.

25 B. Lenman, *The Eclipse of Parliament. Appearance and Reality in British Politics since 1914* (London: Edward Arnold, 1992), p. 74.

26 *Leo Amery Diaries*, 13 October 1922. See also D. H. Close, 'Conservatives and Coalition after the First World War', *Journal of Modern History*, 45 (1973), pp. 240–60.

27 *Bridgeman Diaries*, October 1922.

28 Stubbs, 'The Impact of the Great War on the Conservative Party', p. 15 and P. Goodhart, *The 1922* (London: Macmillan, 1973), pp. 13–31.

29 D. H. Close, 'The Collapse of Resistance to Democracy: Conservatives and Second Chamber Reform, 1911–28', *Historical Journal*, 20 (4) (1977), p. 898 and pp. 904–5.

30 The percentage Conservative seats which were uncontested were: 1922 12.1; 1923 13.5; 1924 3.8; 1929 1.5; 1931 11.8; and 1935 6.0. The number of votes required to win one seat were:

Election	Conservative	Liberal	Labour
1922	15,942	42,296	29,577
1923	21,317	2,704	23,066
1924	19,093	72,500	35,761
1929	33,846	89,830	28,819
1931	25,125	42,424	126,923
1935	27,314	70,000	53,896

31 A. H. Taylor, 'The Effect of Electoral Pacts on the Decline of the Liberal Party', *British Journal of Political Science*, 3 (1973), pp. 243–55. See also W. L. Miller, 'Cross-voting and the Dimensionality of Party Conflict during the Period of Realignment, 1918–1931', *Political Studies*, 29 (1971), pp. 455–61. Liberal candidacies fell from 490 (1922), to 161 (1935).

32 D. Butler and D. Stokes, *Political Change in Britain. The Evolution of Electoral Choice*, 2nd edition (London: Macmillan, 1974), p. 167 and p. 168.

33 Butler and Stokes, *Political Change in Britain*, p. 170.

34 F. W. S. Craig, *British General Election Manifestoes* (London: Macmillan, 1975), p. 37.

35 *BL 111/4/22* and *BL 116/3/3*.

36 *Davidson Papers*, Davidson to Baldwin, 14 January 1929.

37 M. Cowling, *The Impact of Labour, 1920–24. The Beginning of Modern British Politics* (Cambridge: Cambridge University Press, 1971), p. 1.

38 *Davidson Papers*, Davidson to Sam Hoare, 28 December 1923.

39 *Davidson Papers*, Davidson to Neville Chamberlain, 8 January 1929.

40 The largest categories of business connections of Conservative MPs were:

Sector	MPs	Directorships
Banking	16	18
Insurance	43	49
Finance	27	42
Total	86	109

Derived from S. Haxey, *Tory MP* (London: Left Book Club, 1939), pp. 36–7 and p. 176.

41 *Bridgeman Diaries*, Bridgeman to Worthington-Evans, 16 September 1927. Worthington-Evans was in charge of preparing the manifesto.

42 S. Ball, *Baldwin and the Conservative Party. The Crisis of 1929–1931* (London: Yale University Press, 1988), p. 4.

43 'Service' (Leeds Luncheon Club, 13 March 1925), in S Baldwin, *On England and Other Addresses* (London: Philip Allan, 1926), pp. 62–8. This collection underwent two impressions in April and May 1926.

44 Speech at Stourport (12 January 1925), in *On England*, p. 16.

45 'Worcester Memories' (7 November 1923), in *On England*, p. 21.

46 'Democracy and the Empire' (Speech to the Junior Imperial League, 3 May 1924), in *On England*, p. 225.

47 'On England and the West' (Speech to the Royal Society of St George, 6 May 1924), in *On England*, pp. 6–7.

48 'Peace in Industry II (House of Commons, 6 March 1925), in *On England*, pp. 42–3.

49 'Democracy and the Empire' (Speech to the Junior Imperial League, 3 May 1924), in *On England*, p. 22.

50 'Democracy and the Spirit of Service' (Albert Hall, 4 December 1924), in *On England*, pp. 72–3.

51 'The Citizen and the General Strike' (Chippenham, 12 June 1926), in S. Baldwin, *Our Inheritance* (London: Hodder and Stoughton, 1928), pp. 212–21.

52 *Leo Amery Diaries*, 8 May 1926, and *Bridgeman Diaries*, entry for May 1926 and Bridgeman to M. C. Bridgeman, 14 May 1926. See also *National Union Executive Committee*, 13 July 1926 and *NUA 2/1/42*, Minutes of the Annual Conference, 7–8 October 1926.

53 *Davidson Papers*, Davidson to E. Carson, 14 June 1926.

54 *Bridgeman Diaries*, Bridgeman to Baldwin, 7 September 1926.

55 *Bridgeman Diaries*, Bridgeman to Baldwin, 7 September 1926, and *Davidson Papers*, Steel-Maitland to Davidson, 8 September 1926.

56 M. Morris, *The General Strike* (Harmondsworth: Penguin, 1976), pp. 143–50. Sir Robert Horne, a leading City figure and opponent of Baldwin, was rumoured to represent 300 MPs hostile to further compromises with the miners.

57 *Davidson Papers*, Box 9, Davidson to Baldwin, 19 February 1929.

58 P. Williamson, '"Safety First". Baldwin, the Conservative Party and the 1929 General Election', *Historical Journal*, 25 (2) (1982), pp. 400–4.

59 *Davidson Papers*, Memorandum from Pembroke-Wickes to Davidson, 6 July 1926; *Leo Amery Diaries*, Amery to Baldwin, 8 March 1927; and *Bridgeman Diaries*, Bridgeman to Worthington-Evans, 16 September 1927.

60 *Bridgeman Diaries*, Bridgeman to Baldwin, 27 March 1929, p. 218.

61 *Davidson Papers*, Baldwin to Davidson, 1 January 1929.

62 *Bridgeman Diaries*, entry for July 1929. Our emphasis.

63 *Davidson Papers*, Davidson to Baldwin, 23 December 1929.

64 S. Ball, 'Failure of an Opposition?: The Conservative Party in Parliament 1929–1931', *Parliament History*, 5 (1986), pp. 83–98.

65 Ball, *Baldwin and the Conservative Party* provides an in-depth analysis of this period.

66 C. Bridge, 'Conservatism and Indian Reform 1929–1939', *Journal of Imperial and Commonwealth History*, 4 (1975–6), pp. 176–93; S. C. Ghosh, 'Decision-Making and Power in the British Conservative Party: A Case Study of the Indian Problem 1929–34', *Political Studies*, 13 (1965), pp. 198–212; and G. Peele, 'The Revolt over India', in G. Peele and C. Cooks (eds.), *The Politics of Reappraisal, 1918–1939* (London: Macmillan, 1975), pp. 114–45.

67 T. Jones, *A Diary with Letters, 1931–1950* (London: Oxford University Press, 1954), Jones to J. B. Bickersteth, 16 March 1931.

68 There is a vast literature on 1931. Particularly useful on the role of the Conservatives are S. Ball, 'The Conservative Party and the Formation of the National Government: August 1931', *Historical Journal*, 29 (1986), pp. 159–82, and J. D. Fair, 'The Conservative Basis for the Formation of the National Government of 1931', *Journal of British Studies*, 19 (1980), pp. 142–64.

69 J. Stevenson and C. Cook, *The Slump. Society and Politics During the Depression* (London: Quartet Books, 1979), pp. 95–7. See also D. H. Close, 'The Re-Alignment of the British Electorate in 1931', *History*, 67 (1982), pp. 393–404.

70 *Bridgeman Diaries*, Bridgeman to Baldwin, 31 May 1929.

71 On the role of King George V see G. C. Moddie, 'The Monarch and the Selection of a Prime Minister: A Re-examination of the Crisis of 1931', *Political Studies*, 5 (1957), pp. 1–20, and H. Hearder, 'King George V, the General Strike,

and the 1931 Crisis', in H. Hearder and H. R. Loyn (eds.), *British Government and Administration* (Cardiff: Cardiff University Press, 1974), pp. 234–47.

72 Jones, *A Diary with Letters*, 29 September 1931. See also P. Williamson, 'A Bankers' Ramp? Financiers and the British Political Crisis of August 1931', *English Historical Review*, 99 (1984), pp. 770–806.

73 Jones, *A Diary with Letters*, Jones to Gwendoline Davies, 28 October 1931.

3

Conservatism challenged, 1931–1945

Conservatism remained unchallenged until May 1940 when military defeat produced a palace coup which brought Churchill and a Coalition government including Labour to power, thereby altering the political agenda for a generation. From May 1940 Conservatism was on the defensive and Labour's concerns came to dominate the political agenda, resulting in the catastrophic 1945 defeat.

From Baldwin to Chamberlain

Baldwin was the dominant figure in British politics until his retirement in 1937. Ramsay Macdonald remained Prime Minister until 1935 but Baldwin was the chief executive and the National Government was Conservative in all but name. This reflected the attainment of his political objectives of the 1920s, and with the anti-Socialist coalition entrenched in power after 1931 Baldwinism (like Baldwin) seemed exhausted and anachronistic. In the 1930s the party's agenda shifted from containing class conflict to 'the question of the nature of Conservatism'.[1]

1931 led the Conservative Party back towards partisan politics and Baldwin's rhetoric suggests an appreciation that class conflict was biding its time, waiting to re-emerge. Baldwin's speeches display a degree of political pessimism. Athenian democracy failed, Baldwin argued, because its ideals 'were corrupted by demagogues and flatterers' and 'Politicians rivalled one another in bribing the electorate'. Democracy was, however, an accomplished fact and Baldwin believed that British political culture contained obstacles (notably individualism) to the degeneration of democracy and 'that it may be seized and exploited in undemocratic ways for democratic ends'. The central political questions were related to prosperity and this raised the question of the role of the modern state.[2] The democratic state was, Baldwin conceded, redistributionist but 'The redistribution of wealth from the richer to the poorer elements in the country by the machinery of the State has, within limits, obvious advantages'. Sooner or later, however, politicians would have to call a halt, 'then will come the testing time for politicians and for voters, for democracy in short'. Faced by such a crisis Baldwin predicted the need for bi-partisan co-operation to minimise the damage done by partisan electoral co-operation.[3] This would be reinforced by the balancing role of the civil service whose task was to 'translate law into policy'. The civil service was portrayed as a restraint on both the left and right 'and thus keep the Ship of State on an even keel' whilst keeping a due regard to public opinion.[4] Despite the growing restiveness in the party in the mid-1930s Baldwin remained convinced that 'conventional Conservatism could never hold the country ... It is Disraelian Conservatism, and with that you can always win. The Conservative policy should never frighten our people if it means change ... We are going through uncharted seas, economically and industrially, and I would shrink from no methods, nor would my colleagues if they felt they were methods that would help our country. You see those new methods being tried today, we are experimenting and the experiments must go on'.[5] This bi-partisan, pragmatic and statist Conservatism was not enthusiastically embraced by the party.

At the 1934 party conference Major A. F. G. Renton insisted that any positive programme had to be accompanied by a vigorous anti-Socialist campaign, otherwise Socialism would recover. Speaking in the debate on party propaganda Sir Edward Grigg MP condemned ministers who had been introducing bills 'which would certainly have been regarded as rank and barefaced Socialism ... a few years ago'. A third delegate, opposing a resolution on industrial reconstruction proposed by Macmillan, argued 'they were relying too much on the State ... The man in the street saw little difference between Socialist legislation or Conservative legislation ... If an industry could not exist, except for State support, it should be allowed to close down'.[6] For Conservative governments to behave thus was dangerous as it would make Socialism appear less of a threat, and many Conservatives were attracted to a more fundamentalist Conservatism. This is important because the 1930s have been identified as a period in which Conservatives were increasingly favouring greater state intervention which was to provide the basis for post-war Conservatism. In particular, attention has focused on the Tory corporatists.[7]

Baldwinism and Tory corporatism had much in common but parted company over the ability of parliamentary institutions to cope with the economic and political strains of depression.[8] Tory corporatism was not viable because, first, it required a dramatic extension of state control over private property and many Conservatives believed that the state was already too interventionist. Second, proposals for industrial reorganisation and rationalisation, even if in an industry's own interests, raised the spectre of nationalisation and Socialism. Although Conservative governments promoted rationalisation and even nationalisation they did so on a piece-meal basis and never sought to justify their actions as part of restructuring political and industrial power. Third, corporatism's emphasis on manufacturing implied a downgrading of commercial and financial interests which were traditionally very influential in the Conservative Party. Fourth, corporatism's preference for 'bigness' threatened the 'little man', a group particularly influential in the party's grassroots. Finally, despite its emphasis on the subordination of labour corporatism implied an increase in union influence in industry and government. Support for rationalisation was 'non-political' in the sense that it enjoyed support from all parts of the political spectrum. Conservative governments had passed the Industrial Transference Act (1928) and created the Central Electricity Board (1926), but when compulsory reorganisation was mooted (as in the Coal Mines Reorganisation Act, 1930) Conservatives were far less enthusiastic. Conservative intervention was essentially defensive, and taking precedence was the maintenance of financial stability.[9] Whilst the 1930s see a sharp break with Conservative *international* political economy (protection and departure from the Gold Standard) there is no major shift in *domestic* political economic ideas.

By 1935 Labour had recovered remarkably from the disaster of 1931 but its recovery was patchy (it made few inroads in the crucial industrial West Midlands) and its support was strongly correlated with high unemployment. There was also a tendency for Liberals to vote Conservative and Labour's attractiveness was reduced by serious left–right conflict. The electoral 'middle ground' remained dominated by the National Government.[10] In the 1935 general election the swing against the Conservatives was insufficient to erode the National Government's position. The National Government was bound to lose seats (it lost 70) but it nonetheless won 53.7% of the votes cast. The Liberals were the main losers, so the 1935 election pointed to a polarisation of politics, and most serious of all 'was the fact that very few people saw in Labour a viable alternative to the National Government'.[11] This pattern was not disturbed right up to the outbreak of war. By-elections and municipal elections maintained the pattern of 1931–4 and Labour secured some very good results. However, none of the swings (the average in ten by-election victories was 7%) would have produced an overall Labour majority in a general election, and in the by-elections of 1938–9 there was an anti-Labour swing. In the last three contests before the outbreak of war the average swing to Labour was 3.7% and poll data for the year February 1939–February 1940 shows a strengthening support for the government.

Electoral evidence points to the growing strength of the class alignment after 1918, peaking with the cohort which entered the electorate during the Second World War, a trend which was to benefit Labour.[12] There is no evidence that class displaced religion as the major cleavage in British politics before 1918 but between 1910 and 1918 there was a shift to class voting. This 'leads inescapably to the conclusion that the rise of Labour and the decline of Liberals are bound up in the same packet with the substitution of class for religion as the major social division underlying the British party system'. In the 1930s 'the image of politics as the representation of opposing class interests was increasingly accepted as we moved from the pre-1918 to the interwar cohort and reached a peak in the cohort which entered the electorate during the Second World War and its aftermath'.[13]

By 1945 party support was related to perceived class differences and these perceptions were particularly strong amongst Labour working-class voters, although middle-class Conservative voters demonstrated an increased recognition of class politics by 1945 (from 8% to 23%). There was an increasing perception of difference based on class between the Labour and Conservative parties (despite the existence of a 'National' government), a perception which reached its zenith with the inter-war cohort. Similarly, there was a sharp jump in middle-class Conservative perceptions of politics being driven by class interests (+ 15%) compared to only a small increase in the case of working-class Labour voters who were already more convinced of this.[14] The inter-war period saw a long-term electoral realignment on class lines which benefited Labour but which would not have produced a Labour victory in 1940.

Chamberlain became Prime Minister in 1937 because there was no other rival. He enjoyed a meteoric rise, entering Parliament in 1918 aged 50 after a business career and after being sacked by Lloyd George as Director of National Service. In 1920 he joined the Cabinet, by 1929 was recognised as a leading Conservative, and when Churchill rebelled over India he became Baldwin's successor. This status was confirmed by his appointment as Chancellor of the Exchequer. As Minister of Health between 1924 and 1929, as Chancellor, and as Prime Minister he proved to be a clear-thinking, hard-working administrator with a magisterial command of detail. Chamberlain's major political weakness was the perception that he was cold, supercilious, sarcastic, and arrogant, qualities which were to doom his government when war made it necessary to involve Labour. Labour's political and industrial leaders heartily disliked Chamberlain and he was openly contemptuous of them. Chamberlain's disdain prompted Attlee's uncharacteristically vehement judgement that he treated Labour like dirt but in 1926 Chamberlain wrote 'The fact is that intellectually, with a few exceptions, they *are* dirt'.[15] After seeing himself on film Chamberlain agreed that he appeared a most unattractive personality, but he concluded this did not matter. The fact was that Chamberlain enjoyed unassailable control of Parliament and the party, and he knew it. Some Conservatives looked back nostalgically to Baldwin's bi-partisanship (Baldwin cautioned Chamberlain against being too hostile to Labour), far more approved of Chamberlain's aggressive anti-Socialism, and he retained the support of most MPs and the constituencies after his fall.

The study of Conservative politics in the late 1930s is dominated by foreign affairs but no clear line can be drawn between domestic and foreign policy in a liberal democracy preparing for war. Total war on the scale of 1914–18 logically required total mobilisation: a limited war, limited mobilisation. The expected nature of the next war therefore forms the kernel of Chamberlain's foreign and domestic policy, the basis of which was avoiding war and rearming to deter aggression. The Chamberlain government's rearmament programme and the political consent needed to promote it were a function of its conviction that the next war would be limited. The cry 'No More Passchendales' had two obvious consequences: a major European war should be avoided at all costs but if it came Britain's participation would not be via mass armies, and therefore there would be no need for the state to direct production.[16] When Chancellor Chamberlain had been determined to control rearmament costs in order not to disrupt the civilian economy, and as Prime Minister his foreign policy envisioned a limited war confined to the defence of the home islands and Britain's Imperial interests by air and naval power. Again, this would minimise economic and political disruption.[17] Rearmament would peak in 1939–40; if there was no war by then the Treasury believed the economy could not sustain a high level of defence spending.

The Government believed the electorate, the City, and the Conservative backbench would not countenance the high levels of direct taxation needed to finance general rearmament and Chamberlain often referred to financial stability as 'our fourth, and final military arm'. Government spending would increase inflation and labour unrest; the resulting financial and industrial crisis, Chamberlain feared, might bring Labour to power. Politicians doubted the existence of the consent required to legitimise the political and industrial mobilisation needed to prepare for a continental war, and the party would not accept a level of mobilisation which would require the labour movement's participation in government. Chamberlain's policy depended on avoiding war and so both domestic and Conservative politics revolved around the appeasement of Nazi Germany. The failure of appeasement, therefore, implied a major political restructuring. Until appeasement failed Chamberlain was secure. Any challenge required a political 'third force' and the scale of the Conservative victory in 1935 meant that this would have to come from a split in the Conservative Party capable of attracting non-Conservatives.

Eden's resignation as Foreign Secretary (April 1938) meant he was widely seen as the embodiment of an alternative policy of mobilisation of the nation's resources to resist the dictators, and as Chamberlain's replacement.[18] Resignation brought Eden no widespread support in Parliament and he was anxious not to be regarded as the leader of the opposition to Chamberlain as he wished to make a comeback. Macmillan (one of the leading dissidents) noted in his diary that 'Chamberlain's position was not seriously shaken' by Eden's resignation. There is no evidence that 'the party as a whole was much concerned and there were many who were beginning now to realise the terrible position into which we were drifting'.[19] The major figure was, of course, Churchill. His appeal, however, was confined to a tiny group of Conservatives and the bulk of the parliamentary party (including Eden and Macmillan) believed his behaviour over India and during the Abdication Crisis showed him to be dangerously unstable. Churchill's all-party anti-Nazi group, *The Focus*, had few Conservative members: it embraced trade unionists, Socialists, pacifists, and League of Nation enthusiasts with whom mainstream Conservatives would not be caught dead.[20]

Dissidents' groups began to coalesce in the summer of 1938 but Eden's resignation did not produce 'a pivot round which dissenting members of the Conservative Party could more readily form'.[21] Their lack of impact points to their marginality in Conservative politics: the dissidents were few and disunited. Churchill's group (what Macmillan dubbed the 'Old Guard'), consisted of Brendan Bracken, Duncan Sandys, and Robert Boothby, none of whom could be described as being in the mainstream of Conservatism. Their association with Churchill condemned them in the eyes of Chamberlain, the Whips' office, and the party.[22] Eden's group ('the Glamour Boys') had about sixteen members but none of them was politically significant; some (for example, Harold Nicolson) were not Conservatives and of the dissidents identified by Macmillan in the summer of 1938 only Churchill, Macmillan, Sandys, Bracken, and Eden were to achieve high office. Eden was suspicious of Churchill and kept his distance but remained in close contact with Baldwin. Baldwin warned Eden to beware of Churchill and Eden agreed with his suggestion that he 'make a few big speeches on such general topics as Democracy and Young England, in which (while avoiding current topics in Foreign Affairs) he will clearly indicate that he stands for postwar England against the old men'.[23]

Even after Munich the dissidents failed to formulate a coherent strategy and their activities took on aspects of a schoolboy secret society. Harold Nicolson reported attending a 'hush-hush' meeting with Eden in November 1938 composed of 'good tories and sensible men' who were distinct from the Churchill group. These good and sensible men decided 'not to advertise ourselves as a group or even call ourselves a group. We should meet together from time to time, exchange views, and organise ourselves for a revolt if needed'. The leaders of this un-group 'do not mean to do anything rash or violent' and sought to distance themselves from Churchill who gave the impression of being bitter rather than determined. Not surprisingly a political ineffectual like Nicolson concluded he would 'be happy and at ease with this group'.[24] In the September 1938 debate on the creation of a Ministry of Supply Churchill appealed for fifty Conservatives to join him in voting against the government, but only Bracken and Macmillan followed where he led. This suggests that Churchill was beyond the pale even for those Conservatives who opposed the Munich Agreement. On the eve of the war the dissidents were thrown into turmoil by rumours of a general election: 'They did not feel they could stand in support of the Government. Should they act as Independent Conservatives? Or should they seek to try to create a new Independent party? What, above all, should be their relations with Churchill?'.[25]

The dissidents' attractiveness was limited by their consorting with Labour. Macmillan was the go-between. As the most left-wing of the dissidents and as MP for a depressed north-east industrial constituency he was more likely to be acceptable to Labour politicians than Churchill or Bracken. During the summer and autumn of 1938 Macmillan, with Churchill's approval, held informal talks with Hugh Dalton (the shadow Foreign Secretary and an anti-appeaser) on the possibility of Labour co-operating with the dissidents with the object of removing Chamberlain or restructuring the government along National lines. Dalton refused to be drawn, correctly estimating the dissidents were too weak to deflect government policy let alone bring Chamberlain down. Furthermore, he judged the obstacles to electoral co-operation were insuperable, and concluded Labour's interests were best served by maintaining its political independence.[26] The dissidents were fully aware that the labour movement would under no circumstances enter a Chamberlain government. These conversations were regarded as profoundly disloyal by the party, the backbench, and the Whips, confirming the 'unsoundness' of the dissidents.

The Munich Agreement which dismembered Czechoslovakia reinforced Chamberlain's dominance, producing relief and adulation even amongst the rebels.[27]. Despite talk of a Cabinet rebellion only Duff Cooper resigned and Chamberlain's coup threw the rebels into confusion. Chamberlain's popularity led his opponents to fear he would call a snap general election which led Churchill to try and create a platform around collective security and national unity. This failed because electoral co-operation between dissident Conservatives and the Labour Party was not feasible and the reaction of the constituencies to Conservatives conspiring with Socialists against Chamberlain can be imagined. The domestic political effect of the Munich Agreement was to significantly entrench Chamberlain's dominance by forcing the dissidents on to the defensive.[28] Chamberlain's prestige and the authority of his government was now irrevocably bound up with the success of his foreign policy. Munich polarised opinion into those hoping for success and those predicting its failure. This latter group now included Labour, so Munich accelerated the return to party politics heralded by Chamberlain's accession to the Premiership. Senior ministers urged Chamberlain to create a National Government or at least bring Eden back, advice which was not accepted.

Chamberlain believed Munich had made war less, not more, likely and the fruition of the rearmament programme reinforced this. Thus, there was no need to broaden the government base, no need for a Ministry of Supply to organise war production, and Treasury fears about financial stability beyond 1940 reinforced Chamberlain's refusal to change course. However, Hitler's incorporation of the remnant of Czechoslovakia and of Memel into the Reich (15 and 22 March 1939) led the British government to guarantee Poland's independence. This signalled the failure of Munich and renewed the dissidents' hopes for a National Government. Politically Chamberlain was in a difficult position as he could not call a general election without it becoming a referendum on appeasement or being interpreted as an attempt to hijack the war for party purposes. Chamberlain still refused to broaden his government but as Labour remained deeply hostile to Chamberlain his assumption that any offer of participation would be rejected was correct. Chamberlain gave no ground to his critics, and the harsh political reality was that despite the failure of appeasement Chamberlain's grip on the Conservative Party was unshaken. The country's and the party's natural reaction would be to rally to the government. The dissidents were political has-beens and young rebels, a political force totally incapable of mounting a coup against Chamberlain. There was nothing here to worry Chamberlain and it is hard to disagree with Boothby's comment on the dissidents: 'On the whole they were a sorry lot'.[29]

War, Coalition and Conservative politics

The crisis of 8–10 May 1940 was of pivotal importance for British and Conservative politics.[30] From early 1938 the inclusion of Labour and the unions in the Government was a powerful undercurrent in domestic politics. Immediately after Munich both Baldwin and Halifax urged Chamberlain to use the temporary euphoria to bring Labour into his government: a suggestion he rejected. Chamberlain's closest adviser and *eminence grise*, Sir Horace Wilson, bolstered the Premier's anti-Labourism. Chamberlain's response to Halifax's urging was, ' "I am not sure about that. You had better speak to Horace about it". And Horace did not approve'.[31] Baldwin told Lord Reith that Chamberlain's government was too right-wing and was squandering the fund of national loyalty that he, Baldwin, had done so much to forge. Behind this refusal was a recognition that British participation in a continental war would generate large-scale political and economic change. This explains the Chancellor of the Exchequer's (Sir John Simon) policy to 'keep our industry on a peace footing [so] that it will be less difficult to return to normal conditions after the war'.[32] Chamberlain's fall and Churchill's appointment was the result of the failure of the Norway Campaign and Hitler's invasion of the Low Countries. The catalyst for change was the small group of Conservative dissidents who, by moderating their anti-Social-ism in the interests of creating an anti-Hitler coalition, drew Labour into their orbit. Chamberlain's failure to include Labour was condemned even by loyal Chamberlainites.[33]

Symbolic of the political transformation was Churchill's appointment of Ernest Bevin as Minister of Labour. 'I thought', Bevin commented, perhaps tongue-in-cheek, 'it would help the prestige of the Trade Union Movement and the Ministry of Labour if I went in'. Bevin was determined to transform the unions' influence in Whitehall: 'They say Gladstone was at the Treasury from 1860 to 1930. I'm going to be at the Ministry of Labour from 1940 to 1990'.[34] Bevin joined the War Cabinet in October 1940 following Cham-berlain's resignation through ill-health, becoming after Churchill the most powerful Coalition minister. The war offered a major opportunity: 'there has been, and will have to be, a great re-casting of values. The conception that those who produce or manipulate are inferior, and must accept a lower status than the speculator must go'.[35]

Labour made Churchill Prime Minister.[36] Between 1940 and 1945 Churchill was in an anomalous position being both the national leader and Conservative party leader. His prime object, winning the war, required the preservation of the Coalition which necessitated concessions to Labour, con-cessions which antagonised the Conservative Party. In the early desperate months this did not worry Churchill. After entering Chamberlain's govern-ment Churchill enjoyed limited support amongst Conservatives and this remained so when he became Prime Minister, but the Conservative Party was his only party base. Churchill did not purge the 'Men of Munich' as this would have been 'destructive of national unity' and complicate his relations with the Conservative Party. Despite his history Churchill was a party-man who, as Lloyd George predicted in July 1940, 'will not smash the Tory Party ... as I smashed the Liberal Party'.[37] Churchill inevitably became the focal point for Conservative political hopes but his partisan role was restricted by the demands of Coalition politics and he could not provide the Conservative Party with a clear political lead. Deprived of leadership the party lost coher-ence as the political agenda was increasingly determined by Labour.

For many Conservatives (as well as public opinion) Churchill was not first choice as Chamberlain's replacement. Shocked by the débâcle in Norway and the Low Countries, and the need to bring Labour into government the parliamentary party acquiesced in Chamberlain's replacement, but when Churchill first entered the Commons as Prime Minister it was the Labour benches which cheered and the Conservatives remained silent.[38] Churchill recognised his elevation was 'very unpleasant' to many Conservatives 'after all my long years of criticism and fierce reproach'; many would not accept him as a true Conservative as much of his political life 'had been passed in friction or actual strife with the Conservative Party'. As Prime Minister, however, he identified himself with the Disraelian mainstream: 'the Tory Party was the strength of the country: Few things need to be changed quickly and drastically; what conservatism, as envisaged by Disraeli, stood for was the gradual increase of amenities for any ever larger number of people, who should enjoy the benefits previously reserved for a very few (i.e. a levelling upwards, not a levelling downwards)'.[39]

Chamberlain resigned as Prime Minister in May but remained party leader until leaving politics in October. Churchill decided he must take the leadership even though this conflicted with his national role. Addressing the 1922 Committee he reconciled these two roles within the Conservative tradition: 'I have always faithfully served two supreme public causes – the maintenance of the enduring greatness of Britain and her Empire and the historic certainty of our Island life'. These 'public causes' were Conservative interests, the Coalition was not inimical to Conservatism as 'Alone among the peoples we have reconciled democracy and tradition' and the Conservative Party, as the embodiment of the nation and leading political force in society 'will not allow any party to excel it in the sacrifice of party interests and party feelings'. In November Churchill explained why he had accepted the leadership while head of a Coalition government: 'the Conservative Party has an absolutely vital and indispensable part to play in the future turn of events that I felt I should accept the great honour which it sought to confer upon me, and I am most anxious that there should be in this Country a strong Conservative Party'.[40] Churchill's emphasis on the Disraelian idiom was important because it provided a standard for the party to rally around and offered an alternative perspective on the emerging reformist political agenda.

The Conservative Party was the obvious organisation to resist 'war socialism'. Sir Robert Topping, the Central Office Director General warned the war would transform politics, and Sir Douglas Hacking, the Party Chairman was determined that the party should challenge the growth of Socialism.[41] The Conservatives' inclination was to support the government but neither the Labour nor the Liberal parties were part of the government, and remained free to criticise the Government. On the outbreak of war the National Union expressed disquiet that so many constituencies had closed down as 'the Labour and Liberal organisations are working hard' and by the spring of 1940 the party was 'as dead as makes no difference'.[42] The National Union Executive expressed concern at the political gains being made by the opposition and the Chairman, Sir Eugene Ramsden, warned all associations of Labour's claim to be the alternative government.

As long as criticism did not undermine the government's authority, the National Union agreed to 'abstain from provoking party feeling'.[43] Disquiet was expressed, however, at 'Socialist Party propaganda' in Parliament and the media but the invasion of the Low Countries and the arrival of the Coalition meant nothing could be done. Chamberlain (still party leader) warned the Executive of 'the necessity of maintaining the party organisation in the Constituencies, and that it should not be allowed under the pressure of events to fall into disorganisation as in the last war'.[44]

Conservatives accepted Labour's participation strengthened the war effort but it also had serious political implications. In the summer of 1940 R. A. Butler's constituency chairman warned of 'the socialistic mess we shall have to clear up' and the demands of war 'will mean the final collapse of the upper middle class ... and the end of the old social [order]'. The main beneficiaries would be the organised working class. The Chief Whip, David Margesson, reported that a speech by Bevin attacking profit had annoyed Conservative MPs, commenting 'There would be terrible trouble if Conservative Ministers went about denouncing socialism and proclaimed their panaceas for the future'.[45]

As early as November 1940 the scale of Labour's political influence was described as 'extremely depressing' but little could be done 'to keep Conservatism alive without workers and without money'. Conservatives were already dancing to Labour's tune, 'chaos is looming ahead: all the cranks and faddists are getting ready to put things right, and the so called Conservatives are playing up to them – we are to have a "better Britain" after the war; "there must be no going back to the status quo", etc etc – and no one appears to know what is to be done except that there must be no more profit making and that everything must be nationalised'.[46] Behind the facade of national unity the government's Home Intelligence reports found serious class conflict and 'a general expectation that this war must bring the end of class conflict and the abolition of great inequalities of wealth ... rationing and shortages affect the rich very little, since they can pay the extra prices and feed in well-stocked restaurants ... Employers and Labour both claim that the other is profiting from the war'.[47]

Between May 1940 and May 1942 Conservatives were paralysed politically. 'I always feel in despair', Headlam wrote, 'when I attend meetings of the Executive ... it always appears to be so utterly out of touch with the realities of politics ... still living in the atmosphere of the Primrose League'.[48] This has been ascribed to Conservatism's ideological and political obsolescence when the war required interventionism and collectivism. Wartime domestic politics aroused Conservative fears in four areas: high taxation; state control; trade union power; and backdoor Socialism. These were challenged directly by personal responsibility, liberty, and free enterprise. War would take the country further towards Socialism under the guise of winning the war, a trend that would be impossible to reverse. Conservative fears were exacerbated by the party's loss of self-confidence and the constraints of Coalition politics which tempered the party's anti-Socialism. Conservatives were facing what *The Times* termed 'Progressive Democracy' in which 'The aim of the 20th century electorate ... is to expand equality of political rights into a new equality of social and economic opportunity. This is the inevitable trend of mass democracy'. Also inevitable was the decline of the individual, *laisser-faire* and the minimal state as 'the economic life of the country is controlled by a small number of powerful and closely organised groups, each struggling to harness the power of the State to uphold and further its own particular interest'.[49]

Despite agreement that there should be reform, the Coalition divided on party lines over its extent and timing.[50] Central to this was Churchill's conviction that controversial legislation should be postponed until after the war. So, if the Cabinet agreed to present a bill to Parliament it was *ipso facto* non-controversial and all Coalition parties were obliged to support it. This definition of non-controversial was deeply disliked by many Conservatives who felt that Labour was using its influence to have controversial matters redefined as non-controversial. In 1943 James Stuart (the Conservative Chief Whip), goaded by Beaverbrook's taunts that the party was surrendering to Labour, retorted that if his 'original instructions were to be altered it would be quite simple to engineer the collapse of the National War Government within 48 hours'. The Coalition's difficulties were revealed in the controversies surrounding the Beveridge Report: 'The Labour people were ... very angry that the Government did not accept Beveridge's recommendations en bloc – others of us thought they were accepting too much of them'.[51]

To restrain Labour's enthusiasm and offer a sop to his backbenchers Churchill appointed Lord Woolton Minister of Reconstruction in November 1943. Woolton had been highly successful as Minister of Food and although seen as a non-party figure, he was, in fact, a Conservative whose business career made him sceptical of ambitious (and costly) schemes of social reform. Woolton was appointed to restrain Labour's ambitions whilst building a reform consensus amongst sceptical and hostile Conservatives. Woolton's approach was to appeal to their self-interest. At the Constitutional Club in June 1943 Woolton told a 'large and somewhat dyed-in-the-wool body of Conservatives that it was no use thinking that things could go on as they did before the war – that we had failed as a Government to handle the post-war situation in 1918 ... we must not fail them again'. The mass of the population would accept no more unfulfilled promises; despite the cost of these reforms it was in the wider Conservative interest to accept reform and control its implementation.[52] The leftwards shift in domestic politics imposed considerable strains on the staunchly anti-Socialist Conservative backbench elected in 1935. Even before May 1940 the 1922 Committee was seized by the fear that Labour was getting the best of both worlds, acting as both an opposition whilst gaining kudos from its new govern-mental influence. The 1922 were convinced Labour benefited from left-wing propaganda emanating from the BBC and the Ministry of Information. After the Conservatives' loss of the Grantham by-election (March 1942) to an Independent Labour candidate there were demands from the 1922 for greater resistance.[53]

Dalton's plans to reorganise coal production and impose coal rationing were seized upon by Conservative MPs as a surreptitious attempt to nation-alise the coal industry. One MP warned: 'The party to which I belong did not wake up to the fact that other people had strong opinions and were pressing them, and now some of us are beginning to wonder whether we might not have our opinions'. Churchill initially favoured rationing but changed his mind when the party Chairman warned him the party was opposed and Stuart estimated up to 100 MPs would vote against and more would abstain. The rationing scheme was then withdrawn.[54] The back-benches' growing negative power in 1942 was directly related to the end of the invasion threat and led to some recovery of confidence. One Conserva-tive dismissed *Guilty Men* as an 'adolescent triumph' and declared his belief in the value of the Munich Agreement and others disputed the need for a new post-war world. Such expressions led Aneurin Bevan to proclaim, 'We can see the Conservatives crawling out of their holes. In 1940 and 1941 they would not have dared to say these things'.[55]

The most serious Conservative rebellion came over Bevin's Catering Wages Bill which was seen as symptomatic of Labour's use of the Coalition to promote Socialism. The rebels' leader, Sir Douglas Hacking (a former Party Chairman), claiming the support of 200 MPs, the party, and indus-try, argued the Bill 'originated solely from the personal desire of the Minis-ter to impose regulation on an industry the individuality and complexity of which have so far puzzled those who would like to see every industry con-trolled and regulated'.[56] The issue was not wage setting in restaurants but the preservation of free enterprise, a principle on which there could be no compromise between Labour and Conservative: 'he (Bevin) would desire to interfere with private enterprise in any circumstances while I would say that you should never interfere with private enterprise until you have proved that it is not doing its job'. For its opponents the bill symbolised where power lay within the Coalition. Conservative ministers 'have come to heel ... because the Minister of Labour has cracked the whip' even though they knew the bill was 'the first step towards ... nationalisation'.[57] Despite the revolt of 116 Conservative MPs, the largest Conservative rebellion in the war, the Whips' writ still ran and Bevin's bill was forced through.

The 1944 Town and Country Planning Bill was equally 'non-controver-sial' but it too generated enormous Conservative hostility. The compensa-tion schedule for compulsory purchase was, in particular, perceived as undermining property rights and individual freedom. Kenneth Pickthorn used the bill to deliver a disquisition on the proper (i.e. limited) functions of government ('defence, and the maintenance of the currency'), condemning the bill as 'a gross piece of injustice'. Land and property ownership was described by Sir Robert Tasker MP as the fundamental political question. 'This is a Bill', he thundered, 'which threatens the rights of individuals and deprives people of their freedom ... this Bill I regard quite frankly as another step in the direction of National Socialism'.[58] Commander Bower lambasted 'high falutin' talk and ... those wonderful new principles' preferring more down-to-earth values: 'since the dawn of history it has been a laudable and commendable thing for a man to own his little bit of property ... Members on either side ... who are so devoted to the great god Plan that they never seem to think of the poor blighters who are being "planned"'.[59] This resistance infuriated Churchill but he nonetheless withdrew the compensation clauses. When they were debated again in October Churchill was visiting Stalin, on his return he deployed his prestige to reduce the threatened rebellion of 70 to 100 MPs, but 56 Conservatives defied Churchill and voted against the schedules.[60]

In 1940 Douglas Hacking had asked Butler to take over the party's drastically reduced research effort 'with a view eventually to adjusting the Party's outlook to the radically different trends of thought which prevail at a time like this', but little was done until March 1941.[61] In March 1941 the Executive and the Central Council decided the party must prepare plans 'in view of the War-time activities in the Constituencies of Socialists, Communists and certain subversive Societies'. In May Butler proposed the Executive appoint a committee to collate the party's views on reform. A memorandum would then be presented to Churchill. This was agreed and at the end of May Topping wrote to Butler asking him to chair the committee.[62] In July 1941 an *ad hoc* Reconstruction Committee (soon renamed the Post War Problems Consultative Committee becoming the Post War Problems Central Committee in July 1942 (PWPCC)) was established, its composition reflecting the need to cater for all factions in the party. As well as Butler (already identified as a leading reformer by his contemporaneous appointment to the Board of Education) the PWPCC consisted of Erskine-Hill (Chairman of the 1922), Douglas Hacking (a former Party Chairman), James Stuart (Chief Whip), Sir Cuthbert Headlam (a traditionalist backbencher), and Topping as secretary. These were joined by twelve others organised into eight sub-committees: Consultative; Reconstruction; Agricultural; Industry and Finance; Education and Social Services; Constitutional and Administrative Reform; National Security; and Imperial matters. Sub-committee reports would go first to the Central Committee who would then pass them to Churchill and the relevant minister. Butler would report generally on progress to the Executive and the Central Council.[63]

Progress was slow but 1942 was a turning point. Responding to the PWPCC, the Central Council resolved in March 1942 that the party truce was not incompatible with the Conservative Party 'mak[ing] known to the public its general attitude on broad lines to post-war problems'.[64] The new Party Chairman, Tommy Dugdale, warned of 'the difficulties being met by Conservatives in counteracting adverse party propaganda', urging the party to greater efforts. The Executive received several complaints about the BBC's Socialist bias and that 'the subtle propaganda of our opponents ... is having such a damaging effect on our Party, and advocates measures to counter such propaganda being put in hand at once rather than wait until the end of the war'.[65] Suspicion of the PWPCC, of Butler, and of reform was, however, never far below the surface leading the Executive to request interim reports be produced for discussion within the party to ensure they conformed to Conservative principles. One document, *Plan for Youth*, was described by Major P. Petherick MP as 'typical of the pink "slop" which for years had been infecting the Conservative Party'.[66] Churchill sanctioned sufficient reform to keep Labour on side whilst insisting its leaders deliver the movement's support for the war effort. The Conservative Party tended to see only the former. A further difficulty was that whatever policy preparations the party undertook only the party leader could define authoritatively party policy, and Churchill adamantly refused to do this. Typical of his statements was that of July 1942. Reconstruction would require unity around a common policy, and Churchill wished to avoid a partisan approach, so the scope of reconstruction remained vague: 'our aim will be to build a society in which there will be wealth and culture, but where wealth shall not prey on commonwealth nor culture degenerate into class pride'.[67]

The popular acclaim which greeted the publication of the Beveridge Report (November 1942) and the tardiness of the Cabinet's response (the result of divisions within the government) and the tensions revealed in the Commons debate of 16–18 February forced Churchill to make a statement on reconstruction in a radio broadcast on 21 March 1943.[68] 'We must', he told his audience, 'be wary of trying to build a society in which nobody counts for anything except a politician or an official, a society where enterprise gains no reward and thrift no privileges'. Equally, the mistakes made after 1918 would not be repeated which was why the Coalition was carefully preparing for a peace in which 'The modern state will increasingly concern itself with the economic well-being of the nation'. In this speech Churchill floated the idea of a four-year plan 'to cover five or six large measures of a practical character'. After the end of the war this plan would be put to the country in a general election by a Coalition or even a non-party government 'comprising the best men in all parties who are willing to serve'. Beveridge was not mentioned but Churchill spoke approvingly of

social insurance 'from the cradle to the grave', of full employment, part-
nership in industry and with the state, and even nationalisation. There
would be, he pledged, dramatic improvement in housing, education, and
health care. That this speech represented a definitive statement of both
Coalition and party policy can be seen in Churchill's comment to the editor
of *The Times* 'that the Tory Party would fight on that'.[69]

Despite Churchill's broadcast the party continued to 'call for a bold and
constructive policy from the Leadership of the Party'.[70] To damp down disquiet and rally support the Executive agreed to call a Conference, the first
since 1937. The Conference's main purpose was to endorse Beveridge and
Churchill's broadcast which was presented as an alternative to Socialism
embracing the interests of the whole nation. In Churchill's absence (he was
in Washington) Eden delivered the key note address, arguing that the country's single-minded pursuit of victory must be applied to the peace. Eden
argued that the One Nation tradition gave Conservatives a natural sympathy for reform and repeated Churchill's hope that reconstruction would be
overseen by a Coalition. Eden, like Churchill, made no specific commitments, concentrating instead on broad aspirations. This was challenged on
the second day by those who felt definite plans should be made so as to challenge Labour. Captain Quintin Hogg, for example, insisted the forces
'wanted the assurance of decent well-paid, and reasonably secure jobs and
decent homes ... they wanted education not Education Bills'.[71]

Churchill's absence meant the party could be given no authoritative lead.
The Executive endorsed the Conference's call for a policy statement, a
request forwarded to Churchill. The Executive also urged government 'to
recognise that each interference with the complete liberty and independence
of the individual can only be justified by the greater need of the community
in every instance ... while plans now for the Post-War period are desirable,
they should not involve either avoidable restrictions or bureaucratic control'.[72] This tension between individualism and collectivism bedevilled
wartime Conservative politics. Through 1944, whilst Churchill's attention
was concentrated on the approaching invasion of Europe, the party chafed
at the absence of any clear lead which allowed Labour policy to be presented
as 'the only policy for the internal and economic reconstruction of Britain
after the War, and feels that the failure of the Conservative Party to declare
a post-war policy is placing its members and supporters at a great disadvantage and causing a general tendency to lean towards the left'.[73] Party
officials refused to allow the resolution to go further, regarding it as an
attack on Churchill, who was himself unhappy about the party's attitude.
During the rebellion over the Town and Country Planning Bill Churchill
threatened 'he would resign the leadership of the Conservative Party' in
protest at its attitude over reconstruction.[74]

Conservative electoral defeat

The approach of the war's end led Dugdale to announce 'that the time had now come for stimulating Party Organisation throughout the country ... with the object of putting forward the Conservative point of view'.[75] Studies have tended to focus on the Tory Reform Group and ignored the strength of Conservative free market liberalism.

The Tory Reform Group (TRG) was formed in March 1943 in response to the Conservative revolt against the Catering Wages Bill. Chaired by Viscount Hinchingbrooke it had some thirty-six members who believed the Conservative Party was misinterpreting the nation's mood. The government's tardy response to Beveridge sparked the debate on post-war politics and had an enormous effect on younger MPs, especially those who had served in the forces. In fact what the TRG advocated was perceived to be more difficult for orthodox Conservatism than it was. A leading member, Lord Hailsham, identified himself with Macmillan's 'middle way' but had an equally strong belief in free enterprise. The Group's philosophy has been described as 'Publicly organised social services, privately owned industry'. The Tory Reform Group was important because it 'fused the old Tory tradition of state intervention with the more recent ideas of Harold Macmillan and other radical Conservatives of the 1930s and was, therefore, more in tune with the wider climate of opinion'.[76]

The TRG had little impact on government or party thinking. One backbencher noted acerbically 'whenever "Young Tories" try to be "progressive" they quote Dizzy and produce a watered down Socialist programme, very much like the Conservative Party programme only expounded vigorously – sometimes almost ferociously – as something entirely new'.[77] The Tory Reform Group's dispute with Conservative ministers was not over content but their 'pussy footing over the Beveridge Report [which] was unduly unconstructive and unimaginative'.[78] Its members' volubility provoked a powerful reaction amongst more traditional Conservatives.

Reversing war Socialism would require a supreme effort from the Conservative Party which 'should be ready to stand firmly upon an unequivocal and constructive programme, and be prepared to go down to temporary defeat upon it'. Sound policies required balancing the defects of democracy ('irresponsibility, instability, inefficiency and corruption') with individual freedom and liberty, citizenship, and the party programme should concentrate on individual enterprise: 'state interference, bureaucracy, and taxation must be regarded as necessary but unavoidable harms, to be kept as light as possible'. One MP wrote, 'socialism is war, and war is socialism ... the war is landing us with all sorts, or most sorts of Socialism ... we ought to make sure that every bit of war-time socialism is labelled as such, so that it may have no chance to go on in peace-time unchallenged ... we ought to resist it ... [and] consider every positive assistance to free enterprise'. In education and health matters the party was urged to take its stand on 'individuality', oppose planning, and actively challenge the view that 'the tendency to socialisation' was inevitable.[79] Conservatives were concerned at the fate of 'the little man' crushed between the state, big capital, and organised labour. This, as a 1922 sub-committee report argued, was a 'prime question of policy for the Conservative Party'. The defence of the small man was not only intrinsically important but also because 'the Party numbers among its supporters very many of the independent businessmen whose future is in jeopardy'.[80] If Labour had no qualms about advancing the interests of its constituency, neither should the Conservative Party. This underpinned the founding of the National League for Freedom (April 1943), itself a reaction to the TRG. The League would 'protect the interests of manufacturers, farmers, traders, small-holders, small shopkeepers, housewives and others of individual responsibility and initiative' against state control.[81]

Although avowedly non-party, sixteen of the thirty-five officers and council members were Conservative MPs and amongst these were leading Central Office figures, notably Sir Douglas Hacking (ex-Party Chairman), Sir Patrick Hannon (Chairman of the Midland Group of MPs and of the National Union of Manufacturers), and Sir Waldron Smithers (a longstanding free-marketeer). The League's Manifesto pledged it would 'fight the growing threat to British liberty, represented by the host of Government officials who today shut down businesses, pry into private affairs, issue endless forms, "coupon" the housewife to distraction, and are slowly strangling not only trade but liberty'.[82] Excessive bureaucracy diverted resources from productive industry and bureaucrats, having no practical experience or common sense, who ran the system were doing irreparable damage to commerce and industry. The growth in wartime bureaucracy, the League argued, was no different to the process whereby the state in pre-war Italy and Germany had taken control of the individual.[83] In January 1943 a similar body, The Society of Individualists, was founded by the publisher Sir Ernest Benn. Relations between the two were uneasy as the League, dominated by MPs, was constrained by the needs of party politics which led Benn to condemn it for having 'the typical pinkish Conservative attitude' but the two merged in January 1945.[84]

The League found the Conservative Party was not a congenial environment for faction politics as the natural instinct of the majority was to rally to the leadership even if they were advocating policies of which the MPs disapproved. Party leaders tended to elevate the electoral success of the party above the triumph of abstract ideas so Conservative politics were electorally pragmatic and this was a major obstacle to faction politics. Senior Cabinet ministers (for example, Woolton) and backbenchers were attracted by neo-Liberal ideas but would not allow this to jeopardise their position in the party or its electoral chances.[85] The League was part of a wider upsurge in neo-Liberal thinking: in 1943 Kalecki published his *Political Quarterly* article which suggested that Keynesian demand management techniques offered permanent government to the party skilled in their use, and in 1944 Hayek's *The Road to Serfdom* was published with its famous dedication 'To the Socialists in all parties'. Replying to a letter asking about the creation of a League branch in Birmingham Hannon wrote 'The plain fact is that we already have too many organisations in Birmingham ... [which] ... include the removal of controls as part of their working programme'. These organisations included the National Association of Manufacturers, the Institute of Exports, the Chamber of Commerce, and the Empire Industries Associations, as well as the Birmingham and Midland Group of MPs.[86]

The League's influence is impossible to estimate but it was more influential than the TRG as it went with the grain of Conservative politics. Butler's frequent conflicts with the 1922 and the Executive contributed to his decision in July 1943 to hand over the PWPCC to his deputy, Major David Maxwell-Fyfe, and concentrate on the passage of the Education Bill. Interestingly, the upsurge in neo-Liberal ideas coincided with Maxwell-Fyfe's tenure of the PWPCC where he was far more combative, anti-Socialist, and more interested in party propaganda than Butler.[87] With the benefit of hindsight Conservative defeat seems inevitable and the evidence for this was available at the time but was ignored by all. The British Institute of Public Opinion (BIPO, later Gallup) published its polls in the *News Chronicle* which measured, albeit imperfectly and sporadically, the pro-Labour nature of public opinion. In January 1946 Churchill's doctor told him of the *News Chronicle*'s polls and Churchill confessed he had never heard of them. He found their support for himself coupled with dislike of the Conservatives to be incomprehensible.[88] Before the March 1945 Conference party leaders were in a buoyant mood, confident of victory because of Churchill's popularity and Labour's unsuitability as a government. Headlam doubted Churchill's popularity would last beyond the end of the war, pointing out that the Labour Party did not look futile to the many members of the electorate who liked the idea of socialism. Returning to Britain in May 1945 after two years in the Middle East Macmillan found opinion altered to a degree that 'middle way' Conservatism was unlikely to satisfy the electorate.[89] Conservative electoral strategy was influenced by Churchill's confidante, Lord Beaverbrook, whose approach 'was to base everything on Churchill's name', a strategy endorsed by senior Conservatives (notably Bracken, Stuart, and to a lesser extent Assheton). Woolton's formulation was typical: 'The mixture we want is Churchill the war-winner, Churchill, the British bull-dog breed in international conference, and Churchill, the leader of a Government with a programme of social reform'.[90]

The 1945 Conference launched the Conservative election campaign; its themes were individual freedom, and Churchill. Churchill's speech as leader was of enormous significance defining not only the party's electoral appeal but the tenor of post-war Conservatism. In fact his speech (and the 1945 manifesto) scarcely departed from the March 1943 radio address. Churchill began by congratulating the party on its forbearance in the face of years of Socialist propaganda and misrepresentation whilst regretting Labour's dissolution of the Coalition. Churchill then repeated his 1943 proposal for a Four Year Plan and a non-party government under his leadership, a proposal which alarmed many Conservatives not just because of a dislike of Coalition but because many believed Conservatives had been underrepresented in government since the February 1942 reshuffle. Whilst his government would be reformist and would implement the Coalition's agreed plans Churchill refused to promise immediate benefits. 'The Conservative Party', he declared, 'had far better go down telling the truth and acting in accordance with the verities of our position than gain a span of shabbily bought office by easy and fickle froth and chatter'. Reconstruction and reform depended on economic recovery which in turn depended on the speedy relaxation of controls, Churchill argued. Continuing controls after the war would promote totalitarianism and prosperity would come from free enterprise and strict controls on public spending. Churchill drew a sharp line between the Labour and Conservative parties over nationalisation. Whilst there was common ground on, for example, social policy there could be no compromise on the structure of economic power. Nationalisation, he argued, 'impl[ied] not only the destruction of the whole of our existing society, and of life, and of labour, but the creation and enforcement of another system or other systems borrowed from foreign lands and alien minds'.[91] These points were reiterated in the 1945 manifesto. He declared 'This is the time for freeing energies, not stifling them. Britain's greatness has been built on character and daring, not on docility to a state machine'. Despite repeated assurances that Conservatives accepted the Coalition's plans these were subordinate to 'Confidence in sound Government – mutual co-operation between industry and the State, rather than control by the State – a lightening of the burdens of excessive taxation – these are the first essentials'.[92] Churchill's tone and the party's mood were closer to that of the League than the TRG.

The Conservative defeat in the Chelmsford by-election (April 1945) by Commonwealth shook the confidence of Churchill's campaign team. Beaverbrook, Bracken, Stuart, and Assheton 'were at once summoned for a lengthy conclave' with Churchill. To Headlam defeat came as no surprise; he could not understand 'why our Conservative pundits are so blind to the situation – their faith in the magic of Winston's name is to me rather pathetic'. Two weeks earlier he had written, 'Once the war is won, his war record will be forgotten and his past misdeeds will be remembered. He was never a popular politician with the people'.[93] Compared to the excitements of running the war Churchill recognised peacetime politics was not his natural habitat. 'I have no message', he told his doctor, 'I had a message. Now I only say "fight the damned socialists". I do not believe in this brave new world'.[94] The election failed to stir his imagination but despite the poor reception of his 4 June speech which charged that Labour would need to create a Gestapo to implement its policies, he continued to believe the Conservatives would win. In mid-July Beaverbrook and Assheton confirmed Margesson's estimate of a majority of 100 and as late as the 23rd Beaverbrook repeated his prediction of a Conservative majority.[95]

The Conservative defeat was of 1906 proportions: a 12% swing to Labour which gained 227 seats and a net loss of 185 Conservative seats, but despite Labour polling 49.05% of votes cast, the Conservative share of the vote held up well (41.5%). Six days after the Conservative defeat Beaverbrook wrote, 'The truth is that the British public have been conceiving for a long time an immense dislike of the Tory Party, the Tory Members of Parliament and many of the Tory ideas. They were bored and wanted a change'. Cuthbert Headlam, who survived the deluge, agreed 'the people wanted a change and, no longer being afraid, voted for a Labour Party filled with young half baked young men – mainly from the RAF'. When Parliament met his worst fears seemed confirmed: 'The House was a strange sight – full to the brim with the new boys – the flight lieutenants and other callow youths who are to rule us all for the next five years at least – my heart rather sank within me when I saw their eager, excited young faces and the smug grinning faces of Morrison and his colleagues on the Front Bench'.[96] Could the Conservatives recover?

Notes

1 T. Stannage, *Baldwin Thwarts the Opposition. The British General Election of 1935* (London: Croom Helm, 1980), p. 13.
2 'Authentic Note of Democracy', in Earl Baldwin of Bewdley, *This Torch of Freedom*, 4th edition (London: Hodder and Stoughton, 1937), pp. 43–7.
3 'Authentic Note of Democracy', pp. 56–7.
4 'The Civil Service' in *This Torch of Freedom* (26 October 1933), p. 62.
5 *The Times*, 7 October 1933.
6 NUA 2/1/49, Minutes of the Annual Conference, 4–5 October 1934, pp. 21, 37, and 40.
7 L. P. Carpenter, 'Corporatism in Britain, 1930–1945', *Journal of Contemporary History*, 11 (1976), p. 5. The best examination of Tory corporatism is N. Harris, *Competition and the Corporate Society. British Conservatives, the State and Industry, 1945–1964* (London: Methuen, 1972).
8 For example, R. Boothby, H. Macmillan, J. De V Loder and O. Stanley, *Industry and the State. A Conservative View* (London: Macmillan, 1927), W. S.

Churchill, *Parliamentary Government and the Economic Problem* (Oxford: Claren-don Press, 1930), and H. Macmillan, *Reconstruction* (London: Macmillan, 1933).

9 M. Kirby, 'Industrial Policy', in S. Glynn and A. Booth (eds.), *The Road to Full Employment* (London: Allen and Unwin 1987), pp. 131–5, and A. Booth, 'Britain in the 1930s: A Managed Economy', *Economic History Review*, 40 (3) (1987), pp. 499–522.

10 J. Stevenson and C. Cook, *The Slump. Society and Politics during the Depression* (London: Quartet, 1979), pp. 120–3.

11 Stevenson and Cook, *The Slump*, pp. 257 and 260.

12 D. Butler and D. Stokes, *Political Change in Britain. The Evolution of Electoral Choice*, 2nd edition (London: Macmillan, 1974), p. 175 and p. 186. The data is,

Net Increase in Labour Strength (% manual workers in each cohort)

| Cohort | Exchanges with: | | Recruitment of non-aligned voters |
	Liberals	Conservatives	
Pre-1918	14.6	5.5	13.3
Inter-war	6.3	4.3	20.7
1945	2.4	1.6	16.4
1951–1964	0.3	0.3	15.7

Source: Butler and Stokes, *Political Change in Britain*, Table 8.5, p. 178.

13 K. D. Wald, *Crosses on the Ballot. Patterns of British Voter Alignment since 1885* (Princeton: Princeton University Press, 1983), pp. 214–15, and Butler and Stokes, *Political Change in Britain*, p. 200.

14 A simulation conducted by Wald confirms Butler and Stokes' cohort analysis (*Crosses on the Ballot*, pp. 245–6).

15 F. Williams, *A Prime Minister Remembers* (London: Heinemann, 1961), p. 12, and P. F. Clarke, *A Question of Leadership* (Harmondsworth: Penguin, 1992), p. 118.

16 K. Feiling, *The Life of Neville Chamberlain* (London: Macmillan, 1946), pp. 313–14.

17 J. Charmley, *Chamberlain and the Lost Peace* (London: Macmillan, 1989), p. 29.

18 R. Rhodes James, *Anthony Eden* (London: Macmillan, 1987), pp. 196–8.

19 H. Macmillan, *Winds of Change, 1914–1939* (London: Macmillan, 1966), p. 538.

20 Charmley, *Chamberlain and the Lost Peace*, p. 55, and Macmillan, *Winds of Change*, p. 569.

21 Macmillan, *Winds of Change*, p. 548.

22 Macmillan, *Winds of Change*, p. 548 and R. Boothby, *Recollections of a Rebel* (London: Hutchinson, 1978), p. 128. Boothby also identifies the 'Amery Group' as well as the Eden and Churchill groups but there was a considerable overlap between them.

23 Rhodes James, *Anthony Eden*, pp. 203–4, and H. Nicolson, *Diaries and Letters 1930–39* (London: Collins, 1966), 11 April 1938.

24 Nicolson, *Diaries and Letters, 1930–39*, letter to V. Sackville-West, 9 November

1938.

25 Macmillan, *Winds of Change*, p. 601. Eden estimated only 30 Conservative MPs opposed the Government's policy. Rhodes James, *Anthony Eden*, p. 208.

26 B. Pimlott, *Hugh Dalton* (London: Macmillan, 1985), pp. 257–61 for these links. Dalton also had talks with dissident members of the Foreign Office.

27 Macmillan, *Winds of Change*, p. 562.

28 Macmillan, *Winds of Change*, pp. 568 and 569. Further meetings were held in the summer of 1938 but Labour preferred to wait on events. Amery cautioned hotheads like Macmillan that there was as yet no possibility of removing Chamberlain.

29 Boothby, *Recollections of a Rebel*, p. 134. Boothby exonerated Churchill and Amery from this judgement; Macmillan also concedes this, admitting the dissidents could not force Chamberlain to go and even then would the resulting government have been any more effective? (*Winds of Change*, p. 550).

30 J. M. Lee, *The Churchill Coalition, 1940–45* (London: Batsford, 1980), p. 31 and T. Jones, *A Diary with Letters, 1931–1950* (London: Oxford University Press, 1954), p. 397.

31 K. Middlemas and J. Barnes, *Baldwin* (London: Macmillan, 1969), p. 1045 and Feiling, *The Life of Neville Chamberlain*, p. 385. For Wilson's role see B. Pimlott (ed.), *The Second World War Diary of Hugh Dalton* (hereafter *Dalton Diaries*), (London: Cape, 1986), 8 January 1941. When Labour joined the Coalition it insisted Wilson be removed from all Government positions.

32 Middlemas and Barnes, *Baldwin*, p. 1047 and J. Colville, *The Fringes of Power. Downing Street Diaries, 1939–1955* (London, Hodder and Stoughton, 1985), 31 January 1940.

33 Feiling, *The Life of Neville Chamberlain*, pp. 420–1, and *D/HE 36 Headlam Diary*, 1 July 1940.

34 *Dalton Diaries*, 3 October 1940 and F. Williams, *Ernest Bevin* (London: Hutchinson, 1952), p. 217.

35 Bevin's foreword to J. Price, *Labour and the War* (Harmondsworth: Penguin, 1940), p. v.

36 R. Blake, 'How Churchill Became Prime Minister', in R. Blake and W. Roger Louis, *Churchill* (Oxford: Oxford University Press, 1994), pp. 257–73.

37 W. S. Churchill, *The Second World War Volume II. Their Finest Hour* (London: Cassell, 1949), p. 10 and Jones, *A Diary with Letters, 1931–50*, p. 465.

38 *D/HE 36 Diary 1940*, 21 January, 9 May, and 10 May 1940, and *Dalton Diaries*, 18 June 1940.

39 Churchill, *Their Finest Hour*, p. 9, and Colville, *The Fringes of Power*, 10 August 1940.

40 Colville, *The Fringes of Power*, 9 October 1940, and *NUEC*, 13 November 1940.

41 *CCO 4/1/86*, Political Organisation and Structure. Director General's Memorandum on the Possible Effect of War on Political Life and Organisation, 14 November 1939, p. 4 and *NUEC*, 20 September 1939.

42 *D/HE 36 Headlam Diary*, 26 October 1939, and *Diary 37*, 20 March 1940.

43 Ramsden to all Constituency Associations, *NUEC*, 13 December 1939 and *NUEC*, 13 March 1940.

44 *NUEC*, 27 June 1940.

45 A. Howard, *RAB. The Life of R. A. Butler* (London: Macmillan, 1987), p. 90 and *D/HE 35 Headlam Diary* 28 September and 1 October 1940, and Colville, *The Fringes of Power*, 21 November 1940.

46 *D/HE 36 Headlam Diary*, 30 November 1940.

47 Colville, *The Fringes of Power*, 5 February 1941.

48 *D/HE 38 Headlam Diary*, 26 May 1942.

49 *The Times*, 2 January 1943.

50 There is no need to go into detail about the Coalition's reconstruction efforts. See K. Jeffrey, *The Churchill Coalition and Wartime Politics, 1940–45* (Manchester: Manchester University Press, 1991), chapter 5.

51 J. Stuart, *Within the Fringe* (London: Bodley Head, 1967), pp. 134–5, and *D/HE 39 Diary, 1943*, 16 February 1943.

52 Lord Woolton, *Memoirs* (London: Cassell, 1959), pp. 276–7, and *MS Woolton 3*: Diary 18 September 1942–June 1960 57, 3 June 1943.

53 P. Goodhart, *The 1922* (London: Macmillan, 1973), pp. 99, 105, and 124.

54 *5s H. C. Debs 380*, 10 June 1942, col 1139 (Charles Williams MP), and *Dalton Diaries*, 12 May 1942.

55 *5s H. C. Debs 377*, 28–29 January 1942, col 776 (Beverley Baxter MP), and *5s H. C. Debs 38*, 12 November 1942, col 138.

56 *The Times*, 14 January 1943.

57 *5s H. C. Debs 386*, 9 February 1942, col 1211 (Sir Douglas Hacking MP), and col 1939 (Captain Peter Macdonald MP).

58 *5s H. C. Debs 401*, 11 July 1944, cols 1637 and 1640 and 12 July 1944, col 1831.

59 *5s H. C. Debs 404*, 25 October 1944, cols 212–13.

60 *The Times*, 26 October 1944.

61 J. Ramsden, *The Making of Conservative Party Policy: the Conservative Research Department since 1929* (London: Longman, 1980), p. 96: Chamberlain closed CRD down in 1940.

62 *Central Council*, 27 March, and *NUEC*, 14 May 1941.

63 *Post War Problems*, Sir Eugene Ramsden's Report to the National Union Executive Committee, 9 July 1941. Butler quickly took the opportunity to warn the party that Conservatives had no choice other than to respond positively to the popular demand for change. See *Central Council*, 2 October 1941. Butler's warning was published as *Looking Ahead*.

64 *NUEC*, 13 May 1942.

65 *ARE 8/1/2*, Home Counties North Annual Meeting, 18 June 1942, and *NUEC*, 8 July 1942.

66 *NUEC*, 13 May 1942, and *The Times*, 3 October 1942. The PWPCC's discussion paper on education had been published before the Executive had been given a chance to comment.

67 'The Atlantic Charter', *Notes of Speakers* (1st series), July 1942, pp. 1–2.

68 On the Beveridge phenomenon see J. Jacobs, 'December 1942: Beveridge Observed. Mass-Observation and the Beveridge Report', in J. Jacobs (ed.), *Beveridge 1942–1992* (London: Whiting and Birch, 1992), pp. 20–31.

69 'Reconstruction of British Industry', *Notes of Speakers* (1st series), March 1943,

p. 2, *The Times*, 22 March 1943 and M. Gilbert, *Winston Churchill Volume VI. The Road to Victory 1941–45* (London: Heinemann, 1976), p. 372.

70 *NUEC*, 14 April 1943.

71 *The Times*, 21 and 22 May 1943.

72 *NUEC*, 8 July 1943.

73 *NUEC*, 14 March 1944.

74 Gilbert, *The Road to Victory*, p. 1037.

75 *NUEC*, 27 July 1944.

76 Lord Hailsham, *A Sparrow's Flight. Memoirs* (London: Collins, 1990), pp. 209–10, and Ramsden, *The Making of Conservative Party Policy*, p. 99.

77 *D/HE 40, Headlam Diary*, 11 October 1944.

78 Woolton, *Memoirs*, p. 295, and Hailsham, *A Sparrow's Flight*, p. 216.

79 *Davidson Papers*, Memoranda on a Post-War Programme (Wing Commander A. H. James MP and K. Pickering MP), September 1941.

80 Hannon Papers *H61/1*, Report on the Sub-Committee on Small Traders, 1942.

81 *The Times*, 16 April 1943.

82 *H82/5* National League for Freedom. Objects and Manifesto.

83 *The Times*, 16 April 1943.

84 D. Abel, *Ernest Benn. Counsel for Liberty* (London: Ernest Benn, 1960), pp. 116–17, and *H82/5*, National League for Freedom, 16 November 1944 for the merger talks.

85 Benn Diary, 4 May 1942 (meeting with Woolton) and 5 November 1943 (Sir Geoffrey Shakespeare MP), in Abel, *Counsel for Liberty*, pp. 106 and 120. After the war Benn saw his most important task as 'rooting Socialism out of the Conservative Party' (p. 131).

86 *H82/5*, Sir Patrick Hannon to Lieutenant General A. N. Floyer-Acland, 24 February 1944. M Kalecki, 'Political Aspects of Full Employment', *Political Quarterly*, 14, 1943, and F. Hayek, *The Road to Serfdom* (London: Routledge & Kegan Paul, 1944).

87 Howard, *RAB*, pp. 142–3.

88 R. Sibley, 'The Swing to Labour During the Second World War: When and Why?', *Labour History Review*, 55 (1) 1990, pp. 23–34 explores the change in public opinion. See Lord Moran, *Winston Churchill. The Struggle for Survival* (London: Sphere Books, 1966), p. 335 for Churchill's ignorance of these polls.

89 *D/HE 41*, 14 March 1945 and Horne, *Macmillan 1894–1956 Volume I of the Official Biography* (London: Macmillan, 1988), pp. 283–4.

90 A. J. P. Taylor, *Beaverbrook* (Harmondsworth, Penguin, 1974), p. 723. Butler describes the PWPCC's work as sporadic, having little or no impact on the party, Conservative ministers, or public opinion. Lord Butler, *The Art of the Possible* (London: Hamish Hamilton, 1971), p. 127. Butler's memoirs are almost totally silent on the PWPCC.

91 *The Times*, 16 March 1945.

92 'Mr Churchill's Address to the Electors', in F. W. S. Craig, *British General Election Manifestoes, 1900–1975* (London: Macmillan, 1978), p. 115.

93 Colville, *Fringes of Power*, 27 April 1945 and *D/HE 41*, 27 April and 12 April 1945.

94 Moran, *Winston Churchill*, 20 September 1944.

95 Moran, *Winston Churchill*, 20 May, 4 June, 11 July, 16 July, and 23 July 1945.
96 Taylor, *Beaverbrook*, p. 727 and *D/HE 41*, 26 July and 1 August 1945.

4

Conservatism remade,
1945–1953

Conservative politics in this period can be divided into three phases. Between 1945 and 1947 the modernisers filled the vacuum created by defeat in 1945. This period ends with the publication of *The Industrial Charter*. 1947–9 sees a reaction reflecting the Labour government's declining fortunes after 1947 and the return of Conservative political self-confidence. This period ends with the publication of *The Right Road for Britain* (1949). Third, after 1951 government policy was dominated by the closeness of the election result and economic crisis. The government thrashed out, in a pragmatic and piecemeal fashion, a response to post-war politics, helped by an upsurge in economic growth and prosperity which owed more to the end of the Korean War than any government policy. The remaking of Conservatism has been exaggerated; the most significant adaptation took place at elite level and its penetration into the mass of the party was limited. Disquiet was managed by economic and political success.

Defeat and the demand for change

Pressure for change did not suddenly appear on the morrow of defeat.[1] Reforming the Conservative Party was a complicated process composed of three aspects: organisational reform under Lord Woolton (Party Chairman) who oversaw the creation of a mass party oriented towards electoral mobilisation; candidate selection reform; and policy innovation. Cumulatively these reforms are portrayed as not only modernising the party but signifying the victory of 'New' Conservatism.[2] The accuracy of this interpretation can be disputed.

Lord Woolton ('Uncle Fred') joined the Party on the morrow of defeat, a gesture which touched Churchill deeply.[3] His original reaction to the party's organisation when appointed Chairman in July 1946 was to scrap it and start again. Woolton secured a free hand from Churchill as a condition of his appointment but quickly recognised that scrapping the organisation would mortally offend the constituency activists upon whom the success of the party depended. Woolton drew three conclusions: voluntary effort and constituency autonomy were essential to the party's vitality and should be preserved; function was more important than organisational neatness; and the main function of party organisation was to win elections. Woolton's objectives were members and money ('The Fighting Fund') so as to win power. He deliberately set a high financial target (£1 million) as a spur to party effort and by December the target had been achieved. In April 1948 he appealed for 1 million members and by June 1948 the target was secured; by 1951 the party had 1.5 million members. Achieving these targets boosted party morale.[4]

Many of Woolton's reforms were under way before he took over and their origins can be discerned before 1939.[5] In October 1945 party candidates, the Central Council and the party Executive called for the reform of the party organisation. Woolton took advantage of a widespread desire for change which reduces the 'revolutionary' aspect of the reforms. The implosion of the party organisation in the war meant that even without defeat considerable change was inevitable and a Labour government was bound to lead to an upsurge in party membership and improved finances. Woolton was a great self-publicist and used the organisational reforms to build up his own and the party's image implying that greater changes were under way than was actually the case.

Traditionally candidate selection, especially in safe seats, depended on handsome contributions to constituency funds. This restricted candidates to a narrow social strata and made it difficult (not impossible) for poor but talented Conservatives to secure nomination; it also led to a lack of organisational vigour. The 1947 Conference set up three committees on aspects of constituency organisation which submitted their recommendations to a central committee chaired by David Maxwell-Fyfe.[6] In 1948 this produced an Interim Report (the Maxwell-Fyfe Report) which recommended the constituency be responsible for election expenses; candidates were forbidden to contribute more than £25 (MPs £50) a year to their party; finance was not to be factor in selection; and unless a very good case could be made constituencies were not to make demands on central funds. These reforms were approved by the 1948 and 1949 Conferences. Did the Maxwell-Fyfe Report mark a sea-change in internal party politics as well as a potent symbol of the new Conservatism?

The report had little effect on candidate selection until 1955 and there is no evidence of any shift in the party's social structure that can be traced directly to the report. It did have a major effect on the constituencies in that they strengthened their autonomy vis-à-vis Central Office and many became more efficient and active. However, as time went on associations selected candidates who reflected the view of the selection committees not the wider interests of the party. This had the effect of narrowing the ideological base of the parliamentary party.[7]

Many of the measures introduced by the government derived from the Coalition and Churchill was determined to maintain a bi-partisan approach on foreign policy. Outright resistance would have opened the Conservatives to the charge of lack of faith when in the Coalition and of now being reactionary. On many occasions the Conservative front bench found themselves criticising the details of bills whose principles were disliked by broad swathes of Conservative opinion. This was made all the more complex by the Consultative Committee's (shadow cabinet) view that if a measure had been contained in Labour's 1945 manifesto parliamentary resistance should cease after second reading. This meant that the Conservatives could not use their majority in the House of Lords to its maximum effect under the Parliament Act (1911). When the Conservatives did use their majority to delay steel nationalisation, the government retaliated by reducing the House of Lords, delaying power to one year. This implicit complicity with Labour caused disquiet amongst the Conservatives who wanted aggressive opposition.

After his defeat Churchill told Lord Camrose (proprietor of the *Daily Telegraph*) of his intention to retire but that he would continue as leader for the time being.[8] Churchill found the loss of office very hard to bear, fearing Labour would be in government for twenty years and his confidence was not helped by his failure to better Attlee in the House of Commons. The very strength of his support in the party was interpreted by one observer as a measure of the depth of the Conservative predicament: 'after all, without him what's left?'[9]

Butler was instrumental in the revival of the Conservative Research Department (CRD), the Advisory Committee on Publicity and Political Education (ACPPE) for propaganda and publicity, and the Conservative Political Centre (CPC) whose responsibility for internal party political education masked a more serious purpose. The CPC's *The Two-Way Movement of Ideas* established study groups to consider policy briefs provided by CPC and feed their conclusions back into the policy process. This involved the party grassroots and encouraged them to elicit *non*-party opinion, keeping the centre aware of mass opinion and reactions to proposed policies. ACPPE, CRD, and CPC operated with a high degree of autonomy from both Central Office and the party leader, acting as a counterweight to Churchill's resistance to detail. Their influence was helped by the fact that Butler went out of his way to attract recruits not of the usual party apparatchik type. As Butler told the ACPPE at its preliminary meeting, their task was to transmit Conservative ideas in a climate dominated by 'Leftist intellectualism'.[10]

From the early months of opposition there were suggestions 'That it is very greatly to be desired that Conservative principles should be re-stated as

a basis for future policy'.[11] Churchill was content with making vague dec-
larations, as in Edinburgh in May 1946 when he defined Conservatism as
'Liberty with security; stability combined with progress; the maintenance of
religion, the Crown, the Parliamentary Government'. Churchill believed
these meaningless phrases were adequate given the length of time before the
next election but they failed to ease the disquiet in the party, leading
Churchill to write in exasperation that 'it would be a great help if those who
are pressing for a more detailed programme would kindly state precisely
what they have in mind in the light of the statement I made in Edinburgh'.[12]

Butler was conscious of the party's negative power. The PWPCC had been
hamstrung as a sub-committee of the National Union and the resulting need
was to conciliate various factions in the party. ACPPE was part of the CRD,
its members selected by Butler and then approved by the Executive. His
speech to the Central Council in March 1946, ostensibly concerned with
political education ranged much wider, being Butler's first public pro-
nouncement on the 'New Conservatism'. The electorate, he contended,
wanted neither Socialism nor *laisser-faire* but an alternative which recognised the state's positive role in the life of the individual and the community. Such statements revived the fears of 'pink socialism' which had so
damaged the PWPCC and Butler always had to take this into account even
in the more favourable post-war atmosphere.[13] The 1946 Conference
pressed the leadership to respond: but none of the eight resolutions seeking
for a statement of policy had been called for debate. This criticism led the
Chairman to give 'an assurance that the Executive would consider the point
about resolutions [and] he would arrange for one of the motions on policy
to be discussed before the end of Conference'.[14]

The ACPPE's report to Conference stressed the requirement for 'an analysis of the industrial situation as a basis for the revision of our industrial
policy in the light of modern conditions'. More sensitive were the principles
on which this would be based. These should 'retain the inspiration which
comes from personal responsibility and we should rob public planning of
that cramping grip which results in paralysis of effort. We are the only Party
which can conscientiously hope to achieve success along these lines since
we are sincere in our faith in free enterprise'. The battleground for the
defence of personal responsibility and free enterprise was nationalisation but
Butler made no commitment to wholesale denationalisation. Policy must be
'largely concerned with defining the relationship between Government,
industry and the individual. All these partners have their part to play in
raising the well-being of the nation. We must lay down clearly the duties
appropriate to each and the boundaries of their respective spheres'. So far,
so platitudinous, but given the earthquake of 1945 what were to be the
objectives of Conservative policy? Butler identified three: increase the standard of living by greater efficiency; maintain a high and stable level of

employment; and increase the workers' status.[15] One delegate condemned the ACPPE's report as 'weak, vacillating and compromising', particularly with reference to nationalisation. Anxious to avoid a controversy Butler condemned nationalisation and the reference back was withdrawn.

'The objective of Socialism', Eden told Conference, 'is state ownership of all the means of production, distribution and exchange. Our objective is a nation-wide property-owning democracy ... Whereas the Socialist purpose is the concentration of ownership in the hands of the state, ours is the distribution of ownership over the widest practicable number of individuals'. The property-owning democracy was the golden thread which could unite all forms of Conservatism and distinguish Conservatism clearly from Socialism and the collectivist temper of the times. Central to realisation of the property-owning democracy, Eden believed, was greater quality of status. 'The worker in industry', Eden declared, 'should have the status of an individual and not a mere cog in a soulless machine. To substitute the state for the private employer as boss won't give the worker status. He will never have it under Socialism. Nor will he achieve it ... under a system of free enterprise unless we are prepared to foster and encourage schemes for the distribution of capital ownership over a wide area and for giving men and women a closer interest and share in the purpose and operation of the industry that employs them'.[16] The realisation of Eden's vision required a Conservative government promoting and perhaps imposing co-partnership, profit-sharing and worker share-ownership schemes. Similar suggestions in the past had foundered on the indifference of employers who, with a few exceptions, had shown little interest and the scepticism of the party grass-roots who felt it was not a Conservative government's job to interfere with the structure of economic power and the distribution of profits and dividends.

Churchill delivered a sustained rhetorical assault on the Labour government but he too eulogised the property-owning democracy. Its purpose was to promote class compromise rather than class conflict and Churchill, an ex-Liberal Home Secretary and Coalition Prime Minister, claimed the welfare state for the Conservatives who had nothing to fear from the state defending society's weakest. Lambasting Labour 'in the most lurid colours' did not answer the question: what does Conservatism stand for? The scale of Labour's victory meant 'there can be no intransigent or reactionary reply' and, *The Times* thought, Churchill was wrong when he asserted the next election would be between those who sang The Red Flag or Land of Hope and Glory as the war and the election had shifted the political centre of gravity. Irrespective of which party was in government it had 'to strike the most fruitful balance, according to its faith, between the free activities of the individual ... and the power, indeed the duty, of the community to participate directly in the organisation of national wealth and welfare'. This was

Eden's message (endorsed by Churchill) but whilst acknowledging the need for a policy statement Churchill refused to go beyond generalities even though 'the (Leader's) first task is now the mapping of the road back to power'.[17]

The New Conservatism

The Industrial Charter is 'generally regarded as the most important post-war policy document produced by the Conservatives'.[18] The PWPCC experience suggested a single document would have a greater impact than several statements and CRD aimed to produce a document by the spring of 1947 covering employer–employee relations and the relationship between the state, industry, and the individual.[19] CRD was conscious Churchill had only reluctantly agreed to a statement and in November he sanctioned the appointment of the Industry Policy Committee (IPC).[20] The difficulty facing the Conservative front bench was the absence of a strategic overview of Conservatism's relationship to post-war politics and a positive alternative to anti-Socialism. Churchill's political instincts were liberal and non-interventionist and he opposed detailed policy-making but felt the IPC would divert his critics and that it would have little effect.[21]

The IPC was chaired by Butler. It had four front bench members (Oliver Stanley, Oliver Lyttleton, David Maxwell-Fyfe, and Harold Macmillan), four backbenchers (Derick Heathcoat-Amory, David Eccles, Sir Peter Bennet, and Colonel James Hutchinson), and CRD provided research and secretarial support (David Clarke, Reginald Maudling, and Michael Fraser). Technically, Stanley was senior to Butler and so Butler's appointment as chairman was seen as recognition that he was now the party's 'philosopher-in-chief'.[22] In fact Butler's appointment was logical given his centrality to the party's research effort. The ACPPE timetable was tight but was adhered to and *The Industrial Charter* was published in May 1947. This suggests there existed a prior general agreement on its content although IPC consulted industrialists, businessmen, trade unionists and party activists.

The *Charter* sought to free industry from unnecessary controls and institute a spirit of free enterprise to reconcile the needs of industry, the individual and the community. *The Industrial Charter* was derived in part from the policies of the Coalition but with an emphasis on voluntary co-operation in planning economic recovery. Cuts in public spending would finance tax cuts to boost private investment and individual initiative. Nationalisation was opposed in principle but it accepted the nationalisation of the Bank of England, coal, and railways but road haulage and steel nationalisation would be reversed. It envisaged no interference in established collective bargaining or industrial relations but recognised that this had implications for inflation and economic management. The new government role as regulator and guarantor of full employment meant it could not contemplate restrictive practices but it remained vague as to what could be done to promote productivity. *The Industrial Charter* recommended a process of education and increased worker security which would cushion the slow abandonment of restrictive practices. The *Charter* was critical of trade union militancy, threatening legislation on the closed shop and the political levy. Part III of the document, *The Worker's Charter*, sought to foster a united purpose and co-operation in industry which would eventually lead to cultural change in industry.[23] The publication of *The Industrial Charter* attracted considerable attention but was criticised as 'milk and water socialism' by the *Daily Express* and *Daily Herald*. This led the IPC to conclude they had the balance about right. Hogg's judgement was that irrespective of the criticism the *Charter* was valuable 'in that the Party could not be accused of being reactionary'.[24]

Churchill was potentially a major obstacle. Macmillan was 'surprised at the attention [Churchill] gave' to the *Charter*, claiming he indicated general approval.[25] This, however, is not the recollection of others and there is evidence that Churchill never read *The Industrial Charter*. When it was then submitted to Churchill 'Silence ensued ...', Butler wrote, 'his ultimate imprimatur was not so much obtained as divined. At a dinner party for his senior colleagues he placed me on his right hand, plied me with cognac and said several agreeable and no disagreeable things about my work'. On this slender evidence of approval Butler published the *Charter* with its status undefined.[26] Maudling, a CRD researcher and IPC secretary, doubled as a speech-writer for Churchill and Eden and provides further evidence of Churchill's lack of involvement in *The Industrial Charter*. On the eve of his Conference speech Churchill summoned Maudling:

> 'Give me five lines, Maudling', he said, 'explaining what the Industrial Charter
>   says'. This I did. He read it with care and then said. 'But I do not agree with
>   a word of this'.
> 'Well, sir', I said, 'this is what the Conference has adopted'.
> 'Oh well', he said, 'leave it in'.

Churchill read out the offending lines 'with calculated coolness'.[27]

The IPC's consultations were intended to placate opinion and neutralise any claim that the *Charter* had been foisted on the party. Centre-right IPC members (Maxwell-Fyfe, Stanley, and Heathcoat-Amory) and figures trusted in the party (Sir Peter Bennett and Colonel Hutchinson) were vital as they 'gave invaluable support when later we were *pushing the Charter through the party conference* and were being accused of having a rather "pink" document'.[28] Maudling notes that 'there was still a good deal of antipathy to it [the *Charter*] among the traditionalists' and Butler acknowledges the suspicion in the party from Churchill downwards meant the *Charter* 'was indeed "broad" rather than detailed, vague where it might have been specific and restrained instead of following the simple, connected line that I wanted'.[29] Potentially a powerful anti-*Charter* coalition existed and the focal point of their distrust was *The Industrial Charter*'s acceptance of the inevitability of a much enlarged state. This opposition failed to coalesce and its influence was reduced by the shock of defeat and the clamour for a policy statement. Those who had to be won over, or at least to be persuaded to acquiesce in *The Industrial Charter* and what it represented were the centre-right, the natural political home of the vast majority of MPs and the party members.[30]

Defeat did not clear out the Conservative dead-wood. In fact, 'defeat *fell hardest* on those Conservative MPs whose education, occupation, and social rank were more typical of the social composition of British society as a whole'.[31] Macleod's biographer, a key figure in the CRD, notes the unfavourable material with which the reformers had to work, 'the Conservative membership in the new House of Commons consisted largely, though not of course exclusively, of brigadiers and colonels and landowners and their sons. They represented the selection committees which had chosen them, but they were unlikely to alter the policies or the appearance of the Conservative Party'.[32] The much vaunted Two Way Movement of Ideas had no impact on *The Industrial Charter*. In its first phase only two of the five topics under consideration had any relevance to the *Charter* and the consultation did not end until after the *Charter* had been written, so the information it produced could not have affected the IPC's deliberations.[33]

The IPC was determined that Conference should not accept the *Charter* as a basis for discussion by sponsoring an amendment in September that it be accepted as a statement of policy. This was moved by Maudling (in his capacity as prospective parliamentary candidate for Barnet), the conference Chairman was Harold Macmillan, and Butler responded to the debate. The mover of the original resolution (welcoming the *Charter* as 'a basis for discussion') was prevailed upon to accept Maudling's amendment and the substantive resolution was passed with only three dissentients. This has been described as 'one of the more naked pieces of Conservative Conference stage-management'. Accepting the decision Churchill pressed a glass of Pol Roget champagne on Butler with the comment, 'Well, old cock, you have definitely won through'.[34] However, Churchill seems to have remained unconvinced. He remained impatient with demands for detailed policy, arguing 'The job of the leader of the Opposition ... is to attack the Government – that and no more'.[35]

The myth is that the *Charter* transformed Conservative doctrine but the recollections of participants give a different picture. Butler accepted the *Charter* was a compromise and at least one IPC member (Heathcoat-Amory) made no secret of his belief that the exercise had little substance. Furthermore by the time it was published *The Industrial Charter* was addressing problems which seemed to be no longer so pressing given the difficulties facing the Labour government. Butler concedes *The Industrial Charter* had little discernible effect on legislation.[36] This contrasts with Macmillan's assessment of it as a 'land mark in the history of the party' even though he admitted that of its recommendations 'many proved impossible to put into legislative form'.[37] Lord Kilmuir argues the *Charters* 'were not only important in clearing our minds and letting the thinking public know ... our approach', they were also important as a means of energising the party in the battle against Socialism.[38] Furthermore, the *Charter* had a limited impact. The *Charter* had 'failed to provide that clear concrete alternative policy to Socialism' and a Mass Observation report on its impact found widespread ignorance not just of the Charter's content but its existence.[39] In July 1948 Butler expressed disquiet at the party's failure to follow up the *Charter's* launch. Statements of general principle needed more specific proposals if public opinion was to be persuaded but 'the main difficulty was the need for an authoritative interpretation of policy'. This could only come from Churchill who remained reluctant so to do.[40]

There were complaints from MPs about the failure to exploit *The Industrial Charter* especially in industrial areas and that many MPs failed to appreciate its importance.[41] The *Charter's* impact was blunted further by the refusal of companies implementing its provisions to have this publicised. CRD estimated that 100 leading companies were implementing aspects of the *Charter* and were willing to supply details on condition they were not publicised.[42] Aims of Industry gathered information on the *Charter's* implementation but Central Office could not publish this data 'owing to the danger of it being considered as a boost for certain individual firms ... and in general as an advertisement for "big business"'. Any dissemination would therefore have to be covert and confined to circulation within the party which defeated the *Charter's* object.[43]

As early as 1949 the *Charter's* central weakness was identified by Colonel Hutchinson, 'we have got to let industry know that we are serious about the Industrial *Charter's* recommendations. I have heard a number of MPs say that industry won't easily accept it and we won't have the strength to impose it'.[44] This proved to be the case and in government Conservatives were vulnerable to the charge that the *Charter* had been abandoned. The party's trade union organisation, for example, argued it was being implemented without the need for legislation by individual employers and that should it prove necessary legislation would be forthcoming after consultation with employers and unions.[45] This was disingenuous. Legislation to implement the *Charter* would have been a serious breach of the principle of voluntarism – the government did not interfere directly with the internal operation of industry or unions – and invited conflict with both employers and unions. CRD attempted to persuade ministers to issue a statement on implementation before the 1954 party Conference as part of the preparations for the election but none was forthcoming.[46]

Macmillan believes *The Industrial Charter* did have a positive long-term influence in that 'The principles laid down in this document guided our policies in the future Conservative Government'. In support of this he cites the control of monopolies ('at least to some degree'), measures to increase the status of employees (Contracts of Employment Act 1963 and the Redundancy Payments Act 1963), and the abolition of resale price maintenance as direct results of *The Industrial Charter*. Even if this is accepted at face value it is a meagre show for so important a statement. Macmillan implies that legislation was not the *Charter*'s prime purpose and its importance 'lies not so much in the detailed proposals as in their general tone and temper'.[47] This calls into question the radicalism of the entire rethink sponsored by Butler who described his approach as being 'to wield a pruning knife rather than an axe'. Enoch Powell's biographer describes the work as 'more cosmetic than substantial' and that Powell (surely someone suited to radical, even iconoclastic, thinking) was not engaged in original work but supporting party leaders striving to come to terms with Attlee's reforms.[48]

The Industrial Charter's importance lies not in what it said, nor in its impact on Conservative governments but in that what it said was said by the Conservative Party. It enabled the Conservative Party to sever itself from 1945 and the legacy of the 1930s and it represents the end, not the beginning, of an era in Conservative politics.[49] It marks the high point of the influence of those who, like Macmillan, wished to persuade the party to embrace the state: conventional Disraelian One Nation Conservatives (for example, Eden) who wished the party to bind itself to the working class and pragmatists (for example, Butler) who interpreted 1945 as a warning that the party must accommodate itself to a new political reality. *The Industrial Charter*'s publication date is itself significant; May 1947 was half-way through Labour's 'annus terribilis'.[50] The winter of 1947 sees a marked recovery in the political confidence of the Conservative Party and a resurgence of hostility to the Conservatism in vogue after defeat in 1945 and expressed in *The Industrial Charter*. The *Charter* did not conclude the debate on party strategy but signalled the beginning of a new phase which culminated with the publication of *The Right for Britain* in July 1949.[51]

The Conservative response to Labour's dominance

The ejection from office of a party accustomed to seeing itself as the natural party of government is bound to be traumatic. The initial Conservative response to blame the electorate soon gave way to an acceptance that the electorate wanted a change and that the passage of time would demonstrate the futility of Socialism.[52] Despite his gloom Churchill confessed that defeat might prove to be a blessing for the country and party as 'there is no doubt that a Conservative Government would have been very roughly treated by the Left-Wing elements and strikes and Labour troubles would have made our path one of extreme difficulty'.[53] If Labour could manage the strains of post-war readjustment the Conservatives could avoid unpopular decisions and if Labour failed the Conservatives would benefit from the reaction against Labour. Austerity, the Cold War, and the government's errors and mistakes made Labour's ejection from office at the next election inevitable. After the Bexley by-election in July 1946 *The Times* concluded 'it is difficult to resist the impression that the Government have, at least for the moment, disappointed a large section of those who helped to bring them to power'.[54] The Conservative Party's attacks on Labour's domestic policies focused on the unpopularity of Socialism, controls, and nationalisation. These issues demarcated the parties providing clear political choice for public and electoral opinion. Public opinion accepted controls as a fact of life; although disliked they were familiar as the population had been subject to them since 1939. Familiarity did not breed contempt: 'the apparatus of war-time control, though willingly accepted as equitable and desirable so long as scarcity continues, remains in the public eye a necessary evil'.[55] If the Conservatives did not reap their expected political reward, the charge that Labour was building a Socialist society seemed more promising. An average of 46% agreed the government was too Socialist, 31% believed they had got the balance about right. Opinion was initially favourably disposed to the general idea of nationalisation but by 1950 there was substantial hostility to further nationalisation, and iron and steel nationalisation was opposed by a ratio of 2:1, although one in five of those asked had no opinion. In October 1948 7% thought nationalisation was the best thing done by the government since 1945, 20% thought it the worst.

There was, however, a major defect in the Conservative pendulum theory of politics: the pendulum refused to swing. The failure of popular revulsion at the Labour government to appear is one of the most remarkable features of this period. Despite organisational and doctrinal reform and a 'feeling of constriction as well as restriction ... the feeling that the hand of the Socialist State pressed on the community like thunder clouds on a heavy and oppressive day', the electorate remained curiously unmoved.[56] Evelyn Waugh's description of post-war Britain as a country under foreign occupation, and the picture of a Britain dominated by the spiv and a Whitehall bureaucracy determined to force the population to subsist on a diet of snoek and regulation portrayed in the best-selling novels of Angela Thirkell reflects the power of the class cleavage at this time.[57] The middle and upper classes and the professions were hostile to Labour but they had never been its strongest supporters and the government retained its working-class base. It was, remembered Maxwell-Fyfe,

an uphill struggle, for disillusionment with the Labour Party, although growing had not reached the point when we could foresee a major breakthrough,
which, in fact, was not achieved until 1952 or 1953. This fact needs to be
emphasised again and again. *It took us not five or six years to destroy the Labour
grip over half the electorate, but nearly 10 years.*[58]

The Conservative return to office was neither speedily or easily achieved.

Labour's by-election record has been described rightly as remarkable.[59]
Labour lost no seats between October 1945 and October 1951, except for
Glasgow Camlachie in January 1948 where splits between Labour, the Independent Labour Party (ILP), and the Communist Party allowed the Conservatives to take the seat on a minority vote. At a time when it is axiomatic
that governments lose by-elections Labour's ability to retain seats won in
the high tide of 1945 is astonishing. Opinion fell into two camps: 'there had
been no By-elections in Constituencies where we had the slightest chance
of reversing the Labour majority'; alternatively, 'We had discontinued political propaganda while Labour continued with it during the war'.[60] The Conservative failure to win Gravesend despite a 6.8% swing and the adverse
publicity caused by the expulsion of the sitting MP and by Dalton's resignation as Chancellor of the Exchequer came as a shock. Not surprisingly,
'the Conservatives are in a heart-searching mood'.[61] Woolton claimed the
result revealed 'a progressive improvement which would give us a working
majority at the next General Election', an analysis which was disputed by
some Executive members. Gravesend was blamed on the party's poor image,
a widespread perception that high money wages and full employment were
the product of a Labour government, and that welfare provision 'would be
reduced by the Conservatives'. The Conservatives' image and 'the difficulties in counteracting the lack of faith in the Conservative Party ... were due
to misrepresentation of the pre-war years'. Despite the increase in the standard of living between 1918 and 1939 Hugh Molson (an ex-Tory Reform
Group member) lamented 'they would always be remembered for their large
number of unemployed' for which the Conservatives were blamed.[62] These
factors had also been identified in the Liverpool Edge Hill by-election where
it was noted 'there has been little alteration in the general temper of the
electorate since 1945'.[63]

'Conservatism cannot now wait', *The Times* argued, 'as many an Opposition has done in the past, for the Government to defeat themselves by their
own errors and shortcomings. Conservatism can and must present itself as
a policy in its own right'.[64] This indictment was delivered seven months after
The Industrial Charter's publication and was particularly relevant in the
Hammersmith South by-election of February 1949. Hammersmith had been
Conservative except for 1929–31 and Labour's 1945 majority was only
3,458; the Conservatives confidently expected to win. They devoted considerable resources to the campaign, including a tour by Churchill. Despite this

Labour retained the seat with a reduced majority of 1,613. The Conservatives were again dismayed as Hammersmith was precisely the sort of constituency the Conservatives had to win if they were to form a government. Hammersmith focused internal discontent over the party's appeal and image as 'In the by-election there was no apathy ... The Conservatives raised their proportion of the vote but lost the fight. The general signs are still that the electors are not sufficiently inspired by the Opposition to seek a change over in Westminster'.[65] Labour was perceived as the party of nationalisation and austerity, the Conservatives as the party of poverty and mass unemployment. Public opinion judged life under Labour to be bad but that it would be a whole lot worse under the Conservatives.

The Right Road for Britain

Hammersmith 'produced the most serious crisis of confidence in Churchill's leadership since 1945'. The 1922's post-mortem identified the lack of a positive programme and reliance on 'negative snarling' as the explanations for the Conservative failure. Churchill disputed this, arguing Hammersmith was a hiccough on the road to recovery but conceded the need for a new policy statement.[66] Churchill tended to take the party for granted (in December 1945 he described the new intake as 'no more than a set of pink pansies') and the party acquiesced, but by 1949 backbenchers were coming close to charging Churchill and Eden with dereliction of duty. In March Churchill's wife warned him that backbenchers believed he was too often out of the country, failing to give a clear lead. He was advised to cement his links with the backbench; the advice was taken.[67]

Constituency resolutions seeking greater aggression and a declaration of principles are a feature of Executive agendas at this time. The Eton and Slough Conservatives criticised the 'lack of an offensive policy', charging that the leadership was out of touch: 'the gloves must be taken off, the Socialists and Communists will stop at nothing ... they must be politically attacked on all occasion' (*sic*) with 'bold, clear, simple programs'. The party seemed reliant on the glories of the past which evoked no response among young voters. The *Charters* were dismissed 'as the basis for discussion but have no real value either as a political programme or as an appeal to the general public'. The property-owning democracy appeal had not been promoted, a failure symptomatic of Conservatism's inability to challenge Labour's 'personal appeal to human feelings' and 'we are being out-manoeuvred and playing right into the hands of the Socialists'. The working-class voter remained convinced 'that Labour represents the masses whilst the Tories represent the privileged'. This impression must be corrected by 'our leaders to convince the people that Conservatism is the only way to safeguard the best interests of each and every class'.[68]

Butler warned the ACPPE 'of the growing opposition to documents on the Charter lines and the general concern about the necessity for producing material as a basis for an election programme'.[69] In the month before the Hammersmith by-election the Tactical Staff Committee agreed 'that they were finding increasing difficulty in their work by reason of the lack of any sufficiently defined Conservative Party policy'.[70] Disenchantment with 'Charter-itis' was picked up by the Two Way Movement of Ideas and was reflected in the 1922 and the National Union. The vacuum could only be filled by Churchill making the sort of powerful endorsement which had been so noticeably lacking with *The Industrial Charter* but this was a response to defeat and had been published when the Labour government was in serious trouble and opinion appeared to be shifting decisively. This encouraged anti-collectivism which party strategists feared might go too far. David Gammans wrote 'the Conservative Party was again on the defensive throughout the country. He ... viewed the future with grave apprehension since, if things got better, the Socialist Party in 1950 would be able to point to the fact that it had pulled the country through the crisis and would say the Conservative Party had done nothing constructive, but had only criticised the government's efforts'.[71] Although made in the aftermath of the crisis of 1946–7 and the publication of *The Industrial Charter* this assessment was still opposite in 1949. Too great a lurch to the right might push a nervous electorate into Labour's hands but, equally, the party had to be satisfied. *The Right Road for Britain*'s gestation was long and complex. Butler took great care to liaise with the 1922, Churchill was much more closely involved as was Lord Woolton, but drafting was controlled by those anxious about too sharp rightwards moves.[72]

The Right Road for Britain was published on 23 July 1949 and endorsed by Churchill before an audience of 40,000 at Wolverhampton Wanderers football ground. Churchill attacked Labour for degrading the country from the heights of victory by nationalisation, high spending, and ruinous taxation, claiming the country was on the verge of economic and political bankruptcy. He did not commit the party to wholesale denationalisation or deep cuts in social spending, nor an attack on the unions. Churchill distinguished Conservatism from Socialism which was portrayed as differing only in degree from Communism:

> The first essential step is to regain our economic independence by earning our own livelihood ... We mean to set the people free, so far as possible, from wrong-headed planning and from official interference with our daily life.
>
> We shall return to a system which provides incentives for effort, enterprise, self-denial, initiative and good housekeeping ... But we also must strive to maintain the social services ... which assure the whole mass of the people, whether successful or not, a minimum standard of life and labour below which no one is let fall.[73]

This was an amplification of earlier statements but it expressed subtle but important differences. Anti-monopoly measures, wage-fixing, and priorities for basic industries (for example) were downgraded and replaced by reliance on free enterprise to deliver growth, nationalised industries (except for iron and steel) were to remain but would be reformed and decentralised. *The Right Road for Britain* emphasised property ownership as the basis of individual freedom and responsibility.[74]

The Right Road for Britain was not an paean to free markets; it accepted the welfare state, full employment and some controls, drawing the line on nationalisation and the role of the state.[75] The tone of *The Right Road for Britain* was more neo-Liberal than *The Industrial Charter*: 'The hot white light of free enterprise was present in *The Industrial Charter*, but it was blurred by a reddish filter ... In *The Right Road* the white light burned as before but, to extend the analogy, the reddish filter was replaced with one of a fainter hue'.[76] This fainter hue was more to the taste of the party.

Despite Churchill's 'authoritative exposition' at Wolverhampton it still required Conference's approval. The careful preparation, Churchill's launch and its tone ensured there was no need for the management of Conference and *The Right Road for Britain* was approved with only eight dissentients.[77] Its main purpose was to unite the party and provide the basis for the Conservative election appeal. Butler thought it 'the most comprehensive of the *Charters*, whose main proposals it incorporated and the first to be proof-corrected by the Churchill pen and dignified by a Churchillian foreword'.[78] Conservative politics were now dominated by preparations for the forthcoming election and *The Right Road for Britain* ended the debate over the nature of Conservatism, providing a common platform for all elements in the party.[79]

The Right Road for Britain's tone reflected the party's rightwards move after 1947 but the electoral attractiveness of this shift was unclear. Central Office's Public Opinion Research Department (PORD) found the swing to the right had begun in late 1946 and despite fluctuations the overall trend remained favourable. Using Gallup data PORD estimated there had been an 8% swing to the Conservatives by June 1949, by-elections pointed to a 7% swing and the 1949 municipal elections a swing of 8% on 1945. PORD predicted a nationwide swing of 5% in a general election which would give the Conservatives a majority of votes.[80] This overestimated the swing by a factor of two: in 1950 the swing was 2.9% which gave the Conservatives the largest number of votes but not seats.

The 1950 and 1951 general elections are amongst the most important in British political history because of the ambiguity of the results and Labour's continuing strength. In 1950 and 1951 Labour polled more votes than in 1945 and in 1951 polled 443,288 more votes than the Conservatives but won fewer seats. The reason for the Conservative victory in 1951 lay in the behaviour of the Liberal vote which collapsed from 9% to 2.6%

in 1951. Sufficient Liberals voted Conservative to cost Labour 20 seats which, with other Conservative gains as seats lost in 1945 returned to their historical allegiance, gave the Conservatives their majority.[81] This confirmed what many feared: the Liberal vote could keep Labour in office. This concern with the Liberal vote was a key element in Conservative calculations down to 1955, renewing Churchill's infatuation with anti-Socialist pacts and fusion with the Liberals.[82] It was, the Conservatives contended, in the interests of both parties and the country to co-operate in defeating Socialism. This led to the negotiation of several informal and two formal pacts (in Bolton and Huddersfield) in which the Conservative withdrew in favour of a sympathetic Liberal.[83]

Woolton's support for 'a united front against Socialism which he had been striving to bring about since coming to Central Office', aroused the party's traditional dislike of co-operation. When, for example, the Conservative candidate in Montgomery stood down to allow Clement Davies a clear fight against Labour, William van Straubanzee sought assurances that no Central Office pressure had been brought to bear and that there was no Liberal–Conservative pact. Woolton responded that the Montgomery CUA had come to its own decision but that 'he did give a little private advice' on the value to the party of such a decision. Churchill's predilection for cross-party politics also caused alarm. In January 1951 Henry Brooke MP raised the persistent rumours of coalition which were circulating in the party, asking 'whether some informal guidance could be given to the Leader of the Party'. Woolton conveyed the Executive's concern to Churchill. Despite winning only 2.5% of the vote and six seats Churchill remained anxious to win Liberal support to bolster his majority, offering the Education ministry to Clement Davies who wanted to accept but was over-ruled by his party.[84]

The Conservatives believed nationalisation would win them votes but felt themselves vulnerable on the cost of living, food subsidies and full employment. On food subsidies, for example, it was suggested that 'until the case for reduction ... can be proved, subsidies would not be touched by a Conservative government'. In the key Birmingham constituencies the Conservative chances in 1950 were estimated to be 50/50 but one MP predicted an overall majority of forty. Churchill, who took an active role in preparing the manifesto, *This Is The Road*, was anxious that whilst the party should attack the Socialist threat to liberty it should not stage an overtly ideological assault.[85] Butler described the manifesto as a 'policy of enterprise without selfishness' but against expectations the Conservatives lost. Labour's victory was ascribed to full employment and unscrupulous tactics, such as the *Daily Mirror*'s 'Whose Finger On The Trigger' lead, the day before polling, which implied a Churchill government was more likely to embroil the country in World War III. Churchill sued and won damages. Many new MPs concluded the election had been fought on the memory of mass unemployment and fear about what a Conservative government would do to full employment and the welfare state.[86]

The Conservative failure and Labour's narrow victory produced a significant change in tactics. Kilmuir paints a vivid picture of the Conservative mood in this 'heated and hectic interlude':

> Relations between the parties became exceedingly bitter, and the spectacle of aged Labour Members muffled up in rugs being pushed through the division lobbies in bathchairs was not a pleasant one ... Our hatred of the Government was deep and sincere, we had many old scores to pay off, and the price which the Labour Party had to pay for their arrogance and abuse after 1945 was a heavy one.

Macmillan was so depressed by the 1950 result and concerned about the direction of politics he refused to invite Labour politicians to his daughter Catherine's wedding.[87] Hostilities were suspended on the outbreak of the Korean War in June but were renewed when the government introduced its iron and steel nationalisation bill in December. In early 1951 a controversial disruption campaign began. In the first week of February the Opposition tabled three censure motions, in March the Conservatives entered an unholy alliance with Labour left-wingers to vote against the Reserve Forces Bill, and on 8 March the Opposition tabled seven Prayers forcing an all night sitting, a tactic repeated three times in the next week. Disruption continued after the Easter recess and the government's troubles were worsened by the resignation of Aneurin Bevin and Harold Wilson over prescription charges (April) and then the Burgess and Maclean defection to Moscow (June). Despite this Labour survived, leading Churchill to comment to Oliver Lyttelton that 'It looks as though these bastards can stay in as long as they like'. At the 1922 in June Churchill agreed 'our first object was to turn out the Government' but he was ambivalent towards the disruption campaign because whilst this guerrilla war was popular with the party it was damaging the Conservative image. The disruption tactics were seen as poor sportsmanship and even unpatriotic given the fighting in Korea. As an election could not be long postponed this was a significant consideration.[88]

In public the Conservatives trumpeted their 1951 victory but in private were more circumspect. Before the election Macmillan wrote 'I am impressed by the class solidarity of the Labour vote. They grouse and tell the Gallup Poll man that they will never vote Socialist again – but when the election comes, they vote the party ticket'. Woolton 'hated to think that the country was almost divided into two classes'. 'This was not good. It was not the Britain that we wanted. Now the Conservatives were in office they must strive to create in all people a sense of belonging to one nation'.[89] During the election Churchill, worried by the declining pull of his name, feared the Conservatives were seen as the party of the rich. Conservative trade unionists found the working-class and trade union electorate were deeply influenced by 'warmongering, unemployment and the economy cuts which would be suffered if the Conservatives had a large majority'.[90] Despite six years hard Labour the closeness of the result and the near equal division of votes impressed and worried many Conservatives:

> At first sight, therefore, one can only form the most gloomy forebodings about the future. What will happen, after three or four years of Tory Government, with the inevitable mistakes and failures? Moreover, what will happen with so many almost insoluble problems crowding on us, at home and abroad? Will there be a terrible reaction at the next election, and another 200 majority for Labour, with Bevan this time (not Attlee) at the head?[91]

Churchill, whose initial optimism was buoyed by the wholly unreliable predictions of Lord Beaverbrook, became gloomy as his early lead slipped away.

The close balance of electoral support complicated Cabinet making. Churchill had intended to appoint Oliver Lyttleton as Chancellor of the Exchequer but opted instead for Butler who would be better able to handle the House of Commons and whose moderate image would reassure the country. Lyttleton was seen as too close to the City and too orthodox in his economics. David Maxwell-Fyfe's appointment to the Ministry of Labour was reconsidered after he made a number of speeches in the election hinting at trade union reform; he was replaced by the 'non-party' figure of Sir Walter Monckton whose instructions not to antagonise the unions came directly from Churchill.[92] This sensitivity to the implications of the 1951 election result was to have a significant impact on party strategy and government policy in the 1950s, predisposing them to caution. Nonetheless, some Conservatives discerned in their unfavourable inheritance a historic opportunity. Labour had fought on the electorate's fear of a Conservative government, however, 'If, before the next election, none of these fears have proved reasonable, we may be able to force the Opposition to fight on Socialism. Then we can win'.[93]

This prognostication was based on the Conservative identification of a large floating vote of an aspirant, affluent, upwardly mobile, politically pragmatic ex-Labour partisans with a weak attraction to Conservatism. This floating vote was estimated to number five million, a high proportion of whom were women. They were concentrated at the higher end of the working class in terms of income and were married; about 30% were home owners with a slightly higher than national average level of car ownership. They had steady jobs, anticipated no difficulty in keeping them, and about one-third were trade unionists. Some 23% stated the Liberals were closest to their way of thinking but only 2.5% had voted Liberal in 1945. PORD estimated 3.5–4 million votes had to some degree defected from Labour since 1945 but only one-third had come over to the Conservatives. These voters could deny or give victory to the Conservatives but they would not be attracted by 'an unrelieved recital of failures of the Labour Party'; they were, after all, former Labour voters and would not take kindly to being branded as dupes 'and if we do not provide these people with sufficient incentive the chances of a Conservative victory will hang on nothing more substantial than the number of ex-Socialists who abstain from voting altogether'.[94]

Another segment of the electorate targeted by the Conservatives were trade unionists. The industrial working class seemed immune from the general swing against Labour because of high cash wages, job security, a feeling that Labour was 'their' party, and a perception that the Conservative Party was the bosses' party. The vast majority of trade unionists were not convinced Socialists and large numbers already voted Conservative, so there was no reason why the Conservative union vote should not increase substantially.[95] This, it was readily acknowledged, was a long-term project but a start could be made by attacking the 'soft' union vote, especially the better paid worker. The proposed strategy was put to the Executive in May 1950 and was based on four points: the perception that the Conservative Party was anti-union had to be broken down, party thinking on industrial relations issues had to be clarified and communicated effectively, and the party should strive to recruit more unionists as party members. The Conservative Party would appeal to the 'large section of trade unionists who are not Socialists by conviction but who "vote the Labour ticket" because of environment, pressure of local opinion or a misguided sense of class loyalty'.[96] In short, the Conservatives discovered the affluent working class and from the late 1940s to the early 1950s these became the focal point of Conservative strategy.

Crisis to consensus, 1951–1953

The Conservative government found its room for manoeuvre limited by the narrowness of its victory and its economic legacy: a £600 million balance of payments deficit and public spending running out of control. Churchill described his inheritance as 'appalling', 'the financial position is almost irretrievable: the country has lost its way. In the worst of the war I could always see how to do it. Today's problems are elusive and intangible, and it would be a bold man who could look forward to certain success'.[97] Butler was shocked by blood-curdling warnings from Edward Bridges and William Armstrong (senior Treasury civil servants) over lunch at the Athenaeum the day before the first meeting of the new Cabinet about an economic crisis potentially worse than 1931. Macmillan compared the crisis to 1940 without the bombs but also without the sense of national unity.[98] In these circumstances it is not surprising Churchill was cautious. His policy, Churchill told his private secretary, Jock Colville, and son-in-law, Duncan Sandys, was, '"Houses and meat and not being scuppered" ... perhaps "not being broke" is going to be our major difficulty and preoccupation'.[99]

An embryonic radical Conservatism based on denationalisation and Operation ROBOT (a proposal to float the pound) which enjoyed support at both elite and grassroots level in the party posed a major threat to the government's position. These policies, with the exception of the denationalisation of steel and road haulage, stood little chance. This left the Conservative Party the only option of working within the post-war settlement.[100]

After the election the Conservatives' fragile lead in the opinion polls evaporated reaching a nadir in July 1952 but from that point the Conservatives recovered. Dissatisfaction with the government so soon after the general election deeply worried the government. Conservative losses in the 1952 London County Council elections expressed the country's hope that 'a Tory Government would mean relaxations and much more food: in fact it has meant controls as stringent as ever and severer rationing'. So depressed did Churchill become he talked of the need for a coalition.[101] Woolton stressed the apathy of Conservative voters who abstained 'because they are not very pleased with us'. Central Office concluded that the local government elections and the Gallup polls would produce a Labour victory of 1945 proportions and that any MP with a majority under 4,000 was in danger. The government was dangerously out of touch: 'It is no use ... treating the electorate as if they were all middle-class with the property qualification ... [T]he country is tired of party politics. This means they do not want us to denationalise just for the sake of it ... It is no use our harping on freedom and opportunity. It makes a very limited appeal to a nation which is security-minded.[102]

The key was the economy. Butler's March 1952 and April 1953 budgets mark not only the revival of Conservative fortunes but also established the subsequent pattern of Conservative politics and government. Butler quickly realised the Treasury and Bank of England had been too pessimistic. The Bank, for example, had predicted reserves would fall to $1.3 billion by mid-1952; in fact they stood at $1.6 billion, rising to $1.8 billion by December. Butler's first budget was necessarily restricted and was generally welcomed as Butler 'managed to make a Budget that made no net change in the tax burden an interesting and exciting one'.[103] This approach was maintained in 1953 but taxes were cut, reflecting, as Butler stated in his speech, the economy's changed circumstances. This was the first budget since 1945 which introduced no new taxes, cutting both direct and indirect taxation. The 1952 and 1953 budgets were important because they established Butler's political stature and signified the end of austerity. In June 1953 Oliver Franks, the UK's Washington ambassador, came as 'a breath of fresh air':

He thought everybody too gloomy. We must edge our way out of the crisis: the balance of payments had begun to improve, as he said it would, in May; time was needed for remedial measures to take effect. People talked a lot of the popular insensitiveness to our plight; but as four-fifths of the population had known seven years of prosperity and a standard of living higher than ever before, it was not surprising they paid little attention to cries of economic alarm. Successive Chancellors of the Exchequer spoke as if the impoverishment felt by one-fifth of the people was an experience shared by all.[104]

The affluent four-fifths (which included millions of Labour voters) were, Franks was implying, the Conservatives' natural constituency. The 1953 budget marked the beginning of economic expansion.[105]

It was in this context that the Conservatives captured Sunderland from Labour in May 1953. Labour appealed to memories of the 1930s and Butler's reduction of purchase tax on mink coats caused the Conservatives some difficulties but Labour's programme was not clearly defined. The Conservatives pointed to the steady abolition of rationing, increasing prosperity, the fruition of its housing programme, and the maintenance of full employment and the welfare state. Canvassers noted the Conservatives were doing well amongst young voters on the new housing estates and their majority of 1,175 was described as a 'striking success'. This victory signalled the 'New Conservatism' as this was the first time since 1924 that a government had won an opposition seat in a by-election. The real significance of Sunderland, *The Times* argued, was the Conservative Party's rediscovery of its historic role.[106] Despite crushing victories (1906, 1945) centre-left parties had not secured long, unbroken spells in government and each political earthquake was followed by a period of consolidation in which the Conservative Party's 'eternal and indispensable role is to criticise and mould the latest heresy ... in the name of tradition, as tradition has itself has been enriched and moulded by all the transient theories of the past'. 'In performing this function', *The Times*, argued, 'the Conservative Party always accepts the revolution which it had previously resisted and which deprived it of its power'.[107] The remaking of the Conservative Party had now created a policy and appeal to which Labour had no answer and until it had, it would be excluded from office.

Notes

1 Central Office predicted that the war would, for example, lead to the democratisation of candidate selection. See *CCO 4/1/86* Director General's Memorandum on the Possible Effect of the War on Political Life and Organisation, 14 November 1939.

2 This is the dominant interpretation in the party histories, ministerial memoirs and biographies.

3 Lord Woolton, *Memoirs* (London: Cassell 1959), chapter 20, and J. D. Hoffman, *The Conservative Party in Opposition 1945–1951* (London: MacGibbon and Kee 1964), chapter 4.

4 In April 1947 320 constituency associations submitted returns on Woolton's membership drive reporting 233,001 new members and membership returns from 438 associations indicated a total membership of 905,662, *National Union Executive Committee*, 17 April 1947.

5 J. Ramsden, 'A Party for Owners or a Party for Earners? How far did the British Conservative Party really change after 1945?', *Transactions of the Royal Historical Society* 5th series, 37 (1987), pp. 49–63.

6 Hoffman, *The Conservative Party in Opposition*, pp. 90–117.

7 Earl of Kilmuir (David Maxwell-Fyfe), *Political Adventure* (London: Weidenfeld and Nicolson, 1964) makes this point. For the 'embourgeoisement' of the Conservative Party, see D. Butler and M. Pinto-Duschinsky, 'The Conservative Elite 1919–1978. Does Unrepresentativeness Matter?', in Z. Layton-Henry (ed.), *Conservative Party Politics* (London: Macmillan, 1980), pp. 186–209.

8 M. Gilbert, *Winston S. Churchill, Volume VIII 'Never Despair' 1945–1965* (London: Heinemann, 1988), p. 125.

9 Lord Moran, *Winston Churchill. The Struggle for Survival, 1940–1965* (London: Sphere Books, 1966), 2 August 1945, and Gilbert, *Winston Churchill, VIII*, pp. 163–4.

10 *ACPPE*, 19 February 1946.

11 *Central Council Meeting*, 27 March 1946.

12 *National Union Executive Committee*, 9 May 1946.

13 R. A. Butler, *The Art of the Possible* (London: Hamish Hamilton, 1971), p. 134.

14 *NUCUA, 67th Annual Conference, 3–5 October 1946*, p. 2.

15 Report of the ACPPE for 1945/46, *NUCUA 67th Annual Conference, 3–5 October 1946*, pp. 32–5.

16 *The Times*, 7 October 1946.

17 *The Times*, 7 October 1946.

18 T. F. Lindsay and M. Harrington, *The Conservative Party 1918–1979* (London: Macmillan, 1979), p. 151.

19 *ACPPE*, 15 October 1946.

20 *ACPPE*, 12 November 1946.

21 R. Rhodes James, *Anthony Eden* (London: Macmillan, 1986), pp. 317–18.

22 A. Howard, *RAB. The Life of R. A. Butler* (London: Macmillan, 1987), p. 155.

23 *The Industrial Charter* (London: Conservative Central Office 1947). Thereafter came *The Agricultural Charter* (June 1948), *True Balance* (February 1948, 'The Woman's Charter'), *A Policy For Wales* (March 1949), *Imperial Policy* (June 1949), and a *Charter for Scotland* (November 1949).

24 *ACPPE*, 13 May 1947.

25 H. Macmillan, *Tides of Fortune* (London: Macmillan, 1969), p. 301.

26 Butler, *The Art of the Possible*, p. 145.

27 R. Maudling, *Memoirs* (London: Sidgwick and Jackson, 1978), pp. 45–6.

28 Butler, *The Art of the Possible*, p. 143. Our emphasis.

29 Maudling, *Memoirs*, p. 45 and Butler, *The Art of the Possible*, p. 135.

30 A. Gamble, *The Conservative Nation* (London: Routledge & Kegan Paul, 1975),

pp. 44–51.

31 Hoffman, *The Conservative Party in Opposition*, p. 45. Our emphasis.

32 N. Fisher, *Iain Macleod* (London: Deutsch, 1975), p. 59.

33 Hoffman, *The Conservative Party in Opposition*, p. 161.

34 Howard, *RAB*, p. 157, Woolton, *Memoirs*, p. 347 and Butler, *The Art of the Possible*, p. 148.

35 Moran, *The Struggle for Survival*, 7 December 1947.

36 Butler, *The Art of the Possible*, pp. 146–7.

37 Macmillan, *Tides of Fortune*, p. 302.

38 Kilmuir, *Political Adventure*, p. 164.

39 *CRD 2/7/7*, Michael Fraser to David Clarke, 8 January 1948 and 12 January 1948.

40 *ACPPE*, 6 July 1947.

41 *CCO 4/2/83*, Colonel J. R. H. Hutchinson MP to Lord Woolton, 10 March 1949.

42 *CRD 2/7/7*, Fraser to Wills, 28 June 1948.

43 *CCO 4/2/83*, Chapman Walker to Colonel J. R. H. Hutchinson MP, 29 March 1949.

44 *CCO 4/2/83*, Colonel J. R. H. Hutchinson to Mark Chapman-Walker, 30 March 1949.

45 *CCO 4/5/162*, CCTU Bulletin 65 (January) 1953, p. 1.

46 *ACP 3/4/(54)/34b*, Implementation of the Workers' Charter, Michael Fraser to H. Watkinson, 16 July 1954.

47 Macmillan, *Tides of Fortune*, p. 303.

48 Butler, *The Art of the Possible*, p. 131 and P. Cosgrave, *The Lives of Enoch Powell* (London: Bodley Head, 1989), p. 101.

49 N. Harris, *Competition and the Corporate Society. British Conservatives, the State and Industry 1945–64* (London: Methuen, 1972), p. 77.

50 K. O. Morgan, *Labour in Power, 1945–51* (Oxford: Oxford University Press, 1984), chapter 8.

51 This ethos was not confined to the Conservative Party. In November 1948 Harold Wilson, the President of the Board of Trade, lit 'the bonfire of controls' sweeping away physical economic controls.

52 *D/He 41 Headlam Diary*, 26 July 1945.

53 Gilbert, *Winston Churchill VIII*, p. 185.

54 *The Times*, 24 July 1946.

55 *The Times*, 24 July 1946.

56 Kilmuir, *Political Adventure*, p. 140.

57 Blake, *The Conservative Party from Peel to Thatcher* (London: Fontana, 1985), p. 264, and Morgan, *Labour in Power*, chapter 7 explores class and politics.

58 Kilmuir, *Political Adventure*, p. 160. Our emphasis.

59 C. Cook, 'Note: 1945 to 1960', in C. Cook and J. Ramsden (eds.), *By-Elections in British Politics* (London: Macmillan, 1973), p. 192.

60 *National Union Executive Committee*, 10 July 1947.

61 *The Times*, 28 November 1947.

62 *National Union Executive Committee*, 11 December 1947.

63 *The Times*, 15 September 1947.

64 *The Times*, 28 November 1947.

65 *The Times*, 26 February 1949.

66 P. Goodhart, *The 1922* (London: Macmillan, 1973), pp. 146–7.

67 H. Nicolson, *Diaries and Letters 1945–62* (London, Collins, 1968), 19 December 1945 and Gilbert, *Winston Churchill VIII*, pp. 461–2. J. Stuart, *Within The Fringe* (London: Bodley Head, 1967), pp. 145–7, for the suggestion that Churchill retire.

68 *National Union Executive Committee*, Resolutions Submitted by Constituency Associations, April 1949.

69 *ACPPE*, 27 October 1948.

70 *CCO 600*, Tactical Staff Committee, 4 January 1949.

71 *CCO 600*, Tactical Staff Committee, 10 December 1947.

72 Hoffman, *The Conservative Party in Opposition*, pp. 188–9.

73 *The Times*, 25 July 1949.

74 *The Right Road for Britain* (London, Conservative Central Office 1949).

75 *The Times*, 25 July 1949.

76 Hoffman, *The Conservative Party in Opposition*, p. 192.

77 *Central Council Meeting*, 15 July 1949, *The Times*, 23 July 1949, and *NUCUA Annual Conference Report*.

78 Butler, *The Art of the Possible*, p. 151 and Howard, *RAB*, pp. 162–5.

79 Gilbert, *Winston Churchill VIII*, p. 476.

80 *CCO 180/1/4*, 'The Swing to the Right', 14 June 1949.

81 *CCO 181/1/4*, 'Increases and Decreases in the Conservative and Socialist Vote at By-Elections', 23 March 1950.

82 M. Baines, 'A United Anti–Socialist Party? Liberal/Conservative Relations 1945–55', *Contemporary Record* (February 1991), pp. 13–15, Gilbert, *Winston Churchill VIII*, pp. 502–3, and Moran, *The Struggle for Survival*, 15 October 1951, pp. 371–2.

83 B. J. Evans and A. J. Taylor, 'The Rise and Fall of Two-Party Electoral Co-operation', *Political Studies*, 32 (1984), pp. 257–72 for the Bolton and Huddersfield pacts.

84 *National Union Executive Committee*, 17 April 1947 and 11 January 1951, and Gilbert, *Winston Churchill VIII*, p. 655.

85 *National Union Executive Committee*, 12 January 1950, *Hannon 75/1*, Hannon to J. Crowder MP, 24 January 1950, and Gilbert, *Winston Churchill VIII*, pp. 501–3.

86 Butler, *The Art of the Possible*, pp. 152–3, Woolton, *Memoirs*, pp. 355–6 and Fisher, *Macleod*, pp. 87–8.

87 Kilmuir, *Political Adventure*, pp. 171–2, and Horne, *Macmillan. Volume 1, 1894–1956*, p. 326.

88 B. Pimlott (ed.), *The Political Diary of Hugh Dalton* (London: Jonathan Cape, 1988), 15 February 1951, *1922 Committee Minutes, Volume 5 1950–1959*, 22 February and 14 June 1951, and *CRD 2/21/2*, Brig. Clarke to Mr Greville, 3 April 1951.

89 Macmillan, *Tides of Fortune*, p. 355, diary entry for 21 September 1951, and *National Union Executive Committee*, 11 November 1951.

90 Macmillan, *Tides of Fortune*, p. 355, Gilbert, *Winston Churchill VIII*, p. 638 and

CCO 503/2/21, Trade Union National Advisory Council, 19th Meeting, 8 November 1951.

91 Macmillan, *Tides of Fortune*, p. 361, entry for 28 October 1951.

92 Moran, *The Struggle for Survival*, 29 September 1951 and Butler, *The Art of the Possible*, p. 156. For the Cabinet appointments see Viscount Chandos, *Memoirs* (London: Bodley Head, 1962), pp. 243–4, and *Dep Monckton 49*, 40 Autobiographical Fragments.

93 Macmillan, *Tides of Fortune*, p. 361, entry for 28 October 1951.

94 *CRD 2/21/1*, 'The Floating Vote', 28 November 1949 and 'The Approach to the Ex-Socialist Floating Voter', 30 December 1949.

95 *ACP 1/1/3*, Memorandum on Propaganda in Relation to Wage Earners, and *CCO 4/3/55*, 'The Trade Union Vote', R. Catterall to S. H. Pierssene, 19 May 1950.

96 *CCO 4/3/297*, 'The Trade Union Vote: A Plan of Approach', H. V. Armstrong to Mr Watson, 5 May 1950 and *National Union Executive Committee*, 18 May 1950, 'The Trade Union Vote', 11 May 1950.

97 Chandos, *Memoirs*, p. 243. See also Moran, *The Struggle for Survival*, 30 December 1951.

98 Butler, *The Art of the Possible*, pp. 156–7.

99 Colville, *Fringes of Power*, 22–23 March 1953, p. 298.

100 On free market thinking in the Conservative Party in this period see S. J. Procter, 'Floating Convertibility: The Emergence of the Robot Plan 1951–62', *Contemporary Record*, 7 (1) (1993), pp. 24–43, and K. Burk, *The First Privatisation. The Politicians, the City and the Denationalisation of Steel* (London: The Historian's Press, 1980).

101 Colville, *Fringes of Power*, 4 April and 16 May 1952.

102 *MS Woolton 22*, 2 Woolton to Churchill, 9 May 1952, and *Dep Monckton 2*, 225 David Gammans MP to Monckton, 12 June 1952.

103 S. Brittan, *Steering the Economy. The Role of the Treasury* (Harmondsworth: Penguin, 1971), p. 191.

104 Colville, *The Fringes of Power*, 23 June 1953.

105 Howard, *RAB*, p. 194.

106 *The Times*, 14 May 1953.

107 Viscount Hailsham, *The Case for Conservatism* (Harmondsworth: Penguin, 1947), p. 14, and *The Times*, 14 May 1953.

5

Prosperity and political exhaustion, 1955–1964

Between 1955 and 1964 Conservative politics ranged from triumph to defeat and embraces one of the high points of Conservatism: the government of Harold Macmillan. This chapter explores, first, the reasons for the decline and fall of Eden and the emergence of Macmillan as Prime Minister. Second, it considers the central dilemma of the politics of prosperity: how to reconcile full employment and low inflation. Third, the chapter examines the electoral politics of the period and in particular the Conservative attempt to exploit changing mass political loyalties under the impact of affluence. Fourth, the chapter examines the implosion of the Macmillan government after 1961 and its implications for Conservative politics. Finally, it considers the wider consequences of Macmillanite Conservatism for British and Conservative politics.

Suez and the emergence of Macmillan

By the end of 1954 Churchill was under considerable pressure to retire despite his protestation that he was now fit and believed he could contribute significantly to ending the Cold War and averting nuclear war. As Churchill prevaricated Eden's frustration mounted and their personal relations deteriorated.[1] On 1 February Churchill had agreed to resign at Easter but on 27 March he made one last attempt to remain in office provoking a confrontation with Eden. Woolton expressed his unease to Eden, economic problems (especially wage inflation) were mounting 'and we cannot keep dithering on every domestic issue that comes up to the Cabinet whilst we let what is expedient balance what is right'.[2] On 4 April Churchill entertained the Queen to dinner at No.10 to commemorate his retirement:

> When they had all gone, I went up with Winston to his bedroom. He sat on his bed wearing his Garter, Order of Merit and knee-breeches. For several minutes he did not speak and I, imagining that he was sadly contemplating that

this was his last night at Downing Street, was silent. Then suddenly he stared at me and said with vehemence: 'I don't think Anthony can do it'. His prophecies have often tended to borne out by events.[3]

The transition from Churchill to Eden was accomplished smoothly. There was a limited Cabinet reshuffle so as to express continuity and the preservation of an experienced team but it soon became interpreted as Eden failing to impose his will on his government. Eden's Press Secretary William Clark was 'aware of what was to be a continuing, even dominant, theme of my Downing Street days: Eden's indecisiveness and, equally important, his anxiety about being thought indecisive'.[4] Eden was determined to have an early general election: Labour was divided whereas the Conservatives basked in Eden's reflected glow, and economic conditions were favourable – delay would only dissipate these advantages. Eden was convinced he enjoyed a unique rapport with the electorate and was determined to bring to his government a philosophy: 'I believed that a property owning democracy could be encouraged to grow and that it fitted the national character as Socialism did not'. Eden expressed a determination to press ahead with economic modernisation and industrial efficiency which would underpin the welfare state and growing mass affluence. The election was delayed until after Butler's budget (which can be charitably described as expansionary, or uncharitably as a bribe) which was then placed alongside the Conservative record since 1951 and Eden's image as a popular, non-sectarian politician. Whilst this was an attractive package many Conservatives, including Eden, feared a re-run of 1951.[5]

The 1955 election was very quiet compared to 1950 and 1951. There were no great controversies but a significant development was discerned in mass electoral behaviour: 'the growing distance of time, rendered the pre-war myths about the Conservatives with which we were plagued in 1950 and 1951, more or less a dead or unreal issue in which the Socialists were unable to revive any interest'.[6] Labour was unable to present a credible alternative:

> the Socialists were forced back on the argument of the sinister underlying character of the Tories – that they really want mass unemployment, that they are just waiting to cut the social services, etc. This line did not ring very true with people who remembered the unemployment scare of the last election ... Conservatives just said that people were better off and left it at that.

The dissonance between Labour's message and perceived reality produced many Labour abstentions particularly amongst young working-class voters and this disaffection represented a considerable opportunity for the Conservative Party.[7] The increased Conservative majority and the 2.4% swing 'should not be ascribed so much to a movement of opinion in our favour as to a greater number of abstentions on the part of Labour Party supporters', and Labour's reliance on negative campaigning revealed 'They had little or no positive policy of their own and the crusading fervour of past days was gone'. Relying upon Eden's personal popularity, 'our approach was reasoned and sincere'.[8]

There was a widespread perception that Conservative support was changing: 'the results of the Election are proving more profound and pervasive than anybody expected ... the Labour Party ideologically disintegrated by the fact that Keynesian welfare capitalism is proving, for the time being, an adequate substitute for socialism'. One analyst argued that if the Conservatives had truly 'laid the bogey of its past' they would have won a further 20–30 seats; this and the failure of Labour abstainers to vote Conservative indicated many remained unconvinced the leopard had changed its spots. Victory in 1955, however, gave the party an opportunity to realign politics and create a natural Conservative majority.[9] With the welfare state secure and nationalisation unpopular the Labour Party was now in a serious quandary: 'To unite their Party they needed a radical programme [but] to win the election they needed a moderate programme attuned to Britain's new and more hopeful economic circumstances'. This quandary could not be easily resolved so providing the Conservatives with room for manoeuvre, while social change made swathes of Labour support vulnerable. The government's task was to create the conditions in which these voters could be won over.[10]

A flaw in this strategy was the sudden fall in the Eden government's popularity. At the end of 1955 a press campaign against Eden began which led to an unprecedented Gallup poll on Eden's premiership in January 1956. Camrose's *Daily Telegraph* and Randolph Churchill in Beaverbrook's *Evening Standard* were particularly hostile and this deeply affected Eden. In early January the *Daily Telegraph* published a devastating editorial which expressed and crystallised growing doubts about Eden: 'There is a favourite gesture of the Prime Minister's: to emphasise a point he will clench one fist to smack the open palm of the other hand – but the smack is seldom heard ... What are the actual criticisms that are heard whenever politics are discussed? They fall under three heads: changes of mind by the Government; half measures; and the postponement of decisions'.[11] The main complaints were the lack of direction in domestic policy, trade union power and inflation, and little central coherence. Eden's Press Secretary wrote 'I was disappointed by Eden's lack of grip on home affairs; he seemed to know even less about economics than I did, and it was my impression that he did not have much good advice on economic affairs from either of his chancellors, Butler and Macmillan. Eden had never had a home ministry ... it was clear by 1956 that Eden was losing his sense of purpose, and that the government was in serious trouble'.[12] Matters were to get much worse.

In February the Cyprus crisis began, in March Britain's position in the

Middle East was undermined by King Hussein of Jordan's dismissal of General John Glubb, the commander of the Arab Legion. This revived the press campaign and rumours of Cabinet plots. Then came the Suez crisis. On 13 June the last British troops left the Canal Zone under the 1954 Treaty negotiated by Eden, on 26 June Nasser became President of Egypt and, on 26 July, after the United States and Britain refused to finance the Aswan Dam, he nationalised the Suez Canal Company to provide the revenue to build the dam.[13] Suez was a political crisis of the first magnitude comparable to May 1940 with which many, consciously and unconsciously, compared it.

Eden's popularity was ebbing before Suez. Suez increased Eden's popularity in November and December reflecting the country rallying to the government when its troops were about to go into action. Suez wiped out Labour's lead in voting intention and in November–December there was a high degree of net approval not just for Eden but for his policies in the Middle East. Nonetheless, the divisions caused by Suez were dangerous as the polarisation might spill over into domestic politics, especially as the economic consequences of Suez were likely to require harsh remedial measures.

Gaitskell supported government policy in the debate of 2 August but made it clear Labour could not support action without the United Nations' approval, the preferred solution of public opinion. This rejection of force steadily increased and by 12 September Eden was accusing Labour of being unpatriotic. In the 3 November debate Gaitskell called on dissident Conservatives to overthrow Eden, a call he repeated in his broadcast of 4 November following the massive anti-war protest in Trafalgar Square which could be heard in the Cabinet room. The divisions and uncertainties of popular and party opinion were present in the social, bureaucratic, and military elites.[14] Though ministerial resignations were few (notably Edward Boyle and Anthony Nutting) and the government Whips managed discontent very effectively there were deep divisions over Eden's actions. Monckton, the Minister of Defence, the main Cabinet doubter, asked to be relieved of his post but agreed to stay in the government as Postmaster-General, and Lord Mountbatten, the First Sea Lord, twice proposed to resign in protest but was ordered to remain at his post. These intra-elite divisions deeply worried the Americans. The National Security Council noted 'Evidence of the unsettled state of British officialdom' and their conviction that the Eden government would soon fall with resulting complications for the Anglo-American relationship.[15] Soon after the nationalisation of the Suez Canal Macmillan and the Treasury warned that while the economic burden of the military operations was sustainable the inevitable pressure on sterling could not be borne without American support. After the landings on 6 November the foreign currency reserves and sterling came under massive strain and the Americans not only refused to support the pound and blocked the UK's funds at the International Monetary Fund (IMF), but refused to help with oil supplies after the closure of the Suez Canal and the sabotage of oil pipelines. Only when the British had fully accepted and complied with the USA's terms of complete withdrawal were funds and oil released.[16]

Despite his strengthening position as recorded in the polls, and support from the party grassroots and from the backbench, it was clear from 6 November and the cease-fire that Eden could not survive as Prime Minister. Implicit in the American position was the removal of Eden, the man responsible for the invasion. Eden's reputation for poor judgement was exacerbated by his decision (taken on medical advice) to holiday in Jamaica (23 November–14 December) which led Randolph Churchill to compare the crisis to Stalingrad and to note that even Hitler did not winter in Jamaica. Party opinion fell into three groups: those who supported the government whatever it did; those who pressed for decisive action and deplored the retreat; and those who disagreed with the government's policies and expressed their disquiet. Eden did not lack support in the party: his position was analogous to Chamberlain's on 10 May 1940 in that he was unable to mobilise his support and it was the doubts in the parliamentary party and Cabinet which sealed his fate.[17]

Eden's resignation was necessary to maintain the cornerstone of British policy: the American alliance. The Cabinet, led by Butler (again acting Prime Minister in Eden's absence) and Macmillan recognised action independent of the United States was not possible despite vocal anti-Americanism. Good relations with the United States were crucial for Britain's defence, foreign, and economic policies and the restoration of good relations required the removal of Eden. Between 23 November and 14 December while he was in Jamaica a coup was mounted against Eden by Butler and Macmillan with the tacit support of the Eisenhower Administration. On 8 January 1957 Eden resigned on the grounds of ill-health; he died in 1977.[18]

From early November a reconstruction of the government was inevitable. Macmillan told the American Ambassador, Winthrop Aldrich, Eden would resign and Aldrich presumed Butler would become Premier, although he did not rule out Macmillan. Butler was the obvious choice: he was the government's business manager, had varied ministerial experience, was CRD chairman, and had twice acted as Prime Minister. Paradoxically, Butler's management of the post-Suez crisis and his known lack of conviction about the operation ensured he did not become Prime Minister. In an attempt to keep the party together Butler sought to apprise them of the seriousness of Britain's position.

> I dined with twenty influential Conservative members of the Progress Trust, and was very open with them speaking privately of some of the realities of the situation, particularly in relation to sterling, which no one had hitherto done.

The small private room became like a hornets' nest. They all hurried off the Carlton Club to prepare representations to the government. Wherever I moved in the weeks that followed, I felt the party knives sticking into my innocent back.

The delicacy of Butler's position increased after Eden left for Jamaica when he was left 'with the odious duty of withdrawing the troops, re-establishing the pound, salvaging our relations with the US and the UN, and bearing the brunt of the criticism from private members, constituency worthies and the general public for organising a withdrawal, which was a collective responsibility'.[19]

The 1922 Committee meeting on 22 November, addressed by Butler and Macmillan, was crucial. Anxious not to provoke a near mutinous party whilst emphasising the gravity of the situation Butler gave a brief, factual, and sombre assessment and then called on Macmillan to say a few words about oil. Macmillan delivered a carefully prepared performance, complete with expansive gestures which nearly knocked Butler off his chair, which made one observer (Enoch Powell) feel physically sick at its blatant manipulation. Another observer recalled 'Macmillan then got up and made a major speech, said to have already been rehearsed to an audience of Junior Ministers'. Macmillan certainly used the occasion to improve his own prospects but he proved far more sensitive to the party's mood and needs than did Butler: 'the Parliamentary Party were deeply disillusioned and dispirited and he set himself to restore their morale. It was rhetoric and it did border on the "ham" but he contrived to set their present troubles in the framework of the long adventure of politics, full of hard knocks but still a game more worth playing than any other'.[20]

This performance won Macmillan the leadership. His confident lead contrasted sharply with Butler's sombre attitude; during the crisis Macmillan had adopted clear positions (in Harold Wilson's cutting phrase 'first in, first out') whereas Butler prevaricated and let it be known he had doubts while doing nothing about them. On 8 January, after a further bout of ill-health, Eden informed the Queen of his intention to resign and on the 9th the Cabinet was informed. Before 1965 the Conservative Party's leaders 'emerged' through a process of consultation. After the 9 January Cabinet Salisbury went to see Kilmuir. They were senior ministers but as members of the House of Lords they had no personal interest in the succession and they agreed to consult the Cabinet. Using Salisbury's room at the Privy Council Office each minister was called in and Salisbury asked one question: 'Well, which is it, Wab or Hawold?' Edward Heath (Chief Whip) and Oliver Poole (Party Chairman) were consulted and Morrison (Chairman of the 1922) gave his opinion via telephone from the Isle of Islay. Salisbury and Kilmuir found opinion running strongly in Macmillan's favour and advised the

Queen accordingly. Macmillan also enjoyed Churchill's support who saw the Queen on the morning of 10 January. Churchill described the Suez operation as 'the most ill-conceived and ill-executed imaginable ... He also said that if Eden resigned he thought Harold Macmillan would be a better successor than R. A. Butler'.[21]

Suez had little effect on domestic politics, but this was not the perception at the time: Macmillan thought his government might last six months and that if there was a general election the Conservatives would lose and be out of power for twenty years. Macmillan's first object was, therefore, to avoid an election. He concentrated on stabilising party and public opinion, a concern expressed eloquently by Macmillan taking his Chief Whip, Edward Heath, to the Turf Club to celebrate his appointment as Prime Minister with champagne and game pie. In his memoirs Macmillan conveys the impression he was surprised by the press attention; in fact it was a carefully calculated display of insouciance. Here was a new Prime Minister radiating confidence in the future and, in what was to become the defining Macmillan characteristic, exuding unflappability. This bravo performance was repeated on 17 January when Macmillan addressed the nation on television. Macmillan's calmness and resolute tone were crucial in calming the domestic storm of Suez. They contrasted sharply with Eden's hyperactivity and were expressed by the note he pinned on the door of the Cabinet room: 'Quiet calm deliberation disentangles every knot'.

Macmillan set his government six tasks: first, restoring the party's confidence in the government and in themselves; second, overcoming the economic consequences of the Suez crisis and the canal's closure; third, restoring relations with the United States (but with Eden now out of the way this posed no major difficulties); fourth, addressing the economic weaknesses revealed by Suez; fifth, re-evaluating Britain's defence commitments and strategic doctrine; finally, accelerating the shift from Empire to Commonwealth.[22]

Macmillan's immediate problem was resolving the divisions in the Conservative Party. He treated Captain Waterhouse's Suez Group with great caution but the inevitable confrontation came on 13 May when Macmillan announced the government would no longer discourage British shipowners from using the Suez Canal. Before 'the water jump' (Macmillan's description of the two-day Suez debate) action was taken to minimise right-wing opposition: petrol rationing was ended; there had been £100m in tax cuts in the budget; and it was announced Britain had exploded her first nuclear bomb. Nonetheless, the debate began unsteadily for Macmillan but he made the Opposition's motion on the government's policy into a motion of confidence. The question, he argued, was 'whether the prestige and economic interests of Britain are better entrusted to a Socialist or to a Conservative Administration'. There was never any doubt but that the government would win, what mattered were the number of abstentions. If the number was above 20 Macmillan feared a repeat of the 'Norway Syndrome' where the government's majority remained but was reduced to such an extent that its authority was fatally compromised. In the event only 14 Conservatives abstained and the government had a majority of 49, the debate crippled the Suez Group and acted as a catharsis for the party as a whole. Macmillan wrote in his diary, 'the whole Tory party stood up and cheered me. At the speaker's chair, I turned and bowed. It was an extraordinary and spontaneous act of loyalty and touched me very much. How odd the English are! They rather like a gallant failure. Suez has become a sort of Mons retreat. Anyway, we're through this particular trouble – at least for the moment'.[23]

The politics of prosperity

Churchill's domestic goals were simple: houses and red meat. Harold Macmillan, his Housing Minister, delivered the houses and in 1953 rationing came to an end. After 1953 when world commodity prices fell with the end of the Korean War and terms of world trade shifted in the UK's favour there was upsurge in mass prosperity. Between 1951 and 1964 the adult male manual worker saw his weekly wage rise from £8.30 to £17.51, an increase of 53% whilst unemployment averaged 1.8% and never rose above 2.6%. Economic growth averaged a historically respectable 2.8%, achieving over 4% in some years. Affluence was reflected in the production of consumer goods: the production of television sets rose by 67%, vacuum cleaners by 33%, passenger cars 134%, washing machines 40%, and the number of building society borrowers by 43%.

There were, however, serious economic weaknesses. First, the current account balance of payments was in deficit for five of the fourteen years and in surplus on the capital account in only one year. When combined there were deficits in eight of the fourteen years and there were serious sterling crises in 1951, 1955, 1961, and 1964 which led to the 'stop-go' style of economic management. Second, inflation averaged a relatively low 3.6% but this was high by historical standards and was blamed on full employment. Governments in this period searched for a way of controlling inflation whilst maintaining full employment. Third, although public spending as a percentage of GNP remained stable at about 24%, gross public income rose by 40% and expenditure by 49.6%.

The management of the unions and inflation was determined by Churchill's instructions to Monckton not to antagonise the unions. Before the 1951 election the TUC had made it clear they would co-operate with a Conservative government and in preparing the 1952 budget Butler held confidential meetings with Vincent Tewson, the TUC General Secretary. Privately the TUC acknowledged the case for wage restraint but neither they (nor the employers) would countenance government intervention in collective bargaining. Government concentrated on persuading employers and unions to restrict wage and price increases whilst doing all it could to stabilise prices.[24]

Central Office and Conservative MPs had been urged by Monckton not to publicise this as the TUC was trying to co-operate with the government. Central Office agreed with bolstering TUC moderates but what if they could not hold the line? What should be their response? These questions went to the heart of consensus politics. Central Office suggested two responses: wage increases not backed by productivity gains would generate higher inflation and unemployment; or, blame wage claims and industrial unrest on Communists. Lord Swinton (Chancellor of the Duchy of Lancaster), responsible for government propaganda, preferred the former but argued the threat of unemployment should not be emphasised and departments were instructed to make no reference to unemployment as a tool of economic management.[25] Despite their best intentions, union leaders could not resist their members' demands for higher wages while prices, particularly food prices, were rising. By 1955 the TUC found its responsibility for promoting wage moderation contradicted by its affiliates' perceptions about the cost of living, and union leaders were facing competition from shop floor leaders fostered by fifteen years of full employment. Equally, the employers had little confidence in the Ministry of Labour or the tripartite system.[26]

Eden recognised that the country's resources and the demands placed on them had to be aligned, an appreciation balanced by the political orthodoxies of consensus politics: 'The decisions were thought economically right at the time, they were certainly politically odious and cut across our party's philosophy. It is difficult to advocate a property-owning democracy to the tune of "Your kettles will cost you more"'.[27] Eden identified the control of domestic inflation as his government's central economic objective and to support this in December Butler (who was anxious to go) was replaced as Chancellor by Macmillan (who resented leaving the Foreign Office), and Monckton by Macleod as Minister of Labour. Work was already under way on updating the 1944 White Paper. Eden believed that the interconnected problems of inflation and industrial unrest would only be resolved by prolonged public education. In the summer of 1955 a committee was established which laid the foundations for the 1956 White Paper, *The Economic Implications of Full Employment*. At an early meeting of the committee in July Butler, still Chancellor of the Exchequer, suggested a White Paper setting out the economic problems caused by full employment and the case for wage moderation. This was agreed subject to the proviso there be no hint of an incomes policy which the TUC was bound to oppose.[28]

The Treasury debated at length whether unemployment could, or should, be used to deflate union wage bargaining power. The 2% average unemployment since 1945 was insufficient to dampen wage inflation, equally government was unwilling to use unemployment as a tool of economic management. The Treasury recognised union leaders had not made maximum use of their bargaining power so intervention by government would lose the union leadership's goodwill. Hence government's reliance on the indirect approach of persuasion and education which to be successful required stable relations with the unions.[29] Communicating the relationship between unemployment, prices, and wages was 'a very hard task for political leadership. Self-interest, reinforced by group loyalty, is a powerful force to combat, and the voice of reason is at present muffled by a good deal of political suspicion and mistrust'. More seriously there was no evidence 'people will actually behave with greater self-discipline and restraint if they are better informed about the economics of inflation'.[30] The full employment commitment would be retained with an emphasis on increased productivity and wage moderation. The White Paper would appeal to rational economic self-interest. By September a draft of the White Paper was ready and Burke Trend, the group's chairman, wanted the draft circulating throughout Whitehall but the Head of the Treasury, Sir Edward Bridges, expressed concern at the 'political traps' inherent in this and declined.[31]

The Economic Implications of Full Employment (Cmds 9725) did not break with past policy. Full employment with low inflation were the desiderata of economic policy and Cmd. 9725 reiterated neither could be secured by government fiat. Full employment and price stability required a conscious effort and bargainers were warned that failure would inevitably produce higher unemployment. The White Paper was accompanied by a 'price plateau' in which price restrictions in the nationalised industries were matched by price and profit restraint in the private sector. Macmillan's 1956 budget was deflationary with cuts in subsidies following credit restrictions, cuts in public investment and the suspension of investment allowances. Although many union leaders accepted the futility of increased money wages chasing higher prices the TUC refused to circulate the White Paper, seeking increased food subsidies to hold down prices. The unions' growing truculence seemed confirmed by the election of Frank Cousins as TGWU General Secretary in May 1956. Cousins squashed Macmillan's suggestion he attend the 1956 TUC to explain the government's policy and in his speech Cousins issued his famous warning that 'In a period of freedom for all we are part of the all'.[32]

Before becoming Prime Minister Macmillan recognised that traditional anti-inflation politics were failing. The Cabinet rejected deflation and especially unemployment as tools of economic management but recognised the need for a stronger attack on inflation. The government decided to create an authoritative, impartial body to give guidance on the implications of wage settlements and thereby influence the climate of collective bargaining, an idea which had been discussed sporadically since 1954. Thorneycroft, Macmillan's Chancellor, told Macmillan 'Failure to proceed would play into the hands of the more hostile elements in the trade union movement: it would come as a shock to public opinion: and it would leave a vacuum at a time when there is considerable unease at home and abroad about inflation and rising prices'. On 16 July the Cabinet agreed to proceed with the Council on Prices, Productivity, and Incomes (CPPI, known as the Cohen Council after its chairman, or 'The Three Wise Men' after its membership) which would not be involved in the detail of wage negotiation but would restrict itself to influencing the climate of bargaining.[33]

Thorneycroft did not believe CPPI would significantly affect wage bargaining but supported it on pragmatic grounds. In September 1957 another sterling crisis was developing and although inflation was falling Thorneycroft believed inflation was eroding foreign confidence. An important group of officials, including Lord Cobbold (Governor of the Bank of England), Enoch Powell and Nigel Birch (the two junior Treasury Ministers), and Professor Lionel Robbins (an economist) were convinced the answer lay in deflation and a tight monetary policy. Thorneycroft had always considered inflation essentially a monetary phenomenon, the real problem was government spending and general monetary laxity. Union wage demands could have little effect on inflation.[34] This was rejected by Sir Roger Makins (Treasury Permanent Secretary), Sir Robert Hall (Director of the Economic Section) and, of course, by Harold Macmillan. Macmillan was well aware of the threat posed by inflation but deflation would increase unemployment. This dilemma was expressed by Macmillan in the famous Bedford speech (20 July 1957). Thus far, Macmillan implied the consequences of inflation had been evaded but in the long-term the result was inevitable, 'we will be back in the old nightmare of unemployment'.[35] The scene was set for a conflict not just over techniques of economic management but over the contours of British politics.

Confrontation with the unions was out of the question, their co-operation could be won if 'we can stop the flow of the inflationary tide. If we can ever get into slack water, or better still a slight ebb, their task would be much easier'. Macmillan agreed the amount of money in circulation must be reduced and government spending held but did not believe there was much room for cuts other than those planned. Disinflation would in time achieve low prices and low unemployment, and thereby 'we shall lose no votes and injure nobody'. Sharp deflation risked conflict with the unions; if inflation was falling it would be easier to resist the militants and bolster the moderates. Much of Macmillan's analysis, especially stricter monetary policy and public spending control, was welcomed by Thorneycroft. These measures, he believed, would reduce inflation to 2–3 per cent but, he concluded, 'unless we can get away from the idea that over full employment must be supported at all costs we have no hope of curing the inflation'.[36] Without a very public commitment to controlling public sector costs Thorneycroft feared government backsliding and noted the British Employers Confederation (BEC) 'attached the highest importance to the fact that we had said "NO": that we meant "NO": and that we showed no signs of wavering'.[37]

The resignation of the three Treasury Ministers, Thorneycroft, Birch and Powell, on 6 January 1958 had little to do with wage inflation. The crisis exploded on 22 December. Macmillan, worried about the political consequences of the cuts, called a meeting of senior ministers on the 23rd where there was a furious row. Thorneycroft dug in his heels over keeping the following year's public spending total level, in effect a cut of about 3%. Over Christmas Macmillan, faced by Thorneycroft's resignation threat, ordered ministers to get as close as possible to the £153m cut target and by the New Year a further £100m had been found. The £50m gap between the cuts sought by Thorneycroft and those offered by the Cabinet was well within the margin of error for public spending calculations, but Macmillan's dismissal of £50m (1% of public spending) as a matter of no great significance was seen by the Treasury team as symptomatic of his refusal to confront inflation. On 5 January Thorneycroft refused to cut a deal and 'work with the Cabinet', Macmillan feared if he supported Thorneycroft he might lose other ministers from the defence and social ministries and had visions of his government falling apart and Labour taking office. The resignations infuriated Macmillan who, about to depart on a highly publicised Commonwealth tour, felt he was being blackmailed and thought Thorneycroft was in thrall to Powell and Birch, the monetary control fanatics.[38] Careful media presentation (six Cabinet ministers were shipped out to the airport in a spontaneous display of loyalty) and lashings of unflappability (the resignations were dismissed as a little local difficulty) helped defuse the crisis. Macmillan remained anxious about the fallout but was helped by Thorneycroft not using his resignation speech as did later ex-Chancellors to point out their disagreements with their Prime Minister.[39]

There is an important party dimension to Thorneycroft's resignation. Thorneycroft and Fraser had already warned Macmillan inflation was hitting party loyalists. Thorneycroft believed Suez had fuelled a national doubt and disquiet which were infecting the middle classes as their economic security was undermined. Ideologically the Conservative Party was verging on paralysis as electoral strategy focused on consensus politics but there was a widespread dislike of these politics focusing on inflation, trade union power, and economic weakness. Thorneycroft, Birch, and Powell represented this disquiet and despite the success of his 1957 budget Thorneycroft was attracted by the idea of radical change. In the aftermath of Suez Thorneycroft believed Macmillan would not necessarily oppose a re-think. Thorneycroft's September Measures (along with the ceiling on public spending) which *inter alia* raised the bank rate from 5% to 7% were the first stage of this approach. Powell and Birch were intellectually convinced by the Quantity Theory of Money; Thorneycroft was more pragmatic and his policies were closer to orthodox deflation. The September Measures, when coupled with falling inflation, a stabilised exchange rate, and falling money supply did present an opportunity to reorient policy and squeeze inflation out of the system and bring public spending under control so laying the foundations for inflation-free growth.

The conflict was not simply between 'inflationists' and 'deflationists': both sides favoured economic growth but Thorneycroft was convinced that the policies pursued since 1945 must culminate in catastrophe. Macmillan believed these policies were essentially sound and merely required adjustment. Treasury ministers were far more sensitive to the party political consequences of inflation and Macmillan was willing to make concessions as long as the policy set out in 1944 and reiterated in 1956 was untouched. His joust with the Treasury took place on the expectation that a compromise would be reached, but as the Autumn public spending negotiations commenced the Prime Minister and Cabinet suddenly realised Thorneycroft's call for real cuts was not a bargaining ploy, he meant it. Both *The Times* and many backbenchers sympathised with Thorneycroft, blaming Macmillan for not supporting his Chancellor and for breaching the self-imposed principle of keeping the estimates level. The party would undoubtedly rally after the resignations but 'there were rumblings of discontent' on the backbench over welfare spending at a time when defence was being cut. Whilst few on the backbench or in the party were monetarists there was a gut sympathy for its precepts which meshed with the traditional Conservative dislike of public spending and taxation. The government was determined to tackle inflation but this, as Lord Hailsham argued, did not depend on 'marginal differences in the annual estimates'. Thorneycroft's approach, Hailsham argued, would make 'permanent alterations in the shape of social policy' and would 'involve the abandonment of some of the best established of the social policies to which successive Conservative Governments have declared their adherence'. This theme was taken up by Butler who argued Thorneycroft's policies 'meant that the Government would have been asked to overturn, in the course of a few days, policies of social welfare to which some people had devoted the service of their lives'.[40]

The resignations had no discernible effect on policy. Heathcoat-Amory, Thorneycroft's successor, continued his policies and in 1957–8 the economy underwent what was in contemporary terms a severe recession: unemployment rose from 1.6 per cent to 2.2 per cent (1958) to 2.3 per cent (1959), in 1958 there was negative growth, but the balance of payments moved into surplus and inflation slowed markedly. Ironically Heathcoat-Amory's economic ideas were as conservative as Thorneycroft's but he was conscious of the pressure for expansion as the election neared. Macmillan found Heathcoat-Amory far more personally congenial than Thorneycroft and they developed a close working relationship but he was regarded as more malleable than Thorneycroft. Heathcoat-Amory's 1958 budget was delivered with the economy slipping into recession but he rejected a strong stimulus. By early summer Prime Ministerial pressure for reflation was making itself felt. Amory began to make expansionary concessions and Macmillan secured the promise of an expansionary budget for 1959. By early 1959 the economy was recovering rapidly but against his better judgement Amory was held to his promise by Macmillan and delivered a most inappropriate budget which generated an unsustainable boom. At the time, however, Macmillan could point to lower inflation, a balance of payments surplus, and tighter public spending as evidence of greater economic stability. The budgetary stimulus was not necessary as the world and domestic economies were growing rapidly. It was also politically unnecessary. The government's popularity and Macmillan's rating improved markedly, and the Conservatives secured a small but consistent lead in the polls, the average by-election swing against the government fell from 6.6% (1957) to 4.7% (1958), to 2.6% (1959). Macmillan would have won the 1959 election without the stimulus.

Electoral politics, 1957–1963

In 1955 the Conservatives had won 49.7% of the vote which remains the best performance of any party after 1945, but the collapse of the Liberal vote and Labour's disunity were important elements contributing to the Conservative victory. The post-Suez political climate was very complex: Suez had no effect on voting intention but Labour retained a sometimes substantial lead which suggested dissatisfaction with the government. In the by-elections of 1957 there was an average swing of 6.6% to Labour and in early 1958 the Conservatives lost Torrington to the Liberals and Rochdale and Glasgow Kelvingrove to Labour. These results suggested some dangerous weaknesses in the Conservative vote.

At Rochdale there had been a general drift to the Liberals amongst Conservative voters of *all categories*. Rochdale had also revealed significant changes in electioneering, notably 'the obvious fascination exercised by Mr [Ludovic] Kennedy over women, the big impact of TV and the small impact of public meetings, and the big difference between the proportion of Conservatives and all others who considered foreign affairs the main issue in the election'.[41] Analyses of the 1955 election had found little evidence that television had affected political loyalties but had proved successful in promoting the party's and Eden's image. Eden and Macmillan recognised television's potential and made much use of it so Rochdale marked an important step in the 'presidentialisation' of British politics.[42] Macmillan admitted Rochdale came as a 'tremendous shock' and conceded that the government was in trouble. Discontent was fuelled by inflation, party-political bickering, and pensions worries and not by agreement with Liberal policies: only 8% cited these as a reason for voting Liberal compared to 24% dissatisfied with the Conservative candidate, and 36% who expressed dissatisfaction with the government. More worrying was the loss of lower-middle and skilled-working voters – 45% of defectors came from these social classes. Apart from the immediate perturbations caused by Suez and the September Measures 'the main movement is a gradual decline in Conservative popularity since the autumn budget of 1955 of about three or four points a year'.[43]

This pattern was repeated at Torrington, which was taken by the Liberals. The Labour vote fell by 10.3%, the Conservative vote by 27.7%, and the Liberals came from nowhere to 38%. Not surprisingly Macmillan was deeply concerned about the five by-elections to be held on 12 June. The Liberal revival threatened Macmillan's effort to achieve a 'moral ascendancy' in the country after Suez and 'in spite of our bold attempt to ride the storm after the events of 1956 we were still slipping backwards', and he briefly contemplated a snap general election ('riding for a fall but not too severe a one'). Torrington, lost by only 200 votes (a Liberal majority of 2,000–3,000 had been predicted), had been an improvement on Rochdale and the 12 June by-elections continued this trend. The Conservative fear was that in a general election the Liberals would poll sufficiently well to deny the Conservatives a majority. Their by-election record would encourage them to field more candidates than in 1951 or 1955 thereby splitting the anti-Socialist vote. Party strategists discounted this, however, as there were only six Conservative seats with majorities less than 3,000 where a Liberal had stood in 1955, although there had been no Liberal candidate in either Rochdale or Torrington in 1955.[44]

January 1957 to the 1959 general election was a difficult period for the Macmillan government and in it were laid the seeds of electoral disenchantment which flourished after the summer of 1960.[45] Disaffection was concentrated on two groups: the affluent and upwardly mobile skilled and semi-skilled working class who were not committed Conservative voters, and lower-middle class core Conservative voters. Both felt themselves to be suffering from inflation and both resented the organised working class. Controlling inflation so as to jeopardise neither the Conservatives' growing cross-class appeal nor their core voters and activists was a problem which went to the heart of government and party policy. After the Ipswich by-election (September 1957), when the Conservative share of the vote fell by 14.4%, Michael Fraser submitted an analysis of the Conservative predicament to Macmillan. The Conservatives' main asset was that Labour was perceived to be unelectable, but inflation, the credit squeeze, the Rent Act, and the Suez fallout were fuelling a 'middle-class revolt'. The 'main public expression takes the form of demands from the hard core of the Party for "more Conservative policies" and for a "show-down" with the trade unions'. Fraser felt 1955–8 had been wasted because of Suez and 'our political aim in this second period of office should have been to achieve some rehabilitation of the middle class in the widest sense of that word, while not in the process alienating that wider measure of manual-working [class] support upon which we had gained by 1955 and upon which we depend for a reasonable majority'.[46]

This analysis informed the debate between the Prime Minister and Peter Thorneycroft on political-economic strategy. On 1 September Macmillan circulated a memorandum on curing inflation which noted the corrosive effects of inflation were not just economic: it promoted the feeling that the government could not, or would not, do anything to stop price rises. This bred cynicism and weakened social solidarity as the strong sought to protect themselves which in turn generated resentment from those who could not. The government and party had been badly shaken by Suez and although they had survived Macmillan identified two factors which meant the Conservatives could not currently face the electorate with any degree of confidence. First, it was very rare in modern conditions to win two consecutive elections: 'to win three is almost a miracle'. Second, 'while the great mass of the working population and the majority of the entrepreneur class have gained from inflation; those who have been injured by it are disproportionately represented in the Party organisation in the constituencies'. Macmillan's grail was controlling inflation painlessly by a combination of reducing the money supply, public spending restraint, and restraint in wage negotiations. This policy of disinflation rather than deflation meant 'we shall lose no votes and injure nobody'.[47]

Six days later Thorneycroft (who resigned in January) responded. By not tackling inflation head-on the government was courting political and economic disaster. Thorneycroft conceded many were doing well out of inflation but the polls and by-election results produced 'no evidence that we are picking up many recruits from the prosperous majority'. 'What is certain', Thorneycroft contended, 'is that a great number of those suffering are just the people who form the hard-core of the Tory Party – the men and women who do the hard slogging work in the constituencies. My colleagues will know from their own experiences how bitterly such people feel about the way things have gone. To enter a difficult electoral battle with the "old-guard" disaffected is to risk a smashing defeat'. Not only was the government betraying its core supporters it was in danger of betraying Conservative principles and the country's true interests for short-term electoral advantage. It was possible the Conservatives might well lose the next general election but what mattered, Thorneycroft argued, 'was not whether it loses but why'. Thus 'If we are thrown out because we have been too tough ... and have allowed a modest growth in unemployment, we shall be returned again, perhaps quite soon. If we are thrown out because we have flinched from our duty and allowed the economy to drift into disaster I see no reason why we should ever be asked to resume control'.[48]

Thorneycroft's proposal of allowing unemployment to rise not as a regrettable by-product of policy but as integral to anti-inflation policy threatened the edifice of the post-war political settlement. A deliberate but small increase in unemployment would have a dramatic effect on wage bargainers and inflation expectations. Thorneycroft recognised that neither the Prime Minister nor the Cabinet would openly undermine the commitment to full employment and so he shifted the focus of his attack to public spending which was likely to attract wider support. This was the issue on which he would resign in January.[49] These memoranda point clearly to the re-emergence of the debate on the role of the state and disquiet in some sections of the party at the long-term consequences of the Keynesian welfare state and growing disquiet at the direction of Conservative politics in the late 1950s.

There was a marked improvement in the government's electoral position in the summer of 1958. The results, *The Times* suggested, reflected the return of public confidence in the government but conceded there was a long way to go before the Conservatives could face a general election. From this point the government's net approval rating, Macmillan's personal rating, and voting intention all became positive. The Conservative lead over Labour remained fragile but Macmillan and his government enjoyed strong positive ratings, a turn around which showed 'that Macmillan's popularity has vastly increased, that Tory voters are drifting back to voting Tory' which would give them a small majority. Speculation about an early election revived, a course of action rejected by Macmillan as 'slick and unfair' but more likely because the recovery was too fragile, and on 12 September Macmillan took the unusual step of issuing a statement that there would be no autumn election.[50]

Suez allowed a perception to take root 'that the Government was not in control of events, did not know where it was going, and was not in fact doing anything'. Fostering an image of competence by decisive action in foreign and domestic affairs was seen by Macmillan as the key to political recovery. The firm handling of the railway and bus disputes, for example, conveyed the impression of a government determined to act but what impressed the electorate was not what the government did, but the fact that it was acting decisively. This was helped immeasurably by Macmillan's style: 'he is prepared to take action, that he is firm and unruffled, and that he is sincerely trying to solve our problems had undoubtedly had a considerable effect'. Labour's failure to overcome its divisions or present a coherent policy further helped the Conservative recovery. Future electoral prospects required economic growth and action to reinforce the image of competence 'but it might not take much to shake the position'. Confidence remained fragile so successful economic management and tax cuts could be used to boost confidence, and while the full employment commitment should be retained there would be an inevitable, albeit temporary, rise in unemployment. The government must not be panicked into a hasty reflation as this would boost inflation and tarnish its image of competence and rectitude: the government should stick to its current policies – advice which meshed neatly with Macmillan's own preferences.[51]

On the day the Cabinet discussed unemployment Macmillan wrote in his diary,

> It is a heavy responsibility, for the whole future of the Party depends on whether
> (a) we ought to reflate
> (b) we can reflate in time ...
> (a) means can we risk another inflation if we go too far, (b) means how long does it take to stop a slump, if it takes two years, if it takes two years to halt a boom.
> It will be a 'close run thing' – like Waterloo.

The Cabinet chose reflation. Bank rate was reduced to 4% on 20 November after pressure on the Governor of the Bank of England from Macmillan, tax cuts of £200m were agreed, and on 27 December sterling became fully convertible. Over Christmas Macmillan decided this was insufficient, a conviction strengthened by his New Year tour of the North East: 'I feel sure we must do more "reflation" if we are to avoid a serious crisis'. Once again Stockton worked its spell. Macmillan was resisted by Heathcoat-Amory, the Treasury, and the Bank of England and the struggle lasted from 19 January to 3 February when the Cabinet blocked Macmillan's wish for an early budget (he wanted 17 March not 7 April) and agreed £30m extra capital spending instead of the £50m sought by the Prime Minister. With the reflation under his belt Macmillan concluded 'we seemed now safely poised to consider and decide how and when to face "the appeal unto Caesar"'.[52]

On 3 April at a three-hour meeting Butler, Hailsham, Poole, Macleod, Heath, Amory, and Macmillan discussed the election. Every constituency had been analysed, the polls scrutinised, and the Liberals' prospects evaluated: Central Office predicted a majority of 13. This was too close for comfort and on 22 April, secure in the knowledge it would be leaked, Macmillan told the 1922 there would be no spring election, and Hailsham wrote to all constituency chairmen to inform them of this. The delay imposed a further burden on the party which was expecting an election but an early election would have lost the 'helpful and imaginative budget' and there were a number of high profile events due which would help the Conservatives. There was also, Hailsham admitted, a possibility of losing. A summer election was ruled out and it was thought dangerous for a government to go to its full term, which meant an October election was virtually certain giving the government a further five months of campaigning and to allow the reflation to take full effect. On his peregrinations Macmillan sensed an attitude very different to the class hostility of 1945 and 1950–1 which he felt could only be to the Conservative advantage. Macmillan ruthlessly exploited the visit to Europe by President Eisenhower in August. This reached a crescendo in the televised broadcast of Eisenhower and Macmillan seated in armchairs chatting about world affairs. The 'Mac 'n' Ike Show' was deemed a major political coup.[53] On 7 September Macmillan asked the Queen to dissolve Parliament, with election on 8 October.

The budget and the extra months of publicity worked wonders. So buoyant was the party's mood Hailsham wrote to all constituency chairmen warning them, 'We are starting this race hot favourites, and there are disadvantages about this ... Beware of all specious arguments depending on the assumption that the result is certain. The easiest way of losing the election would be if any sizeable proportion of non-Socialist voters assumed that it was already won'.[54] The 1959 election was a personal triumph for Macmillan, confirming his political ascendancy and reports from the party suggested a sea-change was underway in the distribution of political loyalties.

Essex Conservatives reported 'large numbers of Socialists have undergone a complete change and are going to vote Conservative ... they are still Socialist at heart, but at the moment their head warns them of the dangers of Socialist Government ... It might still be possible for the Labour Party to win them back with a powerful emotional appeal'. Lancashire Conservatives emphasised the importance of the 'standard of living, wages and above all security of employment' together with doubts over Labour's tax promises. The Home County Conservatives believed 'the electorate trusted the Tories; it was not willing to risk trusting the Socialists'. The party was 'right to exploit the feeling that things were going well: that so many "never had it so good"'.[55] This conviction of epochal electoral change was reflected in the early studies of electoral behaviour which found that a combination of long-term factors such as social change and the break-up of traditional working-class communities, mass affluence and home ownership, the rise of white collar/service employment, and greater education were eroding the social bases of the Labour vote. These trends were exacerbated by Labour's poor image: it was seen as divided, wedded to outmoded policies, and identified with the increasingly unpopular trade unions.[56]

The skilled and semi-skilled working class were the electoral and ideological battleground. The C2/Ds were two-thirds of the electorate so 'The

Conservatives cannot rule unless they succeed in obtaining considerable support within this group'. In 1959 the Conservatives won about one-third, any losses might be sufficient to deny them office so it was 'no exaggeration to say that the Conservatives govern by permission of the working class and in particular of the lower non-manual worker'.[57] It was to the political and electoral advantage of the Conservative government to advance the material interests of these groups in the hope this would increase their propensity to vote Conservative.

Disgruntled Labour voters tended to abstain or vote Liberal rather than Conservative – they therefore represented both a threat and opportunity. This focused attention on the campaign as many voters did not make up their minds until late in the campaign and the campaign did influence Conservative turnout as the numbers intending to vote Conservative increased during the campaign. It made sense to lavish resources on campaigning, and the issues which influenced centre opinion related to confidence in the government. This meant a centrist appeal which stressed the Conservative ability to deliver an increased standard of living which augmented the tendency of social change to erode the Labour vote. Increased white-collar employment and blue-collar social mobility was destabilising the voter loyalties by creating powerful cross-pressures. CRD was sceptical about predictions of an inevitably middle-class society, but home ownership did have a major and lasting influence on voting. The relationship between housing and voting was particularly strong amongst the working-class; working class home owners being far more likely to vote Conservative than council tenants. Conservatives should appeal to young married couples, promote middle-class consumption patterns and living standards, and win the skilled and semi-skilled working class. To achieve this 'We must keep bright our "image" – competence, opportunity, home ownership, etc.'[58]

Down to 1962 Labour was in crisis over unilateral nuclear disarmament and the reform of Clause IV, disunity was ended by Gaitskell's opposition to membership of the EEC and after his death the new leader, Harold Wilson, proved very effective. After 1961 there was a marked deterioration in the government's by-election performance and the range of swing widened dramatically. Attention focused on the Liberals' performance which influenced the relative strength of the two major parties. Despite producing some creditable results the Liberals had won no seats since Torrington which was recovered by the Conservatives in 1959, but the Orpington by-election (March 1962) was seen as a referendum on the Macmillan government and an indicator of opinion in the Conservative electorate. Lubbock's victory with a majority of 7,855 meant Orpington was identified as a sea-change in politics and was to contribute materially to Macmillan's fall. The first effect of Orpington was that Macmillan made an unscheduled appearance at the Central Council meeting on 15 March to rally the party. Orpington

fuelled the growing conflict within the Cabinet which culminated in the disastrous reshuffle – 'The Night of the Long Knives' – on 13 July 1962.

The decay of the Macmillan government

When once asked what concerned him most as Prime Minister Macmillan
replied 'Events'. Between 1961 and 1964 the Conservative government was
overborne by a never-ending series of 'events' which led one Labour politician to comment to Macmillan's press secretary that if there was only one
banana skin in the country Macmillan would step on it.[59] There was also
something more fundamental at work between 1961 and 1964 in Conservative politics: the exhaustion of One Nation Conservatism. By the summer
of 1960 the economy was again verging on crisis, this time coupled with
an awareness of relative national economic decline compared to France and
Germany. Macmillan opted for a radical response: Britain's application to
join the EEC, incomes policy and indicative planning. Amory's replacement,
Selwyn Lloyd, had been appointed Chancellor precisely because he was
unlikely to pose a major challenge to his master.

Despite Churchill and Eden's early support for European unity, the consensus in the Conservative Party (and British politics) was that Britain's destiny lay wider than Western Europe. Although willing to co-operate on
defence Britain's Imperial/Commonwealth ties and the Special Relationship
with the United States were incompatible with integration in Western
Europe. So when the six-member European Coal and Steel Community
(founded in 1950 without British participation) began negotiations to create
a wider economic union Britain stood aside, despite American promptings,
withdrawing from the Messina Conference in November 1955. Despite
British attempts to undermine Messina the Six put considerable pressure on
Britain to participate but to no avail. The Treaty of Rome was signed in the
following year.[60]

By the end of 1960 the EEC seemed to be delivering substantial benefits
to its members. Britain's attempt to create an alternative free-trade zone
(EFTA) failed. At the Colonial Office Macleod built on Macmillan's 1960
Winds of Change speech in South Africa to accelerate Britain's disengagement from Empire to the fury of the nationalist–imperialist right and to the
chagrin of wider party sentiment. Economic difficulties and a growing sense
of national decline prompted Macmillan, a longstanding Europhile, to look
at EEC membership as a solution to Britain's difficulties. Equally, he strove
to maintain the Special Relationship, securing from President Kennedy at
Nassau in December 1962 an agreement to supply Britain with Polaris
nuclear weapons technology on very favourable terms. This infuriated de
Gaulle who was denied a similar deal and he cited Nassau as one of the reasons why Britain was not ready to join Europe.

In August 1961 Macmillan announced Britain's intention to apply for membership of the EEC. Coming one month after the July economic crisis there was a tendency to see the application as the result of the sterling crisis; this is not so. Macmillan had been considering this since late 1960 and regarded membership as an integral part of his domestic as well as foreign policy. The announcement produced a further outcry from the nationalist–imperialist right and was not popular in the party (or the country as a whole) who saw it as a betrayal of the 'kith-and-kin' in the White Commonwealth: newly independent colonies (for example Ghana and Nigeria) feared they would be excluded from the UK market. Edward Heath, Britain's chief negotiator, pursued his task with great skill and enthusiasm. Macmillan recognised de Gaulle posed the main obstacle and on 14 January 1963 he vetoed Britain's application, kicking away a major pillar of Macmillan's foreign and domestic policies. Furthermore, the application introduced the European virus into the Conservative bloodstream where it was to provoke so much dissension.

The catalyst for incomes policy was the July 1961 sterling crisis. In June the Treasury panicked, predicting the total loss of the reserves by Christmas, and Lloyd's budget of 25 July deflated the economy. In fact Lloyd's deflation was less than that sought by the Treasury, the Bank of England and the IMF at Chequers (20–22 July) and the advice he received ignored the fact that by the third quarter of 1961 there was a current account surplus and domestic demand was not rising quickly. There seemed, however, to be no other option other than deflation. One of the measures agreed at Chequers was a pay freeze. In 1960–1 wage increases were outstripping productivity growth and Lloyd had drawn attention to this in his budget speech. Support for incomes policy was boosted by the OEEC's report, *The Problem of Rising Prices* (May 1961), which argued that wage inflation was a major problem for the UK economy. Its call for an incomes policy had a great effect in the Treasury strengthening those who had long advocated a formal incomes policy as a replacement for CPPI which had done valuable research work but had little effect on wages. As part of the July measures Lloyd announced a pay pause for all public sector workers and those covered by wage councils which the private sector was expected to follow. This was introduced without any consultation with the unions and to soothe them Lloyd promised to work with both sides of industry to find a long-term solution to the problem of pay.[61] The pay pause was to end 1 April 1962 and the Cabinet debated at length what should follow. Despite the TUC's unfavourable response the Cabinet published in February 1962 the White Paper, *National Incomes Policy: The Next Step* (Cmnd 1626). This proposed a 'guiding light' of 2.5% and set out the criteria bargainers ought to take into account in wage negotiations with particular stress on financing pay out of productivity increases.

The White Paper proved controversial. The right regarded incomes policy as contrary to Conservative doctrine and a dangerous escalation of state intervention; the left as a weakening of social-Toryism. Even those Conservatives who accepted the need for a new approach feared the consequences of blatant interference with the unions. The granting of a wage increase to electricity workers which broke the guiding light whilst refusing a nurses wage claim brought the policy into further disrepute. Macmillan believed strongly that such a policy would only work if it was enshrined in institutions but that such institutions had to conform to the British circumstances: they should be non-coercive and independent of government.[62] Frustrated at the delay Macmillan held a meeting of ministers and civil servants from the Treasury and Ministry of Labour to thrash out the details. (One of the by-products of this was Lloyd's dismissal.) The result was the National Incomes Commission (NIC, or 'Nicky') announced on 26 July 1962. Like CPPI the NIC was composed of independent members to review pay matters and examine any settlement referred to it by government. It was not concerned with prices or profits. For this reason the TUC General Council would have nothing to do with it.

A second innovation was the National Economic Development Council (NEDC, or 'Neddy'). Both Macmillan and Lloyd were impressed by French indicative planning which appeared to underpin rapid economic growth: this was reinforced by the Federation of British Industries' (FBI) conference in November 1960 which considered a report, *The Next Five Years*, which expressed approval of planning. During 1961 Lloyd and the FBI met several times to discuss indicative planning. Macmillan, who had made his name as a Conservative planner in the 1930s, was attracted by this but did little to force the pace, leaving it to Lloyd. This hardened into a proposal for a tripartite body to discuss the promotion of economic growth. Again, the energising factor was the July measures; two weeks later Macmillan invited Lloyd to set up a joint planning body but it was not until 24 January 1962 that the TUC agreed to join NEDC and only then on condition that wages were excluded from the NEDC's discussions. Incomes did penetrate the NEDC's discussions by 1963, and more importantly the members quickly came to an agreement in February 1962 on the desirability of an annual growth rate of 4% for 1961–6.[63]

Macmillan's problems were not solely economic. His government endured a spate of security scandals which reached a crescendo with the Profumo Affair. Whatever their consequences for national security these episodes seemed symbolic of the government's decay and that Macmillan was personally out of touch with the modern world. In March 1961 the Portland Spy Ring was imprisoned and one year later George Blake, an SIS officer in Berlin who had betrayed both agents and operations, was sentenced to 42 years in prison. He escaped in 1966. In September 1962 a homosexual cipher clerk at the Admiralty, John Vassall, was arrested and was linked to the Civil Lord of the Admiralty, Tom Galbraith, who resigned. Galbraith was cleared by the Radcliffe Tribunal in April 1963 and returned to government. In January 1963 Kim Philby, the ex-head of the SIS Soviet Section and a Soviet mole who had been cleared by Macmillan in 1955 as the 'Third Man' in the Burgess and Maclean ring, defected to Moscow from Beirut where he had been working for the *Observer*.[64] Embarrassing though these cases were, far more damaging was the Profumo Affair which exploded in March 1963.

On 22 March John Profumo, the War Minister, made a statement to the House of Commons denying any impropriety with Christine Keeler, a 'call-girl'. Speculation mounted over the next three months and on 4 June Profumo resigned admitting he had lied to the House of Commons. This was more than a sex scandal as Keeler had been conducting an affair (though not at the same time as Profumo) with a Captain Ivanov, the Soviet Naval Attache in London and an intelligence officer, and the Security Service had sought to use Keeler in an entrapment operation of which Profumo had no knowledge. Profumo had met Keeler at a party at Lord Astor's estate at Clivden and stories of the proceedings at these and other high society parties titillated the nation over the summer of 1963.[65]

Though this episode damaged the government, Lord Hailsham was correct when he fulminated at Robert McKenzie in a BBC interview on 17 June that 'A great party is not to be brought down because of a scandal by a woman of easy virtue and a proven liar'. The government's problem was that the Profumo Affair encapsulated a perception of national decay and decadence in the highest reaches of society, a perception eloquently expressed in William Rees-Mogg's editorial in *The Times*, 'It IS a Moral Issue'. Eleven years of Conservative rule, Rees-Mogg contended, had spiritually and psychologically drained the country producing a general crisis: 'Today [the people] are faced with a flagging economy, an uncertain future and an end of the illusion that Britain's greatness could be measured by the so-called independence of its so-called deterrent. All this may seem far from Mr Profumo but his admissions could be the last straw'. Rees-Mogg's editorial ended with a thinly veiled appeal to the 'earnest and serious men' (predecessors of the 'men in the grey suits') to think of the country and drop Macmillan.[66] Perhaps most seriously the Profumo Affair encouraged people to laugh at and deride their betters.

The security scandals unsettled an already restive 1922 Committee. Rumours of disaffection with Macmillan were rife and the Whips estimated 60%–70% of MPs preferred Maudling (then Chancellor) as Prime Minister. The backbench felt the government had handled the Profumo crisis badly and in the debate on 17 June, twenty-seven Conservative MPs abstained. Nigel Birch twisted the knife quoting from Browning's *Leader Lost*, '... let him never come back to us!/There would be doubt, hesitation and pain,/Forced praise on our part – the glimmer of twilight,/Never glad confident morning again!' Commenting on Macmillan's performance in the debate his press secretary wrote: 'Alas, the loss of zest is all too obvious. The substance is good, but the manner weary and dispirited: and here and there he tried to interpolate and lost the thread'.[67]

The single most serious blow sustained by the government was self-inflicted. The Cabinet purge of Friday 13 July 1962 – 'The Night of the Long Knives' – seriously eroded Macmillan's authority. Macmillan had been contemplating a major restructuring to breathe new life into his government for some time giving it a younger, more youthful image, a project known as the 'New Approach'. The core was the replacement of Selwyn Lloyd as Chancellor who, Macmillan believed, was burnt out after his long stint at the Foreign Office and Treasury. The suddenness and scale of the butchery has obscured the politics of the reshuffle and the underlying debate over policy. Between April and July Lloyd and Macmillan had become increasingly divided over economic policy, with Macmillan pushing for an incomes policy and reflation and Lloyd resisting. By 6–7 July the Prime Minister had decided to appoint Reginald Maudling as Chancellor and remove six other members of the Cabinet. Lloyd had no inkling of the impending axe stroke.[68]

Press speculation (fuelled by an indiscrete comment by Butler over a convivial lunch with Lord Rothermere, proprietor of the *Daily Mail*, on 11 July), the Leicester by-election (where the Conservatives came third), and difficulties with the Common Market negotiations led Macmillan, on the advice of Martin Redmayne, the Chief Whip, to push the changes through in one day. Three of the seven (Mills, Maclay, and Watkinson) went quietly, the latter had already stated a desire to go back into industry. Hill went quietly but made his disquiet abundantly clear, complaining that what he objected to was not what was done, but how. Neither Eccles (who thought he was being summoned to be appointed Chancellor) nor Kilmuir went quietly and in his memoirs Kilmuir painted a picture of a Prime Minister panicking: 'It astonished me that a man who had kept his head under the most severe stresses and strains should lose both nerve and judgement in this way'. The interview with Lloyd was very difficult with Macmillan repeating frequently that there was a conspiracy against him, implying most improbably Lloyd was a leading participant.[69] The political fallout from the Night of the Long Knives did not seem too severe once the initial shockwave had passed. Birch penned a venomous letter to *The Times* and Jeremy Thorpe spoke his couplet on self-sacrifice, but more serious was the reaction when Macmillan entered the Commons on the Tuesday after the purge. 'It was chilling and daunting', wrote Harold Evans, 'especially since it had been preceded by resounding cheers for Selwyn on taking his seat. This was the first clear indication that the changes – or at any rate the method of making them – had not pleased the backbenchers'. Macmillan never admitted he had made a mistake in sacking Lloyd but did concede that the affair could have been better managed. Whilst Kilmuir and Eccles became members of the anti-Macmillan club, Lloyd, to Macmillan's discomfort, remained a loyal back-bench government supporter. An attempt by Nigel Birch to muster 40–50 abstentions in the vote on the Opposition censure motion in the 26 July debate failed but the damage had been done. Indeed, never glad confident morning again.[70]

The reshuffle transformed the government. Young ministers were promoted but paradoxically this only served to highlight Macmillan's anachronistic image. The policy core of the reshuffle was economic management, so Lloyd's replacement was of enormous significance for the government and the future of Conservatism. Although Maudling and Lloyd entered Parliament after the war (in 1950 and 1945 respectively) they came from different political generations. Lloyd was a conservative, conscientious member of the professional provincial middle classes; Maudling was a professional politician who had entered the party at the elite level, enjoying the patronage of Butler (as one of his CRD backroom boys) and the kudos of being one of Churchill's speech-writers. Temperamentally, Maudling was a gambler and ideologically of the pragmatic-left of the party and was therefore likely to be more congenial to the Prime Minister. Maudling wholeheartedly endorsed Macmillan's basic principle that the purpose of economic policy was to make people better off and that economic orthodoxy held back growth.[71] The Prime Minister had for the first time an instinctively expansionist Chancellor precisely at the time when the price of expansion was being questioned in both government and party.

Growing economic and political difficulties eroded Macmillan's position and Lloyd's precipitate removal strengthened doubts about inflationary economic expansion. At the time of the July purge John Hare, the Minister of Labour, shocked by Lloyd's removal, threatened to resign as he too had been a keen supporter of the Chancellor's anti-inflation policies. As Minister of Labour Hare was a key figure in the government and was well respected by Macmillan so his resignation would cause severe damage. When he threatened to resign if Lloyd's removal signalled a weakening of the fight against inflation Macmillan moved quickly to reassure him. Hare's qualms were shared by many in the government and the party, and after July 1962 they acted as a constraint on Macmillan and Maudling whose main task was to break out of the stop-go cycle without boosting domestic inflation. Lloyd's reluctance to countenance expansion remained and the trust he enjoyed amongst the international financial community ruled out any dramatic policy innovations. A significant shift risked a sterling crisis which Macmillan was, for obvious reasons, determined to avoid. Thus, 'It was important to stress continuity, and to make it clear that while there would be changes of policy, time would be taken about them, and they would be evolutionary rather than revolutionary'.[72] That Maudling became Chancellor after eleven years of Conservative government meant he could hardly repudiate its policy legacy and as he was appointed half-way through the life of the 1959 Parliament limited his room for manoeuvre.

Maudling's economic management was more conservative than has been allowed but the ticking of the electoral clock encouraged the risk-taker in him. Not until November did he sanction purchase tax cuts of some £45m, about half what could have been justified, and some reductions were held over until January 1963. Maudling's position was complicated by a sharp rise in unemployment and his advisors thought he ought to have been more expansionist in 1962–3 while remaining pessimistic about the economy's long-run fortunes. There was, for example, scepticism in the Treasury about the achievability of the NEDC's 4% growth target. Although originally unenthusiastic about NEDC Maudling believed it had important communication and education functions, and as an expansionist he was attracted by the 4% target. By early 1963 Maudling had come to a decision:

> we went for expansion, quite deliberately, with our eyes wide open, recognising the dangers. The prize to be obtained, the prospect of expansion without inflation, the end of stop-go and a break-out from the constrictions of the past, was a glittering one ... the whole policy was deliberate, calculated and coherent. No one could guarantee success, but the chances were high, and the alternatives were drab and depressing.[73]

Unemployment reached 4% in the winter and the 1963 budget was reflationary and sought to win union support for incomes policy. As in 1959, the 1963 budget was badly timed for the economy was recovering and the phased introduction of the tax reliefs delivered a series of stimuli to an overheating economy. A reaction was inevitable. The 1964 budget, by which time Macmillan was no longer Prime Minister and an election was looming, raised taxation by £100m and was portrayed as a middle course between those advocating deflation to attack inflation and those seeking to maintain 'the dash for growth'.

In July Macmillan told the 1922 Committee of his intention of leading the Conservatives into the next election. Macmillan's brokering of the Nuclear Test Ban Treaty in July 1963 was a personal triumph which did something to mitigate the fallout from Profumo's resignation. However, Macmillan was overcome by a lassitude which was the first sign of his prostate trouble. By the summer of 1963 Macmillan's thoughts were turning to his successor as troubles began to mount: Hailsham and Maudling were the front-runners.[74] Macmillan's indecision was resolved by his sudden illness on 7–8 October 1963. Macmillan chaired the Cabinet on the 8th and his ministers, attuned to his hypochondria, recognised something serious was afoot. In considerable discomfort, unable to rely on his own doctor, and convinced he was seriously ill (possibly with cancer) he took the decision to resign (9 October) and enter hospital for an operation (10 October). Macmillan immediately regretted his decision as even in 1963 prostate problems were readily treatable and both Eisenhower and de Gaulle functioned effectively with this complaint.

The leadership battle of 1963 is one of the strangest and most controversial events in Conservative and British politics. The succession crisis (10–18 October) called into question both Conservative policy and its internal processes and was to have revolutionary consequences. Macmillan's first choice as successor was Lord Hailsham who announced he was renouncing his peerage to run for the leadership. On 31 July the Peerage Act received the Royal Assent which allowed hereditary peers to renounce their peerages within one year of the Act becoming law. If Macmillan had gone in early July neither Hailsham nor Home would have been contenders. Hailsham, supported by Randolph Churchill in a conspicuous mirroring of American practice, sought to turn the Blackpool party conference into a nominating convention. This backfired badly. Hailsham was not popular with MPs and was regarded by many as temperamentally unstable and his bid petered out. Of the younger possibilities Macleod had infuriated the right with his colonial policies, which, with his intellect and refusal to tolerate fools gladly, would have made him an unusual choice. Maudling had been mentioned as a leader during the summer but his star waned as his policies worried many MPs and party members as dangerously inflationary. His youth and apparent laziness also counted against him and he ruined his chances by a very poor conference address. This left Butler. In many respects Butler was the obvious candidate: twice he had acted as Prime Minister and in the July 1962 reshuffle he was designated Deputy Prime Minister with the grand but meaningless title of First Secretary of State. Butler was the senior ministerial figure and the leading intellectual figure in postwar Conservatism. The problem was that Macmillan (and many backbenchers) would not have Butler at any price, as Butler himself recognised and was so informed by both the Chief Whip and Chairman of the 1922. Having lost in 1957 Butler appears to have convinced himself that he did not really want the leadership; his vacillations over Suez and a long series of indiscretions had created the impression of a man unsuitable for the supreme office. This prompted Macmillan to contemplate throwing his hat back into the ring but by then it was too late, the only way forward was a carefully managed consultation exercise to produce a unity candidate.

Macmillan's support for the 14th Earl of Home seems strange at first. Home had left the Commons in 1951 (and had not made much of an impact when there) for the Lords, he was a foreign affairs specialist, and was not telegenic. Home fitted neither the new age of televisual politics nor the modernisation ethos, but his absence from the Commons meant he was identified with no faction and his foreign policy expertise meant he was neither a deflationist nor an inflationist. The soundings were entrusted to Dilhorne (Lord Chancellor) who would consult the Cabinet, Martin Redmayne (the Chief Whip) would consult ministers outside the Cabinet and the backbench, Lord St Aldwyn would canvass active peers, and Lord Poole (joint-Party Chairman) would consult the party in the country. The results passed back to Macmillan indicated a preponderance of first choices for Home as each candidate had as many partisans as opponents. Some 300 MPs favoured Home, unsurprisingly the Lords backed Home by two to one, the constituencies split 60/40 for Hailsham and Butler but the speed of Poole's consultation rendered this unreliable. There was, however, a feeling they would swing behind Home. Most controversy attached to Dilhorne's sounding of the Cabinet which can be best described as eccentric (Macleod, for example, was listed as a first voter for Home whereas he was a Butler supporter). Dilhorne's soundings, eccentric or otherwise, indicated Home commanded a majority of Cabinet support so Macmillan recommended the Queen send for Home and invite him to form a government. This was a significant formulation as the emergence of Home produced disquiet and an incipient revolt which eventually faded away when only Powell and Macleod refused to serve under Home. Butler could, perhaps, have scuppered Home's chances by refusing to serve but, as Macmillan predicted, he lacked the killer instinct. On 18 October Macmillan ceased to be Prime Minister.[75]

A sea-change in Conservative politics?

The period between the October 1964 general election and Heath's election as leader in July 1965 is pivotal in recent Conservative politics. It marks the end of the 'Eton/Brigade of Guards' circle's dominance over the leadership. Electing the leader allowed the rise of the lower middle classes (symbolised by Heath and then Thatcher) to the leadership which had consequences for party policy and doctrine. Neo-Liberal ideas had, despite the dominance of One Nation Conservatism, remained the basic values of the party grassroots and between 1961 and 1964 success turned into failure, discontent with One Nation Conservatism flowered in opposition. Heath's election as leader signified seismic social and ideological change in the Conservative Party of a type not seen since Disraeli.

After disclaiming his peerage Home was elected for the safe seat of Kinross and West Perthshire on 8 November. Away from the febrile atmosphere of succession politics Home seemed a peculiar choice (the most unusual political appointment, it was said, since Caligula appointed his horse a Senator), and many Conservatives agreed with Macleod that it was a sad comment that amongst 363 MPs no successor to Macmillan could be found.

Nevertheless, Home had several valuable qualities: he was patently honest and aware of his shortcomings. He was right of centre, the first Conservative leader to be so since Chamberlain, but he inherited a very difficult political legacy. Electioneering dominated Home's government. An election had to be called no later than October 1964, Maudling's advice was to go in February/March and the budget was framed with a May/June election in mind. Maudling's advice was based on the premiss 'There was bound to be a crunch period some time ... the most likely time was the autumn when by tradition sterling always came under considerable pressure'.[76] On the other hand Home was unknown to the electorate and the government was facing a major internal battle over the abolition of Retail Price Maintenance (RPM) which prevented price cutting but whose abolition would hit severely small shop-keepers who were disproportionately represented in Conservative ranks.

The President of the Board of Trade, Edward Heath, had the task of reconciling the Conservative shopocracy with economic efficiency. This proved difficult and Heath solved the problem by ramming the bill through the Cabinet and the House of Commons in the teeth of furious opposition. Twenty Conservatives voted against the bill and 23 abstained, making this the biggest Conservative rebellion since the 1943 Catering Wages Bill. The bill received its third reading on 13 May but Heath made many lasting enemies and the row did the government's public standing no good at all.[77] With these and other difficulties party managers counselled delay in calling an election, advice which Home accepted.

As Prime Minister Home was never comfortable in the Commons and never got to grips with Wilson ('Smart Alec versus Dull Alec') who became Labour leader after Gaitskell's death in January 1963. Home concentrated on speaking around the country and getting himself known and from May 1964 he reduced Labour's poll lead by half. After a brief honeymoon period (November–January) when he enjoyed a huge personal approval Home managed to project a competent image, and from the spring his government's ratings improved. Home worked hard on his television image and recovered some of the ground lost in Macmillan's later years. Nonetheless, there was a perception that Home's government lacked a 'big idea' and was out of tune with contemporary society.

In the early 1960s numerous institutions were challenged and ridiculed as old fashioned. In 1961 the review *Beyond the Fringe*, *Private Eye* (a satirical and frequently irreverent magazine), and BBC TV's *That Was The Week That Was* challenged many of the assumptions of British society. The bookstalls were groaning under the weight of books such as Michael Shanks's *The Stagnant Society* and Penguin's *What's Wrong With ...* series which argued that Britain was sliding into decline. The political personas of Macmillan and Home seemed symptomatic of this climate and since becoming Labour leader Wilson had consciously and with great skill identified his party with modernisation. Whatever the Conservative Party's unsuitability for bearing the gospel of modernisation, it was a message it could not ignore. Heath projected himself as the face of Conservative modernisation but found (as in the case of RPM) that while there was broad agreement on the need for modernisation specific proposals generated massive opposition. Only towards the end of the Home government was modernisation consciously pursued in the creation of the Industrial Training Boards, the establishment of the 'Little Neddies' for individual industries, and regional policy overhauled. Again Heath was the central figure. Home and his party managers opted for an appeal based on the continuation of prosperity under the Conservatives. On 15 September Home announced the election and the Conservative manifesto, *Prosperity with a Purpose*, largely restated the appeal of 1959. Home nearly pulled off a major coup: not until the declaration of the Brecon and Radnor result eighteen hours after the polls closed did Labour have its majority. Labour polled 44.1 per cent of the vote (317 seats), the Conservatives 43.8 per cent (304), and the Liberals 11.2 per cent (13) giving them a majority of 13 over the Conservatives but only 4 overall.

Defeat lead to a post-mortem part of which focused on the leader. As Prime Minister Home's shortcomings in the Commons bear-pit could be portrayed as lofty disdain stemming from a desire not to besmirch his high office. As leader of the Opposition, on the other hand, Home would be expected to 'mix it' on the floor of the House of Commons against an accomplished street-fighter. The unanimous backbench view was that whatever Home's sterling qualities they were not those of an Opposition leader. Labour's narrow majority meant a second election would come soon but not immediately and by July 1964 pressure was building up for a change of leader. The manner of Home's emergence seemed calculated to emphasise the Conservative Party's outdatedness and unfitness to govern in a rapidly changing world. A more severe defeat had been avoided only because of the electorate's fear of the unknown, but if Labour could dispel these fears serious defeat in the next election was facing the Conservatives. So, to limit the damage the Conservative Party, like the country, had to be modernised.

The decline of the Macmillan government and Home's defeat in 1964 are an example of the degenerative tendencies of long-serving governments. That long-serving governments degenerate seems counter-intuitive: they can draw on a fund of experience; fatigue can be balanced by long familiarity with the process of government and so on. However, a number of 'symptoms', or 'indicators' apply to governments in decline.[78] First, degenerating governments display obsessive sensitivity to the press. Both Macmillan's memoirs and those of his press secretary reveal such an obsession which might be the inevitable consequence of Macmillan's decision to cultivate an 'image' which first made ('Supermac') and then unmade ('Edwardian duffer') his government. Home was a victim of this as his term as leader was dominated by the interconnected problems of his poor image and winning the next election.

Second, degenerating governments prefer foreign to domestic triumphs. A glance at Macmillan's voluminous memoirs reveals the extent to which he emphasised foreign adventures and if Home had won in 1964 there seems little doubt that he, as a foreign affairs specialist who confessed he knew little about domestic (and especially economic) policy would have followed the same path. Macmillan did enjoy some major foreign triumphs (for example, the Nassau Agreement on Polaris, decolonisation, the Test Ban Treaty) but he also sustained some serious defeats (notably over the EEC) and, in any case, the issues on which governments are judged are domestic economic issues.

Third, degenerating governments have a high level of mutual suspicion amongst their members. This was clearly revealed in the July Cabinet purge and the emergence of Home as leader. By 1963 Macmillan was obsessed by non-existent Cabinet plots and panicked, Home's emergence brought out into the open the resentments of those who thought themselves to be 'outside' the 'magic circle' in Conservative politics.

Fourth, degenerating governments are unable to think strategically and are dominated by the primacy of the immediate response. This is particularly interesting in Macmillan's case because as Prime Minister he was concerned his government should have a strategic vision. His difficulty was that he had neither the resources (particularly political will) nor the room to implement that vision as events crowded in on his government. Implementation of key aspects of his strategic vision, such as EEC membership or incomes policy, depended on factors (de Gaulle and the TUC) which were outside his control. Once these external factors had neutralised the strategy only the immediate remained. In Home's case, the imminence of the election and the circumstances of his emergence, meant he had no option other than to concentrate on the short term. Only after electoral defeat could Home begin the process of reconsidering party doctrine.

Fifth, a degenerating government tends to make speedy concessions to powerful interest groups. The most visible manifestation of this was the apparent rise of trade union power. This was not a new phenomenon, dating as it did from Monckton's appointment as Minister of Labour, but by the early 1960s the unions had become identified as a major factor in national decline. They had lost public sympathy and many Conservatives were demanding legislative changes. These sentiments seemed to be ignored by a government in thrall to the TUC, making concession after concession to the unions, and refusing to grasp the nettle of union power.

Sixth, in degenerating governments ministers tend to identify with their ministries and prefer bureaucratic to party politics. Despite ministerial changes, the lack of a strategic vision means long-serving governments are dominated by departmentalism with ministers regarding party tasks as a chore, second-best to the real business of governing. Thus, a gap between government and party emerges, with poor communication breeding mutual suspicion.

These factors are invariably complicated by two others. Degenerating governments bear the burden of an accumulation of poor economic decision-making generated by engineering pre-election booms to maintaining 'the feel-good factor'. The consequences of these decisions cannot be blamed on their predecessors. The Chancellorships of Heathcoat-Amory, Lloyd, and Maudling, as well as the expansionist-inflationist sentiments of Macmillan, provide many examples of the political management of the economy. This cannot be blamed entirely on Macmillan: he was the inheritor of a legacy of both bastardised Keynesianism and political manipulation but neither he nor his government could conceive of any alternative as his conflict with Thorneycroft in 1957 showed. A second problem is the primacy of the electoral. Long-serving governments are long-serving because they have won a series of elections: that is the object of politics in a liberal democracy. Over time electorally driven economic management distorts the economy which generates electoral discontent, forcing governments into a frantic search for panaceas (incomes policy, planning, EEC membership). A long-serving government's tendency to adopt panaceas is encouraged by the intangible but undeniable fact that such governments are perceived by the electorate as 'boring'. The effect of change in 'the climate of the times' is not easy to demonstrate but this was an important factor in the government's demise. Long-serving governments are squeezed between two sets of imperatives: securing re-election and maintaining economic growth.

In mass democratic politics there is a tension between the preference of the party membership for policy to be based on party principles, and the perception of party leaders that to do so would endanger their chances of re-election. This assumes the views of the party are more extreme than both the party leadership and the electorate. In the case of the governments of 1951–64 electoral success kept the grassroots in check, allowing ministers to pursue policies disliked by their supporters but these restraints are removed by electoral defeat. Opposition increases the influence of the party and produces demands for a fundamental overhaul of the policies held to be responsible for defeat.

It is not easy to answer the question: to what extent did the party endorse the type of Conservatism pursued by its leaders in government? The obvious starting point would be the motions submitted to, and the decisions of, the annual Conference. The language of motions, the content of the decisions, and the delegates' voting patterns could be used to chart changing

133

party sentiments. Unfortunately this methodology cannot be applied to the Conservative Conference as votes are seldom taken and the motions selected for debate are chosen carefully to maximise internal consensus. Dissent is difficult to quantify and the Conservative Conference is not in any case a policy-making body. Its decisions are not binding on the leadership and it is purely advisory.[79]

The large number of motions submitted cannot be neatly categorised into ideological categories. The most rigorous published study categorises motions into four groups: libertarian/right, collectivist/left, collectivist/right, and libertarian/left, together with a large residual category. With the exception of the first category no attempt is made to define rigorously these categories and the libertarian/left contains few resolutions in this period.[80] This lack of definitional rigour reflects the imprecision of Conservative ideology but despite the data's limitations it does offer an insight into grassroots attitudes between 1945 and 1965.

The libertarian/right category is the most important as this corresponds closely to Selsdon Man and the New Right. This embraces individual freedom, minimal government, low direct taxation, free markets, the sanctity of property, and the rule of law. Neither reject the use of state power to secure these ends. Many of the preferences of the libertarian/right were accepted by the party leadership even if their actions in government seemed contradictory. The numbers fell in 1961 but peaked in 1965 and this suggests a growing interest in attempting to influence the climate of opinion within the party and perhaps a decline of deference amongst the membership. Whether this increase in activism reflects a growing sociological divide between a lower-middle class, even petit bourgeois, membership attracted to neo-Liberal ideas and upper-middle/upper-class leadership stratum wedded to One Nation Conservatism cannot be answered without further detailed research. More important are the ideological currents revealed by these motions.[81]

Neo-Liberal ideas and motions formed the basis of grassroots sentiment after 1945. From the mid-1950s neo-Liberal motions concentrated on economic management, especially the reduction of public spending and taxation. On taxation, public spending, and nationalisation neo-liberal sentiments were dominant throughout this period even though they were not invariably accompanied by demands for the unfettered application of the laws of supply and demand and deregulation. The one exception was trade union reform. Neo-Liberal ideas were dominant in policy areas – taxation, public spending, and union reform – which were central to Heath's recasting of Conservative doctrine after 1965. It is not the case that a neo-Liberal coalition was waiting fully formed within the party held in check by a sociologically and ideologically unrepresentative One Nation leadership stratum.

Neo-Liberal ideas were dominant in some key policy areas by the early 1960s but the leadership had no difficulty in resisting their influence.

Nevertheless, these ideas were the most important single ideological current within the party and if they were restrained by being in government, leaving government loosened these restraints.[82] Planted between 1940 and 1951 the seeds of change were germinating during Macmillan's dominance, indeed his dominance provided the crucial fertiliser. In response to the Attlee government a young engineer working in the Tyneside shipyards resolved to enter politics 'to see socialism decisively reversed'. He thought the nationalised industries an ideological and commercial disaster, he regarded the growth of trade union power as making effective industrial management impossible and promoting inefficiency and low productivity, and he resented high taxation as a disincentive to effort and risk-taking. In 1955 he stood for Parliament and was elected MP for Cirencester and Tewkesbury in 1959 (the same year in which a certain young woman was elected MP for Finchley), in the Commons he became progressively disillusioned with a Conservative government which did nothing about nationalisation, bolstered union power, increased state spending, and interfered in the economy. In the 1960s this young MP, Nicholas Ridley, became a leading member of a small band of Conservatives determined to try to reverse the post-war collectivist tide. The Conservative governments of 1951–64 came to provide a bench-mark of what Conservatism should not be.[83]

The accumulation of failure and disillusionment culminated in defeat in 1964 and 1966. Even before 1963–4 there was a widespread but inchoate discontent within the Conservative Party, neo-Liberal ideas remained very strong at the grassroots and were becoming stronger with every policy failure. Opposition, especially after a long period in government, inevitably generates a mood of introspection and criticism which inevitably focused on those leaders and policies thought responsible for defeat. This laid the foundations for the remaking of Conservative policy under Edward Heath. Thus began a new era in British and Conservative politics.

Notes

1 J. Colville, *The Fringes of Power. Downing Street Diaries, 1939–55* (London: Hodder and Stoughton, 1985), 29 March 1955.
2 *M S Woolton 3*, 139, Woolton to Eden, 8 March 1955.
3 Colville, *Fringes of Power*, 4 April 1955.
4 W. Clark, *From Three Worlds* (London: Sidgwick and Jackson, 1986), p. 148.
5 Earl of Avon, *The Memoirs of Sir Anthony Eden. Full Circle* (London: Cassell, 1960), p. 267, and CRD 2/21/5 Gallup Polls, 14 June 1954, had discerned little or no long-term trend in favour of the Conservatives.
6 *CRD 2/21/5* Untitled Memorandum, Sewill to Fraser, and Gallup Polls, 2 December 1955, and *CRD 2/28/4* Stebbings to Fraser, 9 June 1955.
7 *CRD 2/28/4*, B. Sewill, The General Election 1955, 8 June 1955.
8 *CRD 2/28/54*, General Director's Report to Eden, 22 June 1955.

9 J. Morgan (ed.), *The Backbench Diaries of Richard Crossman* (London: Jonathan Cape, 1981), 15 July 1955 and *CRD 2/28/54* P. B. Bunyan, The British General Election 1955, Appendix: Personal Observations, p. 3.

10 *CRD 2/28/4* M. Fraser, Report on the General Election 1955. Policy and Administration General Assessment of the Campaign, 17 June 1955.

11 Clark, *From Three Worlds*, p. 156 and the *Daily Telegraph*, 3 January 1956. The editorial was written by Donald McLachlan.

12 Clark, *From Three Worlds*, pp. 161–2.

13 The diplomatic and military side of the Suez crisis are covered authoritatively by K. Kyle, *Suez* (London: Weidenfeld & Nicolson, 1991) and W. Scott-Lucas, *Divided We Stand. Britain, the US and the Suez Crisis* (London: Hodder and Stoughton, 1991). The best, indeed only, study of the domestic consequences of Suez is L. D. Epstein, *British Politics in the Suez Crisis* (Pall Mall, 1964).

14 C. P. Snow, *Corridors of Power* (Harmondsworth: Penguin, 1966), p. 112. For the bureaucratic reaction to Suez see P. Hennessy, *Whitehall* (London: Fontana, 1990), pp. 163–8.

15 Nicolson, *Diaries and Letters 1945–1962* (London: Collins, 1966), 8 November 1956, Kyle, *Suez*, p. 304 and pp. 438–9 and *Foreign Relations of the United States 1955–57, Volume XVII The Suez Crisis* (Washington: Government Printing Office 1990), Doc 626, Memorandum of Discussion at the 305th Meeting of the National Security Council, 30 November 1956, p. 1221.

16 L. Johnman, 'Defending the pound: The Economics of the Suez Crisis, 1956', in A. Gorst, L. Johnman and W. Scott-Lucas (eds.), *Post-War Britain 1945–64. Themes and Perspectives* (London: Frances Pinter/ICBH, 1989), pp. 166–88 and D. Kunz, 'The Importance of Having Money: The Economic Diplomacy of the Suez Crisis', in W. Roger Louis and R. Owen (eds.), *Suez 1956. The Crisis and Its Consequences* (Oxford: Clarendon Press, 1989), pp. 215–32. One of the mysteries of Suez is Macmillan's failure to safeguard sterling in early September (as the French did with the franc) by, for example, drawing on the UK's funds in the IMF. The most likely explanation is that he thought it inconceivable his 'old friend' President Eisenhower would oppose actively an invasion of Egypt. If counter-measures had been taken it would have been much more difficult to remove Eden.

17 Lord Beloff, 'The Crisis and the Consequences for the British Conservative Party', in Roger Louis and Owen, *Suez 1956*, pp. 319–34.

18 W. Scott-Lucas, 'Suez, the Americans and the Overthrow of Anthony Eden', *LSE Quarterly*, 1 (3) (Autumn 1987), pp. 227–54.

19 *FRUS 1955–57 XVII*, Doc 593 Aldrich to Department of State, 19 November 1956 and R. A. Butler, *The Art of the Possible*, p. 194.

20 J. Ramsden, 'Rab did sometimes miss tricks which Macmillan managed to take', *The Listener*, 19 March 1987 and A. Howard, *RAB. The Life of R. A. Butler* (London: Macmillan, 1987), pp. 24–41. Butler dates the meeting in early December.

21 Earl of Kilmuir, *Political Adventure* (London: Weidenfeld and Nicolson, 1964), pp. 285–6. Butler estimated three ministers, Monckton, Patrick Buchan-Hepburn, and James Stuart supported him. Thereafter they left the government. Lord Moran, *Winston Churchill. The Struggle for Survival, 1940–1965* (London:

Sphere Books, 1966), 22 November 1956 and Colville, *Fringes of Power*, Appendix II, p. 721. Macmillan was also President Eisenhower's favourite for the succession.

22 Lord Egremont (John Wyndham), *Wyndham and Children First* (London: Macmillan, 1971), p. 170 and H. Macmillan, *Riding the Storm 1956–1959*, pp. 193–200.

23 *5s H C Debs 567*, 16 May 1957, col 698 and Macmillan, *Riding The Storm*, 15 May 1957, p. 238.

24 *LAB 43/179* discusses the political implications for the management of organised labour of the 1952 budget.

25 *PREM 1/314*, David Gammans to Lord Swinton, 11 August and Swinton to Gammans, 21 August 1952.

26 *CAB 129/53* C (53) 276, 9 October 1953, Wages and Prices and *CAB 129,65* C (54) 21, 18 January 1954, Wages and Prices. See *LAB 43/243* Monckton to Butler, 14 July and Butler to Monckton, 20 July 1955 for Butler's scepticism.

27 *CAB 129/76* (55) 123 CP 55 (65), 9 July 1955 The Economic Situation. Memorandum by Chancellor of the Exchequer and Avon, *Memoirs. Full Circle*, p. 316.

28 *CAB 134/1273* Industrial Relations Committee 2nd Meeting, 28 July 1955.

29 *T234/91* 23 March 1955. This need for the indirect approach was the basis of Butler's paper of 9 July 1955. Sir Robert Hall, the Government's Economic Adviser, argued the problem since 1945 was over – full employment and that 2% unemployment would greatly reduce inflationary pressures but which could not be plausibly described as mass unemployment. *CAB 134/1273* IRR (55) 9, Full Employment and Wages Policy, 23 July 1955.

30 *CAB 134/1273* Economic Publicity and Wage Policy, July 1955 and *T234/91* E. P. Wright to Burke Trend, 4 August 1955, Industrial Relations Education.

31 *T234/91* Informal Group on Industrial Relations, First Meeting, 4 August 1955 and *T234/91* Trend to Bridges, 1 September 1955. From this point the draft was taken out of the hands of the informal group.

32 G. Goodman, *The Awkward Warrior* (London: Davis Poynter, 1979), p. 134.

33 *PREM 11/188* E. Maude to F. A. Bishop, 27 June 1957, Thorneycroft to Macmillan, 15 July 1957 and *5s H C Debs 524*, 25 July 1957, cols 650–1.

34 Interview with Lord Thorneycroft.

35 *The Times*, 21 July 1957.

36 *CAB 129/88* C (57) 194, 1 September 1957, The Economic Situation (Memorandum by the Prime Minister), and *CAB 129/88* C (57) 195, 7 September 1957, The Economic Situation (Memorandum by the Chancellor).

37 *CAB 129/89* C (57) 225, 5 October 1957, Explaining the Economic Situation and *CAB 129/89* C (57) 286, 11 November 1957, Wages.

38 Interview with Lord Thorneycroft and A. Horne, *Macmillan 1957–1986 Vol. II of the Official Biography* (London: Macmillan, 1989), p. 73. Powell's role as evil genius has been denied by Powell (the *Spectator*, 24 April 1971) and Thorneycroft who was adamant that he resigned on a matter of principle and was proved correct by later events. See P. Cosgrave, *The Lives of Enoch Powell* (London: Bodley Head, 1989), pp. 158–60 for Powell's account of this event.

39 Lord Egremont *Wyndham and Children First*, p. 179 and M. Cockerell, *Live from Number 10. The Inside Story of Prime Ministers and Television* (London: Faber and Faber, 1988), p. 57.

40 *The Times*, 7 January and 8 January 1958.

41 *CRD 2/21/5* Rochdale By-Election, 27 February 1958 and *CRD 2/21/5* Notes on National Opinion Poll Reports, 27 February 1958, p. 3.

42 *CRD 2/28/4* General Director's Report to Anthony Eden, 22 June 1955, p. 2 and Cockerell, *Live from Number 10*, chapters 3 and 4.

43 Macmillan, *Riding the Storm*, p. 411 and diary entry 22 February 1958, p. 473 and *CRD 2/21/5* Draft Report on Rochdale, February 1958.

44 *CRD 2/21/5* James Douglas and Michael Fraser, 31 March 1958, Macmillan, *Riding The Storm*, p. 719 and *CRD 2/21/5* Gallup Polls and the Liberals, 17 September 1958.

45 *CRD 2/21/5* Public Opinion, 21 February 1958, p. 2.

46 *PREM 11/2248* Michael Fraser, Some Thoughts On The Present Situation, 20 September 1957. See also, Horne, *Macmillan Volume 2*, p. 62.

47 *CAB 129/88* C (57) 194, 1 September 1957, The Economic Situation.

48 *CAB 129/88* C (57), 7 September 1957, The Economic Situation.

49 Interview with Lord Thorneycroft.

50 *The Times*, 14 June 1958 and Morgan, *Backbench Diaries of Richard Crossman*, 11 July 1958. Macmillan, *Riding The Storm*, p. 721.

51 *CRD 2/12/5* Geoffrey Dear to Michael Fraser, Report on Public Opinion, 9 October 1958.

52 Macmillan, *Riding the Storm*, p. 723 (diary 24 October 1958), p. 727, (diary 16 January 1959) and p. 730.

53 Lord Hailsham, *A Sparrow's Flight* (London: Collins 1990), p. 323, *CRD 4/8/104* Hailsham to Constituency Chairmen, 24 April 1959. For Macmillan's inspired use of television see Cockerell, *Live from Number 10*, pp. 66–8.

54 *CCO/4/8/104* Hailsham to all Constituency Chairman, 10 September 1959.

55 *CCO 4/8/113* Fourth Intelligence Report, 16 September 1959, p. 4, *CCO 4/8/107* North West Area Report on the General Election Campaign, 20 October 1959, p. 1 and *CCO4/8/107* Home Counties North, Home Counties South East Report on the General Election, October 1959.

56 See, for example, A. Crosland MP, *Can Labour Win?* Fabian Tract 324 (London: Fabian Society, May 1960), M. Abrams, 'Social Trends and Electoral Behaviour', *British Journal of Sociology*, 13 (1962), pp. 228–42 and most famously, the Socialist Commentary survey published in book form as M. Abrams, R. Rose and R. Hinden, *Must Labour Lose?* (Harmondsworth: Penguin, 1960).

57 *CCO 4/8/104* The General Election 1959, p. 5.

58 *CRD 2/21/6* Report of the Psephology Group, 15 October 1960 and Mr Dear to Mr Fraser, 1 September 1960, Political Lessons.

59 H. Evans, *Downing Street Diary* (London: Hodder and Stoughton, 1981), 7 July 1963.

60 The clearest presentation of Britain's tortuous and tortured relations with Europe is S. George, *Britain and European Integration Since 1945* (Oxford: Blackwell, 1991). Studies of the early years are M. Camps, *Britain and the European Community 1955–1963* (Princeton: Princeton University Press, 1964), R.

Leiber, *British Politics and European Unity* (Berkeley: University of California Press, 1970), and U. Kitzinger, *Diplomacy and Persuasion. How Britain Joined the Common Market* (London: Thames and Hudson, 1973).

61 *5s H C Debs 645*, 25 July 1961, cols 222–3.

62 H. Macmillan, *At The End of the Day, 1961–63* (London: Macmillan, 1973), p. 47 and pp. 84–5. By May 1962 Macmillan privately acknowledged after a threatened dock strike which was settled with an increase of 9% that his guiding light incomes policy was dead. *At The End of the Day*, p. 66.

63 M. Shanks, *Planning and Politics. The British Experience 1960–1976* (Political Economic Planning/G. Allen and Unwin 1977), pp. 17–29 surveys the Conservatives' 'conversion' to planning, and see K. Middlemas, *Industry, Unions and Government. 21 Years of NEDC* (London: Macmillan/NEDC, 1983), pp. 21–40 for the formation of NEDC.

64 N. West, *MI5 1945–72. A Matter of Trust* (London: Coronet, 1983) details these and other cases. It was at this time that Sir Anthony Blunt, the Keeper of the Queen's Pictures, was uncovered as the 'Fourth Man' but this was kept secret in return for Blunt's co-operation with MI5. During the course of the Radcliffe hearings two journalists were imprisoned for refusing to reveal their sources. This poisoned relations between Macmillan and Fleet Street.

65 P. Kightley and C. Kennedy, *An Affair of State. The Profumo Case and the Framing of Stephen Ward* (London: Jonathan Cape, 1987) is a recent account.

66 *The Times*, 11 June 1963 and H. Evans, *Downing Street Diary* (London: Hodder & Stoughton, 1981), p. 274. Earlier in the year the Americans had cancelled the Skybolt missile which Britain was hoping to buy to prevent the obsolescence of the V-bomber fleet. Britain's 'independent' nuclear deterrent was rescued by Macmillan persuading Kennedy at Nassau to supply Polaris submarine and missile technology at a knock-down price.

67 Evans, *Downing Street Diaries*, 23 June.

68 The seven were: Lloyd, Hill (Housing), Maclay (Scotland), Watkinson (Defence), Eccles (Education), Mills (Minister without Portfolio), and Kilmuir (Lord Chancellor). There were corresponding changes amongst the junior ministers.

69 Kilmuir, *Political Adventure*, p. 234 and D. R. Thorpe, *Selwyn Lloyd* (London: Cape, 1989), pp. 342–3. Macmillan also stopped Lloyd using Chequers as a weekend retreat which given his status as a backbencher is understandable, nonetheless it made Macmillan seem petty and mean-spirited.

70 Evans, *Downing Street Diary*, 22 July, and Horne, *Macmillan Volume 2*, pp. 343–7.

71 R. Maudling, *Memoirs* (London: Sidgwick and Jackson, 1978), p. 103.

72 Evans, *The Downing Street Years*, 22 July, and Maudling, *Memoirs*, p. 105.

73 Maudling, *Memoirs*, p. 116.

74 Horne, *Macmillan Volume 2*, pp. 529–31. Macmillan's health was, despite the injuries sustained in the First World War and in a plane crash in Algiers in 1942, surprisingly robust. He was, however, something of a hypochondriac and suffered from recurrent bouts of depression known as 'The Black Dog'.

75 The clearest analysis is R. Shepherd, *The Power Brokers. The Tory Party and Its Leaders* (London: Hutchinson, 1991), pp. 149–59. I. Macleod, 'The Tory Lead-

ership', *Spectator*, 17 January 1964, pp. 65–7, as well as being an important analysis of internal party politics is a splendid example of forensic political journalism and crystallised disquiet with 'the magic circle'.

76 Maudling, *Memoirs*, p. 130. J. F. Lindsay and M. Harrington, *The Conservative Party 1918–1979* (London: Macmillan, 1979), chapter 15 provides a good account of the Home government. P. Hennessy and R. Seldon (eds.), *Ruling Performance* (London: Blackwell, 1987) do not discuss the Home government.

77 J. Campbell, *Edward Heath. A Biography* (London: Jonathan Cape, 1993), pp. 150–7. Dr Beeching's cuts in the railway network had also stirred up Conservative activists in the party's commuter heartlands.

78 This analysis is based on A. Clark, 'The Downing Street Disease', *The Sunday Times*, 26 December 1993.

79 For an exploration of this see R. Garner, *The Conservative Party Conference* (Manchester: Manchester University Press, 1989).

80 This analysis is based on R. Rose, 'Who are the Tory Militants', *Crossbow*, 5 (17), 1961, pp. 35–9 and especially, M. Wilson, 'Grassroots Conservatism: Motions to the Party Conference', in N. Nugent and R. King (eds.), *The British Right* (Farnborough: Saxon House 1977), pp. 64–89. We have supplemented Wilson's analysis with our own work on the period 1945–65 which cannot be included because of lack of space.

81 The sociology of the Conservative Party in this period is not known. There is very little hard data on the party grassroots social characteristics before or after 1945. What is available dates from the 1960s. The conventional wisdom is that party activists became more lower-middle class after 1945. There is better data for MPs and ministers which indicates that despite massive social change and the party's efforts to widen its social base the social structure of the Conservative elite has remained very stable. M. Moran, *Politics and Society in Britain. An Introduction* (London: Macmillan, 1989), pp. 105–6 (party members) and pp. 154–7 (party elite) surveys the limited evidence for this period.

82 Wilson, 'Grassroots Conservatism', p. 85.

83 N. Ridley, *My Style of Government. The Thatcher Years* (London: Hutchinson, 1991), pp. 2–3.

6

Heath and the Heathmen,
1965–1970

Introduction

The view that 1965 represented a watershed in the Conservative Party history is supported by a major figure in the Party's organisation who asserted that 'a new start was made on the reversal of socialism and, despite many differences of style, presentation and method, the Heath–Thatcher period needs to be considered as a whole'.[1] Lord Butler also asserts that 1965 marked the start of a new era in Conservativism in terms of policy and personality.[2] He withdrew from party politics in February to become Master of Trinity College Cambridge.[3] The *Spectator* also defined 1965 as a turning-point and described the new process of selecting a Conservative leader as 'a revolution'. It claimed that the voters who shrank from the 'Eton Boating Song' and the 'grouse moors', but also rejected Socialism, were now being offered a suitable product.[4] In stronger language *The Economist* observed that Heath's election was 'a watershed in the history of the Tory Party, and a pretty precipitate one', because he was 'the biggest departure from the Tory leadership norm since Disraeli'.[5] In short, the conventional interpretation that the emergence of Margaret Thatcher as leader in 1975 constituted a new era in Conservative history is less sustainable than the view that in 1965 there was a break in the attitudes of the membership and a change in the Party's electoral strategy.

Heath's election as party leader coincided with a stage in the party's ideological return to basic principles which was only consummated in the Thatcher era. Many in the party still assumed that it was necessary to contest the 'middle ground' with Labour in order to regain power and defeat the Socialist threat. The electoral defeat of 1966 by Harold Wilson's Labour government, however, intensified a reappraisal of political values which had begun in limited sections of the party earlier in the decade. Before 1965 there had been ideologically consistent groups such as the Institute of Economic Affairs (IEA) outside the party expressing disquiet with the drift of the

Keynesian Welfare State (KWS) and from 1963 the weight of Enoch Powell was added to their campaign for a return to a free-market strategy. The Monday Club had also campaigned within the party since 1961 for a vigorously nationalistic Conservatism. These political expressions were considered inappropriate by the progressive faction of the party, however, which retained control of the leadership for as long as it delivered electoral success.

The 1964 defeat led many Conservatives to re-examine the established policies which were the product of the progressive faction associated with Lord Butler, Sir Edward Boyle, and Macmillan.[6] The progressive Conservatives spawned such organisations as the One Nation Group, Pressure for Economic and Social Toryism (PEST), and the Tory Reform Group. Their position was increasingly challenged because Labour appeared to have pre-empted the role of implementing the consensus of the early 1960s, symbolised by the phrase the 'politics of modernisation'. Labour portrayed itself more plausibly as the instrument of state intervention to modernise the economy and social relations. As a result, Conservatives began the process of ideological renewal, but for many the main influence was not the New Right but rather a reversion to liberal *laisser-faire* and 'sound money' doctrines of an earlier era.

Beginning with individual and isolated voices, developing into an increasingly potent faction and ultimately becoming the authentic voice of British Conservatism the politics of 'Thatcherism' came to replace the politics of managing the post-war settlement. Yet much of the impetus at elite and mass level within the party arose from values and principles with a long pedigree. The electoral and policy failures associated with the demise of Conservatism in 1964 led many in the party to succumb to the yearnings which had long held sway. Compromising with the pressures of mass democracy by claiming to be an effective provider of the mixed economy, the welfare state, full employment, trades union participation in government and the reduction of social inequality was increasingly perceived to be of doubtful electoral utility. Further, the role of pacifying the emerging policy demands of post-war mass democracy was regarded as an unsuitable stance for the party, particularly where it involved tolerating aggressive trade unionism and an expanding state subservient to powerful interest groups. Yet this was not merely a politics of reaction since it was also a product of an interest in the New Right doctrines which increasingly emanated from the United States from the mid-1960s. While the idea of a New Right international is incorrect, British Conservatives noted the triumph of the ultra-conservative wing of the Republican Party in securing the nomination of Senator Barry Goldwater as its Presidential candidate. He wished to return the Republican Party to its traditional principles which the party's progressive faction had usurped. His heavy defeat in the Presidential election of 1964 did not demoralise the conservative Republicans or their British counterparts. They merely waited for more propitious circumstances.

The changing social composition of the rank-and-file activists which became increasingly evident at annual Conferences began to have some policy impact in the 1960s. The party became less dominated by traditional aristocrats and middle-class ladies of leisure while small businessmen and the self-employed became more visible and asserted that their cause had been neglected from 1945. Their impact increased in the 1970s, although there were limits to this change in the party's composition since public school and Oxbridge educated individuals dominate even in the 1990s. Some change in the social background of party activists has taken place since the 1960s, however, which affected the background of Conservative MPs, who are increasingly drawn from state schools and provincial universities. This, in turn, filtered through to party policy.[7] Claims of this nature were made by leading Conservatives as early as 1965. For example, Charles Curran MP argued that as society changed from a pyramid to a diamond shape representing the emerging dominance of the middle class, so the party's social composition widened to become a 'mirror image of the electorate'. It attracted more women, youth, and even some trades unionists. He argued that this more variegated party was adapting in harmony with British society because it 'feels in its bones that it is a Governing Party'.[8] Certainly, the party was revealing the capacity to absorb, as it had throughout its history, diverse fractions of capital. The small business interest was sufficiently significant in the political economy of the late 1960s and the 1970s for even the Labour government to share in an elite consensus about its importance to the British economy. These socio-economic changes should not be overstated, however, as the Conservative Party has an 'extraordinary ability to combine electoral success with social elitism'.[9] Nevertheless, research suggests that membership became more middle class in this period.[10]

The process of returning the Conservative Party to earlier concepts of the state and the economy, after a temporary post-war dalliance with active government and collectivist policies, was delayed by Heath's politics and leadership style. The five main themes analysed here are the election of Heath as party leader, his work at the head of the party's policy-making process, his tactics and style as leader of the Opposition, the nature and consequences of the 1970 general election victory and finally the surge of neo-Liberal, right-wing ideas in the party from the mid-1960s. The recurring theme is the interaction between neo-Liberal and Heathite Conservatism.

The new leader

In November 1964 Home told the 1922 of his desire to change the leadership selection procedure and chaired a committee which opted for simplicity: the electorate would be Conservative MPs with the 1922 chairman in overall charge. The winner on the first ballot would need a majority plus 15% to win, although on the second ballot a simple majority would suffice, and in a third ballot MPs would list their preferences. The 1922 accepted the proposals in March and they were put to the test five months later. Electing the leader was a revolutionary change in Conservative politics. Heath's opponents for the leadership in July 1965 were Reginald Maudling and Enoch Powell. Maudling was perceived as a personal rather than an ideological rival, although all three had worked for the Conservative Research Department (CRD) after 1945 and had belonged to the One Nation Group. Powell's challenge was of great long-term significance, however, because he represented an ideological critique of existing party policy with his heady concoction of *laisser-faire* and the Quantity Theory of Money, anticipating much of the agenda which was to prevail a decade later. Powell's 'derisory' fifteen votes demonstrated that the party's transition was incomplete and that MPs were seeking a moderniser to challenge Harold Wilson with policies that diverged within a common inter-party consensus. Yet Powell's 'Tory Purity' marked a 'fundamental division' in the party which promised future conflict.[11] Labour saw the opportunity to condemn Conservative internal divisions.[12]

There were significant differences between Heath and Maudling and the 'tougher' element voted for Heath. This element could be described as 'the Unit Trust' faction, because Heath was nearer to Powell's *laisser-faire* strategy than Maudling, who was foursquare in the tradition of Lord Butler.[13] Certainly Maudling described himself as 'the apostle of consensus'. This was apparent with incomes policy which Maudling strongly advocated throughout the period from 1961 to 1978, since he considered that such a policy solved the political problem of capitalism.[14] In contrast, Heath was agnostic on incomes policy at this time.[15] Yet comment that Heath was a committed monetarist ideologically opposed to incomes policy was mistaken, since he merely wished to avert open party disunity. It was his association with Europe which gave Heath a distinctive appeal which attracted younger MPs.[16] The differences between Heath and Maudling were minute but the view that there were only differences of style not policy between Heath and Maudling is too superficial. None of the three candidates, however, came from the party's traditional 'magic circle', but Heath's lower-middle-class origins and meritocratic style offered the best riposte to Macleod's criticisms.

Heath certainly offered a more aggressive style of leadership than Maudling. He was a Chamberlain rather than a Baldwin, who had the credentials to take on Wilson.[17] His record as Chief Whip at the time of Suez, his patience as chief EEC negotiator, and his tenacity in handling the divisive Retail Price Maintenance Bill provided him with great ministerial experience. Conservative newspapers supported Heath on the grounds of his leadership style. He was variously described as 'a man of action', 'a tough-minded bachelor', 'aggressive in thought and speech','having the energy of a powerhouse' and as being 'classless and restless'.[18] His acolytes were described as young exponents of efficiency and implausibly as 'heroes of Swinging London'.[19] Yet these qualities were perceived more within the parliamentary party than in the wider electorate where Maudling's persona was more appealing. While the press supported Heath the public supported Maudling. Yet Maudling's bland style reflected a complacency and an enthusiasm for his City directorships and he underestimated the need to fight his corner among Conservative MPs. He justified his external interests with the argument that an independent income insulated him from the Chief Whip and provided him with knowledge of the wealth-creating sector, but also more unusually, because he sought money for his family's security. Yet he sent out the wrong signals to anxious Conservative MPs. As the last Chancellor of the Exchequer he also took the blame for the 1964 defeat.[20] The vote was 150 for Heath and 133 for Maudling, and while short of the required majority plus 15%, Maudling immediately withdrew.[21]

Powell's candidacy was a statement rather than a serious challenge and was part of the campaign which he had waged since refusing to serve under Home's leadership in 1963. His purpose was to return the party to its first principles by a process of re-education.[22] He had already questioned the Party's defence policy, advocated classical Liberal free-market policies and rejected the 'turn to planning' of the Macmillan government in 1961. He was encouraged by a small coterie of able MPs such as Nicholas Ridley and John Biffen.[23] If he was merely leaving his visiting card then it was not a triumph for his mission or re-educating the party, although he believed that in a free vote Conservative MPs would prefer his policies to the 'me-tooism' which the party was then offering. Powell neglected the party's capacity to compromise with the pressures of mass democracy which had enabled it to counter the successive threats of Liberalism and the Labour Party. With a general election imminent few MPs were prepared to take risks.

Yet the political ideology of Powellism was now being discussed. The appearance of an edited collection of his speeches, *A Nation Not Afraid*, led Macleod to predict that Powellism's influence would grow within the party.[24] Yet Goldwater's heavy defeat in the previous year's Presidential election damaged this as many referred to Powellism as British Goldwaterism. If his campaign was premature in the circumstances of 1965, Powell's cause was also damaged because of the closeness of the battle between Heath and Maudling which squeezed his vote. The fifteen supporters which he secured were a foretaste of the alliance which Thatcher successfully constructed to win the leadership, since they were a combination of young free-market enthusiasts such as Ridley and Biffen, together with traditional right-wingers concerned about immigration such as Sir Cyril Osborne,

Harold Gurden, and Peter Griffiths.[25] His low vote was erroneously interpreted as the death of Powellism.[26]

How did Heath manage to interact with the developing right-wing neo-
Liberal pressures in his party? The contemporary references to Heath and
the Heathmen suggest that Heath was a dogmatic ideologue leading a faction of true believers within the party. In reality, his faction was personal-
ist: a group of individuals whom he selected to share in the leadership of the
party and who returned his loyalty. Some were with him from the period
before his leadership election campaign and were accused of attempting a
putsch against Sir Alec Douglas Home; for example, Peter Walker, John-
Macgregor, and David Howell.[27] Given Conservative loyalty to their leader
his support was extensive, but at the highest echelons of the party he
enjoyed a close relationship only with a small group of the converted. While
Heath never became reconciled to Thatcher's leadership, many of his
acolytes transferred their allegiance to her. This underlines the adaptability
of many Conservatives to circumstances and their overriding commitment
to power not ideology.[28]

Andrew Roth argues that Heath's righteous style and his capacity for
dressing up his decisions in dogmatic language led to his reputation as an
ideologue when he became Prime Minister in 1970. It is true that his commitment to the European cause, which became even more strident after
Thatcher became a sceptic about Britain's political involvement in the European Community (EC) in the late 1980s, appeared fervent. Yet Roth suggests that the reasons for Heath's selection as negotiator with the Common
Market on the British government's behalf was that he was perceived,
throughout the 1950s, to be cautious about Europe.[29] The cautious nature
of his Europeanism in the 1950s is significant, however, because it is an
error to transpose later statements by politicians into an assumption that
they represent long-standing commitments. Heath's vision of Europe at this
time was of a national-based 'Europe des Patries'.

The reality of Heath's career is that he moved from a modest attachment
to the party's progressive wing to an adherence to right-wing values in the
1970 general election, to a position on the outer left of the party in the
1990s. Such judgements are difficult, however, since the Conservative
Party's ideological centre of gravity moved to the right during that period.
He has engaged in a progressive shift from an interventionist moderniser
sympathetic to the use of state power between 1965 and 1970, to an
adherent of classic free-market ideas urging the disengagement of government from industry between 1970 and 1971, to a pseudo-corporatist advocacy of governance by tripartite concertation of the state, business, and
trades unions from 1972 to 1974. He subsequently contested the February
1974 general election on a class-based, anti-trades union platform, only to
revert to an appeal to national unity and coalition in the October general

election.[30] His later attachments are blurred by personal pique against Thatcher's leadership.

Heath's self-image as a hero figure, almost regardless of the policies he pursued at any given juncture, was shared by a small group of people in the Shadow Cabinet, the House of Commons and the party in the country. Heath was probably never fully converted to the New Right doctrines which reasserted themselves from the mid-1960s and which are analysed in a later section of this chapter. His volatile pragmatism was a result both of his own lack of clear political values and a reflection of his struggle to come to terms with forces which were hostile and barely comprehended for much of the time that he remained leader.

Policy-making and the Advisory Committee on Policy

Heath replaced Butler as chairman of the Advisory Committee on Policy (ACP) under Home's leadership and continued until 1968. The involvement in detailed policy-making unencumbered by serious philosophical analysis suited his temperament because, other than a desire to strengthen the British economy to allow it to compete successfully in Europe, he had few deep convictions. The task of leading a process of detailed research to develop a programme to win back political power and provide a basis for effective action in government was one which he relished.[31] The tone of the Conservative 1966 manifesto, *Action Not Words*, captured Heath's preference for action on practical policy rather than philosophy. Much of the manifesto's content was shaped by the ACP and by the document which that process had already produced in October 1965, *Putting Britain Right Ahead*. The document used the language of management consultancy, and Heath's aversion to political ideas and his lack of concern for philosophical coherence was evident in his comment: 'As I go around the country I find that people are asking for an entirely fresh approach to the country's problems. They are looking for constructive policies – how do we do things rather than what needs to be done'.[32] Yet Heath's emphasis upon results rather than theory neglected the interconnectedness of theory and practice and the danger that erroneous theories produce faulty results.[33] All political decisions must necessarily be rooted in political values, so the principles should be overt.[34] The lack of theoretical substance created difficulties after 1970 when Heath's government lacked an agreed philosophical base. His weakness was recognised from the outset. A prominent Bow Grouper expressed concern that Heath's mastery of detail concealed an arid mind, a lack of principle, a deficient imagination and a failure to produce grand perspectives.[35]

The absence of principle in *Putting Britain Right Ahead* created interpretative difficulties. *The Economist* defined it as moving the party slightly to the left.[36] While some were unable to detect any Conservative principles in the document, the *Spectator* claimed that on trades unions and immigration it represented a move to the right, but that on Europe and the social services it was moving left.[37] This demonstrates the difficulty in classifying Heath in conventional left–right or One Nation and neo-Liberal terms. *The Economist* had lost its earlier enthusiasm for the state's role in increasing business efficiency and welcomed the particular proposal in *Putting Britain Right Ahead* of reforming industrial relations by imposing collective agreements on unions through legally binding contracts. But the journal considered the document to be cautious in rethinking policy goals, for example, the control of inflation, sterling's role as a reserve currency, the review of Britain's East of Suez military commitments, and the reshaping of social services to ensure the concentration of resources on those most in need. The reform of social services required an end to wage-related sickness benefits, the tying of housing subsidies to individuals not property, and the recasting of flat-rate pensions.

Putting Britain Right Ahead challenged elements of the post-war consensus but did not entirely break with it. This reflected Heath's personal reluctance to discard electorally popular policy, his own antipathy to fundamental analysis, and his wish to avoid 'the risk of ideological disputes between free-market and welfare-state Conservatives'.[38] The commitment to reform the trade unions was 'delphic' but there were clearer signs of divergence from the consensus in the promise to lessen tax burdens on rising earnings, to build a capital-owning democracy, and to ensure 'the closest scrutiny and rigorous control of all branches of public expenditure, to free business activity from the distortions of excessive demand and for expansion to be achieved without the inflationary consequences of an overstretched economy'.[39] Some elements of Heath's Conference speech in the month that *Putting Britain Right Ahead* was published confirmed the view that he sought to present a dynamic policy portraying Labour as the party of the status quo. His language encouraged the Tory right to consider that Heath had shifted more in its direction than he was able or willing to deliver in government. A Labour opponent also claimed that Heath's policy 'was attractive only to young and thrusting businessmen ... it is now clear that he has taken the very big decision to drop the socialistic attitude which crept into Tory policy in the last two years of Macmillan's regime. Heath is going to fight much more for free enterprise; his theme will be Into Europe where British free enterprise can survive'.[40] While Heath concentrated on the ACP's work there was an attempt to involve the mass membership in the policy review process. A mid-term manifesto, *Make Life Better*, was released to the 1968 Conference. This was a more thorough policy review than even that of 1965.[41]

Heath was concerned that the ACP's policy groups should examine means as well as ends, and this detailed policy preparation diverted him from merely seeking electoral support by concentrating upon the short-comings of the Labour government. Yet the ACP could not make policy. It merely advised the leader who took final decisions in consultation with the Shadow Cabinet. More than thirty groups met under the ACP's auspices and their focus ranged from such broad topics as economic policy to such narrow areas as services pensions.[42] Yet the process failed to reconcile the party's contradictory economic policies.[43] In certain respects the drift of policy appeared to offer new directions by shifting the balance of power in industry, curbing union power, making the rich richer by tax relief for managers, so that some Conservatives were anxious about the narrowness of the party's appeal.[44] Yet Heath had no intention of returning to pure *laisser-faire*. The party was doubly hurt, therefore, since its policies were not radical in reality but austere language made them appear 'hard-nosed'.[45]

There were three committees addressing economic policy but the most contentious was concerned with taxation policy. There was a dispute over a proposal to shift the burden of tax from earners to owners and to finance top level tax cuts by a wealth tax. Some of the committee resisted this, arguing that it was an inefficient way of raising revenue, could split the party and offered a Labour government a tool that it could exploit.[46] Macleod jettisoned the idea, but in the absence of a commitment to VAT, and alongside its promise to abandon the Selective Employment Tax (SET), this created a revenue hole.[47]

The committee on trade union reform also involved compromise and the upshot was a commitment to outlaw unofficial strikes by enforcing collective agreements through industrial courts. In order not to disturb the compromise, the policy was not updated despite the changed circumstances produced by the Labour government's failure to reform industrial relations with its modest *In Place of Strife* proposal in 1969. This inflexibility created problems when the Heath government sought to implement its proposals in 1971. The experiences of the late 1960s should have shown it that the proposals had become unrealistic.[48] Once more there was a profound divergence within the party between those who had an emotional dislike of unions and wished to attack the political levy and the closed shop, and those who sought to control excessive labour costs and who considered the unions to be an estate of the realm and wished to assist union leaders to discipline and control their members through enforceable contracts.[49] Thus the policy remained static save for the adoption in *Fair Deal At Work* in 1968 of compulsory cooling-off periods and secret ballots before strikes.[50]

In parallel with the ACP the party also set up a unit to examine ways of enhancing the efficiency of the public sector. The former transport minister Ernest Marples chaired it. The unit was influenced by American managerial ideas.[51] Its work was necessary for the credibility of the party's policy as it sought to demonstrate how tax cuts could be reconciled with increases in expenditure by enhancing economy and efficiency in government. The main methods advocated were the recruitment of more businessmen into the public services and the 'hiving off' of state activities to the private sector.[52] The unit's work was consummated at a seminar held at Sunridge Park in 1969 which involved businessmen, industrial executives, backbenchers, former civil servants and attended by Heath, which examined the reform of the machinery of government. The aim of greater efficiency was to be achieved by creating a small number of federal departments of state and a smaller Cabinet to enable ministers to adopt a strategic perspective.[53] This reflected Heath's lingering enthusiasm for 'corporate whiggery'.[54] His concern to enhance the efficiency of the government machine assumed that the state had a valuable role to play. Evidently intervention to produce growth was 'part of Conservative economic philosophy in the mid-sixties, involving at the very least indicative planning and commitment to specific numbers and growth targets'.[55] Heath's managerial collectivism prevailed over neo-Liberalism.

Heath's enthusiasm to involve external experts to support the Cabinet and improve the quality of government led to the formation of the Central Policy Review Staff (CPRS) in 1971.[56] Whether through confusion, or the desire to avoid intra-party battles, or the appreciation that the party has always sought to balance change with stability, Heath favoured the importation of business experts and improved efficiency to produce spending cuts, and so avoided painful decisions about reducing the role of the state.

An early draft of the document *Make Life Better* appeared to recognise the danger that a technocratic approach needed to be accompanied by partisanship. The draft developed the concept of 'overloaded' government a decade before political scientists, and attributed frustration with parliamentary democracy to the intractable problems of governance, particularly economic management. It asserted that while the case for applying 'technical expertise' to decision-making was strong there was a need to stress a political dimension since a party system is necessary to focus 30 million different views by offering practical alternatives. So while the next Conservative government was ready to use the new tools of decision-making, this was not to displace politics but to identify problems and define the range of solutions. Technical methods could not decide what 'our aims should be'. Politics ensures that the government is responsive and not a mere automaton.[57] An interesting aspect of the Steering Committee's debate on the document was Maudling's insistence that Conference could not vote on it because 'it is the leader who makes Party policy, and it is important to maintain this prerogative and to keep policy-making in the hands of the leadership'.[58]

Heath's most unsatisfactory interaction with the rising forces of neo-Liberalism infiltrating the ACP committee system was on inflation. The schism over incomes policy led a CRD official Brendòn Sewill to seek a compromise. Instead of a formal incomes policy he proposed that all pay claims should be submitted in a single month, that the government should announce an annual national dividend linked to productivity and people should accept the limit laid down. 'The Conservative Party is divided between those who instinctively dislike any form of detailed wages control and those who recognise the existence of cost-push inflation and the impossibility of leaving it unchecked'.[59] As Heath continued to resist, Sewill wrote to him in 1969 noting Maudling's sympathy for incomes policy, and observing that the party had not used its years in Opposition to develop appropriate tools of economic management. Yet a decision had to be taken on the fate of the Prices and Incomes Act of 1966. Sewill agreed that union reform, strict controls over public sector pay, and resistance to a public sector strike for demonstration purposes were necessary but he remained concerned about the vacuum in public policy.[60] The vacuum was apparent at the pre-election Selsdon Park Hotel conference where the participants agreed to say little on economic policy, despite a paper from Sewill, who later claimed that the Conservatives fought the general election of 1970 unprepared for the central problem which faced it.[61] So the entire policy-making exercise was marred by a serious omission.

The purpose of the Selsdon conference was to draw the strands of the ACP process together before the general election. A main motif was one of excitement at the prospect of a tax-cutting and incentive-producing policy tempered by a concern that society's weakest should not be disadvantaged. The views of participants were sometimes surprising and they caution against a rigid classification of political views. Heath stressed economic growth before consumption and Robert Carr claimed that voters recognised the priority of wealth-creation. Barber argued for vagueness on moving towards taxes on expenditure. Joseph surprisingly argued, however, the necessity to 'raise the status, standards and pay of nurses, teachers and the police', to which Macleod responded that the police should be helped, but 'in the case of the teachers there would be difficulties in finding the money', and a danger of 'starting off a round of wage explosions a year or two after the Party was back in power'. Unlike Joseph he opposed raising family allowances to attack poverty but wished to cut taxes.[62] Heath sided with Macleod because it was desirable to do something early in the life of the government that 'the Party is worked up about'.

The Selsdon myth is that it was the occasion when Heath responded to the burgeoning right-wing sentiment in the party by attempting to reconcile it with his own managerial and consensual style. The formation of the Selsdon Group in 1973 to protest at the collectivist drift of the Heath government reinforces the idea that Selsdon was a seminal event in the party's history.[63] Wilson's reaction to the conference, was to invent the concept of

'Selsdon Man' to portray the Conservative programme as neolithic. This erroneously suggested, however, that the Conservatives had an alternative prospectus.[64] In reality, the public relations element of Selsdon was accidental and it was only when the cameras arrived that Macleod struck a populist note by emphasising the issue of law and order.[65] At most Selsdon consummated the party's rightwards movement.[66] A close Thatcher adviser denies that Heath betrayed Selsdon and argues, 'Selsdon was an invention of the press. There were no policy decisions. Selsdon was a myth'.[67] The myth proved potent, however, since even *The Economist* condemned the lack of compassion displayed at Seldson, regretted the passing of the party's 'squirearchical centre' as it represented, 'in a muddled way, the compassion and moral basis of the Tory Party'. Now the Party was run by 'the stainless steel Tories'.[68] The *Spectator* criticised Selsdon, or 'Codex Croydoniensis' as it described it, from the right. While rejecting Powellism it called for immigrants to be spared the attentions of race relations 'do-gooders'.[69] It argued that Conservatives gain votes by sounding like Tories on taxation, law and order, and trade unions.[70] Selsdon was an uninspired conclusion to an extended process of policy analysis.

Heath: leader of the Opposition

The leader of the Opposition must do more than prepare for government. Heath recognised the need to stir up passion against the incumbent Labour government and was sometimes so shrill in his opposition that even Tory commentators urged him to raise the level of inter-party debate, since his 'shrill phrasemaking' was no substitute for economic argument.[71] The nine months' period after Heath's election in 1965 was unhappy for the Conservative Opposition because the Labour government was displaying political skill. Wilson capably fomented Conservative divisions. On the Rhodesia issue, for example, the Unilateral Declaration of Independence (UDI) by the white minority under Ian Smith in November 1965 created problems of disunity for the Conservatives rather than Labour. It was argued, for example, that Heath was unable to control his party, since his problem flowed from the activities of two extreme groups: the Sanctions Group led by Nigel Fisher, Chris Chataway, and Humphrey Berkeley which favoured economic methods to undermine the Rhodesian republic; and the pro-Smith group led by Julian Amery, John Biggs-Davidson, and Anthony Fell which not only sympathised with Ian Smith's actions but advocated his cause at 'Nuremberg type rallies'.[72] Heath moved from support for the government's approach to one of carping criticism, because of his party's three-way split.[73]

Heath failed in his first parliamentary speech as leader to make the impact which the press hyperboles had led observers to expect. Like 'so many debuts, this was a pretty good flop. Heath turned out to be a second-class orator ... and there can't have been many Tories who didn't whisper under their breath, "My God, I see the point of Maudling now"'.[74] Crossman also reported that Wilson had 'the greatest contempt' for Heath.[75] Heath succeeded in his appointments, however, in restoring party harmony. He appointed Maudling as Deputy Leader, Macleod as Shadow Chancellor, and Powell as Defence spokesman. These appointments healed the potential split with his main opponent for the leadership, drew in one of the most talented henchmen to the senior economics portfolio and kept Powell away from economics while giving him an important role.[76] The aim of silencing Powell was doomed, however, and even in his defence capacity he soon began to challenge party policy.

The party's main need after July 1965 was to prepare for an early general election. Encouraged by the Conservative press there was an emphasis upon image rather than substance, which reflected a tendency for British politics to become Presidential. While Heath's stiff personality made it difficult to market him against Wilson's popular style, his lack of patrician and Tory grandee characteristics were perceived by the media and Conservative politicians as making him a more appropriate leader for the times. This was particularly so given the impact of social changes and the trends in popular culture of the 1960s. The theme of economic modernisation could also be more effectively promoted by Heath than by the traditional Tory 'toff' style of leader. Heath did not capture the sceptical or '*Quieta non movere*' ethos of pragmatism for which 'One Nation' Conservatives like Gilmour argued and which Macmillan and Home had practised.[77] Rather his style was optimistic, managerial and utilitarian; and this won support in an approving letter sent by a businessman: 'We are sick of seeing old men dressed in flat caps and bedraggled tweeds strolling about with 12 bores'.[78]

Two pressures pulled the party towards a cautious stance: its empirical tradition encouraged it to persevere with support for the polices of the post-war settlement, and there is a tendency for the parties to converge in a two-party system. While active party members prefer to concentrate on principles, party leaders must seek the votes of those ignorant of or opposed to those principles.[79] It may be an oversimplification that there is merely one debate in each generation, but it is true that at this time the main political argument concerned the valence issue, of which party was better fitted to modernise Britain without jettisoning the post-war policies.[80] Despite such pressures, however, Heath had to offer a distinct approach to modernisation from that of the government if he was to be effective. Gilmour argues that the references in the 1966 Manifesto to reforming the welfare state and the trades unions, ending agricultural subsidies, increasing individual competitiveness, and entering the Common Market were too radical. While conceding that competition and efficiency were essential, he argues that since the party gains half of its votes from the workers who seek authority and security from Conservative governments, it should avoid religious commitments to market forces.[81] The Conservative Party should never be too far ahead of public opinion, but should rather portray itself as 'responding to the natural instincts of the people'.[82]

At this stage in its development the Conservative Party was responding to the challenge of maintaining power in a mass democracy by avoiding a sharp departure from the preferences of the majority of the public. While Heath put a strong emphasis upon the formulation of new policies to retain the support of opinion formers the party continued to invest in techniques, as it had since 1948, to measure public attitudes. The purpose was 'to discover what was palatable, or what might be made palatable'.[83] The party commissioned regular opinion polls from National Opinion Polls (NOP) but also set up a company, Cozreldit Ltd, in November 1965, which later became Opinion Research Centre (ORC). Its goal was to undertake longer-term research by interviewing a small number of voters at length to build a model of the electorate and to seek out the demographic support base of each of the three main parties.[84] The intention was to counterbalance the information derived from party agents and activists and to begin the process, completed in the 1979 general election, of identifying 'target' and 'swing' voters whose behaviour could determine electoral outcomes. The results suggested that they were 5.5 million people in the target category who were defined as younger and less political than the electorate at large and concentrated in the upper-working and lower-middle classes.[85] While these exercises were genuine attempts to discern the changing class and age structure of British society, the party remained schizoid about whether it wished to make policy on the basis of these results, or simply to discover how best to 'present' its preferred policies.[86]

The ideological tone for the 1966 election Manifesto was necessarily determined before the analyses of public opinion could be included; particularly as it was decided, in accordance with the party's hierarchical structure, that the Shadow Cabinet, the 1922 Committee, Central Office, and the top fifty people in the party should be informed of the results first. The Manifesto led one commentator to deny any policy argument between Labour and Conservative.[87] This was compatible with the analysis of one political scientist who doubted whether parties make a difference.[88] But Conservative and Labour were not identical at this time. As Fraser argues theories of the post-war inter-party consensus are simplistic. He draws the analogy with two trains leaving from parallel platforms at a London terminus which then run on broadly parallel lines but heading towards different destinations.[89]

It is fruitful, therefore, to investigate the type of voter that the Conservatives were seeking to appeal to since political parties go 'whoring' after groups of voters in order to build an electoral strategy.[90] The Conservative strategy at this time was to recapture the support of the young managerial and professional technocrats who it was believed Wilson had seduced by his appeal to meritocracy and efficiency. In reality, this group was numerically insignificant and did not determine the outcome of the 1970 election.[91] Yet perceptions are crucial, and Wilson's 'white hot heat of technology' mesmerised the Tories. The *Spectator* argued that Heath could appeal to the 'numerous, influential, educated, unprivileged members of the salariat'.[92] Heath's instinct for power led him to turn the party towards a liberal, modernising and grammar school-led organisation, having overcome the Knights of the Shire and the 'residual anti-Europeans'. Macleod stressed that the party must appeal to the new salariat which had few fixed loyalties and was internationalist, ambitious, and competitive. This was why *Putting Britain Right Ahead* appealed to the 'pacesetters' and he dismissed *The Economist's* jibe that the document was too prone to parade the 'poor bleeding heart of the taxpayer'.[93]

Heath's first Conference was a test for his leadership. By October it was clear that Heath's honeymoon was over. It was ironical that a leader picked because of the lowliness of his birth, and whose working-class roots were indisputable, 'painfully lacked the common touch'.[94] *The Economist* interpreted his speech to Conference as providing the party with a progressive posture, but one different from 1950s Butskellism, since it stressed Liberalism, freer trade and the ending of class distinctions and restrictive practices. Another commentator described Heath's speech as 'flat' and noted that he was a poor debater who had been oversold. He lacked communication skills, a theme to propagate, was afraid of making errors, and was best qualified to be a civil servant as his opposition to the Finance Bill in 1965 revealed.[95]

Heath's behaviour at the Conference represented the new style of political leadership which the party adopted in 1965. He was present throughout, whereas all previous leaders had merely descended on the Conference on the final morning to deliver a speech. Heath also made two speeches and stressed his commitment to political change. It was this rhetoric which led some Conservatives to misinterpret the policy proposals on which the party contested the 1966 election and to fear that Heath was acting in a non-Tory fashion.[96] Despite the main themes of the years 1965–70: tax incentives and a shift towards indirect taxation, the reform of trade union law, greater selectivity in place of universality in the social services and a commitment to EEC membership – Heath's perspective was incrementalist. He sought to build within the existing political and social framework. The language of change was about creating a modern, efficient, and productive economy and convincing the electorate to elect the Conservatives under his leadership.

Heath's behaviour was also significant for avoiding the symbols of traditional deference which prevailed when the party was led by the wealthy and the landed; although as a 'cold, tough, efficient, driving, professional politician', he was incapable anyway of appealing to deference.[97] It is apparent that the party found itself in a transitional position. It had altered its appeal to capture the social changes of the 1960s as it had in previous eras, yet it sought to do so at a time when its members' emotional allegiances still hankered after the grand patrician leaders represented by Churchill, Eden, Macmillan, and Home. Campbell argues that the relationship between Heath and the party at this time 'remained guarded – on both sides. There was in this coolness an undoubted streak of snobbery, never of course stated in public or to his face but expressed in snide remarks behind his back which, inevitably, came to his ears. The Party had chosen him because it was told that it needed someone like him to lead it in the modern world. But in their hearts most Tories did not like his modern world. The social base and outlook of the Party was changing, slowly, but the instincts of most members of most local associations in the 1960s still reflected the traditional predominance of the wealthy and the landed'.[98] The 'thrusting' businessman who celebrated the demise of the 'grouse moor' image was underrepresented at the 1965 Conference where it was the deposed Home who received the loudest applause'.[99]

The Conservatives were also damaged at the 1966 general election because the country still blamed them for economic problems.[100] The Party was also facing financial difficulties. These are a recurring feature of the year immediately following a general election as Lord Archer pointed out with reference to the party's plight in 1993.[101] Yet it was also the case that companies were deterred by the government's proposal to require them to declare their financial contributions. This shortfall in income coincided with the need for more money for market research and advertising.[102] When the general election results were declared Labour had made 47 gains to produce an absolute majority of 96 with 48% of the poll and the Conservatives lost 600,000 votes plunging to their lowest vote since 1945 and gaining just 42% of the poll. While the result was traumatic for Conservatives it was less so than the defeats of 1974. Despite the size of Labour's victory the Conservatives could draw consolation. There was a general understanding that 1966 was an almost unwinnable election, Labour's victory was not based upon a 'terrifying' left-wing platform, and the campaign was a valuable dry run for Heath and the party organisation. Campbell also points out that the outcome provided Heath personally a few years in which to 'set his stamp on the Party more firmly than he had been able to do in the feverish conditions of the previous eight months'.[103]

In retrospect the period from 1965 to 1970 appears to have been one in which the Conservatives inexorably retrieved their 'rightful' position as the dominant party in British politics. The Labour government faced grave economic difficulties and for most of the time the Conservatives enjoyed substantial leads in the national opinion polls, local elections and parliamentary by-elections, climaxing in 1968. The party's own 'deep' private polls also suggested that the electorate was becoming concerned with inflation and trade union power where the Labour Party was on unpopular political territory. The trades union issue was electorally damaging for Labour after Wilson's humiliating climb down over the modest proposals for reform, *In Place of Strife*, in June 1969.[104]

Yet there were uncertainties in the Conservatives' position. Heath constantly ran both behind his party and Wilson in opinion poll ratings, Wilson bettered him in Parliament and the Party was unenthusiastic about his performance.[105] In intra-party terms it became apparent that it took time 'to understand what a middle-class leader is driving at'.[106] Heath also blundered in taking an even more belligerent stance in defence of sterling and resisting devaluation than the government, as well as displaying an even greater commitment to Britain's East of Suez military bases. These positions meant that his economic posture was as unconvincing as the government's and, for a Europhile, he was reluctant to appreciate the implications of Britain's changing position in the international system.[107] Even on the issue of the reform of the House of Lords he backed a government proposal to weaken the hereditary principle that was unable to secure the assent of the House of Commons.[108] There was also some recovery in Labour's fortunes after the balance of payments moved into surplus in 1969 and a good performance in the May 1970 local elections led to 'visible fatalism' on the Conservative benches. There were also continuing divisions over Rhodesia, and Powell embarrassed him both before and after Heath dismissed him from the Shadow Cabinet in April 1968 for making a speech which Heath considered racialist.[109] Heath's capacity to win an election was not always certain, therefore, and errors committed during the period in Opposition later undermined his government.

Heath never overcame at this stage the recurrent Conservative dilemma of whether to portray Labour as Socialist when it is patently not pursuing radical policies, or whether to condemn it for 'centrist' timidity and the betrayal of principles. Clearly on many of the issues of the time such as the devaluation of sterling in November 1967, Britain's post-Imperial military role, the control of inflation and trades union reform, Heath 'worked himself into a passionate condemnation of policies which he would have done better to have broadly supported'.[110] Instead of condemning the belatedness of devaluation he berated the government for its lack of patriotism. *The Times* accused him of 'coming forward in posthumous defence of the old parity'.[111] Heath's 'patriotic' attack on Labour for reducing its East of Suez military commitment suggested his lack of awareness that 'it was in part the unavailing struggle to defend the pound that had made far-flung military commitments finally unsustainable'.[112] Heath committed a further tactical error in opposing the Labour government's trade union reform when he might have embarrassed Wilson with his left-wing and trade union critics by welcoming it. His support for the government 'would have done wonders for the country and still left the Labour Party seething with discontent. I believe that Ted and Ian Macleod should have spotted our opportunity'.[113] The problem flowed from the fact that 'scarcely anyone in the Party understood industrial relations or knew any industrialists, let alone any trades unionists'.[114]

Heath was also deficient in his conduct of intra-party relations. He was aloof with his own backbenchers, at ease only with a small group of intimate subordinates, kept the parliamentary party at bay and relied on a confidential entourage. Some MPs believed that he 'actually despised the Tory Party, and made little attempt to disguise the fact'.[115] Heath also mismanaged the Marples Affair which arose when, having been removed from the front bench Marples volunteered to undertake 'a total systems analysis' review of Conservative Central Office.[116] The Party Chairman Edward DuCann failed to act on the offer and when Marples gave up in despair in February 1967, DuCann claimed that Marples had not 'found it possible to give specific advice'.[117] The episode reflected the party's changing social character and the resulting tensions. One senior Conservative was quoted as saying that Marples, 'is the sort of man who looks as if he is wearing a brown suit even when he is not'.[118] A party activist wrote to the Chairman that there was 'a colossal task to return to power unless Central office recognises people with ability rather than background'.[119] A Young Conservative branch protested at the failure of Central Office to collaborate with Marples. Eldon Griffiths MP also objected to Marples's treatment as 'he has an image that is projected widely in Britain in what I've called the new competitors, the kind of people that both the Labour Party and ourselves are competing to win over'.[120] Heath allowed the problem to fester damagingly.

The 1970 general election

There was a general view that Heath was an electoral liability when Wilson dissolved Parliament in May 1970. Heath remained confident throughout the campaign despite the negative poll ratings which continued until polling day, because of his confidence that the electorate would not vote for the re-election of Wilson.[121] Voters were more irritated by the failures during the Labour government's tenure of office than reassured by the superficial economic improvement in 1970 so Labour's apparent recovery was superficial.

The Conservatives began their planning for the election as early as 1969. The 'Thursday Group', consisting of Antony Barber, Geoffrey Johnson Smith, Brendon Sewill, Geoffrey Tucker (head of publicity), William Whitelaw, Jim Garrett (a commercial film producer), and John Lindsay (head of Central Office's television department) met to plan the campaign.

The group demonstrated that the Conservative Party was now in the vanguard of exploiting the televisual media. It was becoming concerned at the BBC's role in political communication, as it had been since the 1920s.[122] The Thursday Group also used ORC to analyse the public's attitudes and to respond accordingly. ORC advised the party to concentrate on the economy as voters were concerned about taxation and the cost of living, and as in 1959 the party was urged to target the housewives' vote.[123] Data about the reception of party political broadcasts revealed that they were watched by the party's own supporters and that Conservative broadcasts were preferred to Labour's, although this reflected the unpopularity of the government.[124] ORC presented data to the group from a survey revealing that Labour's better image on 'caring' issues was balanced by a 69 to 28% preference for selectivity in the payment of pensions.[125] A further survey demonstrated the role of 'folk memory' in politics. Wilson had succeeded in establishing the image of '13 wasted Conservative years' from 1951 to 1964, plus the idea of a Conservative-created balance of payments deficit in 1964 of £700 m. The report suggested that the Conservatives should campaign on the greater rate of growth achieved in the 1950s compared to the Labour years.[126]

The Conservative Political Centre (CPC) was encouraged to influence the climate of opinion among 'influentials'. It had long existed to engage in political education within and beyond the Conservative Party. Its publications were aimed at opinion formers, curiously defined as MPs, agents, councillors, party workers, the press, radio, television, academics, graduates, estate agents, travelling salesmen, rotary clubs, chambers of commerce, shop stewards, barbers and comedians.[127] Heath recognised the need to promote the pamphlets when he wrote, 'it is not enough just to send pamphlets to people ... they have to be talked to and ginned up beforehand ... (and) bribed and cajoled into giving the pamphlet publicity'.[128]

A first draft of the 1970 Manifesto was put before the ACP and the Steering Committee. One statement was removed before the final version appeared. A comment that 'independent schools are the only safeguard against the state monopoly over the minds of our children' was removed.[129] In foreign policy a CRD official argued that foreign issues were of no electoral impact, and in an area where few votes could be 'swung', it was thought undesirable to tie the hands of a government in advance.[130] The actual campaign was dominated by opinion polls which maintained a Labour lead which did not undermine Heath's dogged conviction that he could win. He stressed economic issues which his advisers told him offered his best prospect and he was aided by the publication of economic statistics which undermined the government's claim that the balance of payments problem had been resolved.[131] This enabled Heath to make an effective last minute broadcast, in which he repeated his claim about the underlying weakness of the economy.[132] Heath also gained from the cost of living issue, through press reports about a statement in a party background briefing paper. He never made the infamous promise to reduce prices 'at a stroke' which has since been claimed, but there was a comment in a briefing document that the Conservatives proposed to break into the wage-price spiral by cutting Selective Employment Tax (SET) and holding down prices in the nationalised industries which, 'would at a stroke, reduce the rise in prices, increase productivity and reduce unemployment'.[133] Acquitting Heath of the charge of pledging to reduce prices at a stroke, ignores the fact that Heath never disavowed the media's presentation of the 'at a stroke' promise. There is also 'poetic justice' in this misrepresentation, since the Conservatives unscrupulously used prices in the election without offering any strategy for dealing with the problem given their disavowal of incomes policy.[134]

The manifesto *A Better Tomorrow* was radical in tone, more so than Selsdon, but less so than Heath's Quiet Revolution speech delivered at the autumn 1970 Conference. The manifesto's repudiation of incomes policy was a hostage to fortune in its statement: 'we utterly reject the philosophy of compulsory wage control'.[135] Another promise which differed from government policy after 1970 was the statement on EEC membership that: 'there is a price which we are not prepared to pay. Our sole commitment is to negotiate, no more, no less'.[136] The manifesto expressed no interest in denationalisation or monetarism.[137]

A final ORC poll placed the Conservatives ahead, upstaging its rivals by undertaking a final survey on election eve and building in a mechanism to allow for differential turnout to favour the Conservatives. Yet the result was not merely the consequence of a late swing. Hurd convincingly suggests, 'the victory was there all the time' but what happened was that 'the press influenced the polls, and the polls influenced the press; each error fed the other. Under the surface people were making up their minds on their impression of Mr Wilson's Government over five years'.[138] The Conservative victory was interpreted as a triumph for Heath. This put him in a powerful position as Prime Minister, but had the unfortunate effect of convincing him that he could ignore his critics. Yet the result did weaken the challenge from Powell and the fundamentalist Tories. The result gave the Conservatives 330 seats, 13 million votes, 46 per cent of the poll and a swing of 4.8 per cent. The 1970 election inaugurated one of the most hyperactive and controversial governments in Conservative history.

Critics on the right

The first upsurge in right-wing ideas after 1965 was not a conscious rejection of 'One Nation Conservatism' or the consensus. The majority of party activists and many of its leaders had 'Thatcherite' yearnings, but these sentiments were submerged for much of the post-war era. Evidently, these ideas did not first capture the party after 1975 with Thatcher's leadership. Few commentators on modern Conservatism recognise that the change among party thinkers and activists dated from the mid-1960s when there was a marked shift to a more uncompromising politics which was resisted by the party's leaders. While they considered such ideas to be too divisive and unpopular, a tougher approach was 'wildly popular with the Conservative rank and file'.[139] In retrospect, it appears that One Nation ideas were ever only significant at leadership level, and were motivated by the imperatives of electoral politics and party competition.

The divergence between rank-and-file and leadership opinion has been characterised by Andrew Gamble as the conflict between the paramount consideration of the leadership which is to secure political support and that of the rank-and-file which is to propound Conservative ideology. Tory activists had long wanted less intervention, restrictions on union power and lower taxes and Heath's policy review was an attempt to 'paper over the cracks'.[140] Gamble argues that Heath's attempt to maintain most of the 'post-1945 Progressive' value system intact was challenged ideologically from the right because it had become exhausted and was inadequate for 'negotiating the politics of support in opposition'.[141] While Gamble tends to underestimate the force and coherence of the right's challenge in the late 1960s, he is correct to assert that it lacked real unity and a single theme 'to orchestrate all the dissident forces in the Party', and that it represented 'no well-defined economic interests'.[142] The challenge in the late 1960s prepared the way for the enthusiastic adoption by Thatcher of the proposals which had been gestating for a decade. While much of the challenge was in theoretical form, there were also pressures which emanated from within the ACP process. Above all there was the influence of Enoch Powell.

The first attack on Heath's technocratic approach to politics came in 1965 from Angus Maude who had long been on the right.[143] He was anxious that the Conservatives had lost their feel for what people wanted, and warned that 'for the Tories to speak simply like technocrats will get them nowhere'. The party should have a solid philosophy to prevent it from being swept along by passing 'fads and fancies' and Conservatives should do more than seek greater material advance. They should challenge trade union power, high taxation and the current administration of the welfare state.[144]

Two young Conservative thinkers captured the direction in which the party was heading, when they demanded in 1966 that it should alter its posture towards trades unions. Timothy Raison asserted that a capitalist ideology was necessary to run a market economy and this required conflict, since there are two opposing sides in industry.[145] David Howell argued that strikes were to be welcomed as evidence that managers were managing rather than capitulating to trade union demands to preserve 'a cosy climate of inefficiency'.[146] Howell's ideological movements since the 1960s are a useful weathervane of the dominant thought within the party. By 1986 he described the Churchill and Heath years as an odd episode in Conservative history in which it accepted sociological analyses and allowed itself to be captured by a 'collectivist civil service'. It forgot the 'modest, middle-owning parts of society' whose ideas provide 'ballast'.[147] Heath had been too much in thrall to large capital.[148] In claiming consistency he can reasonably argue to have introduced the term 'privatisation' into British political discourse as early as 1970, although he suggested the need to 'invent something better'. Urging the achievement of economies by transferring functions to the private sector he saw merit in Peter Drucker's word 'privatisation' to differentiate the process from that of denationalisation.[149]

Joseph's protest that he only became a true Conservative in 1974, ignores his enthusiasms in the late 1960s for a free market and selectivity in the social services. His interventions at the Selsdon Park conference, however, demonstrate his proclivity to agonise about whatever political posture he adopted. The Monday Club widened its criticisms of the drift of post-war Conservatism in the mid-1960s. John Biggs-Davidson, for example, declared: 'under the creeping socialism of a generation we have been stripped well-nigh naked of our monetary, military and moral defences'.[150] He too rejected materialism which differentiated his ideas from 'Thatcherism'. Rhodes Boyson, who was later a strong supporter of Thatcher, also launched a coded attack on Heath's leadership, when he criticised the party's drift towards government control, egalitarianism, and heavy taxation. He urged 'an alternative morality'.[151]

The most potent challenge from the right in this period, however, came from Enoch Powell. His influence with the rank-and-file of the party was considerable until he committed the 'unforgivable sin' of disloyalty. While he appeared to be in the vanguard, he was also popularising ideas which had long been in circulation in the party. Joseph claims that it was Powell who converted both Thatcher and himself to true Conservatism.[152] While the transmission of ideas between individuals is more complex than Joseph recognises, there is little doubt that Powellism was a precursor of Thatcherism. He had less direct influence at the time than he did upon the thinking of those who were to take power in the party in the 1970s, however, because of the extremes to which he took his proposals. This irritated those who broadly agreed with his ideas. Powell's advocacy of total denationalisation made it difficult for Heath to support any at all, and his recommendation that income tax should be reduced to four shillings (20p), discredited the case for lower taxes generally.[153] Yet such politicians are necessary because by advancing 'clear cut alternatives they are available in a political crisis to replace the leaders and the policies that have failed'.[154] Powell's appeal cut across all classes. It consisted of free-market ideas and hostility to immigration and incomes policy to attract the middle classes and the workers respectively.[155] Powell's propositions about economics were too arcane to attract non-activist support, except perhaps for middle-class small businessmen and shop-keepers in the West Midlands. Yet his opposition to immigration gave him a broad social appeal, and his rejection of economic interventionism made him a spokesman for small capital against the interests of big business. His appeal was, therefore, to more than one narrow sectional interest.

Many Tories were censorious about Powell, for example, Barber described him as a 'frustrated fanatic' and a 'traitor'.[156] Heath was his most vehement opponent as he had the most to lose should Powell have succeeded. Not only did Heath dismiss Powell from the Shadow Cabinet over immigration, but he described Powell's speeches on the subject as reflecting 'man's inhumanity to man'.[157] Yet Powell was followed by a group of enthusiastic supporters among Conservative MPs. They lacked effectiveness, however, partly because of their reluctance to challenge the party's established leadership but also because Powell was reluctant to organise a 'faction'. He tended to be 'maverick' in his opinions and was far from being simplistically ultra-right wing, as in his opposition to capital punishment. It followed that the MPs who supported him were themselves divided on the key issues. When Powell's standing with the public was high, his 'loose tendency' of supporters were in disarray. For example, when Powell became opposed to the European Common Market, Nicholas Ridley remained an enthusiast, and while John Biffen agreed with Powell on Europe, he was 'compassionate' on social issues.[158]

Powell was undoubtedly ambitious and Humphrey Berkely describes him as 'messianic'. He first refused office under Churchill in 1952, resigned as Financial Secretary to the Treasury in 1958, refused office from Macmillan in 1959 unless Peter Thorneycroft was readmitted to the Cabinet, rejected office under Home in 1963 in protest against the exclusion of Butler from the leadership and continued to rebuff Home after the 1964 defeat in order to concentrate on returning the party to first principles.[159] On certain issues his credentials were left-wing, for example, his opposition to capital punishment and free medical prescriptions for private patients and his support for homosexual law reform.[160] His views on medical prescriptions were also compatible, however, with a consistently free-market approach since he believed that private medicine should stand or fall independently, and not through an artificially 'rigged' market. He similarly supported the Labour government's proposal to phase out private pay beds from the NHS in 1975, since he considered that private medicine should not be reduced to the undignified role of aiding 'queue jumping'. Powell's undoubted personal ambition, therefore, was not so intense as to undermine this integrity. The one possible exception is that of Europe, where he supported Britain's application in 1965 and urged that a Minister for Europe be appointed.[161] He justified his *volte face* in opposing British membership from 1969, with the claim that he had previously failed to see the political aspirations of the European movement and the potential loss of British sovereignty led him to withdraw his support.

The unifying principle which lay at the roots of his political philosophy was that of patriotism. For Powell, the defence of the British state was at the heart of his Toryism, even to the point of voting Labour in 1974 because of its readiness to hold a referendum on the Common Market.[162] His patriotism led him to describe 'the unbroken life of the English nation over 1,000 years and more' as a 'unique phenomenon in history, the product of a specific set of circumstances' which ensured that 'the deepest instinct of the Englishman ... is for continuity'.[163] This intense patriotism coherently linked Powell's main preoccupations: his support for Ulster's full integration into the United Kingdom, his fear that mass immigration challenged the identity of the nation, his concern that Britain should concentrate on affordable national defences rather than seek a world-wide role, and his rejection of a united Europe. His conception of Conservatism is patriotic, in that it is rooted in 1,000 years of Britain's unique institutions, and lacks the characteristics of a universal dogma such as Socialism.[164]

Powell warned of the perils for the Conservative Party of a contradictory adherence to patriotism and support for European integration. He argued that 'the mental association of patriotism with the Tory Party is strong and persistent', and that the conflict for the party between European integration and patriotism could be 'mortal'.[165] He cited predictions from the President of the European Commission that the Common Market was leading towards a common currency and a Parliament directly elected by universal suffrage, which he argued would lead the Bank of England to become a mere 'local branch office'.[166]

Membership would mean an end of the British people holding their MPs accountable and the demise of Britain as 'a free, independent and self governing nation'.[167] The most striking phenomenon of Powell's opposition to membership, however, was his preference for a Socialist Britain to a united Western Europe. While he was a precursor of 'Thatcherism', it is clear that the Eurosceptics in the 1990s differed from him, in that they put their ultimate allegiance to the Conservative Party above their disdain for the Maastricht Treaty. Even those who were later to lose the Whip saw their status as temporary. The intensity of Powell's opposition to European Economic Community (EEC) membership reveals the degree to which Europe was becoming an ideological 'fault line' in the party; one still evident in 1994.[168]

Powell is associated with the advocacy of a free economy even at a time when this contributed towards his period in exile.[169] Yet the unacceptability of free-market ideas to the party's leadership should not be confused with the view that Powell introduced market principles to an otherwise 'corporatist' Tory party in the 1960s. A large part of 'the Conservative nation' had never lost its allegiance to the free market and Powell articulated and systematised these submerged ideas. He was sympathetic to a measure of social protection and accepted the need for government intervention in non-economic fields such as defence, health and education. He argued governments should found universities or a free medical service if they considered it desirable that people should be well educated or cured of their ailments.[170] It was also reasonable for a government to regulate by determining that it is unacceptable 'to employ persons below a given age', 'to employ women only in certain defined conditions' and to impose 'certain requirements of health and safety'.[171] While the state can legitimately determine that an industry should be prevented in a given area, he argued that individuals acting through the market on the basis of the indices of prices and profits, should make their own decisions. The state is thus prevented from 'directing in detail the economic activity of all the members of the community'.[172] It is evident that despite Powell's reputation for unremitting logic and extremism, he was more sympathetic to state regulation than the Thatcher and Major governments, and he defined the limits of state activity less restrictively than the Conservatives of the 1990s. He was more influenced by the 'compassionate' principles of the post-war settlement than were his later admirers. Indeed, some contemporary Conservatives challenged his position by refuting the clear and logical distinction between intervention and regulation. Rejecting Powell's claim that there is no need to choose between spending on health or on defence while favouring a balanced national budget, Utley asserted that there is an unavoidable choice between guns or butter and between high public expenditure and low taxation. He questioned Powell's free-market credentials because of the judgement that the state should determine which industries should be allowed to develop in a particular location.[173] This is an acute criticism but there are consistent principles in Powell's economic philosophy. These include state regulation but not intervention in the economy; the concentration of government on controlling the money supply; floating exchange rates as a self-correcting mechanism against an over-valued currency, and opposition to prices and incomes policy. He also made an effective defence of the role of high profits within a capitalist society. 'In a capitalist society there is no such thing as a 'just' profit any more than a 'just' price. The only point about price, the only usefulness of price, is to indicate the relationship of supply and demand. There is no justice or injustice about it ... those who talk about fair prices or just profits are talking the language of socialism in which what people do is decreed by the Government'.[174] Although he briefly defended Macmillan's National Incomes Commission (NIC) in 1961 when he held ministerial office, he consistently argued unions were not the cause of inflation. In 1964 he argued the fault lay with governments for yielding to public sector pay demands by printing money.[175] Powell's commitment to monetarism was consistent and predated the widespread reconversion of Conservatives to the monetarist cause after the discovery of Friedman as a rival economic guru to Keynes in the 1970s. In 1968 Powell argued that 'the cash factory' was a major problem, which was 'selling Government securities to the money market and at the same time providing the money market with the wherewithal to purchase them'. This debauching of the currency was the responsibility of government.[176]

A final element in Powell's political economy was denationalisation. He kept this particular faith alive when it appeared that the party's leadership had come to terms with the mixed economy. This kept open the path, with some assistance from Ridley, which later led to the development of privatisation. Powell argued that Conservatives should not accept the myth that the nationalisation of coal, steel, and the railways had been inevitable, since they could have continued in private ownership by raising money on the markets. He teased timid Conservatives with the charge that had the ICI been nationalised then the current leadership would favour retaining it in the public sector.[177] This accusation was justified, since despite Powell's demand for denationalisation at the time, Heath's response was one of 'calling a halt to further nationalisation'.[178] Heath only decided even to mention the issue after an exchange with Brendon Sewill from the CRD at a Steering Committee meeting. After Heath had observed that any proposals for denationalisation would 'displease industrial moderates without pleasing the hard-liners in the Party', Sewill warned that a curious silence on denationalisation created the danger that 'hard liners would raise the issue and say what is going to be done about it'.

Powell's patriotism was compatible with that advanced later by Thatcher in that it shed Imperialist illusions without *angst* over Britain's past. He rejected 'illusions' about the value of the British Commonwealth, and opposed aid to former colonies on moral and economic grounds. The former colonies should rather adopt the free market in order to advance economically.[179] He told the 1965 Conference that defence of the British nation state was vital to Toryism but that this involved the end of Britain's role in South-East Asia.[180] His nationalism diverged from Thatcher's because of his deep-rooted anti-Americanism. He asserted that Britain's passionate American alliance was the result of recent British Prime Ministers having American mothers. He also attacked Labour's Atlanticism, even suggesting that the Labour government would be willing to send troops to support the American effort in the Vietnam War. His patriotic respect for traditional institutions, encouraged Powell to defeat the joint front-bench proposals to reform the House of Lords in 1968.[181]

The issue which transformed Powell from being an arcane right-wing ideologue into a major populist political figure was immigration. New

Commonwealth immigration had expanded rapidly in the 1950s and was a submerged issue in British politics for years before it surfaced in the Smethwick constituency in 1964. Powell is considered to have exploited the immigration issue without warning in his notorious 'Rivers of Blood' speech in April 1968, because of his desire to challenge Heath for the party leadership. Despite his ambition and disdain for Heath, his motives were complex. He avoided supporting many populist positions, and it was his patriotism which committed him to the idea of controlling immigration. Powell had been frightened by the 'colour clash' that he had noted during a visit to the United States in 1967. A leading Birmingham right-wing Conservative MP, Harold Gurden, also urged Powell to lead the anti-immigration campaign which a few fringe MPs were taking up.[182] Powell had also raised the issue previously. In 1967 he stated that 'no amount of misrepresentation, abuse or unpopularity is going to prevent the Tory Party and myself from voicing the dictates of common sense or reason.'[183] He saw himself as representing the back streets of the Midlands against the 'cocooned' upper-class leadership of the Tory party and the Shadow Home Affairs spokesman Quintin Hogg. There was a series of protests from the national membership about Powell's dismissal by Heath at this time. Conservative files demonstrate that many local parties were strong supporters of Powell and were bitter about his treatment, and nineteen out of the nineteen calls from constituency associations supported him rather than the leadership.[184] Yet the Tory leadership was not entirely protected from public sentiment on the race question which explains its opposition in 1968 to the Labour government's anti-race discrimination bill and support for the government's exclusion of British passport-holding Kenyan Asians. It was in this context that Powell inflamed the issue in 1968. The speech damaged Powell's credibility with many Conservative activists, because of its intemperate language, and its challenge to the leadership. Its impact on party disunity was highlighted by the fact that it was circulated to the press, although it had been cleared neither with Heath nor with Hogg. Powell used the classical allusion to the 'River Tiber foaming with much blood', referred to parents urging their children to emigrate because of Britain's dire future unless immigrants were repatriated, described old ladies who had excrement pushed through their letter boxes by immigrant children, and quoted dubious statistical projections. In later speeches he added references to illegal immigrants and Home Office deception of the British people about the problem.[185] *The Times* called for him to be sacked, described his speech as 'evil' and him as a 'racialist'.[186] While Powell was convinced about the need to diminish the immigrant population by subsidised repatriation he was also calculating that his best prospect of leading the party lay in a populist challenge to the Shadow Cabinet.[187]

The evidence that personal ambition was as important as ideological conflict in the contest between Powell and Heath is suggested in the vituperation of the language which Heath used to condemn Powell. Heath suggested that the ultimate logic of Powell's position was 'tyranny', and added that 'it must be fought wherever it rears its ugly presence. It had to be fought in Germany in the 1930s, in America in the 1950s. Wherever it happens today it must be fought'.[188] During the 1970 general election when Powell was linked to Nazism by Tony Benn, Heath was tepid in his condemnation of Benn, which led many non-Powellites to sympathise with Powell.[189] In return, Powell was tepid about Heath. In his late recommendation to voters to support the Conservatives, Powell made it clear that the election was not about a choice between 'a man with a pipe' and 'a man with a boat'.[190] Yet Powell's intervention in the campaign helped the Conservatives. The tide began to turn in Heath's favour in the last week of the campaign after Powell became involved, since he was 'in contact with public opinion'.[191] There is evidence of Powell's activity being marginally beneficial in the West Midlands.[192] Heath's victory finally destroyed Powell's chance of leading the party.

Powell went on to be a vigorous opponent of the Heath government. He was critical of the appointment of John Davis, recruited from the Confederation of British Industry (CBI) as Secretary of State for Industry which he regarded as a futile attempt to depoliticise government.[193] He accused Heath of appeasement in releasing an Arab terrorist, Leila Khaled.[194] Powell was a lone voice condemning the nationalisation of Rolls Royce because it involved the state financing failure. He deplored the view that state ownership was a vehicle to restore profitability in an unsuccessful company since it cast doubt upon free enterprise.[195] When the government retained Giro Bank in public ownership Powell observed that 'from this egg a whole farmyard of lame ducks will be laid'.[196] He attacked Heath's desire to create what he termed a 'Corporate paternalist Japanese type state', suggesting that a managed capitalist state is as undesirable as a Socialist state.[197]

While Powell was the most significant of the many voices urging that the policies associated with the party since 1951 should be curtailed, he tended to alienate intellectuals by his *reductio ad absurdum* positions. A common view was that while Powell's ideas – for example, a defence and foreign policy rooted in Europe, a competitive economic policy and a social policy based on 'humane and generous selectivity' – should be followed by a Conservative Cabinet, it was unimportant that Powell should himself be a member.[198] He had the gift of communicating with an intellectual and a mass audience. If the sprinkling of classical allusions in his media appearances was beyond the comprehension of the masses it reinforced the 'respectability' of his message. It is the dream of many Conservative politicians to forge a genuinely democratic Tory movement, 'to rise to power on a wave of evangelical enthusiasm, to present themselves not in the characteristically Conservative role of safe men with their feet on the ground, but as prophets expressing the native sentiments of simple people in vigorous and intelligible language'.[199] Powell's goal was to make Conservatism a positive creed, by converting it from Imperialism to patriotism and from intervention to the free market.

Utley was a Conservative thinker in the 1960s, who urged a change in direction to avert national decline. Yet in advocating change and a 'radical policy of economic liberalism', he also remained a High Tory.[200] He retained a greater Tory scepticism of a doctrine than Thatcher. He argued in 1981, for example, that in 'reconquering territory which had been lost to State intervention', and in necessarily adopting a messianic tone to achieve that end, she would be better able to carry people with her if her tone became more sceptical and less doctrinal'.[201] He retained doubts about the dogma of the free market. Utley upheld the contradictory principles of the free market and social organicism. His intellectual standing should not be exaggerated as he was essentially a *Daily Telegraph* editorial writer, given to sweeping assertions about the political instincts of the British.

The social services have always been controversial for Conservatives but Geoffrey Howe addressed these issues in the 1960s as social services spokesman. He enquired, 'do we want for ever, to fight a series of pensioneering elections with politicians bidding against each other with promises to raise the basic rate?' He argued that indexed state pensions were inflationary and that the private sector should be more involved.[202] The Young Conservatives (YCs) also challenged Beveridge's universality principle and claimed that the nation could not sustain it given the inadequate production of national wealth. In defence of selectivity the YCs argued that the time had come 'to seek out areas of need and to remedy these'. Their report also sought the abandonment of flat rate family allowances and maternity benefits.[203] Howe extended his radicalism in 1966 to the advocacy of loans instead of grants for higher education, higher charges for further education, and charges for certain health care and motorway tolls. He recognised that voters' flesh might creep but thought it necessary to deal with these issues as Conservatives stood for choice in health and education. Howe confirms that One Nation Conservatism was never deeply rooted in the post-war party and that taxation had never been conceived of to redistribute wealth. He accepts that the party began to shift to a more radical approach in the 1960s, because of union militance and electoral defeat. He also suggests that privatisation was 'bubbling up' at this time.[204]

While Ridley is untypical, his advisory committee on the nationalised industries produced spectacular proposals. Some committee members were less radical than Ridley himself and merely sought more commercial management. But there was a widespread animus against nationalisation and Ridley's plans were actually more far-reaching than the privatisation which had been achieved by 1995. Ridley was not a new convert to denationalisation: he entered politics in 1950 to reverse it. He saw then 'a sloppiness about the way public corporations behaved: early on I realised that they were dominated by their workforce, not their customers. Service was on a "take it or leave it" basis'. Taxpayers' money was also required to raise capital to support the trade union power which 'rampaged unrestrained' in these industries.[205]

The committee's reports on particular industries were bold. The denationalisation of electricity should be accompanied by a regulatory body to enhance efficiency for as long as it remained in public ownership. This involved 'carving up' electricity generation into regional boards to make and supply electricity. The gas industry was more difficult to nationalise, however, because the shift from town to North Sea gas required a greater degree of centralisation. Before full denationalisation took place Ridley urged that the Gas Council should remain as a monopoly with a regulatory commission, although North Sea exploration should be sold off and the Council should lose its monopoly of distribution and become a 'purchaser in the free market instead'. Ridley was confident that the coal industry could be sold off immediately as it was an extractive industry rather than a utility, which weakened its claim for public ownership. He asserted that it would be easy to get competition between coalfields just as coal competed with other fuels. The oversized coal industry had degenerated into a branch of the welfare state. Before privatisation it was necessary to reduce the coal industry to size through pit closures, and a Conservative government should weather the unpopularity that would follow from the emotion generated by the industry's past. He also proposed the denationalisation of steel.[206] While they remained in the nationalised sector, however, Ridley had little doubt that nationalised industries should be scrutinised by a parliamentary Select Committee rather than by the Treasury. If scrutiny was only to be within the Government 'it would be all wrapped up'.[207] While the animus against nationalisation in the party was evident, there was caution at Selsdon Park. Heath and Tony Barber argued that the Party should retain a position of 'responsible silence' on Ridley's proposal and there were strong feelings on the matter 'under the surface' because of Powell's influence. Surprisingly, Joseph urged a 'step by step' strategy while Carr wished to examine the proposals.[208]

There was little stress upon reducing the role of the state in this period, but one constituency report objected that in local government spending decisions were conducted in an atmosphere of violent opposition from the minority beneficiaries of expenditure while the great body of ratepayers were silent. The report also argued that local authorities should not undertake any service which could equally well be carried out in the private sector. This was the thinking which culminated in Thatcherite policies such as rate-capping, the Community Charge, and 'the enabling local authority'.[209]

Many of the policy proposals of the 1980s and 1990s were first aired in Conservative intellectual journals such as *Crossbow*, *Solon*, and the *Swinton Journal*. It was even considered necessary in order to secure a parliamentary nomination in the late 1960s to voice Powellite sentiments. Sir Anthony Meyer, for example, sought to live down his left-wing Conservative image by altering his stance and purporting to adopt monetarism. He started a journal to propound this while attempting to reconcile it with a socially liberal position.[210] He once presented a clumsy paper on monetarism to a group of right-wing Conservative MPs and claims that Nigel Birch, having slept through most of it, only grasped the fact that Meyer had been propounding monetarism. As a result Birch supported Meyer against strong opposition from Michael Howard and Ian Gow to inherit his seat in Flintshire. Monetarism was increasing in vogue within the party but *Solon* was an attempt to 'civilise the backlash'.[211]

The distinctive purpose of *Solon* was to build bridges between Conservatives in politics and education. This was a role for which Meyer was suited, because after losing his seat in 1964, he was employed by Central Office to liaise with the universities, because the party had lost the 'battle of ideas' with the intelligentsia. He first made contact with the monetarist economist Alan Walters, later to become Thatcher's economic guru, and he found Walters 'brilliant' but 'wayward'. From these contacts Meyer acquired his ephemeral interest in monetarism.[212] *Solon*'s first edition asserted that the Conservative Party was moving to the right because of the failures of economic planning and universal state welfare. It was now necessary to challenge the 'omniferous state'.[213] Meyer also proclaimed that the Conservative Party was against equality and for elitism.[214] He also pointed out that class was disappearing as a force in British society and that a vast middle class was emerging which was enjoying rising living standards within capitalist institutions.[215] Otherwise the journal hardly presented a coherent message. It published articles from the right advocating the merits of competition and liberty and cited BUPA membership and public schools as guarantors of freedom. It also published an article by Julian Amery commending Britain's buccaneering spirit as symbolised by Marlborough, Wellington, and Churchill; and a paean from John Biffen to patriotism, condemning the Common Market for its protectionism in contrast to Britain's free enterprise, open society.[216]

The *Swinton Journal* and *Crossbow* also ran articles in the late 1960s and early 1970s which demonstrated the growing assertiveness of the party's right-wing in challenging the drift of post-war Conservative Governments. The Monday Club's journal *Monday's World* also advanced right-wing nationalist and racialist ideas, while the other journals were concerned with economic and social policy. Yet one activist in the left-wing Tory pressure group, Pressure for Economic and Social Toryism, pointed out that the main reason for the Monday Club's success was that while encompassed within the ambit of the Conservative Party, it was able to propound extreme views. The members which it retained in the party's ranks were not worth keeping, as they were intolerant and sought to usurp the real nature of Conservativism. Club members infiltrated the party to secure parliamentary nominations and to oust sitting members, for example, Nigel Fisher.[217] In reality, the traditional authoritarians, imperialists and racists who were involved in the Monday Club were legacies of the Conservative past, whereas the neo-Liberal views expressed in the *Swinton Journal*, *Crossbow*, and *Solon* pointed to the reassertion of political values which were to prove the wave of the future.

Many neo-Liberals were optimistic that in Heath they had the leader ready to implement the strategy of a capital-owning democracy they favoured.[218] One interesting debate taking place within the intellectual Conservative journals concerned the nature of Conservative ideology and its lack of appeal to the intelligentsia. In a confidence building analysis Tibor Szamuely pointed out that such major theorists as Hobbes, Johnson, Burke, Coleridge, Wordsworth, Madison, Hamilton, Peel, Carlyle, Ruskin, Disraeli, and Arnold had been conservatives which disproved the idea that the Conservative Party is the 'stupid' party. Since the war, Popper, Berlin, Sparrow; and among MPs, Powell, Maude, and Hogg were unmatched in their intellectual standing. Szamuely argued that defeat demonstrated that pride in being 'the stupid party' with a working-class appeal was no longer sufficient. Yet he detected encouraging omens in the intellectual climate of the late 1960s. The appeal of coherent, scientific, and collectivist doctrines was being checked with the apostasy of Kingsley Amis, John Braine, Anthony Burgess, John Osborne, John Wain, Simon Raven, and Auberon Waugh. These and other British intellectuals were thoroughly disillusioned with the Labour government with its utilitarian approach to higher education, its threat to university autonomy, and its animus against grammar schools. Yet this process would not continue if Conservatism merely offered a diluted form of Socialism. The Conservative Party should proclaim itself as a capitalist party, with less government, more individualism, and a defence of property. Significantly, given Thatcher's later rejection of libertarian social experimentation, Szamuely also urged that the party should oppose permissiveness in order to promote tradition and the cultural heritage. He claimed that many intellectuals were unenthusiastic about cosmopolitan attitudes.[219] Szamuely clearly struck a chord in the party in 1968 since a number of leading party figures responded. Among party thinkers, for example, Biffen and Howell argued that Szamuely had neglected the notions of 'balance' and 'pragmatism'. This response revealed that the triumph of the ideas of the liberal New Right was not yet complete. Biffen was foreshadowing his call for a 'balanced ticket' in the party's leadership to weaken the domination of Thatcher in the mid-1980s.[220] He was certain that in a two-party system there was never likely to be a total victory either for 'free traders' or 'paternalists'.[221] Howell warned against 'fighting dogma with dogma', arguing that the theory of the free-market economy should be challenged because, as true Conservatives know, 'life is not as simple as political philosophy'.[222]

Significantly, most of the comment in the journal was supportive of Szamuely's position. For example, Roy Lewis argued that while Keynes had transformed the popular support for capitalism, the Conservative Party should now promote the alternative of liberal economics. This required less intervention, lower top rate taxation, and laws to curb the trade unions.[223] Arthur Seldon regretted that the party spoke with two voices. Maudling supported incomes policy, and his ideas, together with Boyle's and John Boyd-Carpenter's on education and social insurance respectively, were difficult to reconcile with the stance taken by Powell, Joseph, Thatcher, Maude, Howe, and Biffen. Yet Seldon still had faith in Heath's leadership and argued that Heath's approach 'causes the heart to beat faster'. Anticipating both aspects of Public Choice Theory and the appeal of Thatcherism, he stressed the importance of the individual, the family and the independent business, as against the mendacity of politicians. Society had developed to the stage where the 'emerging masses' as well as the middle classes sought the freedom to spend their own money. Utley also called for the extension of choice in both the public and the private sectors, advocating the use of vouchers in education. Summarising the debate, Szamuely's conclusions anticipated the Thatcherite commitment to the free economy, and to resistance to individual moral permissiveness. Utley was also revealing about the attitude of the Tory intellectuals to Powellism and offered an explanation why right-wing ideas were becoming more widely expressed. While Powell himself was becoming 'starker' and 'absurd', it was the economic emergency of July 1966 and the government's resort to deflationary measures which had altered the climate in the Conservative Party.[224]

There were signs of a growing suspicion of Heath. Szamuely sensed Heath's preference for the managerial reform of the state rather than its reduction. He argued that more was needed than plans for a smaller Cabinet, federal departments to reduce friction, fewer civil servants, and the introduction of new managerial techniques. These were of no value without the reduction of government. Samuel Brittan demanded policy changes which were more libertarian than those which either Thatcher or Heath would be prepared to accept. He suggested that economic and social liberalism were indivisible and that free enterprise should mean greater overall freedom, including a less rigid attitude to law and order.[225] The intellectual climate had altered and Heath could not ignore the criticism of earlier

Conservative governments, such as Seldon's discussion of the need for the Conservative Party to 'work its way back to trust', after its performance during the thirteen years from 1951 to 1964.

If Szamuely was seen as a significant ally by Conservatives in the 1960s in recapturing the intellectual initiative, by the time of his death in 1973 during Heath's government, his legacy was more contentious. When some in the CPC favoured publishing a posthumous pamphlet, Michael Young of the CRD objected. The pamphlet lauded the Conservative Party as 'the oldest political Party in the world. In 300 years it has amassed an unmatched wealth of political wisdom and practical experience. One feature ... has made it the envy of its opponents ... its extraordinary ability to adapt itself to changing circumstances, its capacity to change its social character whilst retaining its basic principles and to find a place within its ranks for every new social class which has emerged in the course of the country's histori-cal evolution'.[226] The convention existed for all CPC publications to be vetted by the CRD and Young complained about the pamphlet. He was concerned about Szamuely's transference of the politics of the Russian Imperial system to contemporary Britain, his negative views about young people and the British intelligentsia, and his portrayal of the Soviet system as the apotheo-sis of evil while being uncritical of right-wing dictatorships. While Young's views lend credence to Thatcher's later suspicion that the CRD was to the left of the party, the official CRD ruling from Fraser was that the CPC should be allowed to publish as it did not amount to Szamuely's canonisation. Fraser was also conscious that Szamuely was a minor figure whose appeal was mainly to disgruntled left-wing intellectuals who had moved right. Clearly, Szamuely's irascible dislike of the post-war era, and the ease with which his ideas could be portrayed as 'reactionary' created waves in the party in the early 1970s, at a time when its ideological position had become confused.

The proposal to float the pound was advanced two years before the col-lapse of the Bretton Woods agreement in August 1971.[227] It held no more appeal to Heath than did H. C. Elwell's call for private health insurance. Elwell claimed that Institute of Economic Affairs (IEA) research revealed that people preferred self-help to state aid, and so the way forward was to provide tax relief for private health insurance.[228] The strength of the com-mitment of the party's intelligentsia to economic Liberalism was deep, there-fore, and one editorial inverted the argument about contradictions between the free economy and the strong state against the left. It enquired why, if the left sympathised with the freedom in personal life, it rejected it in eco-nomic life?[229]

The Bow Group was a barometer of intellectual tendencies within the party, and *Crossbow* reflected the growing consensus for monetarism and the free market later than either the *Swinton Journal* or *Solon*. In 1971

Crossbow carried a plea that, contrary to the merger mania of the 1964 Labour government, Conservatives should recognise that large combines are slow to innovate, prone to labour troubles, offer a poorer service to their customers, and should be challenged by a tougher monopolies and merger policy. Since state intervention made large firms less competitive, governments should disengage from the economy. It sought the removal of regulations and controls from smaller companies, and the ending of flat rate social benefits. It also urged a more selective recruitment to higher education.[230] Anthony Lejeune also advanced his version of Tory principles, although he shrewdly recognised the British electorate's apathy about ideology. Judging that they were more interested in security than liberty, and asserting that elections are won on the basis of economic circumstances rather than political ideas, he advocated that Tories should introduce self-indulgent policies to satisfy their own preferences. Writing in the summer of 1971, before the U-turn was apparent, Lejeune argued that Conservatives should cease trying to appease their opponents and Heath's Conservative government should win the hearts of party activists. He cited the encouragement of private medicine, vouchers for education, ending the closed shop, the sale of arms to South Africa, and the reintroduction of the second vote for university graduates which had been abolished in the 1940s. He accused Heath of lacking Tory instincts and of providing a future Labour government with instruments that it could use to promote Socialism.[231] At this time the Bow Group expressed concern about its survival given its narrow recruitment base, which consisted primarily of lawyers, accountants, and City employees. Many of its members feared that the Monday Club was having a greater impact upon the party's policy-making.

While the challenge to Heath from the party's right was substantial between 1965 and 1972, it is incorrect to argue that the Selsdon Conference was concerned to achieve a compromise between the right's policy demands and Heath's managerialism. Macleod opposed the commitment to provide 100,000 training places, even though it was central to Heath's desire to strengthen the national economy. This was not because Macleod was a committed neo-Liberal, but because he considered elaborate training schemes to be 'unrealistic', and judged that 'there are not many votes in it'.[232] Macleod's emphasis on law and order was also electorally motivated. He argued that 'ordinary people are getting angry at the sight of scroungers on National Assistance and of demonstrators punching policemen'. Macleod's sympathy for 'the pacesetters' and 'opportunity' only constituted a partial conversion to the party's rightward surge. As he said about Powellite economics, 'I'm a fellow-traveller, but I prefer to get out one or two stops before the train crashes into the buffers at the terminus'.[233] The suggestions about greater selectivity in the social services at the Selsdon meeting were also motivated by the need to finance tax cuts rather than by a

'Thatcherite' antipathy to 'dependency culture'. In any event, Heath resisted the pressure and argued that selectivity could be difficult because it means 'different things to the different services, one thing in housing and another in education'. Yet such comments did not still the concerns about the level of public expenditure. Brian Reading wrote a paper posing the question, 'how far should we go in scrapping various types of universal subsidies in order to make room for tax cuts?' He also proposed selectivity, the payment of family allowances only to those below tax levels, the provision of housing subsidy only to people in need not to bricks and mortar, and ending such indiscriminate supports as investment grants, regional employment premiums, and agricultural subsidies.[234]

The right-wing challenge was generalised and theoretical in character from the mid-1960s and mainly a product of the party's intelligentsia. Some ideas, however, were translated into the key appropriate for political action. Powell also evoked enthusiasm from the predominantly right-wing rank-and-file. Heath responded by occupying the party with the ACP and by making limited concessions. To appease the membership of the National Union he made outspokenly right-wing comments after Powell's Rivers of Blood speech in April 1968, and he also adhered stubbornly to certain 'hard' policies for a brief period in government after June 1970. This phenomenon became apparent with Heath's dogged determination to introduce admission charges to museums and art galleries.[235] The 'coming out' of the party's true ideological preference was the result of electoral defeat, national economic difficulty, and a decline in deference. The growth of small business pressures in the party in the 1970s added an economic interest to underpin the ideological changes which culminated in Thatcherism, which was a response to deeply held desires among the party's rank-and-file and intelligentsia alike. It was not a dramatic conversion by a powerful leader imposing an alien ideology contrary to party tradition. However valid the criticisms of the Thatcher era by Tory grandees may be, they neglect the atavistic desires of the party to which they belonged in the decade leading up to Thatcher's accession to the leadership.

Notes

1 P. Hennessy and A. Seldon (eds.), *Ruling Performance* (London, Basil Blackwell, 1987), p. 314.
2 John Ramsden, 'From Churchill to Heath' in Lord Butler, *The Conservative Party from its Origins to 1965* (London: Allen and Unwin, 1972), p. 479.
3 A. Howard, *RAB. The Life of R. A. Butler* (London: Macmillan, 1987), p. 339.
4 *Spectator*, 30 July 1965, p. 139.
5 *The Economist*, 31 July 1965, p. 417.
6 This conception draws from the theory of political factions in the Conservative Party advanced by Anthony Seldon in 'The Conservative Party since 1945' in

T. Gourvish and A. O'Day, *Britain Since 1945* (London: Macmillan, 1991), p. 252.

7 Stephen Ingle, *The British Party System* (London: Blackwell, 1987), p. 73.

8 *Spectator*, 15 October 1965.

9 Martin Burch, 'Who are the New Tories?', *New Society*, 11 October 1984.

10 John Ramsden, 'Conservatives since 1945', *Contemporary Record*, 2 (Spring 1988).

11 Roy Hattersley, in *Spectator*, 30 July 1965, p. 143.

12 *Daily Telegraph*, 2 July 1965.

13 Alan Watkins in the *Spectator*, 30 July 1965.

14 See R. Maudling, *Memoirs* (London: Sidgwick and Jackson, 1978), p. 141 and p. 191.

15 John Campbell, *Edward Heath* (London: Jonathan Cape, 1993), pp. 230–1.

16 *Spectator*, 30 July 1965, p. 140.

17 John Ramsden, 'From Churchill to Heath', pp. 470–1.

18 Quotations cited in C. Booker, *The Rise of the Neophiliacs* (London: Collins, 1970), pp. 21–2.

19 *Ibid*, p. 23.

20 Maudling, *Memoirs*, p. 142.

21 Campbell, *Edward Heath*, pp. 182–3.

22 Humphrey Berkely, *The Odyssey of Enoch* (London: Hamilton, 1973), p. 19.

23 Andrew Roth, *Enoch Powell: Tory Tribune* (London: Macdonald, 1970), p. 327.

24 Douglas E. Schoen, *Enoch Powell and the Powellites* (London: Macmillan, 1977), p. 15.

25 *Ibid*, pp. 327–30.

26 *Spectator*, 30 July 1965, p. 142.

27 Booker, *The Rise of the Neophiliacs*, p. 23.

28 Peter Walker, David Howell, John Macgregor and Douglas Hurd all served under Margaret Thatcher's leadership.

29 A. Roth, *Heath and the Heathmen* (London: Routledge, Kegan & Paul, 1972), p. xiv.

30 D. Butler and D. Kavanagh, *The British General Election of 1974* (London: Macmillan 1975), *passim*.

31 Ramsden, 'From Churchill to Heath', pp. 470–1.

32 *Putting Britain Right Ahead*, Central Office pamphlet, No 4778, 1965, Introduction.

33 Ramsden, 'From Churchill to Heath', p. 473.

34 Martin Seliger, *Ideology and Politics* (London: Allen and Unwin, 1976), chapter 4.

35 Booker, *The Rise of the Neophiliacs*.

36 *The Economist*, 9 October 1965, p. 129.

37 *Spectator*, 8 October 1965.

38 Richard Rose, *The Problem of Party Government* (London: Macmillan, 1974), p. 392.

39 *Putting Britain Right Ahead*, Foreword.

40 Richard Crossman, *The Diaries of a Cabinet Minister*, Vol. 1 (London: Hamish Hamilton and Jonathan Cape, 1975), pp. 351–2.

41 'Conservative Party Policy-Making, 1965–1970', *Contemporary Record*, 3 (Spring 1990), pp. 32–4 and 36–8.
42 Rose, *The Problem of Party Government*, p. 394.
43 P. Norton and A. Aughey, *Conservatives and Conservatism* (London: Temple Smith, 1981), p. 148.
44 Robert Rhodes James, *Ambitions and Realities. British Politics 1964–1970* (London: Weidenfeld and Nicolson, 1970), p. 290.
45 Norton and Aughey, *Conservatives and Conservatism*, p. 149.
46 Ramsden, 'Conservatives since 1945', p. 246.
47 Nigel Fisher, *Ian Macleod* (London: Deutsch, 1973), pp. 203–5.
48 Campbell, *Edward Heath*, p. 221.
49 Nigel Harris, *Competition and the Corporate Society* (London: Methuen, 1972), p. 172.
50 Campbell, *Edward Heath*, p. 220.
51 Rose, *The Problem of Party Government*, p. 395.
52 George Hutchinson, *Edward Heath* (London: Longmans, 1970), p. 180.
53 *Ibid.*, pp. 182–3.
54 S. H. Beer, *Modern British Politics* (London: Faber, 1969), p. 59.
55 Maurice Peston, 'Conservative Economic Philosophy', *Political Quarterly*, 44 (1973), pp. 411–24.
56 Peter Hennessy, *Whitehall* (London: Secker and Warburg, 1989), p. 211.
57 SC(68)9, 11 June 1968.
58 *Ibid.*
59 CRD 3/7/4/3; 27 June 1967.
60 *Ibid.*, 27 June 1969.
61 View expressed at the Institute of Contemporary History witness seminar, 4 October 1989.
62 CRD 3/7/7/7, Record of Proceedings of Selsdon Park Meeting, January 1970.
63 Dennis Kavanagh, *Thatcherism and British Politics. The End of Consensus?* (Oxford: Oxford University Press, 1989), p. 4.
64 Norton and Aughey, *Conservatives and Conservatism*, p. 149.
65 *The Economist*, 7 February 1970.
66 Maudling, *Memoirs*, p. 141.
67 Alfred Sherman quoted in John Ranelagh, *Thatcher's People* (London: Fontana, 1991), p. 92.
68 *The Economist*, 7 February 1970, p. 14.
69 *Spectator*, 24 January 1970.
70 *Spectator*, 7 February 1970.
71 *The Economist*, 14 December 1968, p. 10.
72 *Spectator*, 26 November 1965, p. 683.
73 Denis Healey, *The Time of My Life* (London: Joseph, 1989), p. 333.
74 Crossman, *Diaries*, Vol. 1, p. 299.
75 *Ibid.*, p. 334.
76 Fisher, *Ian Macleod*, p. 263.
77 Ian Gilmour, *Body Politic* (London: Hutchinson, 1969), p. 11.
78 Quoted in Ingle, *The British Party System*, p. 40.
79 Gilmour, *Body Politic*, pp. 37–44.

80 Quintin Hailsham, *The Conservative Case* (Harmondsworth: Penguin, revised edition, 1959), p. 169.
81 Gilmour, *Body Politic*, p. 92.
82 Lord Butler, *The Conservative Party*, p. 17.
83 D. Butler and A. King, *The British General Election of 1966* (London: Macmillan, 1966), p. 65.
84 *The Sunday Times*, 28 November 1965.
85 Butler and King, *The British General Election of 1966*, p. 68.
86 Conservative Political Centre, *The New Conservatism* (London, 1955), p. 15.
87 Alan Watkins in *Spectator*, 8 October 1965, p. 438.
88 Rose, *The Problem of Party Government*, p. 421.
89 Quoted in Hennessy and Seldon, *Ruling Performance*, p. 310.
90 Jim Bulpitt, 'The Discipline of the New Democracy', *Political Studies*, 34 (1986), pp. 19–39.
91 John Ramsden, *The Making of Conservative Party Policy* (London: Longman, 1980), p. 234.
92 *Spectator*, 30 July 1965, p. 139.
93 *Spectator*, 15 October 1965, p. 470.
94 Ben Pimlott, *Harold Wilson* (London: Harper Collins, 1992), p. 395; but see also p. 8.
95 *Spectator*, 15 October 1965, p. 470.
96 Crossman, *Diaries*, Vol. 1, pp. 351–2.
97 *Ibid.*
98 Campbell, *Edward Heath*, p. 199.
99 *The Times*, 14 October 1965.
100 Butler and King, *The British General Election of 1966*, pp. 265–6.
101 Lord Archer interviewed on *The World at One*, BBC Radio 4, 8 September 1993.
102 *The Sunday Telegraph*, 1 and 22 August 1965.
103 Campbell, *Edward Heath*, p. 210.
104 Barbara Castle, *The Castle Diaries* (London: Macmillan, 1990), pp. 345–7.
105 *The Economist*, 15 October 1966, p. 228.
106 *Ibid.*
107 Campbell, *Edward Heath*, pp. 224–8.
108 *The Economist*, 9 November 1968, p. 19.
109 *The Listener*, 25 April 1968.
110 Campbell, *Edward Heath*, p. 224.
111 *The Times*, 21 November 1967.
112 Campbell, *Edward Heath*, p. 227.
113 Jim Prior, *A Balance of Power* (London: Hamilton, 1986), p. 48.
114 *Ibid.*, p. 72.
115 Campbell, *Edward Heath*, p. 216. See also, Prior, *A Balance of Power*, p. 25.
116 Letter from Marples to Heath, CCO/20/1/15, 3 May 1966.
117 Letter from DuCann to Marples, 12 February 1967, CCO/20/1/15.
118 Note in CCO/20/1/15.
119 Letter, 8 February 1967.
120 Radio Interview summarised in CCO/20/1/15.
121 Conversations with leading Conservatives.

122 CCO 500/27/7, undated documents.
123 A. Alexander and A. Watkins, *The Making of the Prime Minister: 1970* (London: Macdonald, 1970), p. 62.
124 CPC 500/27/7.
125 CCO 4/10/255, 18 July 1968.
126 CRD 3/9/69, 21 January 1969.
127 CPC 12/9/71.
128 Edward Heath to Roy Lewis, 9 April 1968.
129 Alexander and Watkins, *The Making of the Prime Minister*, p. 168.
130 CRD 3/9/69.
131 Campbell, *Edward Heath*, p. 277.
132 David Butler and Michael Pinto-Duchinsky, *The British General Election of 1970* (London: Macmillan, 1971), p. 167.
133 *The Times*, 17 June 1970.
134 Campbell, *Edward Heath*, p. 282.
135 The Conservative Party, *A Better Tomorrow*, 1970, p. 11.
136 *Ibid.*, pp. 28–9.
137 Ranelagh, *Thatcher's People*, pp. 28–9.
138 Douglas Hurd, *An End To Promises* (London: Collins, 1979), p. 25.
139 A. Seldon, *UK Political Parties* (London: Philip Allan, 1990), p. 31.
140 *Ibid.*, p. 32.
141 A. Gamble, *The Conservative Nation* (London: Routledge & Kegan Paul, 1974), p. 91.
142 *Ibid.*, p. 92.
143 *The Times*, Obituary, 11 November 1993.
144 *Spectator*, 14 January 1966.
145 Gamble, *The Conservative Nation*, pp. 93–6.
146 Quoted in Hugh Young, *One of Us* (London: Pan, 1990), p. 57.
147 David Howell, *The Conservative Tradition and the 1980s: Three Gifts of Insight Restored* (Centre for Policy Studies, 1986), p. 3.
148 *Ibid.*
149 David Howell, *A New Style of Government*, Conservative Political Centre pamphlet (May 1970), p. 8.
150 Quoted in Howell, *A New Style of Government*, p. 58.
151 Young, *One of Us*, p. 60.
152 Institute of Contemporary History Symposium, reported in *Contemporary Record*, 3 (Spring, 1990).
153 John O'Sullivan, *Swinton Journal* (Autumn 1968), p. 40.
154 Gamble, *The Conservative Nation*, p. 115.
155 T. E. Utley, *Enoch Powell: The Man and His Thinking* (London: William Kimber, 1968), p. 172.
156 Patrick Cosgrave, *The Lives of Enoch Powell* (London: Bodley Head, 1989), p. 193.
157 *Ibid.*, p. 270.
158 *Ibid.*, p. 261.
159 Berkely, *The Odyssey of Enoch*, p. 19.
160 *Ibid.*, p. 25.

161 Andrew Roth, *Enoch Powell*, p. 328.
162 Roy Lewis, *Enoch Powell: Principle in Politics* (London: Cassell, 1979), p. 12.
163 Cited in Enoch Powell, *Freedom and Reality* (London: Batsford, 1969), p. 257.
164 Enoch Powell, 'Conservatism and Social Problems', *Swinton Journal* (Autumn 1968), p. 8.
165 Enoch Powell, *Common Market: Renegotiate or Come Out* (Kingswood: Paperfront Books, 1973), p. 108.
166 *Ibid.*, pp. 15–17.
167 *Ibid.*, p. 57.
168 *Financial Times*, 2 February 1994.
169 Kenneth Baker, *The Turbulent Years: My Life in Politics* (London: Faber, 1993), p. 300.
170 Roth, *Enoch Powell*, p. 225.
171 Speech delivered to Cambridge University Union, February 1969, cited in Berkely, *The Odyssey of Enoch*, p. 110.
172 *Ibid.*
173 *Ibid.*
174 Powell, *Freedom and Reality*, p. 18.
175 Lewis, *Enoch Powell*, p. 63.
176 *Ibid.*, p. 55.
177 *Ibid.*, p. 70.
178 Alexander and Watkins, *The Making of the Prime Minister: 1970*, p. 104.
179 Powell, *Freedom and Reality*, p. 212.
180 Roth, *Enoch Powell*, p. 335.
181 *Ibid.*, p. 363.
182 *Ibid.*, p. 341.
183 *Ibid.*, p. 341.
184 CCO/500/32, 11 April to July 1968.
185 Berkely, *The Odyssey of Enoch*, pp. 78–83.
186 *The Times*, 22 April 1968.
187 Lewis, *Enoch Powell*, p. 107.
188 Alexander and Watkins, *The Making of the Prime Minister: 1970*, p. 102.
189 *Ibid.*, p. 195.
190 *Ibid.*, p. 198.
191 *Spectator*, 20 June 1970.
192 Cosgrave, *Lives of Enoch Powell*, pp. 284–90, and Schoen, *Powell and the Powellites*, pp. 55–6.
193 Lewis, *Enoch Powell*, p. 170.
194 Cosgrave, *Lives of Enoch Powell*, p. 308.
195 *Hansard*, 8 February 1971, cols 80–3, p. 103.
196 Cosgrave, *Lives of Enoch Powell*, p. 374.
197 Lewis, *Enoch Powell*, p. 191.
198 Michael Harrington, *Swinton Journal* (Summer 1969), p. 42.
199 Utley, *Enoch Powell*, p. 43.
200 Charles Moore and Simon Heffer, *A Tory Seer* (London: Hamilton, 1989), Foreword.
201 *Ibid.*, p. 68.

202 Judy Hillman, *Geoffrey Howe: A Quiet Revolutionary* (London: Weidenfeld and Nicolson, 1988), p. 73.

203 CCO 4/2/45, The Chair of the Group was Sydney Chapman and the other members were David Adams, Eric Chalker, and Keith Speed.

204 In conversation.

205 Nicholas Ridley, *My Style of Government. The Thatcher Years* (London: Hutchinson, 1991), pp. 2–3.

206 CRD 3/17/11, Report from Nicholas Ridley, 28 May 1968.

207 The other members of the Committee were Frank Corfield, Michael Allison, John Eden, Stephen Hastings, Christopher Tugenhadt, and Tony Newton and the only non-MP was Professor Wiseman of York University.

208 CRD 3/7/7/7, Selsdon Park proceedings, January 1970.

209 CCO/4, General Correspondence 1967 to 1974, 1 February 1970.

210 Anthony Meyer, *Stand Up and Be Counted* (London: Heinemann, 1990), p. 54.

211 *Ibid.*, p. 55.

212 Meyer actually left the Conservative Research Department (CRD) in 1968 and duly launched the short-lived *Solon* and sought a Parliamentary nomination. He left the CRD in 1968 after it refused to finance Professor Parry Lewis of Manchester University in a policy study aiming to revitalise run-down inner-city areas with subsidies or tax bonuses for the smartening up of shops, pubs, and the planting of grass. Meyer complains that even Tories at this time were more interested in promoting tower block housing.

213 *Solon*, 1 (1) (October 1969), p. 4.

214 *Solon*, 1 (3) (April 1970), p. 4.

215 *Ibid.*, p. 43.

216 *Solon, ibid.*, p. 35 and 1 (2) (January 1970), p. 6 and 1 (1) (October 1969), p. 23.

217 *Crossbow* (January 1971), p. 26.

218 *Swinton Journal* (Spring 1986), Editorial.

219 *Ibid.*, pp. 5–14.

220 Young, *One Of Us*, p. 496.

221 *Swinton Journal* (Summer 1968), p. 9.

222 *Ibid.*, p. 15.

223 *Ibid.*, p. 17.

224 *Swinton Journal* (Autumn 1968), p. 40.

225 S. Brittan, *Left or Right: The Bogus Dilemma* (London: Secker and Warburg, 1968), *passim*.

226 CCO File, 6/76, documents and pamphlet proofs relating to 1971.

227 *Swinton Journal* (Summer 1969), p. 4.

228 *Swinton Journal* (Summer 1968), p. 28.

229 *Swinton Journal* (Summer 1970), p. 33.

230 *Crossbow* (April 1971), p. 8.

231 *Crossbow* (July 1971), p. 8.

232 Minutes of meeting of Election Steering Committee, 12 March 1970.

233 Boyle in Fisher, *Ian Macleod*, p. 17.

234 Conservative Research Department paper prepared for the party's election steering committee in 1969. File SC(69)6.

235 Campbell, *Edward Heath*, p. 391.

7

Managing party tensions,
1970–1979

Heath's confidence was soon tested by the problems of governance, the loss of popular support, and the resulting need to manage party and electoral tensions. The first section of this chapter has two main purposes. First, it examines the problems of governance, particularly economic management, in the government's first year. It reveals a serious attempt to follow the ideological path defined in Heath's Quiet Revolution speech to the 1970 Conference and demonstrates that the U-turn which reversed it, came as early as one year into the government's life. The second purpose is to examine the Conservative Party's struggle to manage the political tensions which arose in the party and the electorate from 1970 to the Peasant's Revolt which lost Heath the leadership in 1975.

The Quiet Revolution

The Selsdon programme and the 1970 Manifesto were ambiguous, but Heath removed doubts in his first Prime Ministerial speech, on the theme of the 'Quiet Revolution', delivered at the October Conference. It was because his government reneged on these promises that right-wing Conservative activists had grounds for disillusionment. It was from the bench-mark of the 'Quiet Revolution' rather than Selsdon that a policy U-turn occurred. Heath later chose to demonstrate that he had carried out the Selsdon Park programme, rather than to measure his performance against the Quiet Revolution. He was correct that Selsdon had not produced an anti-interventionist economic policy and could point to a pledge in *A Better Tomorrow* for 'an advanced regional policy'.[1] The *Daily Telegraph* could not accept, however, Heath's 'straightfaced insistence' that his policies were consistent with his earlier pledges. It commented accurately that 'it is as well for Mr Heath that the British electorate is not much concerned about ideology'.[2] The true believers were biding their time to observe whether Heath could succeed. By 1974 the prospectus of the Quiet Revolution had become a 'passing and embarrassing aberration', owing to 'the realities of government in the modern world'.[3]

It was in domestic economic management, particularly prices and incomes policy, that the greatest U-turn took place. Heath's Quiet Revolution asserted that 'we were returned to office to change the course of history of this nation, nothing less'. He promised to tackle 'heavy international indebtedness ... enormous and increasing public expenditure ... a high and damaging level of taxation ... outmoded industrial relations ... wildly excessive wage demands ... a stagnant economy and roaring inflation ... defeatist attitudes after continuing retreat and a new style of government'. He pointed out that his government had already abolished the Land Commission, introduced pensions for the over 80s, and published proposals for the reform of industrial relations. He stressed his desire to reform government, to improve decision-making about public expenditure and avoid arbitrariness in the redirection of government spending. The speech proposed that 'government withdraws from all those activities no longer necessary either because of the passage of time or because they should rightly be carried on, if wanted at all, by individual or by voluntary effort ... Our strategy is to encourage individual citizens more and more to take their own decisions, to stand on their own feet, to accept responsibility for themselves and their families'. He promised to resist inflationary pay settlements in the public sector while disavowing incomes policy. In the private sector, Heath threatened firms which acceded to 'irresponsible wage demands', that he would not 'step in and rescue them from the consequences of their own actions'. Finally, Heath promised: 'a revolution so quiet yet so total, that it will go far beyond the programme for a Parliament ... far beyond this decade and way into the future'.[4] This was before Heath faced the full exigencies of government. The pledges suggested a commitment to the principles later associated with Thatcherism. *The Economist* published a mock Queen's Speech in 1979 which mixed elements from Heath's first in 1970 with Thatcher's first in 1979, to demonstrate the similarity.[5]

The Quiet Revolution was not about increasing efficiency, but ensuring that there should be *less government*. 'It [reform] becomes ... a key instrument to transferring functions and activities back to the private sector or running them down altogether'.[6] The revolution was 'anti-collectivist and pro-business, and ... (expressed) a new and vigilant hostility to public spending'.[7] The main contrast between the Quiet Revolution and Thatcher's ideas was Heath's Europeanism. This is supported by Nigel Lawson, who subscribed to everything which Heath offered at the time except for regretting, as early as 1967, the absence of nationalism. The Conservatives must appeal as the national party to avoid an exclusive association with 'individualism' and the 'middle classes'.[8]

It is significant that the idea of a U-turn is not referred to in the memoirs

184

of the leading Heathmen.[9] There is strong evidence for the U-turn, however, and the controversy is about when it took place. Heath remained faithful to his programme for a year, and 'the general impression in the Summer of 1971, whether welcome or unwelcome, was that the Heath administration had established an unusually clean break with the past. At this stage commentators agreed that the government had demonstrated abnormal fidelity to the convictions it had presented to the electorate'.[10] Soon after, however, the Quiet Revolution 'had been decently interred and the government's policy went into rapid reverse'.[11] Bruce-Gardyne is ambiguous about when it occurred. While the statutory prices and incomes policy of November 1972 was the final indignity, he sees the start of the U-turn in the summer of 1971. He refers to growing ministerial anxiety about the effects of government policy, foreshadowed by the definition of Glasgow, Tyneside, and Wearside as special development areas in January 1971, although they had been devised for remote places afflicted by pit closures.[12] The decisive reversal came with a special budget in July 1971 which involved 'a big departure' in macro-economic strategy and of 'the whole course of relationships between Government and the nationalised industries since financial targets were first introduced in 1958'.[13] The abolition of financial targets meant the abandonment of commercial discipline. The budget also provided a substantial stimulus to the economy.

The U-turn is central to Campbell's analysis of the Heath government, but he presents it as a gradual phenomenon.[14] The term entered popular debate during 1972, and some still claim 1972 as the date when the U-turn took place.[15] While the Conservative tradition has always embraced Liberalism and collectivism and all Conservative governments have sought to merge both strands, with one or other predominant, the Heath government uniquely moved from a Liberalism to collectivism during the same administration. Campbell points to Heath's 1971 Conference speech as the time when he started to abandon his goals. 'For all his lofty talk of "stamina" and "destiny" ... the emphasis ... signalled that the Government had already significantly changed tack'.[16] The U-turn was discreet until the middle of 1972 when 'the complete reversal of the "hands off" philosophy on which the Government had been elected became plain and undeniable'.[17] The U-turn was consummated by the incomes policy in October 1972.[18] There is an agreement, therefore, about a 'change of tack' in mid-1971. A new £100 million public works programme to tackle unemployment in the development areas was announced in July which reflected anxiety about the announcement of three-quarters of a million unemployed, and demonstrated a departure from earlier statements that ministers would wait for the spring budget measures to take effect.[19]

Some Conservatives suggest that the U-turn took place because Heath lacked the will and commitment to implement the Quiet Revolution.

Ministers' memoirs portray a government besieged by problems but responding to them energetically. The themes of inflation and unemployment loom largest. Heath admitted that price restraint was 'hardly in keeping with earlier speeches about encouraging free enterprise and refraining from interference in the free market', but he portrayed price restraint as a sign that his government was free from 'doctrinaire attitudes'. Similarly, Home linked the problems of inflation and unemployment by urging that wage increases should be linked to productivity and that unemployment was best avoided by ending 'spendthrift' wage settlements.[20]

Others stress the malign combination of politicians driven by the dictates of the electoral cycle and their preference for quick and easy solutions, coupled with the readiness of civil servants to offer instant remedies. These solutions bore little relationship to the policies which the politicians prepared in opposition. It was the Treasury's attachment to economic forecasting, concern with the balance of payments, demand-management and incomes policy, which drove the government off-course. There was a gap in the Conservative strategy on addressing the inflationary stampede then developing which left government vulnerable to Treasury solutions. Cuts in indirect taxes were jettisoned. In return for CBI promises to curb private sector prices, the government restrained nationalised industry prices which conflicted with commercial decision-making in this sector.[21] As predictions about unemployment worsened, the Heath government moved inexorably towards stimulating the economy, and its initial strategy was derailed by the politicians' demand for quick results, and the reluctance of bureaucrats to recognise the limits of their skills.[22]

The U-turn resulted from Heath's brief experiment with an anti-collectivist policy which contributed to the simultaneous rise in unemployment and inflation.[23] The term U-turn covers a broad range of policies such as reflation, public expenditure increases, intervention in industry and incomes policy. It was also a response to external developments. Determination alone was not enough to carry out the Quiet Revolution. Heath's real purpose was not to dismantle the post-war settlement but to reform it at the edges to make it function better. His government lost its room for manoeuvre, owing to inflation, strikes, and rising world commodity prices.[24]

The interpretation that Heath was beleaguered by events and that his Cabinet resorted to civil service preferences is not sufficiently penetrating. It neglects that Heath's earlier career proved him a technocratic problem-solver rather than a right-wing ideologue. He was unlikely, therefore, to pursue the Quiet Revolution if it threatened national unity. The electorate was also less willing to bear the social costs of high unemployment than in the different circumstances of the 1980s. In retrospect, the early 1970s appear to be a time of transition in the popular mood. While New Right ideas were well developed among many Conservatives, it was only after

1975 that they became common in the party and country. If in the early 1970s the popular intellectual climate was becoming suspicious of collectivist policies, it was not yet ready to bear the consequences of a tough anti-consensual programme. Heath's first Cabinet was more socially representative of the party's changing rank-and-file than previous Conservative governments, representing a shift towards the Party's middle class. A significant appointment, not foreseen at the time, was Thatcher as Minister of Education and Science. Macleod went to the Treasury until his death which damaged the party's attempts to communicate effectively with a mass audience.

The government's early actions were compatible with neo-Liberalism, with public expenditure cuts, the abolition of investment grants, the phasing out of the Regional Employment Premium, and the abolition of the Industrial Reconstruction Corporation. There was a proposal to shift housing finance from public support for local authority housing and the subsidisation of rents, towards support for housing costs paid to individuals in the Housing Finance Bill. Charges for museums and for dental treatment were brought in and free school milk for the over-sevens was ended.[25] For a government becoming aware of the inflationary challenge, these decisions were politically damaging as they imposed costs on workers who were then likely to increase wage demands.

The short-term problem confronting the government was labour relations, particularly public sector unrest. Heath's government stood firm against this challenge with a policy of de-escalating public sector wages as an example to the private sector. The policy was described as 'n-1', as each settlement was intended to be less than its predecessors.[26] As monetarism was still a minority taste, Conservatives were anxious to resist high wage demands from the public sector. Even the neo-Liberal right, which from the mid-1960s had been urging the market economy, lower taxes, and denationalisation, backed Heath in standing firm against union pressure.[27] The government was determined not to intervene in pay negotiations.[28] It remained distant in an early dispute between dustmen and their local authority employers, despite the outcome that arbitration produced a compromise which appeased the workers' demands. Soon after the government faced a major challenge when power station workers voted to 'work to rule' in support of a pay claim. Although there was little public support for the strikers, the government set up a committee of enquiry under Lord Wilberforce. *The Economist* was censorious and complained that the committee was economically illiterate, and that the combination of a judge and a pro-labour trades unionist (Jim Mortimer), did not inspire confidence. The result was a 10.9% reward for an illegal electricity go-slow. Since the report lost touch with economic reality, the journal urged the Employment Secretary to reject it as 'a farrago of uneconomic rubbish'.[29] The government

withstood a strike by the postmen who had public sympathy but little industrial muscle. Its record was mixed in resisting inflationary pay settlements
during the first year.

The Economist advocated the adoption of an incomes policy from the
outset. It criticised the 'ideologues' who preferred to curb inflation by
restraining the money supply which caused bankruptcies and redundancies.
Monetarists believed that all that was necessary was for 'the Old Lady of
Threadneeedle Street to reduce money'.[30] The monetarist solution was can-
vassed by Powell, Biffen, and Ridley. *The Economist* sought a wage and prices
freeze, however, and was censorious of those who argued for a price but not
a wages freeze because wages were rising at 14%, production at 2% and
prices at 8%. Securing an incomes policy was more important than the
Industrial Relations Bill with which the government was then preoccu-
pied.[31] Voluntary concordats with the TUC were non-enforceable so an
incomes policy was inevitable with the demand likely to come from 'the
heart of the Cabinet and the comfortable belly of the party' which were 'less
brilliant than Heath but also less wayward'.[32]

The nationalisation of Rolls Royce in 1971 was uncontroversial. Its
impact was softened because it was preceded by the denationalisation of the
travel agents Thomas Cook and the Carlisle breweries. The government's
legal officers also advised that there was no alternative owing to contractual arrangements between the company and the United States.[33] Hurd
described the decision as a major intervention for a Conservative government, but not 'in principle unconservative'. 'A Conservative government
will in practice always hold itself ready to act in the national interest when
things go badly wrong with the economy'.[34] Powell opposed the rescue, but
even Tebbitt accepted that Rolls Royce was a flagship company.[35] The irony
was intensified, however, by the Industry Minister's speech which proclaimed a 'hands-off' strategy towards industry. The statement was interpreted as meaning that no more 'lame ducks' would be saved although the
actual remark was, 'I will not bolster up or bail out companies where I can
see no end to the process of propping them up'.[36]

During the first year Heath made progress on his goal of taking Britain
into the European Economic Community (EEC). The negotiations succeeded
because President Pompidou did not have an *idée fixe* against British entry,
unlike de Gaulle.[37] By June 1971 the log-jam was broken, but anticipating
the problems which the issue could create, Heath stressed he was not a
European federalist and that he sympathised with the notion of independence in a *Europe des Patries*.[38] The greatest difficulty arose with the Industrial Relations Bill. Heath demonstrated his complacency: 'I do not believe
for one moment that the unions are likely to put themselves in breach of
the law'.[39] Citing the doctrine of the mandate he was determined on radical
reform, when a gradualist approach was preferable. This created a political

dogfight disproportionate to the Bill's value.[40] During the first year the unions devised the tactic of refusing to register under the Act.

Heath did not recognise his change of direction in July 1971, but it was a departure from the uneasy compromise which he had struck with the party's right wing a year previously. Powell rapidly detected a 'betrayal'. The remainder of Heath's government was dominated by a reversion to 'One Nation', 'corporatist' policies. His standing was such that the majority of the party gave this strategy one more trial, although the dissidents were not silenced and lived to fight again.

Propaganda and organisation

The Conservative Party's professionalism in membership recruitment, constituency organisation, and media management was evident at this time. While the membership was larger, younger, and more active than in 1995 it was suffering from the malaise of being the party in government at a difficult time. Its cause was not assisted by Heath's lack of 'sympathy with the passions and prejudices of the retired majors, small businessmen, and hatted ladies who organised fetes, stuffed envelopes in the constituencies and demanded tougher penalties for criminals every year at Conference'.[41] Nor were there many ministers, particularly after Macleod's death who could speak to the Party's 'soul'. Many MPs yearned for Powell. Given the difficulties, the party proclaimed 1972 Support the Conservatives year, to raise finance and revitalise the organisation. The Conservative Political Centre's (CPC) Campaign News participated through spreading good practice by focusing on successful constituency work. The Party Chairman Peter Thomas urged a membership recruitment competition between local parties, with a trophy for the most successful. He provided associations with a special pamphlet to assist them.[42] This stressed the party's age, democratic local autonomy, flexible lack of 'a rigid and doctrinaire philosophy' and even the claim that it was unlike a political party. Conservatives always seek to enjoy the benefits of ideological identity, however, while claiming to be non-ideological; believing only in *principles*, such as individual choice, lower taxes, decentralisation, and a property owning democracy.

One local association refused to use Thomas's pamphlet on the grounds that people were disillusioned with party politics. Instead it employed the 'sociological approach'. This recognised that, '80% of the people supporting a voluntary organisation, be it charitable or political, do so initially for personal or social rather than for organisational reasons'.[43] It decided to adopt a 'soft sell' approach and to advertise the social reasons for membership. Its recruitment leaflet was, 'Your Passport to the Whole New World of Faces and Places'. Other local associations experimented with events to attract new members, such as Keighley's 'Lollipop Fair' for young mothers, and

Dover's series of talks on 'Discovering Old Dover'.

Local activists were as concerned about the role of the media as was the leadership. Oxford was anxious about the way the minister responsible for broadcasting accepted the biased nominations to regional BBC Advisory Councils. Oxford's protest was that, 'no single member of the Radio Council is known to be a member of the Conservative Party let alone a party activist ... and the Chair is a cranky worker priest, a socialist member of Oxford City Council and one of the most disruptive influences in Oxford'.[44] Stimulated by the grassroots, ministers addressed the media's political presentation. At the Central Council meeting in April 1971, attended by the chairs and agents of the national party, Peter Walker, Tony Barber, Keith Joseph, Robert Carr, Geoffrey Rippon and Heath himself, it was asserted that the government should influence who should be invited to appear to put its case.[45] Conservative Central Office's Tactical Committee expressed concern over perceived media bias and the high number of shadow ministers who appeared on television during the course of November 1971. It was acknowledged that television companies only invite government representatives when they are promoting a new initiative.[46] There was also concern that Labour was receiving more publicity over the Housing Finance Bill and the government's case in favour of fair rents was not being aired. Fraser suggested that the party should concentrate on its areas of strength; for example, the difference between the growth of the standard of living under Labour and Conservative governments, measured by the level of real net disposable income. This demonstrated little increase between 1945 and 1951 and 1964 and 1970, in contrast to an annual growth rate of 3.2% from 1951 to 1964.[47]

Double standards emerged at a later meeting when members suggested a cessation of set-piece attacks on Labour as the majority of voters reacted adversely to bickering. The sentiment was contradicted when it was proposed that Labour should be attacked for its inadequate policies on inflation and unions, and particularly nationalisation, which appealed only to a small minority of committed Socialists.[48] Some positive ideas were also put forward, for example, that campaigners should replace national claims about the efficacy of Conservative policy and seek to emphasise the way in which individuals and communities were personally affected. It was suggested that the CRD could produce data showing how individual constituencies were affected by spending on schools, hospitals, roads and regional development projects, and voters were more likely to be impressed by evidence that their local services were being enhanced. Parliamentary questions could be arranged to enable individual constituencies to be highlighted.[49] Concern about the failure to make the Conservative case nationally was motivated by opinion poll results. Heath's honeymoon was soon over as by the end of 1970 the Opinion Research Centre (ORC) gave Labour a five-point lead, with 40% considering that Heath was doing a bad job.[50] The party's attention to its effectiveness in conveying its message developed more vigorously as the signs of government unpopularity grew. By mid-1972 the polls revealed a Labour lead of between 8 and 13%.[51] At the end of the year when the Conservatives lost the safe seat of Sutton and Cheam to the Liberals, Central Office sought information from ORC which, influenced by the Liberal Party's use of 'community politics', urged the Conservatives to adopt a similar strategy. ORC advised that leaflets and meetings were of no value, but canvassing was, since people liked to be 'wooed'. It was important to project the leader as 'sincere and wise' and desirable to stress particular local improvements ensuing from national policy. The Party was urged to avoid 'mudslinging' as 'people are tired of shifty politicians', particularly when the policy differences between the parties were perceived to be small. The benefit of being in government should be used to gain credit for national policy initiatives such as a new lavatory or an extension to a school.[52] A local agent reinforced the view that the public were ignorant of the government's achievements.[53]

Party workers were invited to assist with the evaluation of media bias by becoming broadcasting monitors.[54] Party officials were concerned about how the government's U-turn in restoring a statutory policy in November 1972 would play with both party and public. There was anxiety that the trade unions were projecting the message that prices were continuing to rise while wages were being held down.[55] In reality, local associations pressed Tory MPs to support the government. This was because of the atmosphere of crisis, irritation with the unions for the time fruitlessly spent negotiating, and the tendency for activists to be loyal to the leadership; even if it involved suppressing ideological doubts. Francis Pym was effective in the Whip's Office, even though Heath did not much consult him. Only Powell voted against the measure, although Biffen and Bruce-Gardyne abstained. Maxwell Hyslop and Sir Richard Body both voted for the Bill, despite opposing it at the 1922. Ridley justified his vote with the *post hoc* argument that supporting the Bill enabled him to become a member of the Standing Committee to undermine it.[56] This is unconvincing, because Biffen served on the committee despite having abstained. There were signs of backbench discontent with Heath's authoritarian style of leadership, however, with the election of three backbenchers to party committee chairs: Ridley to finance; Biffen to industry; and DuCann to the 1922.

The leadership often responded with *déjà vu* to ORC data. Carrington responded to information that the party was failing to attract the support of youth, the Scots and the Welsh, with the comment that 'one might have drawn up an identical list five years ago'.[57] Audience reaction to a party political broadcast (PPB) in December 1972 revealed that 12 million viewers watched it, 50% were committed to the party and there was a positive rating of 26%. Two important findings emerged from such analyses. PPBs were specifically viewed by party supporters and there was a close correlation between a favourable response and a party's popular standing at the time.[58] An analysis of a *Panorama* interview with Heath, revealed that 8 million people watched it, of whom 57% were Conservative voters as against 22% who were Labour. The survey revealed that Heath scored highly on trustworthiness, ability and concern; but there was cynicism about the efficacy of incomes policy.[59]

A Central Office official expressed surprise after one ACP meeting because 'the committee were rather untypically full of ideas', but another time he commented, 'the ACP is not a bad sounding board of party opinion'.[60] The ACP's sub-committee on Policy Correspondence swung into action in the autumn of 1972 to prepare for a general election. It represented the parliamentary party, with members drawn from the Lords and Commons. (The MPs were Sir Harry Legge-Bourke, John Page, Norman St John Stevas, Sir Frederick Bennett, and John Selwyn Gummer.) There were also eight members from the National Union including a Young Conservative, three ex-officio members, a deputy chair of the party organisation, and the director of the CPC. There were also six co-opted members. A discussion on social policy led by Joseph generated little interest, because Conservatives have difficulty in conveying their concern to the electorate as 'the social services are not one of the subjects which Conservatives get worked up about'.[61]

Predictably the issue which did generate heat was that of immigration particularly because of the Ugandan Asians. Some members expressed anxiety about the ease with which they had entered Britain and the ease of access of Irish immigrants in contrast to the position of people from the old Commonwealth. The concern was shared by MPs, but the National Union representatives' opinions were summed up as 'while we had been able to get away with the Uganda problem it was seen as an unexpected crisis', and there was great 'apprehension and anxiety about the extent of our legal and moral obligations'.[62]

In parallel with the ACP there was a committee on party policy liaising with ministers to prepare a manifesto. Each minister was asked to nominate a policy proposal. It was agreed that the principle of selectivity in the social services would appear. A Central Office official argued that while in Opposition policy-making was easy, because the CRD was close to shadow ministers and knew their forward thinking; in government, 'the exercise is more difficult as it has to be tied in with departmental forward thinking of which ... we obviously do not have as full a grasp as ... in Opposition'.[63] Brendon Sewill questioned the value of the exercise. As most of the government's election promises had not been fulfilled, and as unemployment, inflation, and growth were all unsatisfactory, it was hardly appropriate to return to the people and say, 'sorry chums our ideas didn't work out. Please re-elect us so we can try something different'. He urged the government to concentrate on solving inflation rather than thinking about the election. 'If we can think of the answer, let's do it rather than going back to the electorate for permission to do it'. In any event, Sewill argued that there was a widespread belief among voters that the Conservatives had been elected to control prices and 'the government is now in a very strong position to take any measures that look like helping to achieve that objective'. His argument was that effective government action was most likely to regain votes.[64]

Sewill's advice was ignored and ministers produced ideas. Thatcher pointed to the improvement of primary schools, the raising of the school leaving age as a 'contribution towards educational and social equality' and a move towards more home-based students in higher education, as residence was expensive to support.[65] There was also discussion about the policy of negative income tax. Sewill urged caution here, since a tax credit scheme would not produce more help for those in need. Yet the discussion was unclear, since members wished to combine compassion for the poor and incentives for the rich. These matters were being seriously examined, however, with references to academic studies such as Friedman's on National Income and Polanyi's Minimum Income Guarantee.[66]

The party organisation was also concerned to improve electioneering techniques at constituency level. From the late 1960s Central Office recommended survey canvassing. This enabled canvassers to be sensitive to the opinions of voters and tease out the genuinely doubtful to concentrate upon them when general elections came round. Survey canvassing was less opportunistic and created an impression of democratic caring. Webster regarded survey canvassing as vital for critical seats. It required 8–10 calls per man hour, and eliminated the 17% who professed allegiance but had no intention of voting Conservative. Their elimination prevented the futility of taking opposition party voters to the polling booths. He reported one constituency where the Tory vote emerged as 41% on a survey and 57% on a traditional canvass.[67]

In the period leading up to the two 1974 elections, individual constituency surveys written by regional organisers, a significant group within the party, were consulted. Their surveys are forthright about the situation in individual constituencies. One was concerned about a local agent's bad relations with the chairman, who was himself 'pompous but enthusiastic'.[68] An MP was condemned for spending too much time with certain members, and since becoming a minister for spending little time in the constituency. The constituency was described as 'a new town combined with some very rural areas and the prejudices which result from the two types of people'. While the local agent worked hard to keep the peace between the urban and rural membership, his task was difficult, because the local association was run by 'a small clique'.[69] A report from Newark showed an early appreciation that Nottinghamshire miners were not antipathetic to Conservatism and argued that even in a constituency with three large council house estates, with only a 20% middle-class composition and 20% engaged in mining, the seat could be won. Another local candidate was said to be prone to 'speak off the cuff', and as his press officer was 'a frail reed', he needed Central Office television training. There was concern that his wife was perceived as a 'snob', and that the Association had 'a shocking and depressing history of rows and disunity'.[70] A further local agent was described as 'ridiculously over-committed coping with the routine administration of two constituencies ... with one overworked secretary.'

The party's concern with the Liberal threat increased after the Rochdale, Sutton and Cheam and Ely by-elections in late 1972 and 1973, and the major breakthrough to 19% of the national vote in the February 1974 general election. Research into the Liberal vote concluded that it was 'an anti-vote against the two main parties, and particularly us. The research showed that Liberal policies had made no impact – most people did not know what they were; that Liberal candidates had made no particular impact'; and community politics was localised in its effects.[71] Fraser stressed that a vote for the Liberals equalled a vote for Labour.[72] The Liberal threat was addressed by Michael Woolf, newly appointed to the position of party Director-General, which Heath imposed upon such long-serving party professionals as Fraser and Webster.[73] He considered the case for an agreement with the Liberals; pointing to policy convergences on Europe, statutory incomes policy, and opposition to nationalisation. He recognised that the Conservatives rejected some Liberal policy, for example, their anti-inflation tax, the statutory minimum wage, and support for universal comprehensive education. Apart from policy differences, however, such Liberals as Des Wilson and Peter Hain were completely opposed to collaboration with Conservatives. Woolf also pointed out that the Young Liberal conference had attacked political moderation and their leader Ruth Addison asserted that 'too often the Liberals are the system proppers and not the system breakers'. Finally, Woolf asserted that Liberals were hypocritical in their condemnation of 'slanging matches'.[74] The party also carried out a survey of Conservative voters who had recently defected to the Liberals in four seats: Newbury, Brighton, Loughborough, and Bodmin. It revealed that 55% of defectors might return. Reasons for defection included housing, Conservative business links, and a belief that Conservatism lacked heart in its attitudes towards the sick and the poor. In contrast, Liberals were perceived as representing 'the broad interests of the nation' and 'direct partisan attacks on them may well be counter productive'. Defectors favoured Conservative policies but were wary of the party's image. It recommended a new appeal of national unity. This influenced Heath's thinking about the autumn election. The middle-class focus which the report also advocated, however, was compatible with traditional Conservatism and Thatcher's strategy.[75] The idea of Conservative–Liberal electoral pacts was also considered provided that 'pacts entered into should be at Association level and not dictated from the centre'.[76] A later memorandum asserted, however, that pacts were undesirable. The Liberals were described as a rump of traditional Liberals plus transients recruited during revivals. They ranged across the political spectrum unlike supporters of the two main parties. This explained why, when Liberal policies were published, the voters faded away. Their substantial vote was based upon disillusionment and because Liberals, unconstrained by office, can behave irresponsibly. Nationally they should be dealt with as 'a joke crew', but because their constituency impact varied they should be dealt with on a constituency basis.[77] When Heath announced his proposed Government of National Unity, Conservative organisers were confident that the Liberal case was weakened by Heath's invitation to people from other parties to join his government.[78]

Confidence was less apparent in Sir David Renton's letter to Heath arguing that if there were a stalemate in the autumn election Heath should offer a Speakers' Conference on proportional representation (PR). Renton wanted the Conservatives to write a commitment to PR in their manifesto as the country needed a period of coalition government. This was because, 'the greatest evil which this country has to face is the possibility in the foreseeable future of a Labour government with a clear majority propelled by a Marxist left-wing. The best way to prevent it would be to end the two party system'.[79] A chasm was now opening up between Heathites, who despite defeat at the hands of the miners were anxious to preserve national unity and co-operate with responsible trade unionism, and elements on the right who were becoming apocalyptic about what the democratic process might yield. Heath talked to the 1922 and DuCann reported that while it was worthwhile, there was uncertainty about the Government of National Unity. DuCann considered it valuable 'if you could define it at some stage, preferably as early in the campaign as possible, the way in which discussions with persons of good will would take if we were successful in winning'.[80] Particularly revealing was the admission that DuCann was in contact with 'General Walker's people'.[81] This is surprising given that it was a group of 'non-class militia', similar to Colonel Stirling's 'non-party, non-class organisation of apprehensive patriots'. These derided groups toyed with the idea of a military coup. DuCann informed Heath that Walker's people were anxious to know how the government would deal with the Scanlon threat, how industrial blackmail could be defeated, whether the Conservatives were committed to stopping social security payments to the dependants of strikers, and whether there was any plan to legislate to enforce peaceful picketing?[82]

Europe's capacity to divide the party emerged in 1961. While Heath's passion for entry stifled much opposition, Conservatives were conscious that they stood for Empire and the Union Jack. One die-hard opponent of British entry to the EEC, Robin Turton, was threatened with deselection in Thirsk and Malton. Central Office was anxious to prevent local associations becoming too assertive, and to avoid a by-election in which the party could be accused of stifling its internal dissent. Its advice to the local party chairman was to avoid deselection, to prevent anti-marketeers claiming that they were being pressurised.[83] Another opponent, Neil Marten, implied that the CPC had refused to publish his pamphlet presenting the case against entry. Heath argues that he allowed free discussion, which could explain Marten's letter of July 1972 where he stated that Heath had given approval to the pamphlet's publication. He was pleased at 'this change of direction by the CPC which can now restore its original reputation which (it is widely recognised) has been sadly and seriously tarnished over the Common Market issue'.[84] The CPC refuted the 'smear' that it was censoring the debate.[85] Yet Marten was justified as an earlier memorandum revealed that the CPC was subordinate to Central Office, and as a result was presenting a one-sided perspective. The CPC had planned to produce a pamphlet presenting both sides of the argument about a referendum on the EEC as recently as the summer of 1970. The new memorandum stated that 'the party has moved'. It was also apparent that the Europe Co-ordinating Committee of Central Office, chaired by Fraser, refused to agree to the pamphlet's publication, and argued that the party could not give the impression of being 'indecisive' on either the EEC or on a referendum, and that the CPC should not be controversial. As a result, Lewis wrote that the 'tactical position assumed during the election of merely supporting negotiations could hardly set the tone for a campaign which the party was preparing to shift opinion in favour of its European policy and in support of the terms which Geoffrey Rippon brings back probably in July 1971'.[86] The CPC was happier with a pamphlet on 'The Housewife and the Common Market' which argued that prices were not higher on the Continent, there was better pay and holidays for 'their men', Britain would not be flooded with Italians and social welfare would be strong. Only commercial laws would be harmonised.[87] As significant for the future as the railroading through of EEC membership was a letter from Ralph Harris of the Institute of Economic Affairs (IEA) in which he admitted his uncertainty about Britain's membership of the EEC because liberal economists were split on whether the EEC would extend the market economy.[88]

More characteristic of the CPC's role was a propaganda pamphlet which cited the words of politicians on the subject. It used earlier expressions of support by Wilson to demonstrate Labour's inconsistency, but it included a revealing comment by Heath relevant for the party divisions of the 1990s. He stressed patriotic reasons for joining, arguing that the EEC's political development could not be characterised as federalism or confederalism, since it was a case of creating the institutions to suit Europe's needs. He urged a pragmatic approach in which member countries would 'start working closely together and in 10 years a learned constitutional lawyer from a university would be able to define where we had got to'.[89] The notion that Europe *would* develop politically was implicit in Rippon's comment that Britain should be 'joining the Community not just as shareholders but as directors. We could have a major influence at every stage on both control and direction, and inevitably I think we must note that we should have far more control than if we remained outside'.[90] Yet opposition remained. Marten wrote to Carrington in September 1972, with Britain's accession imminent, asserting that half the electors think that a clear-cut anti-market policy helped Labour to win, against 29% who thought otherwise. The same opinion survey revealed that 67% considered that the government did not reflect the people's values on Europe. It is striking that many Conservatives disliked Britain's very membership of the EEC, but that the views of sceptics were entirely disregarded at the time.[91] The Conservative capacity to manage its Conference was important in ensuring that Europe was not an issue in 1971, as delegates accepted that the government wanted no argument.[92]

Britain's entry in 1973 submerged the issue until the second defeat of October 1974 when the resentment against Heath spilled over to the EEC. This was when the Labour government's proposal to hold a referendum appeared on the agenda. While Heath was primarily interested in working with organisations which were campaigning for a 'Yes' vote in a referendum, the CRD concentrated upon short-term tactics. A discussion paper considered the options of opposing the principle of the referendum which would lead to the charge of being anti-democratic or adopting a nationalistic posture which would be perceived as cynical in temporarily opposing Labour, while not jeopardising Britain's membership. The paper predicted that a renegotiated package would be presented to Parliament, but wrongly foresaw resignations from the government by failing to predict that Wilson would suspend collective Cabinet responsibility. Europe divided both major parties at this time, and the tendency for all parties in Opposition to exploit anti-European sentiment for political ends was evident in the paper's final recommendation. This departed from the pro-European stance from 1970 to 1974, proposing that on balance 'it might be best to let our MPs have a free vote and a free hand in this matter – since this is an issue on which MPs would vote according to their conscience'.[93]

The party was concerned with organisational issues between February and October 1974, and officials were confident that the critical seats strategy had worked because the swing to Labour in February was 0.4% against an average national swing of 1.4%. It was decided that these seats would be visited by Prior, Walker or Barber and there was a briefing course for representatives of these constituencies at Swinton College in June.[94] The efforts in Preston North demonstrated a readiness to appeal to special groups and to tailor the message accordingly. The Irish and even the nuns' vote was stressed. There was concern to appeal to older women with literature focusing on their needs as they would have more time on their hands and so might read it. Pensions policy for single women and law and order should be stressed. There should also be appeals to working women, emphasising equal pay, creches, and nursery provision. Reflecting the labour market of the time the local party was urged to avoid suggestions that working mothers neglected children and in wards where a high proportion of women worked there should be evening canvassing.[95]

The CRD rejected a proposal from a marketing organisation to undertake a survey into the branch level organisation of the party after the 1974 defeat. The firm argued that the Conservative message was best transmitted through the branches or, 'the meaning and purpose of the Party will never be translated into votes at the polling booth'.[96] The main problem at branch level was that committee membership was traditional and that the image conveyed was one of a hereditary upper/middle class party, and 'basically the party has not attempted to get itself involved at any stage with the mass electorate. It has relied on the supposedly magnetic power of the mass media, big names and occasional sorties by ministers into various constituencies to get over the message to the electorate'.[97]

Heath set up a Leaders Consultative Committee immediately after the February election to find 'nuggets' for the next manifesto. His own favoured vice-chairman Sara Morrison stressed the importance of Heath communicating with the 1922 and the Central Council. She also stressed the importance of policy groups and commended Thatcher's enthusiasm for the work of the housing group.[98] The mood of the time is captured by a letter from Sir David Eccles to Heath about a dinner in which his wife met Labour's Chancellor of the Exchequer, Denis Healey. Healey 'drank a lot and said they would stick at nothing to win the election, after which (speaking in the context of education policy) they could destroy the middle class. He said, "we must do it. This is the key to our chances"'. Eccles noted that the middle classes, including those who would like to be, now realise that a construction worker earns more than a middle manager. He added that Heath should 'pull the middle classes out of their bolt holes to fight for their interests'. The problem of inflation was real but more serious was the decline in moral behaviour. Eccles described the Ulster workers strike as 'a bell tolling for us all'.[99] Also characteristic of the time was discussion about negotiating the defection of Ray Gunter, former Minister of Labour in Labour governments of the 1960s, to the Conservatives. In return, Gunter could be offered an 'invented' advisory role on industrial relations. Heath, Prior, or

Whitelaw were thought to be the right people to approach him.[100] This is redolent of events under Thatcher's leadership. More characteristic of Heath was his response to Eccles, in which he said that the message could be conveyed without any resort to 'scaremongering'.[101] Conservative anxiety at this time made it a crucial period in party management.

The politics of the 'U-turn' and the rise of Thatcher

The rise in unemployment accounted for Heath's policy reversals, and the Queen's Speech in November 1971 was explicit that the government's 'first care will be to increase employment'.[102] Heath may well have survived the political impact of the rise in unemployment as did Thatcher, but he was a product of the shibboleths of the 1930s. His fear of inflation was also a source of the U-turn but unemployment was paramount. He feared the effect on social disorder, and was personally compassionate, as is to be expected from a politician who defines Eden, Butler, and Macmillan as his main influences.[103] The decision to bale out the Upper Clyde shipbuilders in 1972 after six months manoeuvring between the government and the workers engaged in a sit-in, was less a U-turn than a product of the warnings of the chief constable of Glasgow that the closure of the shipyards would lead to disorder. The context of 1 million registered unemployed led to the decision to find £35 million to keep the yards open. Ridley and Sir John Eden, the junior ministers at the Department of Trade and Industry (DTI), warned against an obsession with unemployment and they were the authentic voices of the rank-and-file unconstrained by loyalty to Heath's 'strong leadership'.[104]

There is little doubt that from 1971 Heath developed into a corporate interventionist. He personally set the tone of his government and sought to solve problems of long-standing. The reform of industrial relations, for example, had long been on the agenda and party members were keen to have the problem tackled. Heath's failure to negotiate with the unions and his conviction that he had a mandate, led to the Industrial Relations Act. Conservatives such as Jim Prior and Sir Anthony Meyer argue that he should have implemented Labour's 1969 proposals *In Place of Strife* which would have made it difficult for Labour to oppose it. Heath denies this, arguing that Labour would still have opposed it, that his reforms were better as they had been worked out after fifty meetings, and had he won the 1974 election they would have endured.[105] From the outset unions refused to register under the Act, and determined resistance from dockers when the Act was applied against them, crippled it.[106] Its undermining was assisted by Lord Denning's rulings in the High Court, which some Conservatives attributed to his irritation with the major role played by Lord Donaldson's Industrial Court.[107] A flawed aspect of the legislation was that it was conceived as a means of tackling inflation by reducing the incidence of unofficial strikes, but this was not an effective way of dealing with inflation or improving the climate of industrial relations.

Heath's government was dominated until 1972 with the task of taking Britain into the EEC. This was always a personal preoccupation, and Heath failed to spell out the popular case for shared sovereignty. The party was divided then but only a couple of dozen rebels were deeply moved by the issue to the extent of threatening to vote with Labour. The successful outcome of the negotiations did not guarantee that the measure would pass the House of Commons. The White Paper justifying entry emphasised that entry would enhance the country's standing in the world.[108] By that stage internal Conservative opposition was weakening, although Heath was assisted by Labour's disarray on the subject. Despite Powell's defence of national sovereignty, the pro-market motion was carried by an eight to one majority at Conference. Heath remained concerned that entry to the EEC should be achieved by the votes of his own supporters and favoured a three-line Whip. Wiser counsels prevailed, however, and on a free vote the motion passed the Commons by 356 to 244 votes in October 1971. The size of the majority was achieved by 69 Labour MPs voting for the motion, with 39 Tories voting against.[109] The government secured formal entry by 1 January 1973.

Heath's proclivity for promoting the British economy by resorting to corporate policies was reinforced by events. The first miners' strike in the winter of 1972 proved to be important in the re-evaluation of incomes policy to which he resorted at the end of 1972, just as the unemployment figures reaching 1 million in January 1972 led him to adopt an expansionary policy.

The capacity of the miners to defeat the government and to secure a generous settlement from the Wilberforce tribunal humiliated Heath, but the unemployment figure had a deeper effect. The Treasury lost Heath's favour and he turned to a committee of officials led by Sir William Armstrong, to 'strengthen our industrial capacity so as to take advantage of membership of the Common Market'.[110] This was the basis of the Industry Act and the highly expansionary 1972 budget. That budget was based on a 'dash for growth' and a repudiation of unemployment as an anti-inflationary weapon. It was very much Heath's budget, it disregarded Treasury advice, and while its tax cuts were compatible with the previous manifesto, its use of encouragements to industry to invest violated earlier pledges.[111] M3 (money in circulation plus current account bank deposits) rose by 28% in 1972 and 29% in 1973.[112] Heath and his officials next resorted to incomes policy.[113] In June, faced with a severe run on the reserves, mounting inflation and balance of payments anxieties, the government floated the pound. This intensified the demand for incomes policy since the float was a surrender to events. The Bank of England and the Treasury considered it to be 'a surrender to a perennial political temptation to evade a fixed-rate discipline' leaving no alternative to the restoration of wage discipline.[114] Heath's later critics singled out the reflation of the economy in 1972 as the cause of rampant inflation in 1974/75. It was thought to prove the monetarist critique of Keynesianism and the futility of governments spending their way back to full employment, facilitated by the removal of fixed exchange rates.[115]

The interventionist Industry Act, the expansionary budget, the floating of the pound and the restoration of tripartite bargaining to secure an incomes policy, confirmed the U-turn. The Industry Act permitted such large-scale intervention in the economy that the Labour government was handed an instrument to extend state control over manufacturing firms without further legislation.[116] This contrasted with the abolition of the Industrial Reorganisation Corporation (IRC) in 1970. The Act extended the principle of regional aid so that the entire country virtually became a development area. It led to the dismissal of Eden and Ridley as junior ministers, despite Ridley's claim that he resigned.[117] The DTI's strategy resulted in greater support for large companies at the expense of small risk-taking organisations.[118] The CBI consequently split on the issue. The Act stimulated the neo-Liberal upsurge of the 1970s but Heath is unrepentant and argues that the introduction of regional policy in 1993 vindicated him.[119]

The resort to incomes policy was a response to rising inflation, and a recognition that confrontation with unions was ineffective. The inflationary situation was created by government policy. The expansionary economic policy was overlaid upon a downward trend in the figures from 10% in 1971 to 6.5% in 1972.[120] The intellectual climate was one which assumed that the impetus for inflation came from wages rather than monetary growth, and the press urged Heath to adopt wage restraint.[121] The party's monetarists in the late 1970s were using hindsight and as Howe recognises, tested monetarism to destruction as Heath had incomes policy.[122] It is unnecessary to recount the arduous negotiations with both the TUC and the CBI during 1972 as Heath sought to build a tripartite consensus. When the TUC refused to accept his terms Heath resorted to a statutory policy in November 1972. His patient attempt to secure union support won him sympathy in the party and country. Bruce-Gardyne is correct to assert that the union representatives could never have delivered a binding pledge to enforce a voluntary agreement on their members, and even had their negotiators agreed they would have been replaced by less compliant colleagues.[123] The policy was in three phases. First, a complete freeze, followed by a second phase of an egalitarian across the board increase, and a stage three based on a percentage increase of 7 per cent up to a limit of £350 per annum, but including threshold agreements compensating people for inflation above that rate. Heath was adamant that his incomes policy would increase real earnings.[124] It was only with the unveiling of the complicated stage three package in October 1973 that doubts emerged. These were the first signs of the strategy which was to become the new Conservative orthodoxy. Stage three was 'a complicated sieve' allowing the miners to drive 'a coach and horses' though it.[125] A year previously John Biffen and Ridley rebelled against a statutory policy and Ridley claims that Thatcher congratulated them while refusing to join them.[126]

The Heath government was plagued by ill luck externally, such as the rise in world commodity prices and the fourfold increase in the price of oil after the Yom Kippur War in the autumn of 1973. The inflationary effects of these events weakened Heath's attempts to carry out stage three against the National Union of Mineworkers (NUM). Heath had resisted American pressures to use British bases in Cyprus during the Yom Kippur War.[127] Such foreign policy successes, including the negotiation of Britain's entry into the EEC, counted little with the electorate, against the worsening economic background. The growth strategy, now represented in Conservative demonology as the 'Barber Boom', came unstuck, as public expenditure cuts were announced in December 1973. The miners' action against stage three created a crisis atmosphere, particularly after Heath proclaimed a three-day working week to conserve energy.

There is controversy about whether Heath should have offered the NUM's negotiators a higher settlement, and there is evidence that he was uneasy with his more 'gung-ho' colleagues who relished the confrontation. These included the Party Chairman Lord Carrington, who was certain that the Conservatives could win a 'who governs?' election. There is debate about whether Heath should have accepted a TUC offer to hold the line against further pay claims, in breach of stage three, if the miners were allowed a higher increase. Heath was probably correct to judge, however, that the TUC could not fulfil the bargain. His blunder was to delay the election until the end of February when the polling evidence suggests that he could have won earlier. His tragedy is that the left regard him as confrontational because of the Quiet Revolution, and the Who Governs? election, while the Thatcherite right denounce him for his dirigiste policies. His *dirigisme* was stimulated by the post-war political tradition and the example of interventionist European states.[128] Heath had the advantages of a united Cabinet, a loyal press, an inherited balance of payments surplus and able advisers. These advantages were outweighed, however, by 'a popular and intellectual mood increasingly hostile to collectivism but not yet prepared for tough anti-consensual policies'.[129] The right argues that it was the influence of Sir William Armstrong, head of the home Civil Service, which undermined the government.

Heath could not control the course of the February 1974 campaign to ensure that his favoured theme remained central. While the Conservatives held the initiative at first on 'Who Governs?', the Labour Party shifted the ground to the issue of rising prices. Yet a Tory official had only recently warned of this danger, commenting that, 'a snap Election because of a particularly compulsive set of circumstances ... is not a decision that a government should take lightly, however, because ... with a modern mass electorate ... no General Election has been confined to a single issue and ... it would be the object of our opponents to muddy the waters and prevent one theme running throughout the necessary number of days and weeks'.[130] In a class-confrontational campaign it was the Liberals who benefited, securing 6 million votes by emphasising their ill-defined 'moderation', in contrast to the mud-slinging of the other parties.[131] It was ironic that this vote for consensus set off a series of events which undermined it. These included the early collapse of the power-sharing executive in Ulster, the release of Scottish and Welsh nationalism, and the discrediting of incomes policy in favour of monetarism. These events ended decades of relative consensus in British political economy.

The election result was ambiguous, in that Heath won more votes than Labour, 37.9% to 37.1%; but four fewer seats. Instead of accepting the verdict, Heath sought to retain power by forging an anti-Socialist coalition with the Liberals. This helped crystallise Thatcher's opposition to Heath's leadership, since he would not exclude consideration of proportional representation.[132] The Liberals rejected his offer.

In the opening days of the short Parliament Maurice Macmillan and Julian Amery called for a national government, which delayed a new strategy because people round Heath 'interpreted them as unwelcome back-seat driving from Birch Grove where Harold Macmillan lived in retirement'.[133] Conservatives who were fighting Liberals in the country were particularly disgruntled. In June, however, Heath acceded to the idea of a coalitional appeal, remarking, 'I am now going to take the politics out of politics'.[134] This was not cosmetic, as part of him believed that Conservatives should work for national unity. Heath's proposed Government of National Unity evolved as an ill-defined phenomenon but appealed to many desperate to stop Labour by all possible means. His intra-party critics dissented, however, with the formation by Thatcher and Joseph of the Centre for Policy Studies (CPS). Heath agreed to this on the understanding that it would not compete for funds with the party and would merely examine foreign economies. The CPS soon developed into a hard-edged rival to the CRD.[135] Joseph also broke ranks with a speech which diminished the importance of unemployment, demonstrating that the circumstances had arrived for Conservatives to 'go public' on the ideas which had been gestating since the 1960s.[136] Thatcher was already expressing her concern about the rating system at this stage but advocated shifting teacher and police pay to the centre rather than a new tax. Her animus against local government became clear, however, in asserting that 'one of the major problems faced by the last government in its attempts to control public expenditure was the way those intentions had been frustrated by local authorities'.[137]

Heath's idea of a coalition for national unity enabled him to do well, and removed some of his reputation for divisiveness. The result was 35.8% for the Conservatives, 39.2% for Labour, and the capture of 277 seats against 319 for Labour. This was defeat, however, and he had lost three out of four elections. Heath then failed to read the party's mood and ignored the conviction of his enemies that he should step down. Edward DuCann's friends in the 'Milk St Mafia' were at the centre of the challenge.[138] Heath had lost the support of the right, but many who sympathised with his general approach found him difficult, while close associates were 'in thrall to his baleful influence'.[139] Acolytes such as Whitelaw were mesmerised by the continued loyalty of the constituencies, with both the majority of party members and voters wanting him to stay. The Tory faithful dislike the parliamentary party exercising its prerogative of changing the leader.[140] As Joseph and DuCann ruled themselves out by foolish speeches and controversial business affairs respectively, all that was needed to remove Heath was a resolute challenger for the crown.

The Thatcher leadership

Thatcher was elected to the Conservative Party leadership because she was not Heath. Even Lawson, an enthusiastic supporter of her policies, accepts that her victory was achieved on personal grounds. He was one of the few who voted for her on political and economic grounds.[141] Her campaign was shrewdly managed by Airey Neave who skilfully underestimated her support, to secure the votes of those who wanted her to perform well enough to force Heath to resign, in order to promote another candidate. Many of the votes that she secured on the first ballot were calculated, but her strong performance enabled her to consolidate support in the second ballot, and make the other candidates appear both timid and opportunistic.

Thatcher began her leadership campaign in February 1975 with the advantage of having performed effectively in opposing the Labour government's Finance Bill. When the Chancellor, Denis Healey, accused her of being, 'la Pasionaria of privilege' she responded that 'some Chancellors are macro-economic. Other Chancellors are fiscal. This one is just cheap'. Such an attack heartened the Conservatives who were still recovering from the October 1974 defeat.[142] Neave's underestimation of Thatcher's popularity is supported by Parkinson, who was misinformed that Heath was going to win, by Neave's synthetic concern that Thatcher should be given a post commensurate with her new status in the party. This black propaganda secured the votes of MPs anxious about Heath's arrogance.[143]

The Conservative Party carries the two ideological legacies of Toryism and Whiggery which respectively contribute traditionalism and capitalism. The Tory tradition highlights authority and community and the promotion of an orderly, stable society. The Whigs promote the interests of property and the free market, and give priority to economic development, if necessary by state intervention. The Tory tradition can further be bifurcated into progressive and traditional, and the Whigs into liberal and corporatist. If traditionalist Tories stress order and discipline, progressive Tories emphasise paternalism and endorse the post-war system. Similarly, while liberal Whigs encourage economic growth by a neo-Liberal strategy of the free market, progressive Whigs adopt a more corporatist approach, and are prepared to employ planning and state subsidies to encourage economic success. Heath was a corporate Whig, diluted by progressive Toryism, while Thatcher is a liberal Whig diluted by traditional Toryism. Thatcher drew support from both traditional Tories and liberal Whigs. While only a minority of Conservative MPs combined the ingredients of their Conservatism in the same way as Thatcher, she drew support from others who were enthusiastic about one or other of those two positions. Thatcher underestimated the degree of support for her ideas in the parliamentary party when she contested the leadership. On the first ballot she secured 130 votes, Heath 119, and the rank outsider Hugh Fraser gained 16. Despite the late entrants to the second ballot, Thatcher had become unstoppable. She secured 146 votes, Whitelaw 79, Howe 19, Prior 19, and Peyton 11.[144]

Thatcher appointed Lord Thorneycroft to the party chairmanship. He separated fund raising from financial control and appointed Alastair McAlpine as Treasurer, to raise contributions, particularly from small business.[145] Thorneycroft's appointment was symbolically important because of his resignation in 1958, at the height of Macmillan's deviation from sound finance, on quasi-monetarist grounds. Thatcher believed that he could run Central Office and organise a general election campaign as she knew little about the work of the party headquarters. Thorneycroft, together with Thatcher's new acolyte Whitelaw, Humphry Atkins as Chief Whip, and Joseph as political mentor provided Thatcher with a central team covering all aspects of organisation and policy. Neave continued to organise her office.

Thatcher's success in leading the party was assisted by her admiration for the party in the country. This is an unusual trait among post-war leaders. Her sympathy with the sentiments of the rank-and-file was revealed by her enthusiastic support for the prejudices aired at Conference on law and order and capital punishment. Her empathy for the party helped to sustain her influence when the going got rough.[146] 'Harold Macmillan had a contempt for the party, Alec Home tolerated it, Ted Heath loathed it. Margaret genuinely liked it. She felt a communion with it'.[147] It is a comment on the inbred loyalty of Conservatives to their leader, that Heath was the preferred choice of most of the rank-and-file membership in February 1975. The pattern was not entirely uniform, however, since developing support for Thatcher in certain regions was a reflection of a growing middle-class panic, whether real or manufactured by the media, which provided the backdrop of Thatcher's espousal of traditional Conservative prejudices.

The Conference is a means of Conservative leaders remaining in touch with middle-class opinion in the country.[148] This was a time of middle-class assertiveness. The Middle Class Association was formed in November 1974 and in the same year the National Federation of the Self-Employed (NFSE) came into being to protest about National Insurance rates and VAT levied on them. Inflation was portrayed as threatening those on fixed incomes. General Sir Walter Walker launched Civil Assistance to defend the state against the strike threat, at this time. In 1975 Lord Chalfont's television programme, *Who Says It Can't Happen Here?* asserted that Marx's aspirations were coming true in Labour Britain. By 1976 many of these organisations and individuals coalesced in the National Association for Freedom (NAFF). This attracted members from long-standing right-wing organisations, such as the Aims of Industry and the Institute of Economic Affairs, as well as from the new militants. Its ideology was the defence of economic freedom against collectivism. Its publicity against trade unionism was apocalyptic. It adopted Grunwick's cause, defending the employer's derecognition of trade unions at his film processing plant. There were long, occasionally violent, picket line protests. Extensive litigation upheld the right of the workers to organise, but the employer had sacked the strikers and refused to re-instate them. The result was that the NAFF claimed victory, hijacking the concept of liberty in favour an employer's right to refuse to recognise unions.

The proximity of Thatcher's Conservatism to the NAFF is evident. She shared its antipathy to Heath, and its wish for a different sort of Toryism. Her speech at the NAFF's inauguration in 1977 stressed the indivisibility of freedom and the danger of collectivism.[149] That the right-wing mood which affected much of the party in the 1960s was now pervasive among opinion formers and sections of public opinion is suggested by Thatcher's capacity to attack the Labour government for collectivist Socialism at a time when it was presiding over mounting unemployment, and incomes policy, monetary and public expenditure targets to satisfy the International Monetary Fund and a populist campaign led by Callaghan to restore traditional curricula in schools. The Conservative Party did not cross an ideological watershed in the mid-1970s. Rather the political and economic circumstances of the time brought to the surface the attitudes which had always been present but which had been suppressed by the electoral fear of Labour and the opinions of a party elite formed in the era of mass unemployment.

Programmatic development during Thatcher's leadership of the Opposition was gradual and she only responded incrementally to the intellectual pressures of the radical right. This was partly because of resistance in the party leadership by the heirs of Macmillan and Heath, but also by her own desire to win an election, which she was aware as an outsider to the Tory establishment, would be her only opportunity. In consequence, her preparation for government was ideologically patchy. In areas like the control of public expenditure, unlike the period from 1966 to 1970, a great deal of groundwork was undertaken. A Shadow Treasury team, working in collaboration with the CRD, scrutinised government expenditure and conducted its own shadow expenditure round.[150] Monetary policy was not organised in the tranquillity of opposition, however, as there were disagreements about its relationship to inflation.[151] Monetarist converts reacted against the rapid growth in the quantity of money under Heath, and Joseph's speeches urged repentance. There was no real internal party debate, however, between those who followed Friedman's prescriptions of cutting the money supply through targets, or Hayek's advocacy of an immediate substantial cut. Joseph was Friedman's uncritical disciple. The 1979 Manifesto reflected the confusion: 'To master inflation properly monetary discipline is essential, with publicly stated targets for the growth of the money supply'.[152]

The 1970s entrenched a fundamentalist perspective among the rank-and-file, assisted by the collapse of the Bretton Woods fixed currency exchange system and the quadrupling of the oil price.[153] The Phillips curve, with its trade-off in economic policy between inflation and unemployment appeared invalid, and so the stop-go economic policy had become redundant.[154] Most significant for Conservatives, however, was the apparent inefficacy of incomes policy. Heath's policies from 1972 to 1974 convinced Conservatives to reject Keynesianism. Domestically, union wage-bargaining in the 1970s maintained a rising standard of living, even though Britain's competitiveness was declining. For business, however, the combination of falling national income, wage-push inflation, and high levels of public expenditure was alarming, as Britain suffered from the ravages of inflation and rising unemployment.[155] While the government reverted to an incomes policy, and even monetary control, the crisis led to a more far-reaching commitment to public expenditure cuts, tax cuts, and monetary discipline from the Conservatives.

There were a number of individuals who influenced Thatcher as Opposition leader. Joseph's role was apparent but there was considerable impact from Alfred Sherman and John Hoskyns. Sherman ran the Centre for Policy Studies (CPS) and showered Thatcher with papers. John Hoskyns wielded a more effective influence, however, and by 1978 was her principal source of ideas. He was convinced that the business imperative was the means to Britain's recovery. Such a view was compatible with Conservatism, if unbalanced in overstressing Adam Smith at the expense of Edmund Burke. Hoskyns's central contribution was an assault on trade union power, and together with Norman Strauss he produced the *Stepping Stones* document in 1977.[156] It was a plan to win an election and govern afterwards. It stressed that the Conservatives should not be deterred by the charge of seeking a confrontation. The party should show that Socialism opposed the individual, as the closed shop demonstrated, and that the class struggle and corporatism were outdated. It should explore legislative curbs on unions, such as the freedom to enter legally enforceable wage agreements, the withholding of social security payments, compulsory ballots and contracting in. Union leaders should be divided either into potential allies or political opponents and electors should be appealed to on this issue as 'feelers' rather than 'thinkers'. The document's eccentric tone was increased by the proposal to set up a reformed second chamber in Parliament consisting of a number of union leaders to compensate them for their lost power.[157] A subsequent meeting of the Leaders Steering Committee decided to follow Prior's advice and to withold *Stepping Stones* from journalists.[158] The document maintained the momentum in favour of trade union reform, although its specific proposals were shelved. This reflected the limited impact of the non-party radicals, since Thatcher allowed political reality to prevail over dogma. The record of her leadership defies simple analysis, as there was tension between her militant, value-laden speech and the lack of clarity of her policy statements. This was paralleled by her reliance upon such right-wing advisers as Joseph, Lawson, Tebbitt, Bruce-Gardyne, and Sherman, while appointing a Shadow Cabinet dominated by Heath's closest colleagues. She was constrained in her Shadow Cabinet appointments by the 'collegial cannons' of British politics which meant that radical departures from Heath's policies or personnel would have threatened the leadership's cohesion and the party's chances of electoral victory.[159] Her greatest strength was in the cultivation of the support of backbenchers.

Rhetoric exceeded policy substance in Thatcher's speeches because of electoral and intra-party considerations. Many Conservative MPs were not consciously ideological, others were committed to the policies that united sections of the British elite through the post-war period, and a third group judged it politically unfeasible to challenge 'consensual' policies. Behrens split the party between 1975 and 1979 into 'diehards' and 'ditchers'. The diehards sought to return to Conservative basics and to undermine welfarism. The ditchers believed that circumstances governed principles and that government intervention could still prevent a return to the maladies of pre-war British society.[160] This analysis presumes a simplistic distinction between pragmatic Heathmen, and the ideological Josephites, 'who had taken a crash course on Hayek and Friedman'. Behrens neglects those who move ideologically, who blend views idiosyncratically, or who dissemble

208

their beliefs for career advantage.

The highly committed One Nation or monetarist Conservatives were atypical in their consistency. Circumstances encouraged Thatcher to keep policy options open, even on prices and incomes. The ACP's more formal policy work also became more philosophical and its policy groups ran on a lighter rein. The aim was for a broad approach rather than detailed technicalities.[161]

The demands for fixed targets for the money supply, denationalisation, and the shifting of the burden from direct to indirect taxation came from the rank-and-file and from a group of young MPs, including Lawson, Tebbitt, Ridley and Bruce-Gardyne. Outside Parliament a publication by Walter Eltis, later Director-General of the National Economic Development Office (NEDO), *Too Few Producers*, was influential in presenting the 'crowding-out' thesis of too many wealth-consumers in the public and too few wealth-producers in the private sectors. Sam Brittan widely disseminated ideas of fiscal rectitude and monetary restraint. Thatcher received conflicting advice from immediate colleagues. In October 1975 Howe deplored the government's failure to control the money supply and urged that the Conservatives commit themselves to ending price controls and restrictions on profits, as well as opposing pay policy and supporting widened differentials. He was satisfied that the argument that 'excessive public expenditure was helping to cause inflation and was squeezing the private sector was coming across in the press'.[162] Comments, at meetings of the Economic Reconstruction Policy Group, revealed divisions. Heseltine's opposition to the government's National Enterprise Board (NEB) was couched in terms which defended the Heath government's Industry Bill.[163] There was also confusion about whether to vote against the Labour government's emergency pay policy, with inflation soaring.[164] The Economic Reconstruction Group accepted that there was no painless cure to economic problems, was cautious about increasing VAT, supported a voluntary wage agreement and sympathised with a referendum if there was a militant public sector strike.[165] While neo-Liberal policies emerged long before the Thatcher era, there was caution about adopting them, and Thorneycroft urged 'balance' in economic policy.[166]

The resistance at party elite level to the rise of neo-Liberalism expressed itself in many publications. A self-proclaimed 'centre' Tory argued that, 'the moderates are no longer in control of the party'.[167] He overestimated their resistance, however, in asserting that 'the scene is set for a fierce struggle inside the Tory party – one which will not be resolved simply by it winning the next election'.[168] More perceptively, he noticed the impact of Powellism, recognising that it was the first time that Powell's views were influencing the leader. He noted that the party had split into the two camps of ideologues and pragmatists and argued that the belief that Thatcher would be tamed by the moderates if she won an election was a delusion. The Tory

Reform Group, which emerged in the mid-1970s was no match for the combined efforts of the right-wing Selsdon group and the external 'think-tanks', such as the Centre for Policy Studies and the Adam Smith Institute.

The party's first formal response to the insistent pressures from the right on macro-economic policy, appeared in the ambiguous publication, *The Right Approach to the Economy* in 1977. Howe, Howell, and Prior were influential in its message. It reflected Thatcher's caution; and the diverse authorship of a monetarist in Howe, a convert to monetarism in Howell, and a One Nation Conservative in Prior. While it stressed the control of money and lower taxes except on spending, it only referred obliquely to firm management of government expenditure. Its main genuflection towards the free market was its implication that the state cannot assume full responsibility for economic outcomes or employment.[169] The document emphasised the need to loosen up pay differentials and rejected incomes policy. The case for incomes policy had been advanced within the Shadow Cabinet by Maudling as recently as 1976. He argued that reducing the money supply did not deal with cost-inflation. Economic deflation produced stagnation while creating disparities, as the 'big battalions' were still able to protect their position.[170] Prior's position was subtler. He favoured a voluntary policy plus a clear strategy to deal with the government's own employees. He claims that there was 'a row' on the issue leading to the compromise in *The Right Approach to the Economy* that, 'in framing its monetary and other policies the Government must come to *some* conclusions about the likely scope for pay increases if excess public expenditure or large-scale unemployment is to be avoided; and this estimate can not be concealed from the representatives of employers and unions whom it is consulting'.[171] The document lacked ideological self-confidence. Denationalisation was only wistfully mentioned and increases in indirect taxation were barely discussed. The document was cautious enough to maintain the support of Prior and Joseph.[172]

The issue of labour relations was harder to compromise, however, as both Thatcher and Joseph had a visceral dislike of trade unions while Prior was 'doveish'. Ridley described Prior as in the Monckton mould, believing that if a Tory government annoyed the trade unions they would make the country ungovernable. Ridley deplored Prior's retention in the Shadow Cabinet.[173] Prior's caution prevailed and there was no reference in the *Right Approach to the Economy* to the legislative reform of trade unions. Thatcher considered that she was not yet strong enough to resist Prior's faction. In power she recognised the shallowness of its appeal, and even at Conference before 1979 there was sympathy with Tebbitt's likening of Prior to 'Petain and Laval'.[174] For a period Thatcher allowed Prior to encourage Conservative trade unionists to become active to defeat the militants from within. Since the Conservative Trade Unionists (CTU), and their Director Andrew Rowe, broadly supported Prior rather than Thatcher, they soon lost her favour. The notorious 'Winter of Discontent' of 1978–9 led to a public perception that the industrial system was out of control and government paralysed. It was undoubtedly the unpopularity and overmightiness of the trade unions which contributed to the Conservative electoral victory of 1979 and Thatcher's growing confidence about tackling the issue. She also had the benefit of the negative model of the 1971 strategy.[175]

Ridley and Eden had promoted privatisation in the Heath years, but the time was ripe for its reappearance. At Joseph's request Ridley updated his 1970 statement and insisted that 'privatisation was a popular policy among Tory MPs in 1979'.[176] It was not widely understood at this time, however, and even the Bank of England and the Treasury were more concerned about the fragility of the country's economic structure. From their perspective, 'Thatcherism was a reaction to the real nature of the economic forces weighing on the country'.[177]

There were other issues which emerged to test Thatcher's ideological stance. A Steering Committee meeting debated whether to oppose the second reading of the Race Relations Bill and Gilmour managed to persuade it that the Conservatives should not oppose it.[178] Yet on immigration Thatcher sought to exploit popular concern. The Conservatives established a healthy opinion poll lead in February 1978 after her remark, that she understood fears about being 'swamped by people of a different culture'.[179] She added that there would be 4 million blacks by the end of the century and 'we are not in politics to ignore people's worries, we are in politics to deal with them'.[180]

The party's Steering Committee debated how best to exploit the EEC since it was divisive for the Labour government. When the Steering Committee was informed that Conservatives in the country had voted massively for the EEC, Thatcher claimed that this represented a fear of Labour's left-wingers, Benn and Shore, and not Euro-enthusiasm. At this time the party was more enthusiastic about Europe than was Thatcher, or than it was later to become. The 1975 Conference passed a resolution urging the party to work closely with 'our political allies in Europe' to form 'a centre-right alliance' and to work for direct elections to the European Parliament.[181] There was also discussion about whether to attack the Labour moderates who had linked up with members of other parties in advocating British membership in the referendum. It was decided not to do so as they were popular with the public and attacks on them would encourage Labour to close ranks.[182]

The Conservative mood ebbed and flowed between 1974 and 1979, on the basis of opinion surveys, election results, and the government's performance. In 1978 the government had recovered slightly and there was a concern about the electoral appeal of Callaghan's conservatism. A summer 1978 advertising campaign by Saatchi and Saatchi closed Labour's lead and was important in determining Callaghan to delay calling an autumn election; which was welcome to Conservatives given the uncertain electoral climate. 1978 was an optimum time for Labour economically as the future offered only a troublesome wage round.[183] This was offset, however, by a private Labour poll in marginal seats, which suggested that it was behind. When the government announced a 5% pay norm the Conservatives split at their Conference on whether to support it, and it took Thorneycroft's skill to reunite the party at a Shadow Cabinet meeting behind the formula spelt out in *The Right Approach to the Economy*. The ensuing 'Winter of Discontent' allowed Thatcher to emerge as a Prime Minister in waiting in her January 1979 broadcast, where she seized the initiative, stressing her policy to enforce strike ballots and to tax social security benefits for strikers. The negative outcome of the Scottish and Welsh devolution referendums in March 1979 advantaged the Conservatives, as the Nationalist parties had no further motive to sustain the government and joined the Conservatives in a vote of no confidence, which precipitated the May general election.

The party took the October 1974 vote as the base for the 1979 campaign, and sought to add to it by detaching 'soft' Labour and Liberal supporters among the ranks of the C2s, housewives, and people purchasing their own homes in the campaign. It estimated that these detachable voters would be best appealed to through the *Sun*, ITV, and the Jimmy Young radio show. These were 'soft' presentations aimed at housewives. Thatcher's marketing was crucial as she began the campaign as a less popular leader than Callaghan.[184] Initially, she refused to engage in a debate with him and even her advisers thought that she would perform badly, but as she gained confidence, she became an asset. Her campaign was built around television happenings, as when she picked up a young calf and proudly held it up to the camera. Even before the age of the 'soundbite', therefore, the politically vacuous visual package was used by the Conservatives.[185]

The Conservative Manifesto lacked detailed policy proposals and highlighted themes such as the control of inflation and trade union power, restoring incentives, upholding the rule of law, supporting family life, and strengthening defence. The vagueness on policy reassured electors fearful of change. There was no hint of unemployment, increasing prescription charges, or threatening welfare benefits.[186] This caution was warranted because while the British worried about national economic decline they were broadly contented with their lot.[187] The Conservatives gained 44.9% of the vote against 37.8% for Labour, and secured an overall majority of 43 seats. Analysis suggests that while the Conservatives have always secured a substantial working-class vote, their gains in the 1979 election were spectacular. There was an 11% swing to the Conservatives among skilled workers, particularly in the 24–34 age group, as well as among unskilled workers. There were marked regional variations with the Conservatives performing less well in the urban north.[188] The aspirant workers, rather than those living in areas of economic decline were moving towards the Conservatives. This was for 'secular' reasons of economic ambition but it provided the potential for a more permanent transfer of allegiance.

Labour blamed Conservative expenditure and the 'vulgar' nature of their PR campaign, but the financial differential was solely at a national level and confined to advertising.[189] To some Conservatives the 1979 result marked a decisive break with the post-war consensus of the welfare state, the mixed economy, price and wage controls, and state intervention in industry. Certainly the election offered an unusually stark choice. Some of the Tory programme had a national appeal; for example the sale of council housing, taxation, reform of the unions, and law and order, and the fashion among the intellectual elite had turned to the right for the first time in a generation.[190] Yet caution is needed before assuming that 1979 marked an ideological realignment. The result was not an electoral landslide and public support for Conservative policies was selective. The view that the public converted the Conservatives to economic Liberalism in the 1970s is incorrect.[191] The people's flag was not 'the deepest blue'.[192]

Notes

1 John Campbell, *Edward Heath* (London: Jonathan Cape, 1993), p. 539.
2 *Daily Telegraph*, 15 October 1973.
3 Jock Bruce-Gardyne, *Whatever Happened to the Quiet Revolution?* (Charles Knight, 1974), Preface, p. 1.
4 This summary is drawn from Bruce-Gardyne, pp. 5–7.
5 *The Economist*, 26 May 1979.
6 Bruce-Gardyne, *Whatever Happened*, p. 12.
7 Hugo Young, *One of Us* (London: Pan Books, 1990), p. 66.
8 Nigel Lawson, *The View From Number 11* (London: Corgi Books, 1993), p. 8.
9 See Douglas Hurd, *An End to Promises* (London: Collins, 1979), Peter Walker, *Staying Power* (London: Bloomsbury Press, 1991) and James Prior, *A Balance of Power* (London: Hamilton 1986).
10 Bruce-Gardyne, *Whatever Happend*, p. 54.
11 Kenneth O. Morgan, *The People's Peace: British History 1945–1990* (Oxford: Oxford University Press, 1992), p. 322.
12 Bruce-Gardyne, *Whatever Happend*, p. 68.
13 *Ibid.*, p. 70.
14 Campbell, *Edward Heath*, p. 369.
15 Dennis Kavanagh, *Thatcherism and British Politics. The End of Consensus?* (Oxford: Oxford University Press, 1989), p. 276 and Andrew Gamble, *The Free Economy and the Strong State* (London: Macmillan, 1989), p. 76.
16 Campbell, *Edward Heath*, p. 374.
17 *Ibid.*, p. 442.
18 *Ibid.*, p. 481.
19 *The Observer*, 4 July 1971.

20 *The Observer*, 18 July 1971.
21 Bruce-Gardyne, *Whatever Happend*, p. 62.
22 *Ibid*.
23 Comment by Brendon Sewell of the Conservative Research Department, at a Symposium on Conservative Policy-Making 1965–70, *Contemporary Record*, 3 (3) (February 1990), p. 38. Kavanagh also stresses the effect of 'stagflation'. Kavanagh, *Thatcherism and British Politics*, pp. 194–5. Nicholas Ridley claims that it was rising unemployment alone which produced the U-turn. Nicholas Ridley, *My Style of Government: The Thatcher Years* (London: Hutchinson, 1991), p. 4.
24 Campbell, *Edward Heath*, pp. 313–14.
25 Bruce-Gardyne, *Whatever Happend*, p. 23.
26 *The Economist*, 30 January 1971.
27 Ridley, *My Style of Government*, p. 3.
28 Bruce Gardyne, *Whatever Happend*, p. 27.
29 *The Economist*, 30 January 1971 and 13 February 1971.
30 *The Economist*, 9 January 1971.
31 *The Economist*, 30 January 1971.
32 *The Economist*, 24 April 1971.
33 Morgan, *The People's Peace*, p. 323.
34 Douglas Hurd, *An End to Promises*, p. 92.
35 House of Commons, 8 February 1971.
36 *The Times*, 9 October 1970.
37 Campbell, *Edward Heath*, p. 362.
38 House of Commons, 24 May 1971.
39 *Ibid.*, 15 December 1970.
40 Michael Moran, *The Politics of Industrial Relations* (London: Macmillan, 1971), pp. 162–3.
41 Campbell, *Edward Heath*, p. 509.
42 'So You're Interested?', outlined in CPC, *Campaign News*, 4 (1972).
43 Quoted in *Campaign News*, 3 (1972).
44 Letter to Party Chairman dated 2 September 1970, in CCO/500/27/7.
45 Meeting held on 9 March 1971, CCO20/7/11.
46 Tactical Committee, minutes of meeting held on 4 January 1972, CCO20/7/4.
47 Tactical Committee, minutes, 18 January 1972, CCO20/7/4.
48 CCO20/7/4, 24 January 1972.
49 Letter from Peter Thomas, Party Chairman to Sir Michael Fraser of the Conservative Research Department, 19 January 1972, CCO20/7/4.
50 Campbell, *Edward Heath*, p. 333.
51 *Ibid.*, p. 466.
52 Letter from Taylor to Patten, 11 December 1972, CCO20/27/16.
53 Letter from E. J. Dockerill, 29 February 1972, CCO20/7/4.
54 Internal Memo, 1 November 1972, CCO500/27/8.
55 Humphry Taylor to Lord Carrington, 14 December 1972, CCO20/27/16.
56 Ridley, *My Style of Government*, pp. 4–5.
57 Comment by Lord Carrington on an ORC memo, dated 18 May 1972, CRD3/7/7/7.

58 Memorandum published on 6 December 1972, CRD3/7/7/7.
59 Memorandum, dated 6 November 1972, CRD3/7/7/7.
60 Letter from James Douglas, 22 March 1972, ACP22/3/72.
61 Minutes of meeting held on 8 November 1972, ACP1/22.
62 *Ibid.*
63 Letter dated 6 September 1972, ACP1/22.
64 Letter 11 September 1972, ACP1/22.
65 Letter from Margaret Thatcher, 1 June 1972, ACP1/22.
66 Letter 17 May 1972, ACP1/22.
67 Sir Richard Webster at a briefing meeting held at the end of December 1967, CCO4/10/25.
68 Survey undertaken from 27–29 June 1973, CCO500/26/35.
69 Survey undertaken 22–24 January 1974, CCO500/26/35.
70 Survey undertaken on 14 September 1993, CCO500/26/35.
71 Report published on 18 September 1973, CCO20/7/19.
72 19 March 1974, CCO20/7/20.
73 Campbell, *Edward Heath*, p. 629.
74 Brief from Michael Woolf on the Liberal Party, 26 July 1974, CCP500/25/10.
75 Report, CCO500/25/10.
76 Letter written on 5 May 1974, CCO500/25/10.
77 Undated memo, CCO500/2/10.
78 Memo dated 26 July 1974, CCO20/8/17.
79 Letter from Renton to Heath's Private Office, 7 August 1984, CCO20/7/19.
80 Letter from DuCann to Heath, 13 September 1994, CCO20/7/19.
81 *Ibid.*
82 Letter from DuCann above, CCO20/7/19.
83 Letter after constituency meeting held on 15 March 1971 from Ian Deslandes of Central Office to the local chairman, CCO20/3/12.
84 Letter from Neil Marten to Russell Lewis of the CPC, 15 July 1971, CPC1/11.
85 Letter from Russell Lewis to Neil Marten, 16 July 1971, CPC1/11.
86 CPC1/11.
87 The Conservative Political Centre, 'The Housewife and the Common Market', April 1971.
88 Letter 28 June 1971, CPC1/11.
89 Conservative Political Centre, *Europe – Words to Remember*, September 1971.
90 *Ibid.*
91 Letter from Neil Marten to Lord Carrington, 12 September 1972, CCO20/27/16.
92 Memorandum, 20 September 1971, SC71/10.
93 Paper dated 18 November 1974, LSC/74/17.
94 *Campaign News*, 5, 1974.
95 CCO500/26/4.
96 Document on Proposals Relating to an Investigation into the Current Branch Level Organisation of the Conservative Party, CCO500/26/41.
97 *Ibid.*
98 Minutes of Leaders Consultative Committee, 19 March 1974, CCO20/7/20.
99 Letter from Sir David Eccles to Heath, 8 June 1974, CCO20/8/17.

100 Letter from William Waldegrave to the new Party Chairman William Whitelaw, 22 July 1974, CCO20/8/17.

101 Letter from Heath to Eccles, 14 June 1974, CCO20/8/17.

102 *The Times*, 3 November 1971.

103 In conversation.

104 Campbell, *Edward Heath*, p. 374.

105 Edward Heath in conversation. The view that the Heath government should have taken up Labour's reforms was advanced by Jim Prior in *A Balance of Power*, p. 72.

106 Morgan, *The People's Peace*, pp. 324–5.

107 Leading Conservatives in conversation.

108 *The Times*, 8 July 1971.

109 Campbell, *Edward Heath*, p. 404.

110 *Ibid.*

111 *Ibid.*, p. 444.

112 *Ibid.*, pp. 83–5.

113 Keith Middlemas, *Power, Competition and the State. Threats to the Post-War Settlement: Britain 1961–1974* (London: Macmillan, 1990), p. 333.

114 *Ibid.*, p. 334.

115 Gamble, *The Free Economy and the Strong State*, p. 79.

116 Kavanagh, *Thatcherism and British Politics*, p. 45.

117 Ridley, *My Style of Government*, p. 4.

118 Middlemas, *Power, Competition and the State*, p. 313.

119 *Ibid.*, p. 340.

120 Campbell, *Edward Heath*, p. 469.

121 *The Times*, 7 November 1972. *The Economist*, 14 October 1972.

122 In conversation.

123 Bruce-Gardyne, *Whatever Happened*, p. 92.

124 *The Times*, 6 February 1973.

125 *The Economist*, 13 October 1973.

126 Ridley, *My Style of Government*, p. 6.

127 In conversation.

128 Middlemas, *Power, Competition and the State*, p. 330.

129 *The Independent*, 28 February 1994.

130 SC (73) 17, The Tactical Situation in February 1973, p. 3.

131 D. Butler and D. Kavanagh, *The British General Election of February 1974* (London: Macmillan, 1975), pp. 131–2.

132 Vernon Bogdanor, 'When Heath Lost, Who Won?', *The Independent*, 28 February 1974.

133 Butler and Kavanagh, *The British General Election of February 1974*, p. 43.

134 *Ibid.*, p. 45.

135 Young, *One of Us*, p. 86.

136 Nigel Fisher, *The Tory Leaders* (London: Weidenfeld and Nicolson, 1977), p. 163.

137 LSC (74) 15, 19 July 1974.

138 This was where DuCann's offices Keyser Ullman were located. Phillip Whitehead, *The Writing on the Wall* (London: Michael Joseph, 1986), p. 326.

139 Young, *One Of Us*, p. 95.
140 Morrison Halcrow, *Keith Joseph: A Single Mind* (London: Macmillan, 1989), p. 91.
141 Nigel Lawson, *The View from Number 11*, p. 13.
142 Cecil Parkinson, *Right at the Centre* (London: Weidenfeld and Nicholson, 1992), p. 127.
143 *Ibid.*, p. 128.
144 Young, *One of Us*, p. 98.
145 David Butler and Dennis Kavanagh, *The British General Election of 1979* (London: Macmillan, 1979), p. 71.
146 *The Independent*, 10 October 1994.
147 Lawson, *The View from Number 11*, p. 14.
148 Samuel Beer, *Modern British Politics* (London: Faber, 1969), p. 372.
149 Whitehead, *The Writing on the Wall*, pp. 210–19.
150 Lawson, *The View from Number 11*, p. 17.
151 *Ibid.*, p. 18.
152 *The Conservative Manifesto 1979*, p. 8.
153 The disabling effects of these economic changes on the world economy and particularly on the enfeebled British economy are discussed in a number of texts. A good brief introduction can be found in Middlemas, *Power, Competition and the State*, pp. 332–4. Also Morgan, *The People's Peace*, p. 446–7.
154 Middlemas, *Power, Competition and the State*, p. 335.
155 Ian Budge and David McKay, *The Developing British Political System: The 1990s* (London: Longman, 1993), p. 21.
156 Young, *One of Us*, pp. 113–14.
157 SC (77) 57.
158 LSC (78) 51, 30 January 1978.
159 Howard R. Penniman (ed.), *Britain at the Polls, 1979* (Washington: American Enterprise Institute for Public Policy and Research, 1981), p. 71.
160 Robert Behrens, *The Conservative Party from Heath to Thatcher* (Farnborough: Saxon House, 1980), p. 3.
161 Chris Patten, 'Policy-Making in Opposition' in Zig Layton Henry (ed.), *Conservative Party Politics* (London: Macmillan, 1980), p. 19.
162 SC/75/23, SC76/51, 27 October 1975.
163 LCC/75/65.
164 LSC (75) 38, 7 July 1975.
165 LSC (75) 38, Meeting held on 30 June 1975.
166 *Ibid.*
167 Trevor Russell, *The Tory Party. Its Policies, Divisions and Future* (Harmondsworth: Penguin, 1978), p. 7.
168 *Ibid.*, p. 12.
169 Andrew Gamble, 'Economic Policy' in Zig Layton Henry, *Conservative Party Politics*, pp. 42–3.
170 Reginald Maudling, *Memoirs* (London: Sidgwick and Jackson, 1978), p. 209.
171 Prior, *A Balance of Power*, p. 109.
172 Young, *One of Us*, pp. 107–8.
173 Ridley, *My Style of Government*, pp. 14–15.

174 Cited in Young, *One of Us*, p. 110.
175 Peter Dorey, 'Conservatives and the Unions: Thatcherism's Impact', *Contemporary Record*, 4 (4) (April 1991), p. 9.
176 Ridley, *My Style of Government*, p. 15.
177 Symposium on the publication of Keith Middlemas, *Power, Competition and the State*, reported in *Contemporary Record*, 5 (3) (Winter 1991).
178 CCO 75/23, SC/76/51. Thatcher chaired the Committee which also consisted of Joseph, Hailsham, Carrington, Prior, Peyton, Atkins, Thorneycroft and Ridley. There were apologies from Whitelaw, Maudling, Howe and Maude.
179 I. Crewe, 'Popular attitudes and Electrical Strategy', in Zig Layton Henry, *Conservative Party Politics*.
180 *World in Action*, Granada Television, 30 January 1978.
181 SC (75) 23, annex 1, October 1975.
182 SC (75) 36, 9 June 1975.
183 Butler and Kavanagh, *The British General Election of 1979*, p. 43.
184 Butler and Kavanagh, *The British General Election of 1979*, pp. 138–42.
185 Penniman, *Britain at the Polls*, pp. 141–3.
186 Butler and Kavanagh, *The British General Election of 1979*, pp. 154–7.
187 Morgan, *The People's Peace*, pp. 432–3.
188 Butler and Kavanagh, *The British General Election of 1979*, Appendices 1 and 2.
189 M. Pinto-Duschinsky, 'Financing the General Election', in Penniman, *Britain at the Polls*, pp. 234–5.
190 Ivor Crewe, 'Why the Conservatives Won', in Penniman, *Britain at the Polls*, pp. 302–3.
191 Patrick Seyd, 'Factionalism in the 1970s', in Zig Layton Henry, *Conservative Party Policy*, p. 242.
192 Crewe, 'Why the Conservatives Won', pp. 302–4.

8

The debate about Thatcherism

The interpretation of Thatcher's leadership of the Conservative Party from 1975 to 1990 is undermined by the strong emotions that it produces.[1] There was no unified, static Thatcherite ideology. Ideological change necessarily results from the interaction between fundamental values and political reality, induced by the requirements of government.[2] There were also distinct ideological emphases at different stages of Thatcher's leadership of the party. The events and policies of the Thatcher years are too extensive to describe, but as well as examining the major interpretative issues to which it gave rise a chart reveals the outstanding episodes which occurred. The era is also described in a number of other sources.[3]

The language of Thatcherism altered, although this was as much a change in the justification of policy as a serious shift in the content of policy itself. In the early years of her leadership she stressed puritanical themes, such as 'families must live within their means' and the virtue of 'deferred gratification', but there was a shift towards paeans to affluence, prosperity, and consumer credit after 1985. Disagreements among students of Thatcherism are increased by confusions about which aspects an observer is examining. Commentators focus on different phases between 1975 and 1990, on rhetoric or on particular policies. They differ in their judgement about whether politicians are primarily driven by moral values, political tactics or uncontrollable external economic pressures and by disagreements provoked by the question did Thatcher have long, medium or short-term political aims?

Some of the more challenging analyses of Thatcherism have been written by disillusioned Marxists. Apologists are too close and uncritical, and make the assumption that Thatcherism was an objective necessity. Labour and Liberal opponents are too partisan and prone to analyse the phenomenon as good versus evil. Since former Marxists subscribed to an ambitious and transforming political project, they are most likely to discern one among their opponents. The danger is that they are so influenced by Gramsci's conception of a political 'project' that they underestimate the continuities and the opportunism within Conservatism. Interpretations sympathetic to Thatcherism are discussed first.

The debate

Did the Thatcher governments operate to a preconceived 'New Right' ideological plan, or were they *ad hoc* in character, remaining within the British Conservative tradition? Commentators who reject the view that there was some new plan, fall into three main categories. First there is the view advanced by Willetts that Thatcher's leadership was within the traditions of Conservatism in its concern to promote free markets plus a strong community.[4] Second, Riddell argues that Thatcherism consists of pragmatic policy-making, constrained less by New Right ideas than by prejudices, particularly those which Thatcher acquired in Grantham in the 1930s.[5] Third, Bulpitt proposes that a central concern of the Conservative Party is 'statecraft': stable government, facilitated by 'the autonomy of the centre', and the political problems which confronted central government in 1979 were sufficiently serious to require new policy departures.[6] Each of these perspectives on the Thatcher years are *parti pris* in that they derive from Conservative sympathisers.

A fourth sympathetic analysis has been offered by Letwin. Although she perversely denies that Thatcherism is ideological, she strongly defends Thatcher's programme. Letwin's problem is that like most British Conservatives she has a pejorative view of the word ideology. Thatcherism's purpose was to promote vigorous individualist virtues which Letwin claims is non-ideological, because she regards the encouragement of the 'vigorous virtues' to be a practical response to the historical state of affairs in Britain at the time.[7]

A final perspective is that of the 'wet' or consensual Conservatives, who opposed the party's direction under Thatcher's leadership. This group encompassed Jim Prior, Peter Walker, Francis Pym, and Ian Gilmour, all of whom served for a period in Thatcher governments. Most of their criticisms were expressed in speeches, using 'coded' language, but Pym and Gilmour wrote books describing their philosophy. They argued that Thatcherism was indeed an ideology, and its doctrinaire approach was at odds with the relaxed and pragmatic defence of tradition which is the true essence of Toryism.

The Willetts interpretation

Willetts argues that there is a coherent Conservative philosophical tradition embracing Disraelian 'One Nation' Conservatism and classical Liberal free-market Conservatism; and that Thatcher and Major maintain the continuity. The principles which he argues the Conservative Party has always upheld are individualism and the free market and a commitment to a strong community are just as integral in the Thatcher and Major years as they have been since Edmund Burke. Conservatism has never been solely concerned with the free market, fiscal responsibility, monetary restraint, and the defeat of inflation; but has sought to temper these preoccupations with a concern about the community and social order. People are not merely economic units in a market place, because individuals desire to be loyal to an entity with which they identify. The 'mutual dependence between the community and the free market', has always concerned Conservatives: 'Disraeli's two nations, Salisbury's fears of national disintegration, the One Nation group, John Major's opportunity society all address the question of how to ensure that all British citizens feel that they participate in national life'.[8]

The Conservative manifesto of 1970 was 'more meaty' than those of 1979 and 1983, which demonstrates that Thatcher was not the originator of the ideas she propounded in government.[9] While acknowledging that Heath was undermined by external difficulties, Willetts roots Heath's failure in the technocratic and managerial style of his politics, arguing that Conservatism took a 'wrong turn' in the early 1970s, and that Thatcher reminded the Conservatives of their principles.[10] Willetts suggests that Thatcher carried through a more modest programme than Heath had promised in 1970. In returning the party to its true principles, Thatcher's concern with community led her to maintain the essentials of the welfare state. She did not cut public expenditure in real terms, but delivered better value for money.

Demonstrating that monetarism is no new 'fad or fancy', he quotes Hume's exposition on the monetary causes of inflation (1752). There are three aspects of monetarist theory: keeping the growth in the money supply to the level by which real output increases; an open and explicit financial rule as a discipline for policy-makers; and the use of supply-side reforms such as the deregulation of business. Willetts remains a monetarist and was concerned when in the mid-1980s the government jettisoned the Medium Term Financial Strategy (MTFS) without imposing a new financial rule in its place. Recognising that the government had lost faith in M3 (broad money including bank deposits) as an accurate monetary indicator, and that the target of M0 (narrow money, notes and coins in circulation) was not tested, he deplored the ensuing financial laxity of government policy.

Despite the importance which Willetts ascribes to the communitarian Tory tradition, he clearly regards the 'political cutting edge' and 'intellectual core' of Conservatism as being the free market. He also judges that the market, in liberating business from the encumbrances of the regulatory

221

'nanny state', and facilitating the values of 'freedom', 'choice', 'opportunity', and 'ownership', was the basis of the Conservative electoral success. As if unconvinced that Major has the conviction to persevere with reform, he calls for the spread of the internal market in what remains of the public sector, as well as for further deregulation, the encouragement of technology to hasten privatisation, and the wider spreading of ownership.[11]

Willetts asserts that Conservatives recognise 'man does not live by profit alone'. Consumers always take priority over producers but there are limits to market mechanisms: parents can not sell their children or their vote, neither can jury places be auctioned nor royal events commercially sponsored. Equally, all Conservative governments have preserved the welfare state because they recognise that 'advanced western states need a welfare state in order to function'.[12] Conservative governments have contributed towards the welfare state's incremental growth, and in the 1980s public expenditure on health, social services, social security, and education stood at 21.3% of a greater national income than had been available in 1979, when it only reached 20.4%.[13] The welfare state fits with the theme of moral obligation 'towards fellow members of our community', and even the feckless have a claim to state support by virtue of being compatriots. Yet Willetts is not a 'wet', nor in danger of unbalancing his argument towards the community rather than the market. On the contrary, 'the market argument for the welfare state is that it contributes towards the successful working of the capitalist economy'. It is unusual historically for Conservatives to refer to the welfare state. Willetts uses terminology with which Conservatives have traditionally been happier, when he refers to it as 'an enormous mutual insurance scheme', involving life-cycle transfer payments, rather than a vehicle of redistribution between individuals. There is little risk in a Conservative system of 'moral hazard', since Conservatives discourage individual irresponsibility. Willetts even seeks to distance the Conservative approach from continental Conservatives, and the British welfare state from the German social market economy. In Germany, welfare fulfils a social purpose which is upheld by an all-party consensus. Consensus in Britain is not based on policy convergence, but upon the affinities of a continuously shared culture.[14] Willetts attributes to Thatcher a view of the welfare state which is limited, leaves ample scope for charitable and philanthropic action and ensures that its users do not become so 'dependent on state finance and lose every sense of control over their own lives, that they may not be really integrated into society after all'.[15]

It is through the nurturing of a national identity that a strong community is fostered. The Thatcher governments followed policies to develop British national identity, and their Euro-scepticism was compatible with this goal. Thatcher's own emotional commitment to the country made her a true Conservative. Willetts argues that 'Conservatives are uneasy about the development of Europe ... The real Conservative fear must be that our sense of Britishness, even, dare one say it, our Englishness, is eroded by the EC'. Conservatives can support European co-operation, but the rolling back of the British state cannot be accompanied by the advance of a European state. While Willetts supported the ERM as an anti-inflationary device, he is concerned that there should be no parallel scheme of economic and monetary union implicit in the European Monetary Systems (EMS). In supporting the ERM he, like Thatcher's Chancellor Nigel Lawson, was reverting to 'automatism'; the search for a rule of economic management to overcome the need for discretionary political decision-making.[16]

Thatcher's economic liberalism never veered towards social libertarianism. She never sympathised with the legalisation of drugs or carried individualism to the lengths of supporting personal experimentation and social non-conformity, which placed her squarely in the tradition of British Conservatism, with its respect for traditional institutions and morality.

It is in her regard for the British nation, rather than the welfare state, that Thatcher demonstrated her commitment to the idea of a strong community. Conservatives have always sought to ensure that all citizens become a part of national life. Willetts cites the National Curriculum and the Department of National Heritage as an attempt to sustain national cultural identity.[17] Conservatives are particularly sensitive to Britain's history and institutions and its stable political culture. This conception of nation may only be resonant, however, for middle-class, southern England, or even reflect an 'invented' or 'manufactured' sense of Englishness. That it may only be a part of a Conservative myth of Englishness, however, does not invalidate the importance of the myth for Conservatives.

This explains the difficulty which many Conservatives have with the European Union (EU). After explaining the fidelity of Conservatives to the protection of British sovereignty, Willetts demonstrates why true Conservatives are sceptical towards European integration. It would be 'a terrible mistake for the European community to embark upon grandiose schemes of political, economic or monetary integration without the underlying political culture or economic convergence necessary to sustain them'.[18] British political stability is founded upon cultural integration, and it is the very absence of this integration in Europe which makes federalism so undesirable. Further, he urges a 'variable geometry Europe in which different member-states participate in different sets of policies, chosen from an *à la carte* menu'.[19] He is able to reconcile Thatcher's hostility to further integration with the Maastricht Treaty in 1991.

Willetts rejects the view, therefore, that a set of free-market *arrivistes* have taken over the traditional party of deference, order and authority. This is because Conservatives have always spoken in two different languages: the individual, initiative, enterprise, and freedom; and community, deference, convention, and authority.

Conservatives have responded to the rise of the mass electorate and Socialism by becoming the party of freedom. In the inter-war years, the Party drifted towards economic intervention and 'thought that planners could control the economy like technicians sitting in front of an array of dials at a power station'. Despite his disillusionment with Heath, Willetts also argues that after the Second World War Conservatism came to terms with the economic and social changes of the century, recognising a role for the public sector in the welfare state while avoiding detailed micro-economic intervention. Willetts is adamant that Thatcher scrupulously avoided departures from the paths of British Conservatism and was in harmony with the pattern of post-war Conservatism.

Bulpitt: Thatcherism as statecraft

Bulpitt is at pains to demonstrate that Thatcherism was motivated by an eternal Conservative concern, that of 'statecraft': Thatcherism was more concerned with the traditional goals of winning elections and governing competence than with grand ideological purposes. 'Statecraft' resolves the electoral and governing problems of a party at any particular time and the goal of statecraft is that of 'centre autonomy'.[20] This involves a commitment to the Party winning power at the centre. Once in office the Conservatives have always sought to achieve 'a relative autonomy for the centre' on the matters of 'high politics'. Conservative governments have consistently attempted to exploit Parliament as an intermediary with peripheral social forces, to delegate matters of 'low politics' to agencies away from the centre, and to discover an automatic pilot to depoliticise economic management. By the 1960s Keynesian demand-management was no longer sufficient, and the political fashion was remodernising Britain by state intervention. While the Macmillan government sought to capture the policy initiative for remodernisation, the fact that the Conservatives had been in power for over a decade, and the statist connotations of rapid economic modernisation, benefited Labour. As a result of Labour's successive victories in 1964 and 1966 the Conservatives turned against remodernisation between 1965 and 1970. Heath was a technocrat, however, uncommitted to an anti-remodernisation culture. Partly in order to conceal this he symbolically rejected incomes policy. This left his government without any effective macro-economic strategy, and after two defeats in 1974, the party's prospects appeared bleak.

This was the context in which the quantity theory of money, ideologised as the political theory of monetarism in the 1970s, had so much appeal to Conservatives. If both Keynes and modernisation were ceasing to be effective instruments of 'statecraft', monetarism appeared to offer an alternative strategy for the party. The situation was one in which the Labour government with its Social Contract with the trades unions had a 'statecraft' strategy while the Conservatives appeared to be bereft. Monetarism had little appeal during the years of Heath's leadership, but by the mid-1970s many financial and political journalists had been converted.[21] Monetarism came to have a wide appeal within a Conservative Party troubled with the problem of 'statecraft', with Sir Keith Joseph being particularly influential. Bulpitt is correct that the 'modest little theory of monetarism' was of long standing in a party which had an entrenched commitment to the idea that if governments can effectively control little else, they can control the money supply to counter inflation and protect the currency. The 1970s transformed monetarism, at least in the vulgar version which appealed to Conservatives at the time, into an instrument to tackle inflation in the era of floating exchange rates after 1972. It also preached that trade union wage demands did not determine price levels, even though they might influence the level of employment. This was heady news for a party which had become traumatised by incomes policy. 'Inflation could therefore be controlled by governments acting on their own, without having to resort to incomes policies which involved them in difficult and dangerous bargaining with unions and employers'.[22] The mechanics of controlling the money supply were a simple matter of limiting government spending specifically by the amount that expenditure exceeded tax revenue, or the Public Sector Borrowing Requirement (PSBR). So while monetarism can reasonably be portrayed as an economic theory, a policy framework or even an ideology, Bulpitt correctly asserts that in the mid-1970s it offered 'a superb (or lethal) piece of statecraft.' As the automaticity offered by Keynesian demand management proved unable to conquer 'stagflation' or militant unionism, Friedmanite monetarism filled the vacuum. With the discrediting of the ill-defined coalitional strategy of Heath, the 'wets' had no alternative statecraft to offer. In restoring the capacity of the centre to govern autonomously, the statecraft constructed in the late 1970s involved a reconstruction of the past because it reciprocally offered a degree of autonomy to external groups. His point about the autonomy of external groups should be treated warily, however, since trade unions hardly welcomed the election of the Thatcher government, and they were certainly unable to retain their power during the decade which followed. It was the 1978–79 Winter of Discontent which ensured the success of the Thatcher government's electoral strategy. If the 'wets' had worried about aspects of Thatcher's oppositional prospectus, for example, the signs of moralism, populism, nationalism, and confrontational industrial relations legislation, the events of the Winter of Discontent served only to vindicate monetarism rather than incomes policy.

Bulpitt overstresses monetarism at the expense of other elements in the Conservative Party's appeal. He acknowledges that as leader of the Opposition Thatcher talked about many other matters, ranging from immigration to the need for greater authority, which 'threatened to obscure the simple and important statecraft message'.[23] There were other elements in the Conservative message of the late 1970. Bulpitt's overemphasis upon monetarism and statecraft should not obscure the kernel of truth that the Conservatives needed a strategy to manage union militancy and inflation, while eschewing incomes policy. This restored the rather battered authority of the British central state. Bulpitt concedes the party could not articulate its concern with re-establishing the authority of central government in the context of political argument in Britain at the time and so resorted to other methods of presentation. He is also wrong to claim that the 'automaticity' in monetarism depoliticised the battle against inflation, as he neglects the fact that a monetary policy often requires high interest rates. Interest rates are always highly sensitive, but proved particularly so for Thatcher with her commitment to mortgage holders and to the idea of a 'property owning democracy'.

Letwin: Thatcherism as conviction politics

Letwin's argument is that Thatcher was primarily concerned with action rather than theory, even though as a self-professed 'conviction politician', she clearly had a sense of mission. While Thatcherism practises the primacy of government over pressure groups, it adopted this approach as a practical response to the needs of Britain in the late twentieth century, and not on abstract ideological grounds. Thatcherism was 'not so much an identifiable political outlook as a bundle of attributes, held together by time and place'.[24] She defined Britain's needs as the promotion and encouragement of 'vigorous virtues', and of sturdy individualism. Letwin's proposition is that Thatcher began with the individual, moved to a conception of the family suitable to nurture the personality traits which she upheld, and valued society only if it enabled families to promote vigorous individual virtues. The vigorous virtues she wished to see nurtured are uprightness, self-sufficiency, energy, adventurousness, independence, loyalty to friends and robustness against enemies.[25] These virtues were contrasted with the 'soft' virtues of kindness, humility, gentleness, sympathy, and cheerfulness, which militated against people taking responsibility for their own lives.

Independent individuals did not require a benign state, but contractual relationships upheld by the rule of law.[26] Under Thatcherism people were evaluated on their individual virtues, rather than their profession, education, achievement, wealth, social position, marital status, skills, or views.

Letwin recognises the nationalist dimension to Thatcherism as a post-Imperialist phenomenon. Thatcher felt that Britain's national greatness could only be retrieved by creating a nation where individual vigorous virtues were encouraged, which in turn would revive Britain as an independent island power.[27] As a political method Thatcherism had little faith in the capacity of positive state action, but she considered that government *could* concentrate its firepower against institutions which checked or denigrated vigorous virtues. This explains the attacks by the Thatcher governments on civil servants, the nationalised industries, the BBC, trades unions and local government.[28]

Undermining those institutions which checked the growth of the vigorous virtues required strong government, and Letwin argues that Thatcherism differed from 'middle way' Toryism and *laisser-faire* Liberalism. Thatcher would never support a free market in drugs or oppose policing or public education. Her British Gaullism was far removed from Liberal free-market dogmatism but her interventionism was intended only to ensure an effective and detailed ability to enforce vigorous virtues.

Letwin interprets Thatcher's policies in order to fit her analysis. Privatisation was less a source of government revenue, or a means of increasing economic efficiency, and more a means to spread ownership and encourage individual virtue. More money could have been raised by selling shares to big finance houses, for example, if the true motive had been economic. Share ownership, like the sale of council houses, encouraged popular capitalism; and together they also strengthened the family as a property holding unit. The attack on inflation by monetary methods was less an economic goal, than an attempt to create independence for individuals and families. The Community Charge was an experiment in undermining municipal Socialism without resorting to centralisation, by making individuals responsible for combating high-spending local councils.

Letwin claims that Thatcher was successful because at the end of the period fewer people sought security, and more risk-takers had emerged. Yet Letwin also extends her analysis to explain that Thatcher fell from office because her vigour was leading to a state of 'permanent revolution'.

> After so many years, people in Britain at last came to see the depth of the seriousness of the Thatcherite project. In an incoherent and inarticulate fashion they began to understand that Thatcherism actually aimed to encourage continual vigour and advance. And when Mrs Thatcher kept repeating, 'there's so much more to do', they concluded that 'with that woman around there never would be any peace'.[29]

Thatcherism was a synthesis of freedom and order, designed to respond to a diagnosis of what was wrong with Britain in the later twentieth century, but using a pre-twentieth century morality. It could never adjust to Europe because individualism had never been properly rooted on the continent. This explained the Labour Party's passion for the bureaucratic monolith of the European Community.

Letwin views Thatcherism as non-ideological although she locates ideology solely within the parameters of abstract, dogmatic and eternal doctrines. There appears, by any calculation, to be a system of related ideas within Letwin's account of Thatcherism. Vincent recognises that some versions of Conservatism can be portrayed as non-ideological; for example the pragmatic, the positional, and the dispositional, but his description of these conceptions of Conservatism would permit Letwin's portrayal to be defined as ideological. Letwin's version allows for 'a mesh of interconnected concepts, values and principles ... These link up with conceptions of the structure of society and political leadership'.[30]

Letwin's characterisation of Thatcherism can be criticised for elevating rhetoric about 'individuals and their families', the 'absence of society', and self-reliance above the substance of policy. The Bruges speech of 1988 suggests a denial of European integration but her government's acceptance of the Single European Act in 1986 contradicts much of the Euro-sceptical language. While Gamble has overstressed the enigmatic contradiction involved in the link between the free economy and strong state, Letwin succeeds in reconciling the two with the argument that both were means towards the dissemination of vigorous virtues in Britain. Yet it is an inversion of reality for Letwin to argue that the economic motives for privatisation and monetarism were incidental. Willetts is more realistic in asserting that free-market economics are 'nearly true' as a complete description of Conservatism. Letwin's analysis is too politically based. She neglects the economic as an independent variable in Conservatism, and the interests which it promotes. Her focus on the particular historical and social circumstances of Thatcherism is tautological, since all political leaders propound ideas which purport to respond to the circumstances which confront them. In highlighting individualist vigorous virtues Thatcher was not outside Conservative tradition, but was rather distorting it, by propounding the bourgeois and individualist element within it at the expense of its other components.[31]

The wets: Thatcherism as ideology

The One Nation, Tory progressive or 'wet' politicians in the Conservative Party, such as Ian Gilmour, Francis Pym, or Jim Prior were critical of Thatcher, mainly because she unbalanced Conservatism, by emphasising monetarism and the conquest of inflation, at the expense of a balanced approach to policy-making in tune with Conservative tradition. Gilmour is a clear advocate of the 'disposition' school of Conservatism, although laced also with pragmatic and positional elements. The 'disposition' element is paramount, however, as scepticism, caution, and even languor characterise his political style.

Explaining Thatcher's first words on entering Downing Street on 4 May 1979 in which she promised to bring harmony where there was discord, Gilmour argues that to her 'harmony may have been whatever the free market happened to produce'.[32] Her fervour for *laisser-faire* and the free market, 'chose her friends and enemies for her, ... dictated her goals and it brought about her downfall'.[33] Gilmour points to Thatcher's verbal advocacy of Liberal ideology, and her claim that like the Labour Party, Conservatives needed an ideology against which it could test its policies. He rejects the view of New Right thinkers who challenge Thatcher's allegiance to their cause because her policies sometimes strayed from total purity, when he argues that ideology is merely a guide to policy-making. He adds that for any politician to infuse the laws with the spirit of an ideology is more complex than theoreticians recognise. The Conservative neurosis which always insists that Conservatism is non-ideological, a trait which affects One Nation and neo-Liberal adherents alike, is secondary to Gilmour's charge that Thatcher's belief system was incompatible with traditional Conservative politics.

Thatcherism was too optimistic and too pessimistic. It was too pessimistic in its assumption that everyone is driven by selfish motives; too optimistic in asserting that everyone pursues their self-interest in a rational fashion.[34] This is why Thatcher failed to perceive that pursuing self-interest can involve support for welfare policies, even on the part of the well-off. Gilmour also quoted the leading Conservative philosopher, Michael Oakeshott, who favoured a managerial state, and not one in which citizens are bullied into conformity with a set of goals. Yet the Thatcher government had sought to change attitudes by creating an 'enterprise culture'. This was an explicit attempt to recapture Victorian values, so Thatcherism was neither radical nor Conservative, but reactionary. If the Conservatives continue to wield power on a Thatcherite mandate then Gilmour warns that those who are 'excluded from the benefits of society cannot be expected to remain passive indefinitely'.[35] The state has a duty to preserve everybody's security and a healthy free market depends upon the constructive intervention of the state. 'The limits of government become a matter of judgement and prudence. There is no place at all for dogma'.[36] The free market strategy did not create an enterprising society, but an atmosphere of coarse selfishness. It produced a redistribution from poor to rich which should concern true Conservatives, in Gilmour's view, since the preservation of the social order remains as valid a concern as the new century approaches, as it was in the time of Disraeli. Gilmour's prescription for the party is to eschew the far right in order to return to the centre of the spectrum and the model of European Christian Democracy.

Prior is less clear that Thatcher associated the idea of 'harmony' with the free market, and described her public commitment to the achievement of harmony, as 'the most awful humbug'.[37] Pym also argues that the 'unbalanced' version of Conservatism propounded by the Thatcher government not only created unnecessary political problems but departed from the finest traditions of the British Conservative Party.[38] Prior, Pym. and Gilmour were all critics of Thatcher's policies from within the Cabinet before their dismissal, but were also long-standing advocates of One Nation Conservatism. Their problem was that their defence of the 'muddling through' which characterised public policy in the years before Thatcher's government lacked intellectual force.

Marxists manqué: Thatcherism as hegemony

It is curious that the One Nation Tory critiques of Thatcherism share common perspectives with the critics on the farthest left-wing shores of politics. These judgements include the view that Thatcher was dividing the nation, that she had a clear ideological 'project', and that the weak and poor were compelled to make sacrifices on behalf of the rich and strong. Yet these criticisms are underpinned by their main mistaken judgement, which is that Thatcherism was a dogmatic ideological project which represented a departure from the party's traditions. It is ironic that the view that Thatcherism is a project distinct from the main thrust of British Conservatism, is so widely shared across much of the political spectrum, when much of what happened in the Thatcher years had either been practised or advocated in the party at previous stages in its history. Hall quite deliberately uses 'the Gramscian term "hegemony" in order to foreclose any falling back on the mechanical notion that Thatcherism is merely another name for the exercise of the same, old, familiar class domination by the same, old, familiar ruling class'.[39] Hall assumes that Thatcher set out to create a new political formation to dominate the economy, civil society, intellectual and moral life and culture, as well as government and politics.

Hall's was one of three main critiques from the left. The first, that of authoritarian populism, has its roots in the 1978 article which predicted Thatcher's election: 'The Great Moving Right Show'. Propounded by Hall and Jacques, this rests on the paradox that the disciplinary and directive exercise of state power was being accompanied by a populist politics which harnessed popular discontents, cutting across the divisions of society, to connect with popular experience.[40] This involved creating a national constituency for popular attitudes previously not pandered to by the establishment. These included stirring up suppressed sentiments against unpopular minorities, to which mainstream political leaders had previously not pandered: for example, scroungers, immigrants, and criminals.[41] These views strengthened authoritarianism and justified a growth in the power of the state whose main interest was to protect the interests of business and capital. Such interests were more secure, however, if the support of the poor and the unpropertied in society could be enrolled on their behalf.

The problem with authoritarian populism is that it is situated in the period from 1975 to 1979, when Thatcher's electoral strategy was to maximise her vote to secure power. Once in power, however, the Conservative Party's need for this populist rhetoric diminished, although it was capable of being invoked, if circumstances warranted it, in order to extract the Conservative government from crisis. In its attempt to reconcile the Liberal minimalism of economic policy with the Conservative activism of the strong state, the authoritarian populist interpretation is keen to impute a homogeneity to Thatcherism. This seeks to establish an identity between the themes of monetarism, the strong state, law and order, and the family, rather than to comprehend the changing emphases and contexts of these distinct themes.

Gamble sees 'Thatcherism' as 'the free economy and the strong state'. The chief contradiction in Thatcherism is between economic liberalism on the one hand and social conformity and political centralisation on the other. The elements of economic liberalism are evident enough: consumer sovereignty, the right to own and accumulate wealth, deregulation of the labour market, and the free market. Yet these freedoms have been accompanied by a diminution of many social freedoms, for example, the rhetorical emphasis upon the importance of family life, the rejection of homosexuality, and the promotion of such virtues as thrift and deferred gratification. Gamble neglects the possibility of reconciling these two conflicting strands within the circle of petit bourgeois morality. It is unlikely that Thatcher constructed an *electoral coalition* on that basis, however, since what happened in the 1980s is that a sufficient proportion of the voters were 'satisfied' by increased prosperity rather than by a particular coherent ideological package.

Gamble is on strong ground in asserting the co-existence of free-market economics with a centralist state within Thatcher's strategy. This position is in conflict with one of Thatcher's declared 'gurus', F. A. Hayek, however, who argued that the economic freedoms inherent in *laisser-faire*, provided the foundation for political and democratic liberties. Gamble highlights the incompatibilities between Hayek's theories and those of most British Conservatives.[42] While Gamble sympathises with the interpretation of Thatcherism as 'statecraft', unlike the 'One Nation' version of the strategy, he recognises that 'statecraft' need not be defensive, and that when the authority of the state has been properly restored, 'no compromises with the enemies of Conservatism or freedom are necessary'.[43] Conservatism under Thatcher was less about Hayek's preoccupation with the promotion of the free market as a means towards the sustenance of political freedom, but rather with the creation of a strong state in order to establish the conditions in which a true free market can emerge. While the state may be rolled back in certain areas appropriate for economic freedom such as deregulation and privatisation it has also been rolled forward in the interest of social discipline and the removal of impediments to *laisser-faire*. This is a paradox Gamble does not fully explore.

To decentralise to the market, it is first necessary to centralise power in Westminster and Whitehall. In almost Marxist fashion, as with the dictatorship of the proletariat, therefore, the concentration of power at the state's central apex is a transitional phase. If the rule of the proletariat is necessary to remove bourgeois horizons before Communism can be inscribed on society's banners, then similarly, a phase of a strong central state was needed during Thatcher's years in government, to strip the power from such impediments to free markets as trades unions, local government, *Socialist*-run quangos, the churches, the BBC, and the universities. The transfer of power from unions to employers, and from local authorities to central government, through the instruments of opted-out organisations run by businessmen and accountants, was to encourage an economy based on direct exchanges between employers, employees, and consumers, unmediated as far as possible by public organisations.

Marsh has criticised Gamble for failing to overcome a uni-dimensional analysis of Thatcherism. He claims that in analysing Thatcherism in terms of its enhancement of the capacity of government to stand up to powerful interests and to develop a new accumulation strategy based on the free economy and the strong state under Conservative direction, Gamble fails to link political aspirations to equivalent ideological and economic considerations.[44] Even if Marsh is correct in arguing that Gamble has not sufficiently linked a political focus to ideological and economic considerations, Marsh himself assumes that Thatcherism is an aberration in the history of British Conservatism.

Marsh's claim that Gamble focuses exclusively on the political, is also undermined by Gamble's attempt to relate his account of Thatcher's political strategy to other areas of concern. For example, he deals with the ideological dimension when he considers whether Thatcher managed to change the nation's values. He recognises that while the Thatcher government may have managed to shift the terms of the national policy debate, few of the changes reflected a genuine consensus within the electorate or the policy-making elite. On the contrary, 'major interests ... remained fundamentally opposed and there were only halting signs of the kind of intellectual revolution the government wanted to underpin the new policies'.[45] Equally, Gamble's frequent references to the 'accumulation strategy' of the Thatcher government belies the view that he neglected the economic dimension. He demonstrates that the Thatcher government's economic policies involved a 'shake-out', with the consequence that the future of the British economy was no longer tied to the goal of a manufacturing revival, but to the growth of new forms of wealth creation. These were: a rentier economy with incomes derived from a growing portfolio of overseas investments; internationally tradable services; and the encouragement of inward investment by foreign transnationals establishing plants to assemble products, designed and developed elsewhere, to be sold in European markets. He points out that this was 'a credible and coherent strategy for British capital', although some sections of British capital were weakened by it. Gamble argues that the Thatcher government's economic strategy of abandoning traditional staple industries occurred for three reasons. First, a legitimate recognition that all national economies require change and that many industries must decline rather than be artificially resuscitated, as the failure of government attempts to revive them in the 1970s suggested. Second, a perception that earlier strategies to modernise the manufacturing base of the economy involved political tactics likely to marginalise the Conservative Party. Third, the potency of the new global economy and the crisis which it was experiencing in the later 1970s, as a result of the breakdown of American hegemony, made new thinking obligatory.[46] There is here, therefore, an evident recognition that economic forces interact with party political considerations and ideological development. Further, Gamble links his apparently uni-dimensional political analysis to the Thatcher government's economic or capital accumulation strategy, and makes a judgement about the success of that economic strategy. 'The strong state that is needed so that this economy may remain free is a state able to conduct effective surveillance and policing of the unemployed and the poor, able to confront and defeat any union challenge, able to contain any upsurge of terrorism and public disorder, but it has not yet proved capable of becoming the kind of strong state needed to break out of the cycle of decline'.[47]

Gamble accepts that Thatcher's ideology is 'hardly an alien importation into the Party but a restatement of the libertarian strand of Conservatism, which tended to be eclipsed during the ascendancy of Social Imperialism and Social Democracy, but never entirely disappeared'.[48] Yet his attachment to the interpretation common to that generation of scholars reared in the consensual post-war period, that Thatcherism broke with a social-democratic orientated post-war Conservative Party, actually places him in Marsh's camp.

Marsh's criticism that Gamble fails to achieve an 'inclusive' rather than a partial explanation of Thatcherism is unwarranted, since Gamble does seek to integrate the economic, the political and the ideological. Drawing liberally from Gramsci, Gamble stresses that Thatcher did attempt to establish a new ideological hegemony in Britain. Crucially, however, he argued that 'hegemony is often misrepresented as meaning simply ideological domination, but properly understood it involves the successful interweaving of economic and political as well as ideological domination'.[49]

Jessop's dual nation conception may well be derived from 'dual-labour market' theories, which assert that the labour force is increasingly split under contemporary capitalism into a core of workers in secure and well-remunerated employment, and a periphery of low-wage or part-time workers lacking permanence, and without full employment and pensions rights.[50] The two nations to which Jessop refers, relates to the dichotomy in the labour market. It also links with the idea of a 'sectoral cleavage' between those working in and depending upon the private sector, and those who are employed in and depend upon the services of the public sector. Yet the use of the concept of hegemony demonstrates that Jessop is a Gramscian and assumes that bourgeois capitalist society is sustained by the propagation of ideas, in the form of common sense, which actually conceal the contradictions and irrationalities of capitalism.[51] Ideas are propounded to convince the citizenry that existing economic relations are inevitable, or in Thatcher's case that reforms were needed in order to reproduce those relations. Jessop argues that Thatcherism sought to replace the One Nation Conservative project with one representing business interests but enjoying popular support. The hegemonic strategy is not solely concerned with the propagation of ideas with the assistance of a sympathetic or compliant media, but with small-scale improvements in the living standards and perquisites of a part of society beyond the privileged elite.

Jessop analyses the nature of Thatcher's personal beliefs. He demonstrates the variety of indicators including the attitudes to be expected from a grocer's daughter from Grantham in the 1930s, her zealous political style, the detail of her policies, and her impact on the party and the country. Related to the variety of sources which might indicate Thatcher's political beliefs, Jessop also recognises the fortuitous nature of Thatcherism. This is a corrective to the view that it was inevitable. Historical contingencies are certainly important in explaining Thatcher's rise to dominance. Had Heath held a general election two weeks earlier in 1974 then he would probably have continued as Prime Minister and denied Thatcher her opportunity, had Joseph avoided the *faux pas* of the Preston 'eugenics' speech he would have been the credible challenger to Heath for the leadership in 1975, and had James Callaghan called a general election in October 1978 he might have won it. Equally, after coming to power in 1979, Thatcher was fortunate in the incapacity of her opponents in Cabinet to unite against her, in the invasion of the Falklands, and the failure of more Exocet missiles to hit British ships. Her downfall also had contingent characteristics. Had she delivered her *tour de force* farewell speech in the House of Commons the previous week, she would probably have secured enough votes against Michael Heseltine to have retained the Party leadership. Thatcherism is, therefore, explicable in terms of long- and short-run Conservative history, as well as contingency; and so *contra* Marsh, there are dangers in over-theorising it.

Jessop shares the illusion of the particularity of Thatcherism, but in analysing it as a discrete phenomenon he discerns distinct phases, and emphasises the need to periodise it.[52] The corollary is that 'the most appropriate concepts and tools of analysis for understanding Thatcherism have changed as Thatcherism itself has changed'.[53] Thatcherism is, therefore, a different phenomenon at different times. It first emerged because of concern about Britain's economic decline, and the specific crisis about where Britain should be inserted into the global economy. It was also the product of a governing crisis of the 1970s, whether it is characterised as one of overload, legitimacy, failing experimentation with corporatism or widespread middle-class resentment and insecurity. This phase was completed with electoral victory in May 1979. The second phase was concerned with obtaining actual rather than formal control over the machinery of government. Political power depends upon the securing of political support from the mass electorate, the Cabinet, the party, the government machine, and the social and economic 'Establishment'. This took until 1982. The third phase was the consolidation of Thatcherism and the implementation of a coherent project to reshape the economy, the state, and society. This involved establishing roots to entrench the attack on collectivism, by eliminating those parts of the state inextricably linked to it. This phase lasted from 1982 onwards. It was concerned to create a new social base for Conservatism rather than with the more negative activity of exploiting discontent, which had sufficed previously. Jessop recognises this stage of Thatcherism must itself be subdivided to distinguish the consolidationist and economic phase (1982 to 1987) concerned mainly with the politics of production, from the extension of the project to civil society and the social sphere (after 1987) which was concerned with the politics of consumption.

The periodisation of Thatcherism is valuable, since many of the controversies about its nature often arise because commentators are not focusing on the same phenomena. Jessop's periodisation makes Thatcherism appear to be too calculated and planned. The different stages of Thatcherism suggest the *lack* of a clearly pre-ordained project. Instead, there was considerable *ad hoccery*, and a mix of political values together with new 'appreciations' about the British crisis and the new patterns of the global economy. To portray Thatcherism as the Conservative Party led by Thatcher making up policy as it goes along is itself a distortion, but is a corrective to the theory that it was a coherent blueprint.

Jessop is certain that the Thatcherite project had the clear economic objective of restructuring, so as to advance those economic interests best able to benefit from a situation of footloose international capital, at the expense of those interests best able to profit from a manufacturing orientated Fordist economy. This divided the nation economically, but it linked in with a political strategy, because it sought also to 'consolidate an electoral coalition through redistributive policies and to create new bases of political support whilst resorting to coercion and/or denying basic rights to those outside this electoral block'.[54] Jessop is anxious to differentiate 'One Nation' projects which seek to entice the support of the entire population behind the capitalist state through material concessions to all, as happened in the 'consensus' era, from dual-nation strategies. With the arrival of crisis, the scope for One Nation policies is restricted. There is instead, a resort to a 'two nations' approach, which creates an antagonistic cleavage between the productive and the loyal on the one side who become the favoured nation, and the parasitic and disloyal on the other.[55] Jessop is undoubtedly correct here to examine the effects of the so-called Thatcherite 'project', rather than just to look at its rhetoric.

Thatcherism represented a strategy for capital accumulation, which prioritised financial and international capital over the domestic industrial sector. The deindustrialisation of the North of England was not 'an accidental by-product', since it represented the liberation of the South from the archaic burden of the relics of the Industrial Revolution and the trades unions tied to it. The effect was to transform the British economy in an internationalist direction, making it a convenient offshore location for investment, insurance, and speculation, underpinned by social stability. This neo-Liberal wealth-creation strategy turned Britain into a global service economy. Jessop points to a significant contradiction, since much of Thatcherite rhetoric, particularly in the Opposition phase, appeared to be the revolt of the bourgeoisie and of small and medium capital, against big business and labour. Even in government after 1979, much of the language, and even initiatives such as the Enterprise Allowance Scheme for small business start-ups, appeared to support the small business sector, self-employment, and the domestic service sector. This contradicted the hegemony of international capital in an open economy. Jessop implies that the small business focus was a doctrinal disguise for the real purpose of advancing City of London and multinational interests. He is again falling prey to an analysis that is both uni-dimensional, and unduly based on the idea of a clear Thatcherite project. It is more convincing to interpret the conflict between small-scale domestic capital and international capital, as a dilemma for a government aiming to encourage both interests in an incoherent strategy. Ultimately, however, Jessop is correct to judge that international capital carries the greater weight, which is why government reaffirmed its anti-inflation and sound money goals, even after the Medium Term Financial Strategy (MTFS) and the targeting of £M3 ceased in 1985.[56]

In the later Thatcher years there was a movement towards such supply-side reforms as deregulating and increasing the flexibility of the labour market, and reducing the burdens on business. The abolition of Wages Councils, the reduction of employment rights for part-time workers, and opposition to the European Union's Social Charter, were aspects of this policy. While the policy could be presented as possessing a social dimension, particularly through its claim to create more jobs, it also reinforced the dual labour market, and so connects well with Jessop's overarching interpretation.[57] The use of compulsory competitive tendering in local government and the public sector and the wider emphasis upon market-testing in the civil service are further examples of the control and weakening of organised labour. While this marks a shift towards the 'monetarism is not enough' stance, it was compatible with the dual nations strategy, and could only assist in making British labour practices an attractive investment prospect for the interests of international capital.[58]

Both monetarist and supply-side policies had an uneven impact, and widened divisions between rich and poor, north and south, public and private, and those securely employed and those on the fringes of the labour market. Jessop argues that the Thatcher project ensured that Britain was no longer a single nation, and that a new vertical cleavage divided the productive from such parasitic groups as the unemployed, the disabled, and pensioners. The productive were rewarded through the market while the parasitic were punished. The final stage of Thatcherism, which extended the strategy to civil society, reflected this change in the anti-dependency culture ethos of the social security reforms of the late 1980s.

Jessop detects a further important shift in Thatcherism after 1986, and links it with the phenomenon of 'post-Fordism'. If Fordism was based upon mass production and consumption, post-Fordism is concerned with more flexible forms of production and diverse methods of consumption. Post-Fordism is based upon a recognition of the rise of specialised commodities for niche markets, particularly in the aftermath of micro-electronics and information technology. If Fordism was based upon collective bargaining, a substantial role for public credit, and state intervention, post-Fordism involved the rise of individual and plant bargaining, privatised welfare delivery and consumption, and the consolidation and political institutionalisation of a two nations society. It effectively ended the role of wealth redistribution in politics as cross-class subsidisation was a corollary of the Keynesian welfare state. If Labour was the beneficiary of the Fordist system, the Conservatives were alert to the potentialities in exploiting the post-Fordist transition, and identified themselves with the class interests of those workers associated with it. While manual workers in 'smokestack' industries declined elements of the tertiary service economy expanded. Jessop concludes that Thatcherism was hegemonic, developing a power block to unify the most substantial social forces in the country. Unlike the inequality-reducing character of the post-war era, Thatcherism sought to exploit social division and to mobilise a majority of the satisfied against a dissatisfied minority.

Thatcherism built upon real economic change, particularly the internationalisation of the economy. The management of domestic demand was inappropriate in this context. In Opposition, Thatcher proved to be a rallying force for the worried Establishment, as well as for discontented sectors of the bourgeoisie and the working classes. In power she accentuated the internationalisation of the economy, most dramatically with the final removal of exchange controls in October 1979. While Jessop is correct to regard this policy decision as a significant opening up of the British economy, his consequent theorising about hegemony, however, and his assumption that it was a significant departure from existing trends in the Conservative Party is a misjudgement. In fact, Treasury officials had expected it, it proved easy to carry through, and it became a bipartisan move which was emulated by other countries. Nigel Lawson argues that it enabled the City to remain a major financial centre and assisted British investment overseas. Harold Lever who had belonged to the Wilson and Callaghan governments described the decision as 'a considerable encouragement to a great trading, insurance and banking nation'.[59] Jessop points to the differential benefits which flowed from this strategy, since it produced a *rentier*, coupled with a low-tech, low wage, service economy. The British state is no longer linked to British capital, but to capital operating in Britain. If he is correct here then the market will determine whether this leads to Britain becoming the 51st state of the United States, a Japanese Trojan horse within the EU, or a member of the EU subordinate to Germany. What is apparent is that the state is enmeshed into the constraints imposed by international capital to finance its large balance of payments deficit on manufactured exports.

Thatcherism changed from being a defensive alliance into a new accumulation strategy benefiting multi-national corporations and international finance, sustained by an increasingly authoritarian state. The 1983 and 1987 victories marked the triumph of the privileged against the subordinate nation, in which the nationalist rhetoric failed to fit with the international orientation of the accumulation strategy. Jessop concludes that the project will ultimately stand or fall on its capacity to create economic growth, although the political project could continue for a period even after its economic failure has become evident.[60]

Conclusion

The major left- and right-wing critiques of Thatcherism tend to be unidimensional in character.[61] Many assume that the Thatcher era marks a divergence from the Conservative tradition and that the ideas of the New

Right provided the impulse.[62] Yet New Right ideology in the Thatcher era is best analysed as 'a tool and not a blueprint'.[63] Even then it was a tool which was only sometimes picked up to assist the policy-making process, and used in a fashion conditioned by the traditions of British Conservatism. Uni-dimensional economic analyses of Thatcherism are also partial. Ward explains Thatcherism as a 'bottom-line economism'. He considers Thatch-erism in the context of a crisis of capitalism, and bases his analysis on the theoretical assumption that, 'when the system is at peril the economic needs of capitalism, centring on the maintenance of the accumulation process, powerfully reassert themselves at the political level'. Yet recognising the rel-ative autonomy of the state he adds that it may manipulate taxation and expenditure policy, for example, to forward its own interests, enhance its governing competence, and secure its own re-election.[64]

Less ambitious analyses locate Thatcherism within the traditions of the Conservative Party, and consider her influence to be compatible with the latitude which Conservatives have traditionally permitted their leaders. 'Its behaviour in office provides a precedent for anything: the setting up and the dismantling of Empire, and the creation as well as the dismantling of public ownership. Thatcherism is thus part of the great delta of Conservatism. While Thatcher was not an example of Conservative tranquillity, her posi-tion within the tradition is acceptable because of Conservative eclecticism'.[65] In her stress upon self-help, prosperity, individual responsibility, indepen-dence and freedom to make money Thatcher reflects a doctrinal continuity within Conservatism.[66] Explaining the continuities between Thatcherism and previous Conservative eras Marsh and Rhodes consider policy imple-mentation, and argue that the overestimation of Thatcher's policy effect results from 'a concentration upon legislative change rather than upon changes in policy outcomes'.[67] Yet the Thatcher era lasted for over a decade, and Moon argues that the policy impacts of Thatcher's government were unusually substantial.[68] Moon avoids the untenable extremes of a clear Thatcherite 'project' and the view that her governments lacked coherent direction. He argues that 'the test of coherence and consistency, which no government can meet, ignores the possibility of rolling agendas and of gov-ernments learning to improve their capacity with the experience of office'.[69]

The analyses of Thatcherism presented here are insightful, but should be approached cautiously. It is evident that those which study Thatcherism as a special phenomenon, distinct from Conservative history, are unconvinc-ing. The ingredients of Thatcherism were apparent at earlier stages of the party's history, and even the particular mix of ingredients which were emphasised from 1975 to 1979 formed an ideology which had been ges-tating since the mid-1960s. Powellism was also a precursor of Thatch-erism.[70] Yet despite the insights which commentators bring, they are all flawed and too uni-dimensional.

Willetts is not guilty of distancing Thatcherism from the party's past but is procrustean in his conception of perfect Conservative ideological symmetry throughout the ages. Bulpitt overemphasises the centrality of monetarism and naively ignores the impossibility of depoliticising the battle against inflation. Letwin captures the mood of Thatcher's rhetoric, but neglects the selectivity with which her governments encouraged individuals to assert themselves. The 'wets' overemphasise the Disraeli myth and the rootedness of moderate policies in the party before Thatcher's leadership. They are also on doubtful ground in proclaiming themselves free of doctrine. There were authoritarian and populist elements in Thatcherism, but it is hysterical for Hall and Jacques to imply Fascist associations. Gamble's assertion of the 'free economy, strong state' interpretation has merit, but imposes a *post hoc* order on events that occurred in more serendipitous fashion. Jessop is correct to stress that Thatcher was less concerned to provoke a national populist consensus than to speak to that portion of the electorate that provided her electoral base and gained from her policies. He also comprehends Thatcherism from the perspective of the changing global economy. Yet 'the dual nations hegemonic project' is an oversimplification and if valid, is based upon too benign a view of the so-called one nation Conservatism that preceded Thatcherism. Yet the non-ideological interpretation that there were only rudimentary values underpinning Thatcherism underestimates the ideological consciousness of large sections of the Conservative Party. They had long resisted statism, organised Labour, and Socialism. Thatcherism was the latest episode in the history of a party which, positively explained, recognised the selfish irrationality of people and the imperfectibility of society; and explained negatively, exists to protect the privileged in society, whoever constitutes that group at a given historical moment.

Appendix:
The Thatcher years: main events and turning points

May 1979	Thatcher becomes Prime Minister and appoints Sir Geoffrey Howe and other acolytes to key economic posts.
	Budget begins process of switching from direct to indirect taxation.
November 1979	White Paper proclaims public expenditure to be at the heart of the nation's difficulties.
	Removal of exchange controls liberates the free movement of capital and opens up the British economy.
March 1981	Deflationary budget at a time of deep recession and 364 leading economists protest at this unorthodoxy.
July 1981	Crisis cabinet meeting after a series of urban riots by youths

	fails to alter economic policy but leads to launch of the Youth Training Scheme (YTS) to attack youth unemployment.
September 1981	Thatcher takes control and imposes her authority on the government by a Cabinet purge to dismiss her 'wet' critics and to appoint sympathisers such as Norman Tebbitt and Cecil Parkinson.
March to July 1982	Outbreak and ultimate victory in Falklands War. Thatcher proclaims 'we have ceased to be a nation in retreat', and the electoral dividend of the war begins. It was the perfect metaphor for her 'resolute approach'.
June 1983	Conservative electoral victory, with increased majority.
March 1984–1985	The defeat of the National Union of Mineworkers in a year-long strike weakens all trade unions and the entire public sector.
	Continuation of Trades Union legislation, as having previously outlawed political strikes, extensive picketing and imposed ballots, the 1984 Act challenged union political funds.
	Rates Act introduces rate-capping to penalise high-spending local authorities.
November 1985	Nigel Lawson, Chancellor of the Exchequer announces the formal abandonment of M3 monitoring of the money supply and the weakening of his previous anti-inflationary Medium Term Financial Strategy (MTFS).
January 1986	Resignations of Michael Heseltine from Defence and Leon Brittan from Trade and Industry over the Westland Affair which highlighted deficiencies in the authoritarian style of the Prime Minister.
October 1986	Conservative conference theme defined as 'The Next Moves Forward' to reclaim a positive radical agenda and rebut charges of faltering.
November 1986	Public expenditure statement by Lawson proclaims pre-election increases in education and health expenditure.
	Abolition of the Labour Metropolitan Counties and the Greater London Council.
	The audacious privatisation of British Gas after the precedent of British Telecom. While on the agenda from 1979 the large-scale privatisations demonstrating that the policy could succeed took place in the second term.
June 1987	Third successive election victory. Intra-party disputes

marred the campaign which, despite Conservative nervousness, it was never in danger of losing. There was a slight fall in the majority and Thatcher noted setbacks in the inner cities.

June 1987	Commencement of third term in which Thatcher reveals signs of hubris and pursues a series of free-market driven reforms which contribute to her unpopularity. The period is also marked by a transition from economic boom to slump. This is partly the result of domestic policy, particularly the credit boom which contributed to inflation, and the inflationary budget of 1988 which, contra the 1981 budget reduced taxes when the economy was growing and inflationary pressures were strong, which were then countered by savage interest rate rises which plunged the country into major recession.
1988	Reforms of the education system through the Education Reform Act and the health service through the reforms of that year. Each measure enhanced the role of the market with competition between schools and hospital trusts and differentiated the purchase from the provider.
September 1988	Thatcher's Bruges speech made clear the extent of her antipathy to the further integration of the European Community.
July 1989	Clumsy Cabinet reshuffle removes Geoffrey Howe as Foreign Secretary and creates his discontent.
October 1989	Resignation of Nigel Lawson because of disagreements about whether Britain should enter the European Exchange Rate Mechanism (ERM) and the role of Thatcher's private policy adviser Sir Alan Walters.
November 1989	Sir Anthony Meyer stands against Thatcher for the leadership as a 'stalking horse' candidate.
November 1990	Thatcher is challenged for the leadership by Heseltine after Howe makes a devastating speech attacking Thatcher's European policy.

She secured 204 votes to Heseltine's 156. Cabinet ministers then meet her and overwhelmingly advise her to stand down. The reasons for her downfall were the Poll Tax which was universally unpopular, the developing economic recession, and her negative attitudes to Europe which worried elements in the party and the business community. Her deep unpopularity with the electorate by the autumn of 1990 was demonstrated by the 20% swing to the Liberals in the Eastbourne by-election. Many MPs, who now had a professional approach, in which the needs of their own career took precedence over blind loyalty, were solely concerned to remove her as an electoral liability.

Notes

1 Bob Jessop, Kevin Bonnet et al., *Thatcherism* (London: Polity Press, 1988), pp. 3–4.
2 Martin Seliger, *Ideology and Politics* (London: George Allen and Unwin), Chapter 8.
3 These include Hugo Young, *One of Us*, Peter Jenkins, *Mrs Thatcher's Revolution*, Kenneth O. Morgan, *The People's Peace*, the Nuffield General Election studies for 1983, 1987 and 1992 and the memoirs of the leading participants.
4 David Willetts, *Modern Conservatism* (Harmondsworth: Penguin, 1992), pp. 47–61.
5 Peter Riddell, *The Thatcher Government* (London: Blackwell, 1985, 2nd edn), p. 7.
6 Jim Bulpitt, 'The Discipline of the New Democracy: Mrs Thatcher's Domestic Statecraft', *Political Studies*, 34 (1986), p. 26.
7 Shirley Robin Letwin, *The Anatomy of Thatcherism* (London: Fontana, 1992), p. 31.
8 Willetts, *Modern Conservatism*, p. 182.
9 *Ibid.*, p. 42.
10 *Ibid.*, p. 460.
11 In reality, popular share ownership fell back in the 1980s.
12 Willetts, *Modern Conservatism*, pp. 144–5.
13 *Ibid.*, p. 138.
14 D. Willetts 'Modern Conservatism' in *Political Quarterly*, 63, (4) (Oct–Dec 1992), pp. 419–20.
15 Willetts, *Modern Conservatism*, p. 150.
16 D. Winch, *Economics and Policy* (London: Fontana, 1972), pp. 303–4.
17 Willetts, 'Modern Conservatism', p. 420.
18 Willetts, *Modern Conservatism*, p. 179.
19 *Ibid.*, p. 180.
20 *Ibid.*, p. 26.
21 Martin Holmes, *Political Pressure and Economic Policy. British Government 1970–1974* (Butterworth, 1982), p. 56.
22 Bulpitt, 'The Discipline of the New Democracy', p. 32.
23 *Ibid.*, p. 33.
24 Letwin, *The Anatomy of Thatcherism*, p. 25.
25 *Ibid.*, pp. 32–3.
26 *Ibid.*, pp. 347–50.
27 *Ibid.*, pp. 45–6.
28 *Ibid.*, p. 40.
29 *Ibid.*, p. 33.
30 Andrew Vincent, 'British Conservatism and the Problem of Ideology', *Political*

Studies, 42 (2) (June 1994), p. 206. Vincent defines pragmatic Conservatism as the readiness to adopt any idea which works and is electorally popular, positional Conservatism as a defensive posture to whatever policy arrangements are in place and a Conservative disposition as an anti-philosophical scepticism about the role of reason. Clearly Thatcher, in Letwin's terms, was no unprincipled pragmatist, defender of what she inherited.

31 David Howell MP in conversation.
32 Ian Gilmour, *Dancing with Dogma* (Edinburgh: Pocket Books, Simon and Schuster, 1993), p. 329.
33 *Ibid.*, p. 330.
34 *Ibid.*, p. 333.
35 *Ibid.*, p. 338.
36 *Ibid.*, pp. 338–9.
37 Jim Prior, *A Balance of Power* (London: Hamilton, 1986), p. 113.
38 Francis Pym, *The Politics of Consent* (London: Hamilton, 1994).
39 Stuart Hall, *The Hard Road to Renewal: Thatcherism and the Crisis of the Left* (London: Verso Books, 1988), p. 7.
40 *Ibid.*, p. 6.
41 *Ibid.*, p. 55.
42 Andrew Gamble, *The Free Economy and the Strong State* (London: Macmillan, 1989), p. 144.
43 *Ibid.*, p. 154.
44 David Marsh, 'Explaining Thatcherism: Beyond Uni-Dimensional Explanation', Round table: The Politics of Thatcherism, Political Studies Association Conference (1994). Marsh's argument is that most analyses are marred by over-emphasising a particular perspective, whether political, economic, or ideological. He urges the connection between the three and regrets that writers who attempt to do this remain trapped within one paradigm. The most crudely uni-dimensional explanations highlight leadership, strong government, statecraft and promotion of the interests of capital or particular fractions of capital and the implementation of New Right and/or neo-Liberal ideology.
45 Gamble, *The Free Economy and the Strong State*, p. 219.
46 *Ibid.*, p. 226.
47 *Ibid.*, p. 236.
48 *Ibid.*, p. 238.
49 *Ibid.*, p. 236. Gamble belonged to the Gramscian school which developed its interpretation of British politics in the 1980s in *Marxism Today*. The Hungarian Revolution of 1956, Krushchev's exposure of the evils of Stalinist tyranny, Brezhnev's destruction of the 1968 Prague Spring, the defeat of the New Left uprisings of the 1960s, and the election of Thatcher and Ronald Reagan led pseudo-Marxist commentators to re-examine rather than jettison Marxism. The *Prison Notebooks* of Gramsci, republished in 1971 appeared to offer a Marxist explanation for Thatcherism.
50 The labour market strategy of the Thatcher government is fully explored in Brendan Evans, *The Politics of the Training Market. From Manpower Services Commission to Training and Enterprise Councils*, (London: Routledge & Kegan Paul, 1992). The unacknowledged commitment to a dual labour market is dis-

cernible in the Employment Department's White Paper, *Employment: The Challenge for the Nation* (Cmnd 9474), HMSO, 1985. The conception of a dual labour market has been widely advanced by commentators. See, for example, P. Ainley and M. Corney, *Training for the Future. The Rise and Fall of the MSC* (London: Cassell, 1990); C. Benn and J. Fairley, *Challenging the MSC* (London: Pluto Press, 1986) and Alice Brown, *Labour Market Policy in Britain: A Critical View* (Waverley Papers, Edinburgh University Politics Series, 1988).

51 For a brief discussion of Gramsci's ideas the best source is J. Larrain, *The Concept of Ideology* (London: Hutchinson, 1979), pp. 79–83. The Thatcher government was adept at using the platitudes of common sense to persuade the mass electorate. This was the basis for the statement of 'truisms' such as 'managers must be allowed to manage', 'young people have priced themselves out of jobs', 'a country must live within its means' and 'there is a no alternative'. In this regard Thatcher admitted that 'we had also taken apprenticeships in advertising and learnt how to put a complex, and sophisticated case in direct, clear and simple language. We had been arguing that case for the best part of four years, so our agenda would with luck, strike people as familiar common sense rather than a wild radical project'. Margaret Thatcher, *The Downing Street Years* (London: HarperCollins, 1993), p. 5.

52 Jessop, *Thatcherism*, pp. 59–65.

53 *Ibid.*, p. 67.

54 *Ibid.*, pp. 120–1.

55 B. Jessop, *The Capitalist State* (Martin Robertson, 1982), p. 244.

56 Nigel Lawson, *The View from Number 11* (London: Corgi Books, 1992), pp. 281–2.

57 Thatcher, *The Downing Street Years*, pp. 670–2. This presents a benign view of the policy but is still compatible with a dual labour market and two nations strategy. A further discussion of the enhancement of the right of managers to manage, the deprivileging of public sector employees, and the greater reduction in employment rights experienced by young, part-time and many female workers is available, in D. Fordham, 'Trade Union Policy 1979–89: Restriction or Reform', in Stephen P. Savage and I. Robbins, *Public Policy Under Thatcher* (London: Macmillan, 1990), pp. 65–6.

58 Savage and Robbins, *Public Policy Under Thatcher*, p. 174.

59 Lawson, *The View from Number 11*, pp. 40–2.

60 Jessop, *The Capitalist State*, p. 180.

61 Marsh, 'Explaining Thatcherism'.

62 For example, D. Kavanagh, *Thatcherism and British Politics* (Oxford: Oxford University Press, 1987). Also J. Wolfe, 'State, Power and Ideology in Britain: Mrs Thatcher's Privatisation Programme', *Political Studies*, 39, pp. 237–52. He argues that privatisation was pre-planned. While it is wrong to characterise the entire Thatcher project from one policy area Wolfe is correct that the sale of assets had been undertaken by the Labour government in the 1970s and the incoming Thatcher administration got involved in the process at once. See, for example, the case for using the receipts from privatisation to help balance the books in May 1979. While the policy had not been fully developed at that point the main constraint on more ambitious asset sales was that 'although

government owned shares in British Petroleum could be sold at once, the sale of state-owned assets on a really large scale would need legislation'. Thatcher, *The Downing Street Years*, pp. 49–50. Desmond King in *The New Right*, regards New Right ideas as a main influence on her government, and 'far from irrelevant to the content of political practice'. The main impediment appears to be that of implementation difficulties (King, *The New Right*, p. 199). In a later publication on training policy, however, he shifts towards the more uni-dimensional interpretation that neo-Liberalism is dominant. Kenneth Minogue suggests a combination of New Right ideas and Margaret Thatcher's personality which led her to reject the 'culture of guilt'. K. Minogue, 'The Emergence of the New Right', in R. Skidelsky (ed.), *Thatcherism* (Oxford: Blackwell, 1989), pp. 125–42.

63 Marsh, *Explaining Thatcherism*, p. 816.
64 Ward's analysis is discussed in Marsh, 'Explaining Thatcherism', pp. 822–4.
65 J. Ramsden, 'Thatcher and Conservative History' *Contemporary Record*, 4 (4) (April 1991), pp. 2–3.
66 Michael Bentley, 'Is Mrs Thatcher a Conservative?' *Contemporary Record*, 4 (3) (February 1991), p. 2.
67 David Marsh and R. A. W. Rhodes, *Implementing Thatcherite Policies: Audit of an Era* (Buckingham: Open University Press, 1992), p. 3.
68 Jeremy Moon, 'Evaluating Thatcher', *Politics*, 14 (2) (September 1994), p. 44.
69 *Ibid.*, p. 48.
70 *The Guardian*, 17 August 1994.

9

Conservatism and the 1990s

John Major was bequeathed the difficult legacy of Thatcherism. This created high expectations from the rank-and-file. He had no opportunity to adopt a dispositional Conservatism of merely safeguarding what he had inherited. The party expected a continuation of the excitement which had inspired it in the 1980s, and in Thatcherism they had a yardstick against which to measure the performance of Major's government. While Thatcherism appears coherent in retrospect rather than at the time, it had established a strong faction in the party, and even four years after coming to power Major was struggling to appease it. This is difficult as it is unclear from his actions that he has a personal sense of ideological direction. His dilemma is heightened by the fact that the political climate of the 1990s is different from that of the heyday of Thatcherism, and the electorate does not share the preferences of the party's hard-right faction. Faced with these problems Major has 'dithered', and based his tactics upon the goal of winning elections rather than adhering to principle. Thatcher supported him as her successor believing that, 'the future is assured'.[1] That she was engaging in self-deception is suggested by Major's comment during the leadership campaign that he wished to build on the Thatcherite legacy, but in his own way.[2] One of his campaign team asserted that Major 'provided the happy combination of continuity in policy without the style'.[3] Yet Thatcher was not overthrown solely because of her style as there was also disquiet about policies. Major brought a different style to the role, but there is disagreement about whether he has continued her policies. The evidence suggests that he represents a shift but not a break with Thatcherism; that he is no 'Butskellite' and that he travels light ideologically. It is hard to discern how far his resort to rhetoric to appease the right reflects the nature of his government. There are no grounds for postulating a doctrine of 'Majorism'.

John Major's party 1990–1994: victory and crisis

Major secured a fourth successive election victory for the Conservatives in April 1992, and by the end of that Parliament the party will have been in power continuously since 1979, the longest period of one-party rule since the Great Reform Act of 1832. The outcome confirmed 'the asymmetric pattern of Party fortunes in the 20th century – lengthy spells of Conservative rule interrupted by brief spells of centre-left Government'.[4] Soon after the election victory of April 1992 events turned against the government and the party faced serious internal organisational, membership and financial problems. Power does not automatically protect a party from decline. While Major began by demonstrating a greater sympathy for the party's organisation than his predecessor, in the appointment of Chris Patten and John Cope as Chairman and Deputy Chairman, both of whom had risen to prominence through Central Office, he had a less instinctive relationship to the membership.

John Major's government has been subject to astonishingly varied fortunes. A few years after the victory his was one the most unpopular governments since opinion was measured. Opinion poll deficits of 20 per cent plus were confirmed in disastrous performances in the municipal and European elections of 1994. Press comment urged Major's removal by more powerful figures such as Michael Heseltine, the Secretary of State for Trade and Industry and Kenneth Clarke, the Chancellor of the Exchequer, and commentators proclaimed that 'the Tory jackals have had their day'.[5] A more balanced assessment is that the Conservative Party itself, given its profound divisions over Europe, is the source of Major's problems, rather than the inadequacy of his leadership.[6]

The Conservative Party has a vast capacity to survive and adapt, and its appeal to individualism, patriotism, and family values is enduring. Its malaise in 1994 was undoubtedly deep, however, and there are evident signs of crumbling at the grassroots level as demoralisation spreads. The trend was so serious that a membership of 2.8 million members in 1953 could fall to fewer than 100,000 by the end of the century.[7] The local elections in May 1994 led to the loss of many council seats, even though the previous time when those seats had been contested in 1990 had also been bad electorally. Securing 27% of the votes cast nationally, the same share as that obtained by the Liberal Democrats, was a humiliating performance; as was the achievement of 28% of the vote in the European elections a month later.[8] Major ostentatiously led the local election campaign and claimed that the Party could regain Birmingham; an example of him adopting a cause which he could not win.[9] Reports suggested that in many wards in the local elections of that year, there were few Conservative workers.[10] This reflected the malaise into which the Conservatives sank during the period of Major's leadership of the party.

The electoral dominance which the party has achieved may yet prove enduring and it is possible that the Conservatives could lead Britain into the new millennium. One commentator argues that the millennial celebrations can provide the 'glue for the polity' under Conservative leadership to engage the population. 'In skilful hands ... this kind of talk could be as intoxicating as "the white heat of the technological revolution" sounded 30 years ago'.[11] The signs are not entirely auspicious since the Government not only appears exhausted in the mid-1990s but also seems ideologically directionless. Thatcher herself provides the explanation that Major lacks intellectual certainty and tends to 'blow with the wind'.[12] Major's weaker style of leadership permits the re-emergence of ideological factions within the party's leadership whereas Thatcher left no time for ideological disputation. There are also structural forces at work creating problems for the party beyond the control of any leader. A fourth successive election victory converted the British party system into one characterised by single party dominance, and such party systems produce intra-party factionalism within the governing party as a substitute for inter-party competition.[13] Conservative MPs have also become increasingly professionalised and regard politics as a career. They are unwilling, therefore, to endure unpopularity which threatens their seats, and the 1922 remains a threat to any unsuccessful party leader.[14]

Major has been disadvantaged by Thatcher's legacy in three particular ways. First, she got the party to believe that Conservative governments are radical and purposeful. Second, while the potent mixture of free-market economics and populist nationalist politics proved electorally effective in the 1980s, it had lost its appeal. Finally, she bequeathed a party divided over Europe. While the earlier imperial Tory resistance to Europe represented by the Monday Club had waned, Thatcher exploited Powell's British, perhaps English, nationalism, and enthused a Euro-sceptical faction among the party's elite. This has required Major to indulge in anti-European rhetoric to humour the party's Euro-sceptics. This split was so serious in May 1994 that a former Chief Whip Sir David Renton predicted the possibility of a split into two parties.[15] A survey of Tory MPs revealed that Euro-sceptics comprised a majority, measured by resistance to re-entry into the ERM, opposition to a single currency, and support for the continuing supremacy of Parliament over European legislation.[16] Only opposition to the Social Chapter unites most Tory MPs. The new millennium might witness a fragmentation into two parties, led respectively by Michael Portillo for the Euro-sceptics and Stephen Dorrell for the moderates although it would only happen under a system of proportional representation. Europe is a symbol of the chasm. The conflicting attitudes towards Britain's integration into Europe express 'a darker right-left split between nationalism and internationalism', behind which lies the ideological confrontation over the balance between market forces and the managed economy.[17] There is an anti-European integration, nationalist, and free-market faction characterised by Portillo, and a pro-European, more economically interventionist faction which Clarke represents. Major appears unclear where his loyalty lies in this dispute, which has made the Conservatives 'a beastly Party to manage'.[18] Major is best understood as a post-Thatcherite, who is ready to make a shift away from her agenda, and to offer right-wing rhetoric while creating distance between himself and Portillo. The evidence at the end of 1994 is that Major has problems holding the factions together, as well as enthusing the rank-and-file. Yet an alternative leader would encounter the same dilemma.

Major entered the 1994 Conference, having to respond to a revived Labour Party under Tony Blair. He was faced with the choice between appealing to the minority in his own party with the reassertion of a Conservatism which is European, interested in social reconstruction, and ready to restore local democracy; or pandering to the tax-cutting, anti-European right-wing. A resort to tribal dialect to excite right-wing activists would lose sight of the mood of the nation.[19] It was predicted that he would be unable to break free from the 'ideological tracks of the eighties', to reposition the party in the continental Christian Democratic mainstream, or to stamp any authority or ideology on it.[20] While the right pressed him for tax cuts, the few One Nation members argued for him to 'balance efficiency with humanity' and 'to govern in the interests of the whole of society.[21] The pressures for a neo-Liberal and anti-European stance emerged at the Bournemouth Conference. Portillo provoked enthusiasm when he asserted that 'Europe isn't Working'.[22] He sought 'clear blue water' between the Tories and Labour. There was also evidence that the Conservative Conference was becoming like the Labour Party Conferences of old, with contentious fringe meetings and a plethora of factional organisations such as Conservative Way Forward and the European Foundation. The European issue was the most difficult with the former Chancellor, Normal Lamont, asserting that Britain could contemplate leaving the EU and former Foreign Secretary Sir Geoffrey Howe alleging that such a course would be electorally suicidal.[23] Howe attributed the Euro-sceptical attitude to a residual nostalgia for Thatcher, a contempt for bureaucracy, and an outdated patriotism. He believed that for a 'great nation to remain a great power' it must wield influence; and only by affecting European decisions would Britain also be able to maintain a voice in Washington.[24] Pro-European ministers also joined a new City-funded alliance to promote the case for Britain in Europe.[25] Major's Conference speech ignored Europe but brought the party back on to the centre ground to compete with Blair. While there is evidence that Major simply seeks whatever headline the immediate circumstances warrants, his low-key speech suggested an attempt to restore the 'nation at ease with itself' theme to appeal to Middle England.[26] It appeared that Major has ceased to worry about challenges to his leadership and was no longer going to allow the 'Right to have its head'.[27] Yet the controversy should continue as the Inter-Governmental Conference in 1996 will reveal the desire of many European governments to advance further towards integration. The *Sunday Telegraph* expressed the anxiety that the 1994 Conference had been a 'wasted opportunity' and claimed that an 'unbridgeable' gap had opened up between Conservative leaders and the party. The party's leadership regarded its followers as 'a mob with whom it is impossible to reason' and as 'a sweaty and ignorant multitude'. The same newspaper complained that the leadership was 'mesmerised by the idea of the centre ground' which is described as a metaphor rather than a place. It urged Major to cease the pretence that 'Europe is coming our way', to admit that leaving the EU was 'an option', to hold a referendum and to dismiss Hurd as Foreign Secretary as his pro-European influence was leading the party to defeat.[28]

Major is challenged not just by the diverse and ragged nature of his party. He is also confronted with a marked acceleration of the social changes which began in the Heath and Thatcher years. The Conservatives are no longer dominated by landowners, business leaders and upper-middle class housewives. 'It is more petit-bourgeois, more a Party of managers, small entrepreneurs and skilled workers'.[29] If always predominantly right-wing at its grassroots, this has intensified as the party has fewer 'gentlemanly grandees' and more economically self-interested individuals: politicians such as Tebbitt symbolise this *garagiste* tendency. The newer activists seek a more muscular policy and desire to 'go for the jugular' of opponents. They are less deferential to the leadership and Central Office and are ignorant of the conventions of the party's paternalist past.

The idea that the party has no influence over the policies of its leaders has always been exaggerated. While the annual National Union Conference is stage-managed so little overt controversy occurs there, it also marks the end of a series of important events. These include a myriad of conferences at which the leadership is informed of the party's mood. The Central Council meeting in the spring which represents agents and chairs throughout the country is particularly influential. This hidden Conference system enables ministers to keep in touch with party opinion.[30] While the Conference is primarily a propaganda event, this should not conceal its importance in morale-building and solidarity. Major has been on trial, like Heath before him, for the quality of his Conference keynote speech. *Arriviste* individualism has replaced aristocratic paternalism, and as a result even the party's annual Conference has become less social and more political.[31] The complexity of the relations between the Conference and the leadership means that while Conference shapes activist opinion in the mode desired by the leaders, there are issues of policy where the views of activists are strongly expressed.[32] Crime remains a concern and Europe is the issue of the mid-1990s. The decline of deference has been accompanied by a new breed of Conservative MP less loyal to the leadership and concerned about personal political safety. By the time of Thatcher's downfall, MPs were prone to panic. The party's legendary preoccupation with electoral victory, of which the ruthlessness of its attitudes towards its leaders is symptomatic, was a main motif in government policy from November 1990 to April 1992.

The party's success in the period leading up to the electoral victory of 1992 contrasted with the collapse of the government's authority in the two years afterwards. This demonstrates the need to analyse the two phases separately.

Preparations for the 1992 general election

The first period of Major's leadership before 1992 began with a nervous performance at the dispatch box and the failure to appoint a woman to his Cabinet. His first EC Inter-Governmental Conference (IGC) in December demonstrated that his different tone created a honeymoon period with his partners and not just with the electorate.[33] The changed tone was evident in his pledge that in European affairs, he sought to be 'on the pitch and playing hard'.[34] In Bonn, Major made his classic remark that 'Britain should be at the heart of Europe'.[35]

Major's relaxed political style, symbolised by his remark that he sought 'a country at ease with itself', proved popular. He also restored the collegial role of the Cabinet, in which ministers were free to discuss issues openly. A colleague compared the Cabinet's mood to that of prisoners released into the sunlight in Beethoven's *Fidelio*.[36] Thatcher did not destroy the Cabinet's role permanently, therefore, and even she had run into difficulties over Westland and Lawson's resignation, and the Cabinet's role in her downfall is clear. Cabinet government was, therefore, 'peaky but not poorly'.[37] Initially, MPs allowed Major to set the tone of government. In an early speech he promised a 'softer' approach to Europe and a greater concern for social cohesion, the needs of the inner cities and the north of England.[38] In intra-party terms Major began with an event which enabled him to underpin the 'classlessness' of his appeal with the endorsement of the candidacy of the black Conservative lawyer John Taylor in Cheltenham against local constituency party dissidence. Tebbitt also upheld Taylor's candidacy because 'he thinks of himself as a British Conservative'.[39] The Labour Party's reaction to Major's emergence, that he was the 'son of Thatcher', was weakened by the Poll Tax review and his European policy. Doubts remained as to whether Major was breaking with the past. While Major replaced the moderate Conservative Ian Grist as Under-Secretary for Wales, with Nicholas Bennett of the 'Thatcherite' No Turning Back Group, he also expressed genuine compassion for those who 'needed a helping hand', and announced the reindexation of Child Benefits.[40]

The right maintained pressure on Major. Portillo asserted that the party had to continue to win the battle of ideas and not seek victory through affluence. This involved 'fidelity to the agenda of the 1970s: the independence of the individual, the free operation of the market, and the need for improved incentives. These ideas are scarcely questioned in Britain today'.[41] He also warned that Europe had to be 'a deregulated, freely-trading, single market. But following the Maastricht summit, it is clearer than before that there are conflicting visions about the future of Europe. That conflict is not principally to be found in the Tory Party. The vision of a free-trading Europe in a free-trading world unites the Party ... Within the EC we shall see a re-run of the competition of ideas already played out in Britain'.[42] A Thatcherite group urged Major to persist with the 1980s' agenda which it related to the Conservative traditions of combining 'the best elements of both the great political traditions of Victorian Britain: the Tory respect for time-honoured customs and institutions, and the Liberal emphasis on individual freedom'.[43] The right was confident because of Communism's fall, which encouraged it to maintain the momentum in Britain.[44] The imminence of the election, however, enabled Major to keep the right under control. The Gulf War produced high personal ratings for Major, with 60% asserting that he was doing well in May 1991, but there were continuing by-election disasters in Ribble Valley in March and Monmouth in May, which produced substantial swings to the Liberals and Labour respectively. Similarly, the May local elections led Heseltine to declare that the Conservatives were within 'striking distance' of a fourth victory but not quite there.[45] Election results ensured the Parliament would run its full course.

The politics of 1991 was dominated by the lingering recession despite the persistent assertion by Chancellor Lamont that consumer confidence was recovering. The 1991 recession had hit the south-east and the service sector of the economy. 47,000 small businesses folded during the year, many of which had been brought into being by the support of the Thatcher government.[46] The economic and electoral cycles were out of synchronisation and it was obvious that the party would have to fight an election with the Public Sector Borrowing Requirements (PSBR) in serious deficit, as a result of falling tax revenues and upward pressures on public spending. The Tory press was ambivalent about the government's attempt to hasten the end of recession by loosening controls over public expenditure, but noted the departure from Thatcherite policy in the high ratio of public expenditure to overall national income. It was approaching 42 per cent when in 1988 it had fallen as low as 39.5 per cent.[47] In the absence of recovery the Chancellor's optimistic statements were ridiculed. The trade deficit reached £20 billion and there were problems of poor retail sales and mortgage repossessions.[48] The political problem was the collapse of Lawson's achievement of an ever-declining proportion of national income consumed by public expenditure.[49]

From the outset, Major had been challenged to produce a 'big idea' to give his government a clear identity.[50] By recognising the importance of quality in the public services, rather than having a deep ambivalence towards their existence, the Charter appeared to 'offer an agenda for action which neatly points up the difference between Thatcherism and the policies that the Prime Minister intends to make his own'.[51] Charters lay down standards of service for the rail, gas, water, electricity and telecommunications services, and are consistent with the production of league tables on the performance of schools and hospitals. The ideology is that the customers of services are at the heart of the process. There is continuity between this initiative and the reforms of the Thatcher years. Placing the recipients of services at the centre of the process, it replaced accountability to citizens with consumer rights, and provided no more expenditure. The Charter initiative is an integral element in Major's restructuring of the state. 'Thatcherism' had always involved a commitment to managerial change, better management in public and private sectors, and the more efficient delivery of services through competition and market discipline, privatisation, contracting out and responsiveness to consumer demand. The Thatcher government's reforms of the NHS were similar in that they were an exercise in management accounting.[52] The Charters also relate to Major's concern with privatisation, deregulation, contracting out, market-testing of civil service functions, performance-related pay, quality management, and the extension of the 'Next Steps' agencies for the delivery of public services. This was a clear case of pushing forward with changes which Thatcher had inaugurated.[53] Each Next Steps agency is required to implement a Charter. The Employment Service, for example, reduced waiting times, sought prompt and accurate payment of benefits, and introduced the wearing of staff badges. These reforms were procedural rather than substantive, and it is apparent that 'unemployed people are not consumers able to move elsewhere if they are unhappy with the quality of the service. They are legally obliged to sign on, attend regular compulsory interviews and show that they are available for and actively seeking work'.[54] The Citizen's Charter was mainly cosmetic and failed to excite the electorate.

At the 1991 Conference Major made an attempt to define his version of Conservatism. While he sought to soften the edges of Thatcherism, he also placed emphasis upon tax cuts and wealth creation. He rejected the privatisation of the NHS, a federal Europe and advocated a return to basics in education. Unlike his more ineffective attempts to define Conservatism after the 1992 election this caught the national mood. The *Daily Telegraph* described it as a speech of 'decent Conservatism stripped of the barbed wire girdles' of the right. Yet the newspaper also noted the direct appeals to the right through Major's argument that people should have the power to choose and the right to own.[55] His policies were a minor shift, or were symbolically rather than substantively different from those of Thatcher, but it was to the Conservatives' benefit that voters saw a distinction.[56] A leading Conservative claimed that 'in supermarket terms we want to sell an updated product, not a new brand'.[57]

With the Maastricht Treaty on the EC's future due for negotiation in December, Major had sought to blur differences within the party by alternately advocating that Britain should be 'at the heart of Europe' and then dismissing federalism. In one speech he stressed that Britain could 'strike the right balance between closer co-operation and a proper respect for national institutions and traditions'.[58] At his first Conference he managed both to reduce Thatcher to the status of Heath and Macmillan, point out that she had signed the Single European Act, and avoid a clear commitment to either faction. 'The idea of a single European currency is ... an uncertain prospect ... It is our decision. A single currency cannot be imposed upon us ... but in no circumstances ... will a Conservative Government give up the right, our national right, to take the crucial decisions about our security, our foreign policy and our defence'.[59] She obtained revenge in 1992 when her presence at Conference encouraged MPs to rebellion over Maastricht.[60] Major's ambiguities were necessary because of the party divisions over European Monetary Union (EMU) and the Social Chapter. The government's approach to the Treaty's negotiation was coloured by internal party divisions. In this respect the tactics proved successful. Progress towards political union was limited. Major's proudest achievement, necessary to hold the party together, was securing the excision from the Treaty of the Social Chapter, which the remaining eleven members signed through a separate protocol. The Conservatives feared that the Chapter would harmonise minimum wages, maximum hours and worker participation in industry which could affect industrial competitiveness. Major also secured an opt out from the final stages of monetary union. While he may have been delaying the party's acceptance of European integration, in order to negotiate the election regardless of long-term effects, the outcome diminished the prospect of a damaging split. The peace which the opt outs secured with the backbenchers was a temporary truce and was replaced by the issue of the burgeoning size of the public sector borrowing requirement (PSBR) of £30 million needed to maintain public spending in the run-up to the election. Thatcher had brought national finances 'briefly into surplus'.[61]

The residual split between older One Nation faction and the revived right of the Thatcher era was demonstrated in the different responses to this issue. Thatcher and Parkinson urged 'belt-tightening' to close the deficit, while Clarke asserted that the PSBR must necessarily rise during a recession to protect spending programmes. The former ministers closely associated with Thatcher and now out of public office, such as Tebbitt, Ridley, and Parkinson, were discontented at Major's announcement at the replacement of the Poll Tax by the less regressive Council Tax which combined property and personal elements.[62] Thatcher also accepted in March 1991 the presidencies of the Euro-sceptical 'Bruges Group' as well as the 'Conservative Way Forward' group. The right urged Major to 'come out of the closet'. They were unconvinced that the ERM would address an inflation which was the product of loose money supply and a high PSBR. ERM membership also meant a deflationary policy which exacerbated the recession.[63] Simon Heffer cynically argued that the Conservatives might secure a victory by the moral defeat of allowing public spending to rise as a proportion of GDP and by the 'Pooterism' of the Citizen's Charter.[64] He argued that crime should be stressed and was anxious whether the party could convince people of its capacity to address it, 'particularly all those poor, over burgled C2s on their council estates'.[65] The need to appeal to the C2s was a favourite theme on the right and some deplored the failure to exploit the popularity of Tebbitt, since the C2 voters require 'a real Essex man'.[66] One Conservative claimed that 'the British voters are the most frightful people imaginable, with atavistic longings for cradle to grave services. The C2s particularly, calculate that more education expenditure might save them from paying for school trips and enable them to put the money towards a holiday in Tenerife, and by saving money from prescription charges they could pay for their XR2s more easily'.[67]

As the final pre-election budget approached the possibility of borrowing to finance tax cuts divided right-wing economists. Some monetarists opposed tax cuts based upon borrowing, while others were more relaxed. Thatcher was horrified at such financial imprudence.[68] So the burgeoning PSBR, Europe, and membership of the ERM troubled the right and these matters were linked since the PSBR was defined as 'the price tag' of the ERM.[69] The leading Euro-sceptic Bill Cash asserted that the case against federalism was that it involved 'a concentration of power under German influence'.[70] Right-wing anti-Major factionalism was apparent. The final budget before the general election demonstrated that Lamont was paying greater attention to electoral needs than to the Thatcherites. He found £75 million for loans to the poor and increased spending for health. While Major defended tax cuts alongside greater borrowing, Parkinson attacked the budget's re-establishment of the 20p tax band at the lowest rate of tax-paying.[71] The budget occurred the day before the election was called, but the confirmation of the ballooning PSBR reduced the room for manoeuvre for either of the major parties to make generous promises. The Conservative manifesto avoided spending commitments to enable Major to concentrate his attack on Labour's fiscal imprudence.[72]

Conservatives were united in defence of the Union with Scotland. During the Thatcher years the party turned against devolution. Major's Glasgow speech in February 1992 reaffirmed this. He considered that the case for national unity would draw more votes in Britain in general than would the appeal of devolution to the Scots. Major opposed the 'United Kingdom untied. The bonds that generation after generation of our enemies have sought and failed to break, cast loose, by us, ourselves ... A solitary Scotland means a solitary England, alongside Wales and Northern Ireland. Two proud nations, divorced, marginalised, diminished'.[73] But he was as opposed to devolution. This was because 'so great a change as a new tax-raising Parliament in Scotland could not be a simple bolt-on extra to our constitution ... The danger of Labour's devolution proposals is that they might feed any such grievance, not dispel them. Labour has chosen to ride on a tiger. That tiger, unless soon caged could consume the Union itself'.[74] His right-wing critics were happy with this declaration as an example of his stressing real differences with Labour.[75]

Party preparation before 1992

The preparation for general elections, particularly in government, are based on an interaction between events and propaganda initiatives. While events, particularly economic difficulties, dominated, the Conservative Party addressed its communications and organisational problems. The relationship between party leader and Party Chairman is a key to the party's continuing success. Patten's predecessor commented that the importance of a good relationship between a Conservative Prime Minister and the Party Chairman is as vital as a good relationship between the Prime Minister and the Chancellor of the Exchequer. Bad relations with the Chancellor run the danger that the government will fall apart, but bad relations with the Chairman who has responsibility for the party in the country are also problematical. The Party Chairman should not use the role to create an alternative power base to that of the party leader.[76]

The chairmanship was a poisoned chalice. Patten was faced with a financial deficit of £12 million, plus revelations that large sums had been received into party coffers from foreign financiers from Greece and Hong Kong. There was deep concern from the small, but widely reported Charter Movement, which campaigned for political reform and democratisation within the party. It was formed in 1980 as a symptom of growing disenchantment and declining deference despite the slight support it has achieved.[77] It attacked the party's incompetent financial stewardship in October 1991, particularly for the three-year decline in the proportion of funds derived from constituency parties. Their contribution had fallen from 24% to 7% in the period. The party relied entirely on voluntary donations but their provenance was a cause of concern. If up to two-thirds of the money received came from questionable sources such as the Greek million-aire John Latsis, then the interests of democracy were not being served. The Charter Movement was exercised about a letter sent out from Central Office in September 1991 offering access to the inner counsels of the party in return for a donation of £1,000. The way was being opened for a linkage between political donations and the acquisition of political influence, which helped generate the 'sleaze' accusations which occupied the media in 1994. Central Office's letter stated that, 'we will undertake ... to keep you in touch with our thinking and give you the opportunity to tell us yours through meeting ministers'.[78] The Charter Movement's statement listed some of the largest contributions which the party had received in 1990, including £112,000 from United Biscuits, £110,000 from Allied Lyons, £100,000 from P & O and £80,000 from Hansons.[79]

Patten had to turn the organisation round and inspire the activists who had become disillusioned with Thatcher's ousting.[80] Patten persuaded Major to use the speech-writing talents of Sir Ronald Millar and the advice of Sir Gordon Reece, both of whom had worked closely with Thatcher. He partic-ipated in tactical political meetings with a group of ministers known as the 'Musketeers'.[81] While Baker had succeeded in some aspects of public rela-tions, he had bequeathed 'a bare cupboard' so far as policy and organisa-tional initiatives were concerned. There was criticism of his 1990 'Summer Heat on Labour' campaign for its implausible link between Labour and Com-munism.[82] Patten sought to find a new direction for Conservatism. Since Major was credited with compassionate qualities Patten promoted 'new' Tory themes, most of which were compatible with his traditional One Nation conceptions. The right condemned Patten's advocacy of caring cap-italism and the 'social market'. He stressed that social responsibilities were in harmony with individualism and wished to forget the battles of the 1970s.[83] His assertiveness implied a lack of strategic thinking at Cabinet level.[84] Most seriously the party lacked an election strategy and advertising agency. Baker had concentrated on short-term tactics, as when he por-trayed bad local election results in May 1990 as a success, because the Con-servatives had retained their 'flagship' councils of Westminster and Wandsworth.[85]

The issue of communicating Conservative policy was urgent because Saatchi and Saatchi discontinued its link with the party. A different agency, Allen, Brady and Marsh, had run the Euro-elections in 1989, but their anti-European 'Diet of Brussels' campaign failed. Patten replaced Brendan Bruce as the party's Communications Director with Shaun Woodward from the BBC. Like Patten he regarded Major's arrival as the opportunity to present a new television image. Russ Pipe replaced Harvey Thomas who had cre-ated Thatcher's 'star treatment'.[86] Saatchi and Saatchi returned as the lead advertising agency and the Harris Research Centre was hired to carry out extensive private polls.[87] Patten wished to recapture the creative atmosphere which had prevailed between 1978 and 1979 and the agency enjoyed a central role in the campaigning. He ended the services of the American poll-ster Richard Wirthlin who was expert in negative campaigning.[88] He also placed an agent and a computer in every marginal constituency, although the party's 'doorstep advantage' over Labour was less pronounced than pre-viously.[89] The regional focus was considered important and communications officers were appointed in the twelve regions to liaise with the press and the broadcasting organisations.[90] The Party employed both traditional con-stituency and modern mass communications campaigning.

Patten did not reform Central Office, however, although his successor Sir Norman Fowler conducted the biggest shake-up for over sixty years.[91] His interest was in preparing policy and liaising with the 10 Downing Street Policy Unit, rather than in policy presentation, or in daily administration at Central Office.[92] Patten also sought to retrieve some of the role which the Conservative Research Department had lost during the Thatcher years to independent right-wing think-tanks. He considered the creation of a body to deal with everyday affairs and a think-tank to examine themes for the long term. He found that Major and his Policy Unit under Sarah Hogg also wished to make their mark on the policy process and the Citizen's Charter was their central theme.[93]

In November 1991 the party began preparations for a long campaign. Their concentration upon specific target voters has become more sophisti-cated, and these were then defined as 'former Conservatives and voters who liked John Major but did not support the Party (to a disproportionate extent Liberal Democrats and middle-class women), and middle aged C2 men'.[94] The party's advisers urged concentration on issues, stressing the differences with Labour where Conservatives were strong such as taxation and law and order, and maintaining a low profile on issues on which Labour was trusted, such as health and social security. Having costed Labour's programme the campaign team highlighted a perceived Labour weakness by launching in January 1992 the Labour 'Tax Bombshell' poster. The Saatchi organisation felt that there was little mileage in Patten's social market and Major agreed. Despite his 'softer' style Major was a post-, rather than a non-Thatcherite.[95] The Conservatives were effective in highlighting concerns about Labour's taxation policy even before the campaign began and an opinion poll revealed that the Conservatives were preferred over Labour on tax policy by 18%.[96]

The Conservatives were embarrassed by events during the longer-term campaign. Their financial situation attracted adverse attention. They had to resist pressure to return the donation of £440,000 from Asil Nadir of the bankrupt Polly Peck Company. In the two years up to April 1992, half of the party's income of £35.3 million came from business sources, with about £1.5 million from constituencies and £8 million from wealthy entrepreneurs. Up to £3 million was raised in the final weeks of the campaign by large contributions from individuals such as Sir James Goldsmith, Alan Sugar, and companies such as the recently privatised Thames Water.[97] These contributions undermine the view that the party has become more socially representative and the agent of smaller businesses.

The Conservatives conducted a lacklustre campaign with poor co-ordination of important themes and pointless 'battlebus' journeys by Major. He began the campaign with a good theme which echoed his own and Thatcher's earlier commitment to a classless society by announcing his intention of burying for ever 'the old divisions in Britain – between North and South, blue collar and white collar, polytechnic and university. They're old style, old hat, and we need to be rid of these prejudices'.[98] The manifesto, *The Best Future for Britain*, was dull and its lack of 'zip' reflected the campaign as a whole. It was in Major's interest that a crowd of demonstrators in Luton half-way through the campaign tried to shout him down since it allowed him to appear tough in inviting electors to resist such rowdyism.[99]

This appeal coincided with Major's discovery of the defence of the constitution and the integrity of the United Kingdom. While Labour responded to the Charter 88 'Democracy Day' by dabbling with constitutional reform, Major seized the opportunity to appeal to constitutional caution and the defence of the Union. Whether relying on Conservative instinct or on private polling evidence, he offered the Conservative Party as the Union's defender against threats from Scotland, a Europe of nation states and 'hung Parliaments'. Recognising that the absence of PR had enabled the Conservatives to engage in single party government in the 1980s on a minority vote, and that an increasingly divided party might be prone to a formal schism under the application of PR, he sought to present his opposition patriotically. He accused Liberal and Labour alike as 'trifling with a new voting system – one that would ensure permanent representation in power for the Left ... Let them put their parties first and their country second. We will put the country first, last and always. I will entertain no constitutional changes that will weaken the United Kingdom'.[100] The swing to Labour on 9 April was 2.1%, but it left the Conservatives with 336 seats, more than were required for an absolute majority. The triumph proved short-lived, however, because by the autumn the party had begun its decline into deep unpopularity.

Majorism since 1992: the collapse in confidence

Europe continued to create divisions in the period after 1992, although Major's main achievement was the restructuring of the state.[101] The government pursued its neo-Liberal strategy of reducing the state to an 'inescapable core'.[102] A new Government department was set up after the 1992 general election, the Office of Public Service and Science, to implement the Citizen's Charter and the Next Steps initiative, which transferred functions from the central departments to more commercially driven 'hived off' agencies. The logic of implementing the Next Steps programme opened up a vista of radical possibilities. Departments were required to review their activities and consider five options: abolition, privatisation, contracting out, creating an agency, or remaining in the department.[103] From the autumn of 1992 all government functions have been 'market tested' against the private sector.[104] It is evident that many core civil servants and the threatened Treasury have been reluctant to have their functions transferred to agencies. The agencies are less autonomous in their operations than organisations in the private sector such as the TECs which enjoy the involvement of local businessmen. Both types of organisation generate concern about the rise of non-departmental bodies, or quangos, and the lack of accountability which flows from them. It is in the decline of the central and local state, however, that Major leaves his mark.

The European debate has been dominant, however, since 1992. While in June 1994 Major was described as 'Thatcher without the handbag', after he vetoed the appointment of Jean-Luc Dehane as Commissioner of the European Union (EU), and so managed to re-unite the party temporarily around the concept of a multi-speed Europe, in the previous two years he had often failed to satisfy the Euro-sceptical Conservatives on the party's right by his determination to secure the ratification of the Maastricht Treaty.[105] While Europe is an issue which produces visceral reactions, the fault line which it represents overlaps with other divisive questions. Euro-sceptics condemn the ERM because it prevents a national approach to economic management, and associate it with the corporatist and collectivist versions of political economy prevalent on the continent. Major's position on these key issues is blurred, but after his 1992 victory he appeared more sympathetic to Britain's role in the EU and tried to face down his Euro-sceptic right wing. The trauma of securing the ratification of Maastricht in the summer of 1993, however, led him back to a position of seeking to appease the Thatcherite right.

Britain's position in the ERM of DM 2.95 was Major's decision as Chancellor, and as Prime Minister he adhered doggedly to this fixed rate of exchange, as the only way to combat inflation. Once more the Euro-sceptics blamed the British recession on Britain's decision to enter the ERM, and its members recall Major's role in this.[106] He upheld Britain's position in the ERM even when it was becoming impossible to sustain. Shadowing the DM within the ERM required higher interest rates, because Germany kept its own interest rates up to dampen inflationary pressure at home, in the aftermath of German reunification. The British recession required lower interest rates which could only be achieved by a devaluation against the DM. As speculators perceived that there was no real prospect of economic recovery without devaluation, the pressures on Britain's membership mounted throughout the summer of 1992. The denouncement arrived on 16 September 1992 (Black Wednesday), when a dramatic raising of interest rates was of no avail, and Lamont announced Britain's departure from the ERM. This severely dented both popular and market confidence in the government. The opportunity to devalue the pound within the ERM, and to conduct economic policy more eclectically than through the 'one club' approach of high interest rates, promoted economic recovery. The episode of Britain's precipitate withdrawal from the ERM was humiliating because of Major's protestations to the contrary, and undermined the Conservatives' image of economic competence. The government's economic strategy lay in ruins and Sir Alan Walters was vindicated in his view that both a freely floating currency or an attachment to a given currency such as the DM were preferable to ERM membership.[107] A Conservative newspaper described the ERM as 'the biggest U-turn for decades'.[108] It welcomed the reversion to control by the markets and the probability of lower interest rates. The impact on the party's standing was immediate with Labour's lead in the polls up from 3 to 11%.[109]

To add the intra-party dispute over Maastricht, the failure of Britain's ERM policy, and continuing recession and unemployment, the announcement of a programme of pit closures amounting to a halving of the workforce in October 1992 which was the consequence of the Conservative privatisation of the electricity industry, led to an unprecedented upsurge of popular protest. The public outrage resulted from the additional burden which the closures placed on the unemployment problem. The government appeared unconcerned about the nation's social fabric and its future energy requirements. Local Conservative associations objected and a number of MPs threatened to rebel, but the government rode out the storm.[110] Ministers did ultimately obtain the outcome they sought but not without belated promises to inject financial support into the affected areas and the announcement of an enquiry. Through a deliberate strategy of procrastination the pits closed over the next couple of years. The popular outrage and the recovery in popularity of Arthur Scargill did not undermine the government's confidence in the privatised electricity market, but taught it the need for more deft presentation in future.

The British assumed the presidency of the EC in the second half of 1992 and offered its own European ideals of extending the single market to the EFTA countries and the further liberalisation of trade including amendments to the Common Agricultural Policy (CAP). Even the Euro-sceptics supported this free-market agenda but it was the ratification of Maastricht which alarmed them. Their cause was assisted by the Danish rejection of the treaty and the slender margin by which the French endorsed it.[111] Major's response was to criticise the Euro-sceptical dream of life outside the EU as an 'irrelevant fantasy'.[112] The 1992 Conference proved difficult when Lord Tebbitt asked delegates whether they wished to be citizens of the European Union, which produced a roar of 'no'. Even the pro-European Foreign Secretary Douglas Hurd pandered to anti-European sentiment in rejecting a centralised super state with a single executive and Parliament.[113] Hurd's conflation of Europe and opposition to big government, demonstrates that the European issue is at the crossroads of the two central routes of Thatcherism. Thatcher described Maastricht as 'a ruinous straightjacket' and the ERM as the 'vision of yesterday'.[114] Major's keynote speech to Conference was designed to win the support of the Euro-sceptics, while persisting with policies favoured by the Europhile left. This was described as 'a fudge'.[115] Conservative newspapers noted that Major had used the word 'British' over fifty times in his speech but argued that Tebbitt and Thatcher had overplayed their hand. Ordinary members were confused and unsure as to whether Maastricht was even an important issue. Many delegates, particularly from the small business sector, were far more anxious about inflation, taxation, and unemployment.[116] In the middle of deep economic problems, however, Major placed his emphasis upon securing his authority in the parliamentary party by ensuring the passage of the Maastricht paving Bill. In the November vote, Major's threat to the twenty-plus Euro-rebels who could defeat the Bill, of an imminent general election, was considered ineffective since the party's high command would not permit it.[117] Yet while the country was uninterested, Major continued to concentrate on the passage of the paving Bill, veering between threatening the rebels, launching 'charm offensives', and engaging in the self-defeating manoeuvre of omitting the word Maastricht from the Bill. He won the vote but was less successful when the Bill came up for final ratification in 1993.

Party in-fighting stretched up to the Cabinet and led to opinion polls showing that for the first time the Conservative Party was seen as more divided than Labour. The passage of the European Communities Amendment Bill in July 1993 generated considerable acrimony and the position of the sceptics was strengthened by the government's small majority. The rebels created major tensions, and in alliance with Labour, produced a defeat on an Opposition amendment declaring that ratification should not take place until the government accepted the Social Chapter. The Commons vote was tied at 317 votes. Twenty-two Conservative members voted with the Opposition.[118] The government was then able to win a confidence vote on 23 July, by a majority of forty.[119] A Conservative judgement about the event was that the backbench rebels were 'a bold few ... speaking for the more timid many', including some in Cabinet. The rebels had the support of one in four Conservative activists and the hesitant support of a majority. There were cheers in Tory clubs when the government's defeat was announced, and letters ran twenty to one against Major. The party as a whole was judged to be Euro-sceptical, and an attempt to remould it away from that position would be destructive.[120] The intra-party conflict was such that even the twin opt-outs over Britain's membership of any eventual monetary union and of the Social Chapter were not sufficient to prevent the possibility of a schism.[121] In a leaked off-the-record conversation with a journalist, Major condemned three unspecified 'bastards' in the Cabinet for his problems. (The main candidates for the accolade were Michael Howard, Michael Portillo, John Redwood and Peter Lilley.) More damaging was Major's critical comment about the Thatcher myth, when he complained about leading a party that is 'harking back to a golden age that never was, and is now invented'.[122] In the next session of Parliament Major's supporters attempted to purge the Maastricht rebels from the Executive of the 1922. The shift from tendencies to factions in the party was clear since there were two rival groups of Conservative MPs: the Mainstream and Lollards group. The Mainstream representing the party's centre sought to replace right-wing hard-liners, Sir George Gardiner, Sir Ivan Lawrence, James Pawsey, John Townend, and Sir Rhodes Boyson with a moderate slate. It is revealing of the shift rightwards that it was only Gardiner who was defeated in the election to the Executive.[123]

The party's Euro-sceptic wing regarded Maastricht as an extension of European centralisation and a decline in national sovereignty. In reality, Maastricht did not undermine inter-governmentalism and horse trading between the competing member states. In July 1994 Hurd announced that Conservative divisions over Europe were being resolved. Major concurred and coupled it with an apocalyptic warning against sectionalism reasserting the party's traditional role as an instrument of national unity.[124] Major conceded much to his Euro-sceptical wing in his use of the veto to block the appointment of Jean-Luc Dehane.[125] The contrasting social philosophy between the British Conservatives and the European Christian Democrats, which is symbolised by the uneasy relationship between the two groups in the European Parliament, makes it unlikely that the Euro-sceptical wing will ever reconcile itself to the trend of European politics. Sir Edward Heath remains convinced that Britain will be left behind by the rest of the EU at the 1996 Inter-Governmental Conference (IGC).[126] The left wing of the Conservative Party is undoubtedly small but the potential for its disaffection if Major turns to the right, is real. The Tory Reform Group, for example, advances a different European and economic strategy from that of the right wing to which Major, whatever his real preferences or preferred electoral tactics, must pay attention. The division runs so deep that in a Continental European country a Conservative such as Hurd would be a Christian

Democrat and Portillo 'a liberal nationalist'.[127]

The disquiet of the left openly emerged in 1993. After a decade of promoting a neo-Liberal economic agenda, a leading thinker began to assert the limits of marketisation, to recognise that a deregulated and flexible labour market made the stability necessary to underpin family life hard to achieve and to urge Conservatives to assert their attachment to family and community.[128] A year later, after the emergence of Tony Blair as Labour Party leader, he argued that the 'torch of innovation' has passed to the left as the source of relevant ideas for the late 1990s.[129] He described Majorism as 'Thatcherism on autopilot'. He feared that any one of a number of Major's key policies in the mid-1990s, for example, rail privatisation, VAT on heating fuel, and tax on invalidity benefit 'may turn out to be Major's poll tax'.[130] He urged that Conservatives should confront the 'desolation of communities by unfettered market forces and the spectre of jobless growth producing an ever larger, and increasingly estranged underclass ... As a result British Conservatism today has nothing to say of the political task of the age, which is to reconcile the subversive dynamism of market institutions with the human need for local rootedness and strong and deep forms of common life'.[131] He condemned Conservatives for discarding long-established institutions for the sake of a dubious economic theory. The Thatcher legacy, and the rank-and-file's enthusiasm for Portillo as a future leader prevented Major from jettisoning his radical reforms, since that would be to 'underwrite the image of indecision, dither and U-turn'.[132] He also deplored the Thatcherite 'atavistic rejection of Britain's future as part of a Europe of nations'. The idea of 'withdrawal from the European Union' is 'frivolous and dangerous'.[133]

The party's anxiety as both the 1993 and 1994 Conferences opened was exacerbated by the realisation that the beginnings of economic recovery through growth, a decline in unemployment, an improving balance of payments and low inflation were not yielding the anticipated political dividend. This was because the psychology of the recession had bitten deep. Lamont was ultimately removed as Chancellor in May 1993 after the gaffe in which he commented *je ne regrette rien* about his economic policy. Had Major removed Lamont immediately after Black Wednesday the markets would have been reassured and he would have appeared a strong leader. Lamont's belated dismissal made Major appear weak and turned an ally into an enemy. This was evident in his resignation speech in which he accused the Major government of 'being in office but not in power' and of only looking 36 hours ahead to the next headline.[134]

The loss of Conservative domination of political ideas, the pressure to soften Thatcherism and co-operate with Europe, the continuing demand from the Thatcherite wing for 'pure' policies, and charges that the Conservatives required a period in Opposition to recharge its batteries, led Major to attempt to redefine Conservative philosophy. These attempts did not alter the public perception that he 'has no sense of where he is going'.[135] A leading Thatcherite considered the attempts 'half-baked' and lacking the detailed policy background to give them meaning. There were several attempts, however, including references to social visions which were patently regressive with nostalgic references to 'long shadows on county cricket grounds', 'warm beer', and 'old ladies cycling to church'.[136] The Carlton Club promoted one of Major's attempts to redefine Conservatism as a drawing together of 'the principles and values that underpin Conservatism, linking themes and thinkers of our past with the challenges we must address in the last decade of the 20th century'.[137] Major defined Conservatism as based upon the four principles of choice, ownership, responsibility, and opportunity.[138] He also asserted that the free market did not disrupt community, and exemplified his point by reference to suburbs, villages, and small towns where the local spirit is healthy, in contrast to inner city areas where, with the state dominant, business had fled.[139] Major argued that Conservatives emphasised choice in the welfare state for the consumer.[140] He also doubted whether 'paying unemployment benefit, without offering or requiring any activity in return, serves unemployed people or society well'.[141] The most criticised attempt to define Conservatism was the 'Back to Basics' speech (October 1993). This was soon undermined by the revelation that certain Conservative MPs had been involved in relationships incompatible with family values and over the next year by a series of episodes involving Tory 'sleaze' over financial scandals. Leading Conservatives sought to disassociate the theme of 'Back to Basics' from the behaviour of politicians yet the speech had stressed traditional morality and the theme of 'law and order, the family and suspicion towards Europe'.[142] The theme was about the social ills that worried Conservative 'middle England'; and 'Back to Basics' looked to the traditional family as a social building block, while single parents symbolised social disintegration. The significance of these speeches was that the Conservatives were aware that they were losing the battle of ideas.

The 1993 Conference was marked by speeches in which Conservative leaders played to the right-wing gallery. Tory newspapers were impressed that the speeches highlighted the ideas of property, family, and nation since the assertive rank-and-file condemned state support for illegitimacy and single motherhood.[143] Conservative Central Office was both briefing about the need to reverse the permissive society, and making it apparent that 'Back to Basics' was aimed at challenging fashionable theories on health, education, and crime.[144] There was a welcome for the Back to Basics speech as an advance on Major's ineffective attempt to produce a 'big idea' at the 1992 Conference, when he had focused upon the need for more lavatories on motorways. If 'Back to Basics' was sufficient to quieten delegates at the

Conference there remained many who continued to 'revile him privately'.[145] Many blamed his personal staff, Graham Bright MP, Sarah Hogg, and press secretary Gus O'Donnell; but one Conservative argued that at times of economic difficulty it was unsuitable to have a Prime Minister whose personality made the country feel miserable.[146]

There was a perception that Major had changed tactics to favour manufacturing industry, to restrict public sector pay which 'brought ... the whiff of 1970s style incomes policies', to tolerate high levels of public borrowing which permitted only token tax cuts before the next general election, and to resort to the use of the word 'community'.[147] This change in policy emphasis was real but it ignored elements which had been absorbed into the nation's political fabric, such as weaker trade unions, the need to curb inflation, the importance of competition and enterprise, and the rejection of demand management of the economy. The continuing enigma of Major's government remained, however, as it was proceeding with rail and coal privatisation from which 'even she (Thatcher) shrank'.[148] Toll motorways are also likely, Sunday trading was liberalised, the whole area of middle-class entitlements within the society security budget was challenged and the drive to assert 'subsidiarity' in the EU was continuing. The most likely explanation is that Major is 'a man of unsure political identity, was chosen because his colleagues wanted no more of Thatcher, but did not know what they wanted instead'.[149] One minister complained that 'he is always all things to all men'.[150] Blair's challenge was such that Major capitulated to left-wing opponents of Royal Mail privatisation in November 1994, which was interpreted as the final death of 'post-Thatcherism'.[151]

By early 1995 Major's standing remained low, although it was accepted that he would not be replaced as leader as the division over Europe and market forces was endemic and intensifying as a result of eight Tory MPs temporarily losing the Party Whip and issuing their own Manifesto.[152] The party's changing composition was recognised as increasing the problems of management. A symptom of the party's changing social character is the decline of Eton as a source of MPs and ministers. Churchill's Cabinet had 8 out of 19 Cabinet members drawn from Eton and Thatcher's Cabinet had 6 out of 22, Major's Cabinet, however, has only 2, William Waldegrave and Hurd.[153] Hurd's Etonian background proved a disadvantage in the leadership contest with Major in 1990. Only 34 old Etonians remain in the Commons with a net decline of 9 after the 1992 election. It is significant that the 'glistening hope of the Tory right', Portillo, is a product not of Harrow, but of Harrow County School. This reflects the party in the country which is no longer dominated by big business and landowners. It has become the party of the 'petit bourgeois', 'managers', 'small entrepreneurs', and 'skilled workers'. This has reinforced the right wing.

A major research project into the attitudes of Conservative Party members confirms their right-wing proclivities on crime, law and order, immigration, and opposition to European integration.[154] One MP voted for hanging against his personal convictions to reflect the preferences of his association's members.[155] The survey of members also demonstrates the free-market perspective of the Thatcherites and the rank-and-file; although it claims that members tend to the left of the leadership on welfare state issues, with greater sympathy towards the National Health Service, unemployment benefit and the regulation of the privatised utilities. While some members may favour the welfare state in order to buttress themselves against the vicissitudes of the economy, this finding should be examined critically. First, this type of survey is suspect as respondents do not always reply to questions with the seriousness or understanding that the political scientist assumes. Further, on social welfare it is likely that party members provide either the optimum answer which they believe is acceptable, or express the attitude which they consider necessary for their party's electoral success. On issues which test 'progressiveness', the redistribution of wealth and income and electoral reform, there were large majorities against.[156]

The project's general conclusion is valid, but more generally across the entire range of political issues than the narrow sphere to which they confine it. They stress immigration and capital punishment in concluding that 'Thatcherism may be merely aligned with pre-existing attitudes in the Conservative Party, rather than a force which has shifted opinions in a new direction'.[157] They also conclude that Thatcherism may have been an 'evanescent' phenomenon in the party. Again they make an assumption about the particularity of Thatcherism, and it is debatable whether members are even highly policy-orientated. Membership is often a social phenomenon. A leading party figure asserts that activists will accept any policy which is thrown at them, as long as it leads to electoral success; and another asserts that while activists like to have policies explained to them, they rarely seek to influence the leadership's policy.[158] It is likely that Thatcher tapped a strong vein of attitudes in the party. Among her voters there was little ideological support, however; but enthusiasm for strong leadership, the Falklands effect, and the affluence secured by macro-economic management. This encapsulates Major's dilemma. The activists want right-wing policies and political success, but the two goals are often in conflict. Major is also challenged by a growing tendency for Conservative MPs to rebel. This has been attributed to a reaction against the authoritarian leadership of Edward Heath between 1970 and 1974.[159] The phenomenon mainly results from professionalisation and a changing social background. Since most MPs are career politicians anxious to further their career, or at least retain their seats, 'they are liable to panic'.[160]

Conservative divisions over Europe led to the widespread comment that the 'Conservative administration had worn itself out'.[161] The 1980s' mix of markets and the individual was considered to be an insufficient foundation for governance in the next century. Yet the necessary rethinking could not occur while in government and with the party's two wings far apart. While this was not an entirely new phenomenon, previous Conservative governments had succeeded because one faction prevailed, 'as the liberal nationalists did while ... Thatcher was Prime Minister. The Christian Democrats had their day under Harold Macmillan and Edward Heath ... what we have at present is a daily attempt to create a compromise that will get the Government through the night'.[162] As a result the party found itself pursuing difficult privatisations since it is 'unwilling to switch off a machine it only half understands'. At the same time Major agrees with those ministers who prefer a period of consolidation 'while a rising economy floats it back to acceptability'.[163] While Major had decided to unite the party and strengthen his leadership by 'jingoistic Euro-scepticism', many of its supporters in finance and industry needed successful EU membership, potential inward investors feared peripheralisation, and the City wanted the opportunities provided by Europe. Reconciling these perspectives is impossible. Major's dilemma is that 'the British right is trapped into a commitment to free trade while promoting the distrust of those with whom the country trades'.[164] Portillo's speeches symbolise this in attacking foreigners for selling educational qualifications, while welcoming foreign ownership of the car industry.

The voices advocating either cautious consolidation, or an explicit 'Christian Democratic' strategy, continue to grow. Willetts adjusted his previous views by emphasising that the harsh cutting edge of the free market should be softened by a recognition of the hunger for community, although best provided by strong local institutions rather than the central state. George Walden argued that the pure free market was a dubious blessing as it produced the appalling tabloid newspapers, and Alan Clark pointed to the danger of alienating the entire public sector workforce.[165] Employment Secretary David Hunt worried that young people are becoming 'atomised' and he urged a return to One Nation Conservatism. Stephen Dorrell, the Financial Secretary to the Treasury, echoed Burke's tirade against 'solitary, unconnected, individual, selfish liberty'.[166] The Scottish Secretary Ian Lang warned against the government continuing to offer a pastiche of Thatcher's ideology. He even implied that her ideology had been an afterthought, 'cobbled together to give a spurious air of consistency to an otherwise disparate string of measures'.[167] He feared the vacating of the centre ground. Many MPs, spurred on by the publications of the right-wing 'think-tanks', wanted continuing boldness. In February 1994, for example, the Adam Smith Institute's president Madsen Pirie called for the end of the welfare state as a part of a long-term review of public spending. This was supported by the right-wing group. Some Conservatives argued for a detailed policy on social welfare and certain ministers favoured a sharp alternative to Labour in

Euro-scepticism and tax cuts. The potential for division was clear when in endorsing the free market, Clarke refurbished his One Nation credentials, and stressed that the welfare state was necessary to provide the secure underpinning to enable the middle classes to accept the profound dislocations which the market produces. This was a delicate attempt to address the insecurities of 'middle England'.[168]

The death of the Opposition leader John Smith in May 1994 eased the direct pressure on Major's leadership as did a poor, rather than the expected disastrous, performance in the European elections in June. Major's strength in the party by the 1994 summer recess was clear when he was well received by the end of session meeting of the 1922. He stressed his appeal to the party's right, arguing that there must be clear water between the Conservatives and Labour.[169] Major promised a further squeeze in public expenditure to pave the way for tax cuts and a further battle against inflation. He also appealed to Euro-sceptics with the promise that 'people cannot be taken too far or too fast in a direction they are instinctively loathe to go'.[170] A leading commentator argued that 'the catcalls are dying down. Fewer rotten tomatoes are being flung. It is no longer chic to barrack Major with quite as much enthusiasm'.[171]

The party sought to modernise its organisation and finances in the period after the 1992 general election. The new Chairman Fowler set about a major overhaul. He launched an immediate package of cost-cutting measures and appointed a new Director-General with the function of eradicating the deficit and publishing new financial reports to meet the demand for greater openness. But the main significance was the announcement that party membership had fallen to half a million.[172] The most devastating statistic emerged in July 1994, however, when it was revealed that the average age of the party's membership had risen to 62 years.[173] The problem of the decline of mass parties and the rise of single-issue organisations is general but the problem is particularly acute for Conservatives. When Fowler resigned from the chairmanship in July 1994 the Party's financial situation had improved and it was achieving an annual surplus of £2 million, which enabled it to trim its accumulated deficit from £19 to £16.5 million.[174] The annual accounts published in July 1994 confirmed these figures and demonstrated the imbalance in its sources of income, with £9.3 million coming from donations in contrast to £0.75 million from the constituencies. The trend was alarming as the proportion derived from the local associations was continuing to fall. Fowler confirmed that members were disaffected by the government's performance.[175] The total income of the party averaged £3.5 million annually in the 1966–70 period with two-thirds of the money coming from local associations.[176] The evidence in 1994, however, was that the party was losing activists in a serious way and there were signs of feeble organisation at the local level in the Euro-elections.[177]

Reorganising the finances of the party is a very different proposition, therefore, from reactivating enthusiasm, although an increase in the number of local agents from 220 to 300 was a symptom of the improving financial situation. There were signs of activists losing heart in the summer of 1994 and many were more sympathetic to the Thatcherite organisations, such as the 92 Group and the No Turning Back Group, than to the national party. Despite these signs of malaise party leaders doubt whether the party will break up over Europe, and argue that the leadership remains in touch with opinion in the party and the country. The contrast is drawn with European federalist Christian Democrat leaders whose enthusiasms bear little relationship to the more patriotic views of their supporters.[178] The best prospect for the Conservatives from the perspective of 1995 is for an improving economy, tax cuts, and 'flag-waving' anti-federalist rhetoric while claiming to be centrist, and heavy propaganda against Labour. This could still permit its re-election.

Notes

1 Bruce Anderson, *John Major* (London: Fourth Estate, 1991), p. viii.
2 *Walden*, ITV, 25 November 1990.
3 Michael Pinto-Duschinsky, 'Political Parties', in Peter Catterall (ed.), *Contemporary Britain: An Annual Review, 1991* (Oxford: Blackwell, 1991), p. 44.
4 David Butler and Dennis Kavanagh, *The British General Election of 1992* (London: Macmillan, 1993), p. 274.
5 Hugo Young, *The Guardian*, 31 March 1994.
6 *Financial Times*, 24 May 1994.
7 *The Independent*, 8 October 1994. Summary of a report by Patrick Seyd and Paul Whiteley on Conservative Party membership.
8 *The Guardian*, 13 June 1994.
9 The Right Honourable Edward Heath MP criticised him for this on *Newsnight*, BBC 2 on 6 May 1994.
10 For example, Gary Waller MP on Radio Leeds, 5 May 1994.
11 Joe Rogaly in the *Financial Times*, 29 March 1994.
12 Margaret Thatcher, *The Downing Street Years* (London: HarperCollins, 1994).
13 Giovanni Sartori, *Parties and Party Systems: A Framework for Analysis* (Cambridge: Cambridge University Press, 1976), pp. 72–3.
14 Julian Critchley, *Sunday Telegraph*, 19 October 1992.
15 *The Guardian*, 14 May 1994.
16 Report of ESRC sponsored survey by David Baker, Andrew Gamble and Steve Ludlam of Nottingham Trent and Sheffield Universities.
17 *The Guardian*, 31 March 1994.
18 *Ibid.*
19 *The Independent*, 8 October 1994.
20 *The Observer*, 9 October 1994.
21 Alan Howarth MP, *The Observer*, 9 October 1994.

22 *Daily Telegraph*, 13 October 1994.
23 BBC Radio 4, *The World Tonight*, 15 October 1994.
24 Interviewed on *Walden*, ITV, 16 October 1994.
25 *Sunday Telegraph*, 16 October 1994.
26 *The Independent*, 15 October 1994.
27 *Ibid.*
28 *Ibid.*
29 *The Guardian*, 31 March 1994.
30 R. N. Kelly, *Conservative Party Conferences* (Manchester: Manchester University Press, 1989), p. 23.
31 M. Morgan and M. Burch, 'Who Are the New Tories?', *New Society*, 11 October 1984.
32 Andrew Gamble, *The Conservative Nation* (London: Routledge & Kegan Paul, 1974), p. 14.
33 Peter Catterall, 'Introduction: The Year in Perspective' in *Contemporary Britain: An Annual Review, 1991*, p. 11.
34 *Daily Telegraph*, 30 November 1990.
35 Butler and Kavanagh, *The British General Election of 1992*, p. 39.
36 Bagehot, 'Selling A New Spirit', *The Economist*, 8 December 1990.
37 Peter Hennessy, 'How Much Room at the Top? Margaret Thatcher, the Cabinet and Power Sharing', in P. Norton (ed.), *New Directions in British Politics: Essays on the Evolving Constitution* (London: Elgar, 1991), p. 33.
38 The Press Association, *John Major Prime Minister* (London: Bloomsbury Press, 1991), pp. 180–1.
39 *Daily Telegraph*, 3 December 1990.
40 *Daily Telegraph*, 5 December 1990.
41 Michael Portillo, *A Vision for the 1990s*, Conservative Political Centre, March 1992, p. 6.
42 *Ibid.*, pp. 15–17.
43 Alan Duncan et al., *Bearing the Standard: Themes for a Fourth Term*, Conservative Political Centre, September 1991, p. 3.
44 John Redwood, *Conservative Philosophy in Action*, Conservative Political Centre, September 1991, p. 22.
45 *Daily Telegraph*, 29 April 1991.
46 Catterall, 'Introduction: The Year in Perspective' (*1991*), p. 6.
47 *Daily Telegraph*, 5 May 1991.
48 Butler and Kavanagh, *The British General Election of 1992*, p. 84.
49 Nigel Lawson, *The View From Number 11* (London: Corgi Books, 1992), p. 316.
50 *The Citizen's Charter*, Cm 599, HMSO.
51 *The Independent*, 23 July 1991.
52 This view is explained in Ken Judge and Bill New, 'Health', in Catterall, *Contemporary Britain: An Annual Review, 1991*, pp. 280–93.
53 Kevin Theakston and Geoffrey Fry, 'The Party and the Civil Service' in Anthony Seldon and Stuart Ball, *Conservative Century* (Oxford: Oxford University Press, 1994), p. 400.
54 Unemployment Unit, *Working Brief*, November 1991, p. 3.
55 *Daily Telegraph*, 12 October 1991.

56 Butler and Kavanagh, *The British General Election of 1992*, p. 29.
57 *Ibid.*, p. 39.
58 'The Evolution of Europe', Konrad Adenauer Foundation, Bonn, 11 March 1991, p. 30.
59 'The Power to Choose: The Right to Own', Conservative Party Conference, Blackpool, 11 October 1991, reprinted in *The Power to Choose: The Right to Own*, Conservative Political Centre, November 1991, pp. 84–5.
60 Richard Kelly, 'The Party Conferences', in Seldon and Ball, *Conservative Century*, p. 256.
61 *Daily Telegraph*, 24 February 1992.
62 Kieron Walsh, 'Local Government' in Catterall, *Contemporary Britain: An Annual Review 1992*, p. 57.
63 *Spectator*, 4 January 1992.
64 *Spectator*, 25 January 1992.
65 *Spectator*, 15 February 1992.
66 *Sunday Telegraph*, 26 January 1992
67 *Sunday Telegraph*, 28 March 1992.
68 *Sunday Telegraph*, 23 February 1992.
69 *Sunday Telegraph*, 14 March 1992.
70 *Sunday Telegraph*, 18 January 1992.
71 *Daily Telegraph*, 3 March 1992.
72 *The Guardian*, 22 April 1992.
73 Speech by Right Honourable John Major MP, *Scotland in the United Kingdom*, Conservative Political Centre, 1992, p. 10.
74 *Ibid.*, p. 11.
75 *Spectator*, 7 March 1992, p. 6.
76 Kenneth Baker, *The Turbulent Years: My Life in Politics* (London: Faber, 1993), pp. 281–2.
77 Stuart Ball, 'The National and Regional Party Structure', in A. Seldon and S. Ball, *The Conservative Century* (Oxford: Clarendon Press, 1994), p. 216.
78 *Daily Telegraph*, 7 October 1991.
79 *Ibid.*
80 There was a spate of proposed deselections of Tory MPs who had voted for Michael Heseltine, for example, Cyril Townsend in Bexleyheath on 4 January 1991.
81 Pinto-Duschinsky, 'Political Parties', p. 38.
82 *Sunday Telegraph*, 2 February 1992.
83 *Financial Times*, 31 December 1990.
84 Anthony Seldon, 'Conservative Century', in Seldon and Ball, *Conservative Century*, p. 63.
85 Baker, *The Turbulent Years*, p. 345.
86 Butler and Kavanagh, *The British General Election of 1992*, pp. 34–5.
87 Pinto-Duschinsky, 'Political Parties', p. 40.
88 *Ibid.*, p. 37.
89 *Ibid.*, p. 40.
90 Butler and Kavanagh, *The British General Election of 1992*, p. 35.
91 Simon Burgess, 'The Political Parties', in Catterall, *Contemporary Britain: An*

Annual Review 1993, p. 56.

92 Butler and Kavanagh, *The British General Election of 1992*, p. 32.

93 *Ibid.*, pp. 32–3.

94 *Ibid.*, p. 81.

95 *Ibid.*, p. 83.

96 *Ibid.*, p. 85.

97 Burgess, 'The Political Parties', p. 54.

98 'Trust the People', Conservative Central Council Meeting, Torquay, 14 March 1992, reprinted in *Trust the People: Keynote Speeches of the 1992 General Election Campaign*, Conservative Political Centre, 1992, p. 9, 15 March 1992.

99 Butler and Kavanagh, *The British General Election of 1992*, p. 114.

100 'The Kind of Country We Want', Wembley, 5 April 1992, in *Trust the People: Keynote Speeches*, p. 62.

101 Anthony Seldon and Dennis Kavanagh, *The Major Effect* (Oxford: Oxford University Press, 1994).

102 Stephen Dorrell, *Redefining the Mixed Economy*, Speech to the Centre for Policy Studies, 23 November 1992.

103 Brendan Evans, 'Changing Inter-governmental Relations: The Employment Service and the Training and Enterprise Agencies', *The Waves of Change: Strategic Management in the Public Services*, Conference Proceedings, 5–6 April 1993, pp. 175–87.

104 Office of Public Service and Science, *Competing for Quality*, 17/94.

105 BBC TV *News at Six*, 27 June 1994.

106 *New Statesman and Society*, 1 October 1993.

107 *Daily Telegraph*, 17 September 1994.

108 *Daily Telegraph*, 18 September 1994.

109 *Daily Telegraph*, 5 October 1994.

110 *Daily Telegraph*, 19 October 1992.

111 Peter Catterall, 'Introduction: The Year in Perspective', in *Contemporary Britain: An Annual Review 1993*, p. 6.

112 *Daily Telegraph*, 6 October 1992.

113 *Daily Telegraph*, 7 October 1992.

114 *Daily Telegraph*, 8 October 1992.

115 Sir Alan Walters' phrase.

116 *Daily Telegraph*, 10 October 1992.

117 *Daily Telegraph*, 23 October 1992.

118 House of Commons Debates, Vol. 229, 22 July 1993, cols 604–8.

119 *Ibid.*, 23 July, cols 721–5.

120 *Sunday Telegraph*, 25 July 1993.

121 The tortuous passage of the bill is analysed in Keith Alderman, 'Legislating for Maastricht', in *Contemporary Record*, 7 (3) (Winter 1993), pp. 499–511.

122 Simon Burgess, 'The Political Parties', p. 40.

123 Philip Norton, 'Parliament', in Catterall (ed.), *Contemporary Britain: An Annual Review 1993*.

124 BBC *News*, 2 July 1994.

125 *The Observer*, 3 July 1994.

126 In conversation.

127 *Financial Times*, 18 January 1994.
128 John Gray, *Beyond the New Right: Markets, Government and the Commons Environment* (London: Routledge & Kegan Paul, 1993).
129 *The World This Weekend*, BBC Radio 4, 3 July 1994.
130 *The Guardian*, 4 October 1993.
131 *Ibid.*
132 David McKie in *The Guardian*, 4 October 1993.
133 *The Guardian*, 2 May 1994.
134 *Sunday Telegraph*, 4 July 1994 and Simon Burgess, 'The Political Parties', p. 39.
135 Andrew Gamble, 'In Government but not in Power', *New Statesman*, 1 October 1993.
136 *The Guardian*, 4 October 1993.
137 The Right Honourable Lord Wakeham and Giles Chichester, *The Carlton Lectures*, 1993, Foreword.
138 *Ibid.*, p. 14.
139 *Ibid.*, pp. 16–17.
140 *Ibid.*, p. 26.
141 *Ibid.*, p. 34.
142 *Sunday Telegraph*, 10 October 1993.
143 *Sunday Telegraph*, 3 October 1993.
144 *Sunday Telegraph*, 10 October 1993.
145 *The Guardian*, 4 October 1994.
146 Peregrine Worsthorne, *Sunday Telegraph*, 26 September 1993.
147 *Financial Times*, 22 September 1993.
148 *The Economist*, 30 August 1993.
149 *Financial Times*, 1 June 1993.
150 *The Economist*, 31 July 1993.
151 *The Independent*, 5 November 1994.
152 *The Times*, 19 January, 1995.
153 *The Guardian*, 2 May 1994.
154 Paul F. Whiteley et al., 'Thatcherism and the Conservative Party', *Political Studies*, 42 (2), p. 198.
155 *The Guardian*, 16 July 1994.
156 Whiteley, 'Thatcherism and the Conservative Party', p. 197.
157 *Ibid.*, p. 199.
158 Conversations with the authors.
159 Philip Norton, 'Parliament', in Bill Jones et al., *Politics UK* (Hemel Hempstead: Harvester, 1994), p. 347.
160 *The Guardian*, 31 March 1994.
161 *Financial Times*, 4 February 1994.
162 *Ibid.*
163 *Ibid.*
164 *The Guardian*, 24 March 1994.
165 *The World This Weekend*, BBC Radio 4, 3 July 1994.
166 *Financial Times*, 5 April 1994.
167 *New Statesman*, 8 July 1994.
168 *Financial Times*, 18 July 1994.

169 BBC TV, *Newsnight*, 7 July 1994.
170 *Financial Times*, 8 July 1994.
171 *Ibid.*
172 Michael Pinto-Duschinsky, *A Week in Politics*, Channel 4, 13 October 1994.
173 Edward Heath, in conversation with the author.
174 *Financial Times*, 6 April 1994.
175 *The Guardian*, 16 July 1994.
176 Richard Rose, *The Problem of Party Government* (London: Macmillan, 1974), p. 226.
177 One student researcher, for example, discovered that it was difficult to secure interviews with local Tory activists in contrast to the previous year and the response of the other parties.
178 Lord Lawson in conversation with the authors.

Conclusion

The Conservative Party is undoubtedly the success story of modern British politics. This success is, however, carefully crafted and often disguises an ideological and political ferment in which adaptation is far less easy and more costly than the image of effortless superiority allows.

The Conservative Party's history of ideological ferment belies the jibe that it is the 'stupid party' and it has, in fact, been the source of many of the ideas which have had most impact on the development of British politics in the age of mass democracy. Furthermore, Conservatives have not shown themselves averse to stealing ideas from their opponents and including them in the Conservative 'tradition'. Whilst the Conservative Party's longevity is testament to political continuity, the party's evolution is not simply a smooth adaptation to its changing political environment. As well as powerful elements of continuity, periods of discontinuity can be identified in the party's evolution. Central to the ability of Conservatism to adapt via a process of crisis and response it is important to remember that the Conservative Party is one component in a complex political system, whilst as the dominant party it can and does powerfully influence the political agenda, it does not have an entirely free hand.

There is a tendency to interpret the party's ability to adapt to changing political circumstances by reference to its supposed lack of ideology. This is a mistake: the Conservative Party is an ideological party and its adaptability has, in a large part, stemmed from the constant tension between the One Nation tradition and that of neo-Liberalism. All Conservatives subscribe to the principles of individualism, the free market, patriotism, the sovereignty of the nation state and its political institutions, but these principles in themselves offer no clear answer to which ideological tradition offers the best response to particular policy dilemmas. This tension between One Nation and neo-Liberal Conservatism is most clearly reflected in the changing Conservative orientation towards the state and the use of state power to realise Conservative political objects. The Conservative ambivalence towards the

277

role of the state in politics tends to generate most difficulty when it is linked to Britain's changing place in the world economy: the extent to which the state should promote economic change is a question of perennial difficulty for all Conservatives.

The Conservative dominance over the last century is basically the product of an ability to win elections. First and foremost the Conservative Party is an office-oriented electoral party. Three points flow from this. First, the Conservatives have always placed enormous stress and lavished considerable resources on their relationship with mass democracy. It is not surprising that the Conservative Party has been the most innovative British party in adopting new techniques of electoral management and manipulation, ranging from the Primrose League, through to the use of advertising agencies, public opinion polls and market research, and media training. Second, a central element in the Conservative relationship with mass democracy has been the presentation of an image of unity. It has been an article of faith in the Conservative Party that divided parties are not electorally attractive. This places a premium on both loyalty to leaders and the presentation of a single purpose. Third, organisationally the Conservative Party has worked hard to maintain a close relationship at the grassroots of the political system by maintaining an active and well financed constituency organisation. Whenever this grassroots organisation has been allowed to wither, so have Conservative political fortunes.

The combination of ideological flexibility and organisational activism has meant that the Conservative Party has been able to present itself as the national party. This is more than simply the party 'wrapping itself in the Union Jack', important though this is. It has enabled the Conservative Party to retain the attributes of a cadre party whilst at the same time enjoying a close relationship with mass democracy. The core of this relationship is the creation of a cross-class integrative party: the mechanism of integration might vary from the medieval flummery of the Primrose League, Baldwinism's pastoral myth, Macmillanite affluence, Heath's technocratic meritocracy, to the Thatcherite populism of Essex man (and woman), but its purpose has remained unchanged. That purpose has been to limit so far as was possible the political space available to parties which might seek to challenge the status quo, and a powerful element of continuity in this integrative strategy from the late-nineteenth century onwards has been anti-Socialism and the party's appeal to all those who feared instability and the threat to property rights. These fears are not confined to any one part of the social structure.

Despite this success in dealing with the politics of mass democracy, the Conservative Party has a tendency to doubt the efficacy of its political and electoral strategy. This has often led the Conservative Party to exaggerate the threat from the left for electoral reasons (Salisbury's identification of

Liberalism with incipient Socialism, Law's attacks on the Labour Party as Bolshevist, Churchill's 'Gestapo' speech in 1945, for example), but there is also a private tendency for the party elite to overestimate the threat. This private tendency illustrates an often surprising lack of political confidence in a party supposedly convinced of its natural superiority in dealing with mass democracy. This is apparent in the traditionally cautious approach of the Conservative elite (in contrast to the atavism of the grassroots) to organised labour. Even the quintessentially Thatcherite *Stepping Stones* report of 1977, which advocated making the unions into a political issue for electoral reasons, encased this objective in a remarkably complex and circumspect strategy.

Conservative history suggests the party assumes a different character in its rare interludes in Opposition. As a result of being ejected from government, it exaggerates the threat posed by its opponents being in government. This invariably leads to frequently fatal criticism of the leader who is held responsible for defeat; a demand for a fundamental rethink of policy and a return to Conservative principles; and finally, whilst the Conservative rank-and-file tend to become both more assertive and neo-Liberal in attitude, Conservative support in the business community tends to rally to the party.

This brings us to the party's power structure. A reason often cited for Conservative success is the party's power structure and ethos which gives its leader the ability to modify policy and strategy speedily free from grassroots interference. This is a serious misinterpretation. Parties are organisationally dense and are policy coalitions combined for electoral purposes. This complexity constrains the leadership and encourages a predisposition to adopt policies which maximise agreement but which need not be moderate. This explains the party's elaborate consultative mechanisms which exist to identify support-maximising policies even though the membership do not 'make' policy. No other party institution, however, rivals the leader's centrality. His (or her) influence can be felt in all party institutions and processes and the leader's powers seem incongruous in a mass party. Yet despite the powers and deference accorded the leader, once the leader is perceived to be an electoral liability removal quickly follows.

The leader has four key 'powers': first, wide discretion in formulating policy on which only the leader can pronounce authoritatively. As the party Conference is consultative, until the leader sets out policy the party is essentially 'policy-less' and lacking a clear direction. Second, the leader selects the front bench in and out of government and makes key appointments (notably the Chairman) in the party organisation. These choices are not, however, unfettered as appointment must reflect the party's factional and ideological structure. Third, and more intangibly, the leader sets the party's 'tone' which forms a vital element in both its self, and electoral, image. Changing tone (but not policy) invariably requires a change of leader.

Though intangible, tone-setting is crucial, as failure to 'strike the right note' can cause major internal unrest. Finally, the leader derives enormous strength from the membership's loyalty and deference. Though powerful this is conditional. These are formidable powers, but there are enough discarded leaders to demonstrate the vulnerability of incumbents and the party's unforgiving nature.

To maintain his or her position, the party's dominance, and its adaptive capacity, the leader must balance three factors satisfactorily. First, a clear lead must be given to the parliamentary party, especially the 1922. Whilst parliamentary colleagues cannot substitute for the leader, they can obtain a new leader, a situation not materially affected by the new method of election established in 1965. Second, the leader must satisfy the aspirations and perceptions of the bulk of the grassroots so that they adhere to, and work for the Conservative cause. Third, the leader must hold out the prospect of electoral victory and government. A leader does not, of course, have to deliver all three all of the time.

Policy connects the party and its members to the electorate and, theoretically, Conservative policy (and therefore electoral strategy) is the leader's domain. However, there are three constraints on the choice of policy and strategy. First, the manufacture and preservation of a consensus amongst the front bench is necessary as the resignation of senior colleagues can have profound consequences for the party's electoral image, party management, and governmental coherence. Second, it is important to maintain the confidence and morale of backbenchers who are the critical link with the party in the country. Third, the leader must retain the support of the socio-economic groups which form the bedrock of Conservative electoral support as well as that of the party's representative, voluntary, and bureaucratic institutions which communicate policy, implement strategy, and mobilise support. This embraces the party's relationship with 'public opinion' (or 'the temper of the times') which can be moulded by leadership but which leaders must express and reflect in a way which retains both electoral support and party commitment. The leader's task is to appear credible internally (to the party) and externally (to the electorate).

Leaders are usually able to challenge critics by raising the spectre of electoral defeat. To avoid defeat the leader is permitted considerable freedom, the exercise of which may involve actions and policies not to the party's liking. The party has to accept that its interests and preferences are only one influence, albeit an important one, in the formulation of policy. These views may offer leaders a fresh perspective and suggest new ways of proceeding, but slavish adherence to the views of the party is traditionally regarded as the abrogation of leadership. In the final analysis the leader must bow to the party's will or win it over. If he fails the leader will be removed. Until that happens, however, the party remains loyal. Electoral defeat and political crises are not sufficient reasons for removal as the natural tendency for the party is to unite behind the leader in the face of external threats. Conservative leaders enjoy a remarkable degree of freedom and receive an almost pathological loyalty. Revolt and rejection comes only after an extended period of discontent fuelled by a fear, or actuality, of electoral defeat.

The leader's role and the party's capacity for unity have been major factors in the Conservatives' ability to adapt and to respond effectively to a series of challenges. This is not a process occurring in a vacuum and the party is far from a catch-all party of expediency. It operates on an ideological dimension bounded by pure One Nation Conservatism at one end and rigid neo-Liberal principles at the other, but with neo-Liberal yearnings more frequently evident amongst party activists than amongst the leadership stratum.

The crisis facing the party in the mid-1990s derives from a leader less effective in juggling the complex relationship between strategy, policy, and the black arts of party management which underpin a successful electoral appeal in a mass democracy. The Conservative Party emerged as a response to the challenges posed by the rise of mass democracy; notably organised labour, parliamentary Socialism, and the growth of the state. It has proved remarkably successful in handling what might be broadly described as class politics. In the 1990s, however, traditional class politics and, therefore, the Conservative response, seem less apposite. Major is confronted by the challenge of Europe which has opened a fault-line within the party. This may prove difficult to finesse as patriotism has been a central component in drawing One Nation and neo-Liberal Conservatism together in the fight against Socialism. Now, however, what has been central to Conservative success – the cross-class national integrative appeal – is in danger of splitting Conservatism. On the other hand the history of the Conservative Party cautions against premature obituaries.

Index

Advisory Committee on Policy
(ACP),147–51, 159, 161, 176,
192
Advisory Committee on Publicity and
Political Education (ACPPE),
78–81
Allen, Brady and Marsh, 258
Allied Lyons, 258
Amery, Julian, 152, 171
Amery, Leo, 28
Amis, Kingsley, 172
anti-Socialism, 2, 19–21, 35, 44, 61
Archer, Lord, 156
Armstrong, Sir William, 202
Asquith, H.H., 18, 27
Attlee, Clement, 68, 78

balance of payments, 157, 159, 200,
238
Baldwin, Stanley, 2, 26, 30–8, 40–4,
50–5, 57, 144
Balfour, Arthur, 13–18
Bank of England, 81, 95, 122, 201
Barber, Anthony, 151, 158, 163, 190,
198
BBC, 62–4, 130, 159, 190, 227, 258
Beaverbrook, Lord, 42, 61, 68–70
Benn, Sir Ernest, 67
Benn, Tony, 168
Berkeley, Humphrey, 152, 163
Bevan, Aneurin, 62, 92
Beveridge Report, 61, 65–6, 169

Bevin, Ernest, 58, 60
Biffen, John, 145, 163, 171–3, 188–91
Birch, Nigel, 171
Black Wednesday, 262, 265
Blair, Tony, 250, 265–7
Boddy, Sir Richard, 191
Boer War, 13
Bolshevism, 29–30
Boothby, Robert, 55, 57
Boyle, Sir Edward, 142
Braine, John, 172
British Institute of Public Opinion
(BIPO), 68
British Workers' League (BWL), 27
Brittan, Samuel, 173
Bruce, Brendan, 258
Budgets
1909, 17
1972, 200
Bulpitt, Jim, 220, 224–5
BUPA, 171
Burgess, Anthony, 172
Burke, Edmund, 4, 172, 208
Butler, R.A, 60, 63–4, 68, 78–82,
95–6, 105–6, 141–2, 144, 147
by-elections:
1931–4, 52
1938–9, 52
1942, Grantham, 62
1945, Chelmsford, 69
1953, Sunderland, 96
1972–3,

Ely, 194
Rochdale, 194
Sutton and Cheam, 194

Callaghan, James, 234, 238
Campbell, John, 156, 185
Camrose, Lord, 78
Canning, George, 5
Carlton Club, 31
Carr, Robert, 151, 190
Carrington, Lord, 202
Cash, Bill, 256
Catering Wages Bill, 62, 66
CBI, 168, 186, 201
Central Electricity Board, 52
Centre for Policy Studies (CPS), 203
Central Office, 21, 72, 78, 154, 158,
    171, 191–6, 258–9
Central Policy Review Staff (CPRS),
    150
Chamberlain, Austen, 13–15, 31, 40
Chamberlain, Neville, 2, 42, 53–6,
    56–60, 144
Chartism, 5
Chataway, Chris, 152
Churchill, Lord Randolph, 14, 40,
Churchill, Winston, 50, 53–64, 68–70,
    88–94, 102, 156, 162–3
  assault on Labour, 80
  on foreign policy, 78–9
  threat to resign, 65
Citizen's Charter, 254–6
City, the, 41, 44, 54
Clark, Alan, 269
Clarke, David, 81
Clarke, Kenneth, 248–50, 255
coal industry, 170
Coalition, 30, 50, 59, 69, 78–81
Coal Mines Reorganisation Act, 52
Collectivism, 15, 17
Committee, The 1922, 59–62, 92,
    143–4, 154,
  formation of, 31
Common Agricultural Policy (CAP),
    262
Common Market, 164, 171
Conservative Political Centre (CPC), 78,
    159, 174, 189, 192, 196
Conservative Research Department
    (CRD), 78–84, 144, 151, 159,
    166, 174, 190–8, 203–7
Conservative Trade Unionists (CTU),
    210
Cooper, Duff, 56
Cope, John, 248
Corn Laws, 5–6
Cozreldit Ltd, 154
Crossman, Richard, 153
Curran, Charles, 143
Curzon, Lord, 31, 35
Czechoslovakia, 57

Daily Express, 42, 82
Daily Herald, 82
Daily Mail, 36, 42
Daily Mirror, 91
Daily Telegraph, 78, 103,169, 183, 254
Dalton, Hugh, 56, 62
Davidson, J.C.C, 33, 40, 42
Davidson, John Biggs, 152, 162
Davis, John, 168
de Gaulle, Charles, 122, 188
Dehane, Jean Luc, 261, 264
denationalisation, 95, 166, 170, 187,
    210
Department of Trade and Industry,
    199, 201
Disraeli, Benjamin, 5–11, 14, 16–17,
    21, 31, 59, 141, 172
Dorrell, Stephen, 269
Drucker, Peter, 162
DuCann, Edward, 158, 191, 204
Dugdale, Tommy, 64, 66

Eccles, David, 81
Economist, The, 141, 147–8, 152, 155,
    184, 187–8
economy, 142–3, 184
Eden, Sir John, 54, 57, 65, 80, 87,
    101–3, 156, 199, 201, 211
egalitarianism, 162
Empire, 15–17
Europe, 144–5, 148, 163–4
  divisions over, 248–53, 262–6

European Community (EC), 145–7,
    227, 252–3, 262
European Economic Community (EEC),
    120–1, 132, 160, 164, 188,
    196–7, 202, 211
European Elections, 994, 248
European Monetary System (EMS), 223
European Monetary Union (EMU), 255
European Union (EU), 223, 238, 250,
    263, 267, 269
Evening Standard, 103
Exchange Rate Mechanism (ERM), 223,
    249, 256, 261–2

Factories Bill, 41
Falklands, The, 234
Federation of British Industries (FBI),
    123
Fell, Anthony, 152
Finance Bill 1965, 155
flotation of the Pound, 200
Fowler, Norman, 259, 270
Fraser, Sir Malcolm, 31
Fraser, Sir Michael, 81
Friedman, Milton, 166, 193
full employment, 65, 82, 96, 142

Gaitskell, Hugh, 104
Gallup, 92
Gamble, Andrew, 161, 231–3
Garrett, Jim, 158
general elections:
    1868, 7
    1874, 11
    1880, 11–12, 14
    1886, 12
    1895, 12
    1900, 12
    1906, 12–14, 17–18, 70
    1910, 18
    1918, 29–30
    1922, 28, 32
    1923, 35
    1924, 32, 38
    1929, 40–1
    1931, 32, 44
    1935, 32, 54
    1945, 70,76
    1950, 90
    1951, 90–2
    1955, 102
    1959, 115, 119
    1964, 142–4
    1966, 141, 154–6
    1970, 143–5, 151, 155–8
    Feb 1974, 145, 156, 193–4, 203
    Oct 1974, 145, 156,193
    1979, 154, 211–13, 235
    1983, 238
    1987, 238
    1992, 3, 248, 270
General Strike, 38–9, 41
Germany, 16, 168, 223
Gilmour, Ian, 220
Glubb, John, 104
Gow, Ian, 171
Griffiths, Eldon, 158
Griffiths, Peter, 145
Grigg, Sir Edward, 51
Gulf War, 253
Gurden, Harold, 145, 167

Hacking, Sir Douglas, 59, 62–3, 67
Hailsham, Lord, 66
Hannon, Sir Patrick, 67
Hanson plc, 258
Hayek, F.A, 68, 231
Headlam, Sir Cuthbert, 60, 63, 68–70
Healey, Denis, 204
Heath, Edward, 2–3, 141–52, 160–6,
    175–7, 183–6, 189–90, 195,
    211, 221, 264
    addressing the 1922 committee,
        195, 198
    advised to step down, 204
    in condemnation of Powell, 168
    on the EEC, 188, 196, 200
    election as leader, 129
    use of expansionary policies, 200–1
    and labour relations, 187
    as leader of the opposition, 152–9
    policy reversals, 199
    public opinion of, 191–2
    taking Britain into the EEC, 200

Heathcoat Amery, Derick, 81, 83–4
Heseltine Michael, 248, 253
Hichingbrooke, Viscount, 66
Hitler, Adolf, 57–8
Home, Sir Alec Douglas, 143, 145–7, 153, 156, 163, 186, 205
House of Commons, 5, 30, 32, 42–3, 78, 131, 147,157
House of Lords, 5, 17, 78, 157, 166
Housing Finance Bill, 190
Howard, Michael, 171, 263
Howe, Sir Geoffrey, 169, 173, 210, 250
Howell, David, 145, 161, 173
Hunt, David, 260
Hurd, Douglas, 263–4, 267
Hutchinson, Colonel James, 81

ICI, 166
immigration, 145, 148, 162–7
Independent Labour Party, 87
India, 42, 53–5
Industrial Charter, 81–5, 87–9
Industrial Policy Committee (IPC), 81–3
Industrial Relations Act, 199
Industrial Relations Bill, 188
Industrial Reorganisation Corporation (IRC), 201
Industrial Transference Act (1928), 52
inflation, 54, 81, 148, 157, 165, 184–8, 199–200, 221–5, 261
   cost-push, 150–1
   wage-price spiral, 160
Institute of Economic Affairs (IEA), 141, 174, 196, 206
Inter-Governmental Conference (1990), 252
International Monetary Fund (IMF), 105
interventionism, 163–9
Ireland, 16
Irwin, Lord, 42
ITV, 212

Japan, 238
Jessop, Bob, 236–8

Johnson Smith, Geoffrey, 158, 172
Joseph, Keith, 151, 162, 190–2, 204, 210, 225, 235

Keynes, John Maynard, 173
Keynesianism, 201, 207
   demand management, 68, 224–5
   failure to control stagflation, 225
Keynesian Welfare State, 142, 237
Khaled, Leila, 168
Korean War, 92

Labour Party, 3, 56, 60–8, 96, 141, 145–9, 154–62, 250–60, 265, 271
   on the EEC, 199–202
Lamont, Norman, 250, 253, 265
Lang, Ian, 269
Law, Andrew Bonar, 2, 17–21, 26–8, 31, 36
Lawson, Nigel, 184, 223, 238, 254
Latsis, John, 258
leadership elections
   1965, 144, 152
   1975, 3
Lejeune, Anthony, 175
Lever, Harold, 238
Lewis, Roy, 173, 196
Liberal Democrats, 248, 259,260
Liberalism, 5, 9, 66, 145, 169, 185, 213, 227, 231
Liberal Party, 9, 56–8, 203
Lilley, Peter, 263
Lindsay, John, 158
Lloyd, Selwyn, 123–5
Lloyd George, David, 31, 34–6, 41–2, 53, 58
local elections
   1970, 157
   1990, 248
   1994, 248
London County Council (LCC), 19–20
London Dock Strike (1912), 18
London Municipal Society (LMS), 19–20

Maastricht Summit, 253

Maastricht Treaty (1991), 223, 255, 261–4
Macdonald, Ramsay, 36, 41, 43–4, 50
Macgregor John, 145
Macleod, Iain, 83, 144, 149–52, 158, 175, 187–9
    as Shadow Chancellor, 153–5
Macmillan, Harold, 2–3, 55–6, 68, 81–3, 92–4, 101–6, 142–8, 153–5, 114–15
    decline of, 121–7
    popularity of, 114, 117–19
Macmillan, Maurice, 203
Major, John, 3, 165, 221, 247–51
    on Europe, 250
    post 1992, 261–3
    in preparation for general election, 252–4, 259–60
    on Scotland, 257
Marples, Ernest, 149, 158
Marxism, 168, 230
Maude, Angus, 161, 172–3
Maudling, Reginald, 81–3, 144–5, 150–3
Maxwell Fyfe, David, 68, 72, 86, 93
Meyer, Sir Anthony, 171, 199
miners' strikes
    1912, 20
    1971, 200
Mogg, William Rees, 124
Monckton, Walter, 93
Monday Club, The, 162, 172, 249
monetarism, 144, 160, 165, 171, 187, 221–4
    as a solution to problems of Keynesianism, 225
    uneven impact of, 237
Mortimer, Jim, 187
Munich Agreement, 55–7

Nadir, Asil, 259
National Association for Freedom, 206
National Association of Manufacturers, 68
National Economic Development Council (NEDC), 123
National Enterprise Board (NEB), 209

National Incomes Commission (NIC), 123, 165
Nationalisation, 169
National League for Freedom, 67–9
National Opinion Polls (NOP), 154
neo-Liberalism, 2, 68, 134, 143–5, 148–50, 187, 277
NHS, 163, 254
Nicolson, Harold, 55
NUM, 202

Oakeshott, Michael, 229
Observer, The, 124
Opinion Research Centre (ORC), 154, 159, 190–1
Osborne, Sir Cyril, 145
Osborne, John, 172
Oxford City Council, 190

Party Conferences:
    1945, 68
    1946, 79
    1947, 72
    1948, 72
    1949, 72
    1965, 155–6
    1968, 148
    1970, 160, 183
    1971, 185
    1993, 266
Patten, Chris, 248, 258–9
Peel, Sir Robert, 5–7, 11–15, 21, 31
Petherick, Major P., 64
Pickthorn, Kenneth, 63
Pipe, Russ, 258
P&O, 258
Poland, 57
Polly Peck, 259
Portillo, Michael, 249–50, 264–5
Powell, Enoch, 142–5, 162–5, 170, 176, 188–91, 200
    as Defence Spokesman, 153
    dismissal from Shadow Cabinet, 157, 163
    on immigration, 157, 167
    as a populist figure, 166–7
Powellism, 3, 239

Pressure for Economic and Social
        Toryism (PEST), 142, 172
Prices and Incomes Act (1966), 151
Primrose League, 14, 60, 278
privatisation, 169
protectionism, 171
Public Sector Borrowing Requirement
        (PSBR), 225, 253–6
PWPCC, 63–4, 68, 79, 81
Pym, Francis, 220

Quantity Theory of Money, 144

Race Relations Bill, 211
Ramsden, Sir Eugene, 59
Reading, Brian, 176
recession, 253, 265
Reform Acts:
    1832, 5–6
    1867, 7, 9
    1884, 12
reformism, 2, 5–6
Republican Party, 142
Retail Price Maintenance Bill, 130–1,
    144
Rhodesia, 152, 157
Ridley, Nicholas, 145, 163, 166,
        169–70, 188–91, 199–201
Rippon, Geoffrey, 190
Rolls Royce, 188
Roth, Andrew, 145
Rowe, Andrew, 210

Saatchi and Saatchi, 211, 258
Salisbury, Lord, 2, 9–15, 21
Sandys, Duncan, 55
Selective Employment Tax, 149, 160
Selsdon Group, 151–2, 183
Selsdon Park Hotel Conference, 151,
        162, 175
Sewill, Brendon, 151, 158, 166, 192–3
Single European Act (1986), 228
Smith, Ian, 152
Smith, John, 270
Social Chapter, 249, 255, 263–4
Socialism, 2, 4, 9, 84, 141, 172–5,
        224, 281

Spectator, The, 141, 148, 152, 155
State, the, 2, 4, 65, 79, 143–5, 148,
        238, 260, 266
Statism, 3
Steel-Maitland, Arthur, 19,21, 28
Sterling, 148, 157
Stewart, James, 61,63
Suez Canal, 104–7, 112, 144, 148,
        157
Sun, The, 212
Swinton Journal and Crossbow, 171–2,
        174
Szamuely, Tibor, 172,174

Tasker, Sir Robert, 63
taxation, 95, 134, 149, 152–5,
        159–65, 169
Tebbitt, Norman, 210, 251–2, 263
Thatcher, Margaret, 3, 141–7, 161–6,
        171–3, 193, 221, 240, 249,
        254–5,
    as leader of the Opposition, 204,
        207, 210–112
    as Minister of Education and Science,
        187
    in opposition to Heath's leadership,
        203
Thatcherism, 2–3, 142, 164, 176, 184,
        263
    as conviction politics, 226–7
    the debate about, 219–20
    as hegemony, 230
    as an ideology, 228–9
    as statecraft, 224–5
Thomas, Harvey, 258
Thomas, Peter, 189
Thorneycroft, Peter, 112, 116, 133,
        163, 205
Thursday Group, 158–9
Times, The, 61, 65, 80, 86–7, 96, 113,
        124–5, 167
Topping, Sir Robert, 59, 63
Tory Reform Group, 66, 68–9, 142
Town and Country Planning Bill
        (1944), 62, 65
trade unions, 119, 142, 145, 148,
        152, 155–7, 190, 213, 227

Trade Unions and Trade Disputes Act
(1927), 39
Treasury, the, 122, 170, 201
Trinity College, Cambridge, 141
TUC, 34, 38, 122–3, 133, 188, 202
Tucker, Geoffrey, 158
Turton, Robin, 196

Ulster, 18, 164
unemployment, 30, 33, 38, 52, 127,
160, 186, 199–200, 263–5
Unilateral Declaration of Independence
(UDI), 152
Unionist Labour Movement, 29
Unionist Party, 17, 20
Unionist Social Reform Committee
(USRC), 17, 20
United Biscuits, 258
United States of America, 104–5,
167–8, 238
Utley, T.E, 165, 169

VAT, 149, 265
Vietnam War, 166

Wain, John, 172
Walker, Peter, 145, 190
Walters, Alan, 171
Wandsworth Council, 258
Waugh, Auberon, 172
Waugh, Evelyn, 86
welfare state, 80, 96, 142, 148, 170,
213
Westminster Council, 258
Whitehall, 232
Whitelaw, William, 158
Willetts, David, 220–3, 240, 269
Wilson, Harold, 92, 141, 144, 151–9,
238
'Winter of Discontent', 211, 225
Woodward, Shaun, 258
Woolton, Lord, 61, 67–8, 72, 76,
91–2, 101
Worker's Charter, 82
World War I, 19, 22, 29
World War II, 2, 52–3, 56, 58

Yom Kippur War, 202
Young, Michael, 174
Younger, Sir George, 31